A Luminous Brotherhood

EMILY SUZANNE CLARK

A Luminous Brotherhood

Afro-Creole Spiritualism in
Nineteenth-Century New Orleans

The University of North Carolina Press *Chapel Hill*

This book was published with the assistance of the Fred W. Morrison Fund of the University of North Carolina Press.

© 2016 The University of North Carolina Press
All rights reserved
Set in Arno Pro by Westchester Publishing Services
Manufactured in the United States of America

The University of North Carolina Press has been a member of the
Green Press Initiative since 2003.

Library of Congress Cataloging-in-Publication Data
Names: Clark, Emily Suzanne, 1984–
Title: A luminous brotherhood : Afro-Creole Spiritualism in
    nineteenth-century New Orleans / Emily Suzanne Clark.
Description: Chapel Hill : University of North Carolina Press, [2016] |
    Includes bibliographical references and index.
Identifiers: LCCN 2015040308| ISBN 9781469628783 (cloth : alk. paper) |
    ISBN 9781469628790 (ebook)
Subjects: LCSH: African American Spiritual churches—Louisiana—New Orleans. |
    African Americans—Louisiana—New Orleans—Religion. | Race—Religious
    aspects. | New Orleans (La.)—Church history—19th century. | New Orleans (La.)—
    Religious life and customs.
Classification: LCC BX6194.A464 C53 2016 | DDC 277.63/3508108996073—dc23
    LC record available at http://lccn.loc.gov/2015040308

Jacket illustration: Page from one of René Grandjean's composition books (Item 85–71 in the René Grandjean Collection). Courtesy of the René Grandjean Collection, Louisiana and Special Collections Department, Earl K. Long Library, University of New Orleans.

For my family

Contents

Illustrations

Acknowledgments

I owe gratitude to a lot of people. John Corrigan and Chip Callahan were formative mentors: critical, encouraging, and good at instilling curiosity about American religion. The two of them, along with Ed Blum and Paul Harvey, have made me a better scholar. In fact, a conversation with Ed convinced me that there was a great story to be told with the Cercle Harmonique's records and that I should tell it. A number of people read previous versions of this project and offered helpful advice, asked insightful questions, and raised critiques. This includes John Corrigan, Amanda Porterfield, Mike McVicar, Martin Kavka, Ed Blum, Charlie McCrary, Paul Harvey, and David Kirby. The entire American religion contingent at Florida State University read an early chapter of this project and their feedback gave me perspective on the big picture. In addition, Adam Brasich, Cara Burnidge, Jenny Collins-Elliott, Mike Graziano, Rachel Lindsey, Andy McKee, Adam Park, Brad Stoddard, and Jeff Wheatley closely read sections of an earlier version. Their comments, critiques, and questions were astute and much appreciated.

At my departmental homes, I have been lucky to have smart colleagues who are also friends. My cohort at Florida State University kept me sane through graduate school. My Gonzaga University colleagues helped make my move to a new institution and new job easy and fun. Additionally, Mike Pasquier and Doug Thompson have become wonderful conversation partners and friends.

Elaine Maisner at UNC Press is a keen editor and guided me through the process of a manuscript becoming a book. Elaine's advice and the manuscript's two reviewers made this book better. The publication world is a bit daunting to a first-time author, and Elaine Maisner, Allie Shay, John Corrigan, and Mike McVicar helped me navigate it.

Dr. Florence Jumonville, Connie Phelps, James Hodges, and the rest of the special collections staff at the University of New Orleans's Earl K. Long Library were immensely helpful, as were Sean Benjamin of the Louisiana Research Collection housed at Tulane University, Christopher Harter and Andrew Salinas at the Amistad Research Center at Tulane University, and the staff at the Williams Research Center of the Historic New Orleans

Collection. During my first archival visit to the University of New Orleans, Dr. Jumonville suggested that I start with the séance records; I'm sure glad she did. And thanks to René Grandjean for donating his father-in-law's séance records to UNO and lots of appreciation to Henri Louis Rey for keeping them so dutifully.

The support my family provides is vastly different from that of a mentor, colleague, or archivist but theirs is the most important. The academic world can be rewarding and fun, but it can also be a strange and frustrating place. This is why I'm so grateful to my family. Linda, Phil, Laura, and Ed have been with me from the beginning and buoyed me through everything. Jon is a more recent addition to my family but a key reason why this book exists. Laura and Jon also took a turn reading and copyediting it, and Laura carefully copyedited the page proofs. Advice from the spirit world kept the Cercle Harmonique hard at work, and my family sustains me. They provide unconditional love and unconditional support. Thank you. I love y'all. And big thanks to Chubbs the cat who, while I typed and revised, lounged on my desk and occasionally walked on the keyboard. (Sorry your contributions didn't make it to final print.)

A Luminous Brotherhood

Introduction

Afro-Creole Spiritualism in New Orleans

One effect of the law of association is known as *harmony*; and *harmony* is the
soul and element of *music*. Music is a representation of divine *Order*; and *Order*
is the Wisdom of the Deity. To establish *harmony*, therefore, in society, every
man must be well instructed and properly situated, so that his movements may
accord with the movements of the whole; and thus the movements of the
human race will be in concert.
—Andrew Jackson Davis, *The Principles of Nature, Her Divine Revelations,
and A Voice to Mankind*

The march of these events will bring Progress; the Fusion of the Races will
happen little by little. The antagonistic elements will harmonize and
Concord will triumph over disunity.
—Spirit of French priest Hugues-Félicité Robert de Lamennais to the
Cercle Harmonique, 6 October 1871

In the struggle of good against evil, you have in your world both antagonisms
which continuously fight. My common sense and my heart directed me;
I succumbed under the ball of a fanatical madman if there ever was!
—Spirit of Abraham Lincoln to the Cercle Harmonique, 27 December 1871

According to his spirit, Napoleon Bonaparte was full of regret. Believing himself to be "great" and "powerful" while living, his spirit realized that he was
"nothing" when compared to "the immense majesty" of God. When he
looked back on his life choices, Napoleon's spirit was "sad and in despair," and
he grieved "under the multitude of evils" he caused. He wept and moaned
over the "great wrongs" he committed during his time on earth. It was only
through the grace of God that he experienced any forgiveness. However, in
the same communication, Napoleon's spirit indicated that he was still awaiting God's forgiveness. He cried out for it. While Napoleon did not identify
his present location in his messages, other spirits alluded that Napoleon
thought he was in hell.[1] Wherever he was, he was not happy. He found himself "groaning at the foot of the 'Ladder of Progress'"—a series of steps he

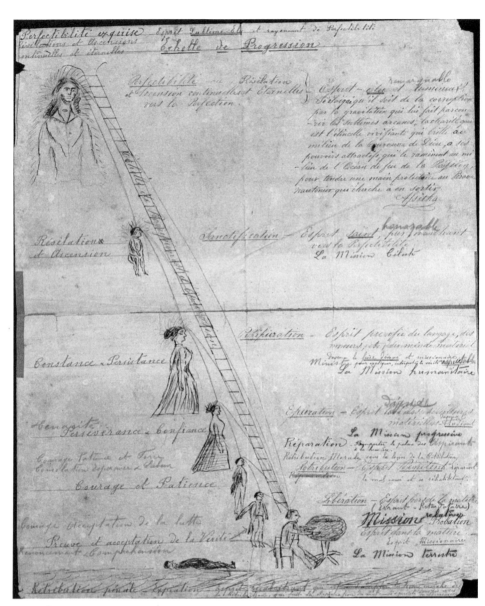

Échelle de Progression, or the Ladder of Progress. This drawing was added to the séance records in the early twentieth century by René Grandjean, the circle's first archivist, who was also the son-in-law of one of the Cercle Harmonique mediums. Courtesy of the René Grandjean Collection, Louisiana and Special Collections Department, Earl K. Long Library, University of New Orleans.

so desperately wanted to climb. If the top of the ladder was paradise, Napoleon was far from it. "The Lords of the Earth," he reported, "are here the last to ascend the luminous Ladder of Progress." His message provided a crystal warning to those with social and political power: "You the first on earth, will be the last here."[2]

Napoleon's spirit delivered this message in February 1869 to the Cercle Harmonique (Harmonic Circle), a community of Afro-Creole Spiritualists who held séances in New Orleans beginning in 1858 as the country anticipated a civil war and concluding in 1877 when southern Reconstruction came to a disappointing end.[3] Led by local Afro-Creoles Henri Louis Rey, François "Petit" Dubuclet, and J. B. Valmour, the Cercle Harmonique's spirit guides included a wide roster. Messages from radical abolitionist John Brown, assassinated president Abraham Lincoln, and Rey's friend Union Army captain André Cailloux abound in the Cercle Harmonique's séance records, along with messages from famed scientist-theologian Emanuel Swedenborg, poverty-fighter Saint Vincent de Paul, and New Orleans's own beloved Father Antonio de Sedella. Even the spirit of Confederate general Robert E. Lee delivered a message once. Other departed friends and family members of the circle frequented the table, as did figures from the French Revolution, such as Terror leader Maximilien de Robespierre and lyrical poet Pierre-Jean de Béranger. Anonymous friends and brothers chimed in too. Together these guides formed a spiritual republic—a body of spirits who governed the world beyond this one with fairness and an eye to future progress.[4]

Consider another message the Cercle Harmonique recorded from the spirit world in February 1869, though this message contains a very different sentiment from Napoleon's. Three days after the death of J. B. Valmour, his friend and fellow Spiritualist Henri Louis Rey received a message from Valmour's spirit at the Louisiana House of Representatives during his term in office. In the message, Valmour covered a range of topics, from personal matters to humanity's progress. He called attention to his "unhappy family" and asked his friend to "pity" them and look after them. However, much of Valmour's message emphasized not his immediate family but rather his world family. He congratulated Rey and other Spiritualist members of the Cercle Harmonique for "the beautiful work" they achieved. As the "soldiers of Progression" they, not emperors like Napoleon, deserved crowns. The Afro-Creole Spiritualists bravely struggled to "discern the truth from error and falsehood," and so they championed the virtues of Spiritualism and equality. They had broken with "the infamous prejudices and ignorance" that blinded so many others. Valmour encouraged them to continue fighting "for the good" and purifying themselves "by good deeds." Much Napoleon's opposite, this would secure them a "reward" after their deaths, even if they were not recognized for their righteousness on earth.[5] Napoleon had only pain and regret, but members of the Cercle Harmonique would find joy in the spirit world.

As a group, the Cercle Harmonique filled over thirty register books with spirit messages, reaching their heyday between 1871 and 1874. While other members came and went, Rey was a devoted Spiritualist and a leader for the whole tenure of the Cercle Harmonique. Even when alone, he would transcribe the messages he received from the spirits. Rey was born a free man in New Orleans to parents from Saint-Domingue; he was a "bright mulatto,"[6] he was educated, and he volunteered in the army during the Civil War. The other Afro-Creoles in the Cercle Harmonique were like Rey: male, free, educated, of mixed heritage, and from Catholic families.[7] They recorded spirit messages almost always in French, indicating that all in attendance at the séances came from similar Afro-Creole backgrounds.[8] The Afro-Creole members of the Cercle Harmonique were part of a politically active community in New Orleans that sought self-determination, even if limited. Together, the messages in Rey's séance books frequently encouraged the Spiritualists to continue their struggle for justice with patience and courage—timely instruction for the city's black population during the Civil War and Reconstruction.

This book contends that the Cercle Harmonique created and inhabited a religious world that intertwined political activism, social reform, and a moral vision for a more egalitarian United States. Through their communication with an authoritative yet democratic spirit world, the Cercle Harmonique envisioned the proper social, political, and religious ordering of the material world. Communing with the world of the wise spirits offered these Afro-Creoles a forum for airing their political grievances and for imagining a more equitable world. Local, national, and global politics shaped the Afro-Creoles' Spiritualist practice, and the messages from the spirits frequently responded to the Cercle Harmonique's contemporary context. The years after the Civil War were a hopeful time for black New Orleanians as it was their first clear entry into the political arena. It was also a dangerous time, punctuated by the violence of white terrorism. Thus, it was an auspicious time for the leaders of the spiritual republic to guide the Cercle Harmonique.

Many of their messages focused on what the spirits called "the Idea"—a concept that meant humanitarian progress, equality, egalitarianism, brotherhood, and harmony. Similar to ideas about millennial progress sweeping across nineteenth-century America, the Idea required the Afro-Creole Spiritualists to work during their material lives and make the world a better place. According to the spirits, God intended the Idea to structure the world and ensure universal liberty. However, the Cercle Harmonique observed a discrepancy between the ideal, egalitarian spirit world and the corrupt, raced material world.

New Orleans Afro-Creoles had difficulty finding a place where they belonged in the mid-nineteenth century. First, this dominantly free black community lived in a legal space between white and slave; then, after the Civil War, they entered a political realm that was both promising and immediately disappointing. In communicating with this spiritual republic, they found where they belonged and that was with Montesquieu, George Washington, and revolutionary French priest Henri Grégoire. With the spirits' guidance, the world inhabited by the Afro-Creole Spiritualists might become the material reflection of that republican, egalitarian spirit world. When the spiritual republic communicated with the Cercle Harmonique it was a vivid, dramatic exchange complete with visions, feelings, and verbal communications. The political and social heroes who delivered these messages offered commentary on local events, warned of future danger, encouraged hopeful outlooks, repackaged revolutionary rhetoric from the Atlantic world, and brought political ideology directly into the Cercle Harmonique's religious practice.

From a close reading of their séance records and noting the spiritual network into which they placed themselves, I map the Afro-Creoles' social, political, racial, and religious goals. Concurrently, the book illuminates how the Cercle Harmonique understood local and national society and politics, as well as hierarchical religious institutions, to be limiting humanity's progress. Tyrannical leaders, corrupt power, and white supremacy worked against the Idea. Through their séances the Cercle Harmonique connected with an idealized society whose members provided the Afro-Creoles with a republican ideology to combat politically destructive forces on earth. This perfect world of the spirits manifested a deep collective identity that linked the members of the Cercle Harmonique to the spirits who spoke to them. Rather than individualized messages from the spirits of the dead about personal issues (though that happened too), the Cercle Harmonique primarily received communications that encouraged them to copy the idealized society of the spiritual world here in the material world.

When describing the appeal of antebellum Spiritualism, religious studies scholar John Modern argued that the practice owed much of its popularity to the way a séance allowed participants to interact with people and social forces outside their immediate surroundings or, as Modern put it, an "abstraction of the public."[9] The Cercle Harmonique's practice engaged an "abstraction of the public" while also being critical of that public.[10] Their séance records contained discourse that criticized dominant society and politics on both the local and national level, and they hoped that discourse would inspire a reconstitution of the social world. The spirits offered visions of proper laws, advised the correct way to organize government, and modeled the perfectly functioning society. Because the spirit world conformed to the Idea, it was harmonious. With its racism, violence, and greed, the material world was not. Members of the Cercle Harmonique hoped the egalitarian republicanism that governed the spirit world could be replicated on earth. If reformed, then the material world could be harmonious too.[11] The Cercle Harmonique considered their religious practice as engagement with a collective body of spirits who lived in harmony together as a community. The Cercle Harmonique's communication with spirits of the French Revolution, spirits extolling the United States' republican promise, and spirits critiquing slavery and the Confederacy allowed circle members to locate themselves in the trajectory of humanity's progress. Their practice furthered the Idea of republican egalitarianism. The knowledge shared by the spirits guided them in their task. While their local and national context shaped the messages the Cercle Harmonique received from the spirit world, they were hardly the only community that communicated with the dead during the nineteenth century.

American Spiritualism

The Afro-Creole members of the Cercle Harmonique were part of a larger, popular religious movement. Broadly put, nineteenth-century Spiritualism was "regular contact with a spirit world."[12] In most cases, this meant the spirits of the dead. Spiritualism first rose in popularity in New Orleans in the 1850s among French émigrés and Creoles and then again in the late 1860s and 1870s with the Cercle Harmonique, but its origin in the United States dates earlier. The historian Jon Butler and others identify Spiritualism as a product of the "antebellum spiritual hothouse"—the widespread acceptance of an active supernatural presence.[13] Spiritualism gained great currency in the United States following the fame and success of the Fox sisters and their Rochester rappings. The sisters communicated with spirits of the dead through interpreting knocks and raps heard in various rooms of their Rochester home. People traveled hundreds of miles to communicate with the dead via the Fox mediums; along with them came those who wanted to expose the women as charlatans. Despite critics, the Fox sisters and numerous other mediums embarked on national tours. Also helping the tradition spread across the United States was its print culture. Journals like New York City's *Spiritual Telegraph* (1852) and *Herald of Progress* (1860), the Boston-based *Banner of Light* (1857), and Chicago's *The Religio-Philosophical Journal* (1865) connected a national network of Spiritualists and helped spread the news of Spiritualist lectures, books, and pamphlets to both practitioners and nonbelievers.[14]

A large part of Spiritualism's appeal came from its ability to straddle the material and spiritual worlds, the natural and the supernatural, the immediate world of those alive and the world of the dead. Historians and scholars of religion include Spiritualism in the broad spectrum of Christianity, though with a unique focus on spirit activity and the possibility of (and desire for) communication with spirits in the invisible world beyond the material one. Spiritualism was popular among Americans of all class backgrounds, and the authority the spirits could bestow was attractive to both those with social power and those desiring it.

While Spiritualism was a product of the antebellum spiritual hothouse, its roots reach back to European scholars who experimented with science, philosophy, and religion. In the eighteenth century, Swedish scientist and theologian Emanuel Swedenborg wrote extensively about the nature of the world and the three heavens—the celestial, the spiritual, and the natural—as revealed to him in his visions and religious experiences. *Heaven and Its Wonders and Hell* (1758) described the afterlife as he saw it: full of spirits organized in ascending spheres according to their spiritual status. Swedenborg's ideas regarding communication with the spirits and the organization of the spiritual cosmos became a core part of American Spiritualism. Another major foreign influence on American Spiritualism came from German physician Franz Anton Mesmer, whose 1766 doctoral dissertation "On the Influence of the Planets" examined the power of planetary magnetic fields and what he called "animal gravity." His theory of animal magnetism suggested that invisible fluids coursing through the bodies of humans connected them with the larger world around them and that good health was a result of keeping those fluids in harmony. Accessing and manipulating these fluids, spirits could affect the bodies of Mesmer's patients, and magnetizers like Mesmer could use the powers of their minds to harmonize the fluids in others. Particularly in France, mesmerism was associated with liberal politics, freethinking, and those who wanted to transform society.[15] In the United States, mesmerism was, as contemporary Emma Hardinge Britten wrote, "wide-spread" and "largely practiced over every part of America."[16] Concepts from Mesmer, Swedenborg, and Andrew Jackson Davis, as well as the spirits of the first two, manifested in the ideas and practices of the Cercle Harmonique.

Andrew Jackson Davis, a prolific writer and predominant American Spiritualist in the late antebellum period, first engaged in the practice of magnetism before channeling spirits from the invisible world through his body. If American Spiritualism had a lead theologian, Davis was it. His 1847 lectures *The Principles of Nature, Her Divine Revelations, and a Voice to Mankind*, which just preceded the Fox sisters' fame, solidified his position as one of the country's foremost Swedenborgians and mesmerists. The volume rambles at times and reads like a stream of consciousness at others because Davis delivered these lectures while in a magnetic, mesmeric trance. His emphasis on the power of the mind, the mind's abilities, and the "spiritual organization" of matter and bodies complemented his interest in communication with the spirits. Significant to all of Davis's writings was his "Harmonial Philosophy," which explained how this world could be improved through the involvement of advanced spirit societies in other "spheres." God and other spirits resided in these spheres, and spirits would progress through the spirit world's levels or spheres toward God: the "Great Positive Mind."[17]

Jackson's Spiritualist theology reflected his utopian vision for U.S. society.[18] He advocated the creation of a perfect society and the perfection of individuals on spiritual quests. For a perfect society, harmony would be key. This harmony required egalitarianism. While Swedenborg's understanding of the spiritual cosmos was a static one in which one's spirit was fixed to a particular sphere with no potential for upward mobility, Davis and most American Spiritualists, including the Cercle Harmonique, believed that spirits could and would progress to higher spheres. This is particularly where Davis and others' understanding of a spiritual republic becomes clear. The spirit world was based on equality in the sense that it was a meritocracy rather than aristocracy. Echoing the millennial ethos of the nineteenth century, Davis believed that the United States was the best place on earth to reflect this spiritual republic. He described his country as "a supernal promise of the happiest land,—the foundation and perfect prophecy of a true Spiritual Republic."[19] Davis developed what religious studies scholar Bret Carroll called a "spiritual republicanism" that "avoided the extremes of individualism and authoritarianism, by emphasizing spiritual freedom, democracy, and equality on the one hand and self-restraint, social obligation, and the rule of natural law, and moral order on the other."[20] According to another nineteenth-century Spiritualist, the spirit world was "the beau ideal of a republic" because "virtue and mind give respect" and "ascendancy is founded on real merit."[21]

In the wake of the Fox sisters' popularity and notoriety, mediums, trance healers, mesmerists, and others who combined these identities traveled the country to give lectures and share their practice with others. In particular, connecting with the spirit world and communicating with the dead—be they deceased loved ones or celebrity figures from history—brought the power of the supernatural in close proximity with everyday Americans. Though Margaret Fox later identified her work as a hoax, Spiritualism continued to spread, bolstered by its appeals to science. Many sought scientific evidence for the existence of the spirit world and its involvement in the material. Spirit photography fulfilled this demand for some. Others, like Davis, used the language of electricity and circuits to explain Spiritualism's scientific validity. Spiritualists also encouraged skeptics to try Spiritualism for themselves, and chemistry-professor-turned-Spiritualist Robert Hare saw no distinction among the mind, matter, and spirit, concluding that the natural and the supernatural were not exclusive.[22] In short, evidence for the spirit world could be found in the material world in both science and humanity's progress toward republican enlightenment.

Answers to immediate queries and issues could be found in Spiritualism. The spirits could suggest whom to marry or how to invest money and provide guidance for both everyday life and major decisions. The spirits were present in larger, more significant ways too. With their guidance, the spirits helped move along the progress of humanity by advising those on earth. Davis explained, "the intercourse between minds in this world and minds in the other, is just as possible as the oceanic commerce between Europe and America, or as the more common interchange of social sympathies, between man and man, in every-day life."[23] The progress that the spirits advocated was typically one of reform, including abolition, women's rights, health reform, and labor reform.[24] Spiritualists could observe the spirit world, take notes, and apply these observations to the material world. From the spirits, Spiritualists gained "a code of governance that guaranteed freedom on earth."[25] Spiritualism taught that humans on earth were not alone, and the spirits who guided them lived in harmonious societies built on fraternal brotherhood.

This analysis of the Cercle Harmonique challenges the racial, geographic, and denominational assumptions about American Spiritualism. The Cercle Harmonique was black, not white; in New Orleans, not the northeast United States; and from Catholic backgrounds, not Protestant ones. Additionally, in the study of nineteenth-century American Spiritualism, most books provide an overview of the practice and its practitioners, examine its esoteric elements, or focus on leaders such as Davis. This text sits readers at the séance table with the Cercle Harmonique.[26] As such, *A Luminous Brotherhood* is one of the first texts to closely examine the séance practices of a group, providing a deep analysis of messages, spirits, and significance while still touching upon big picture issues such as politics, race, and gender. The topics discussed by the spirits visiting the Afro-Creoles' circle had everyday significance to members of the Cercle Harmonique and offered a corrective to white supremacy and its social hierarchy.

Power and Politics; Religion and Race

The "spiritual republicanism" that Bret Carroll attributed to Andrew Jackson Davis resonated with the Cercle Harmonique too. Davis extolled the "REPUBLIC of SPIRIT embosomed and gestating in the dominant political organism" and linked the religious reform of American Spiritualism with political republicanism.[27] Carroll described the spiritual republicanism of antebellum Spiritualists as similar to "its political counterpart" because it "avoided the extremes of individualism and authoritarianism by emphasizing spiritual freedom, democracy, and equality on the one hand and self-restraint, social obligation, the rule of natural law, and moral order on the other."[28] The spirits who came to the table of the Cercle Harmonique echoed the spiritual republicanism that Carroll identified in antebellum Spiritualism, but *A Luminous Brotherhood* engages this spiritual republicanism in both broad and specific ways. Spiritual republicanism was a general force universally needed in the whole world, and the Cercle Harmonique's immediate environment required it too. The spirits directly commented on contemporary issues, and so this text discusses local and national Reconstruction politics as well as international events. Liberty, which governed the spirit world, was supposed to rule the material world too. For example, the circle's anticlericalism demonstrates one way this spiritual republicanism manifested in the Cercle Harmonique. Out from under the yoke of the Catholic institution's tyranny, Afro-Creole Spiritualists believed they were on the road to truth and right. This pertained to both their spiritual understanding of the world and the egalitarianism they desired in society, politics, and religious authority. Afro-Creole Spiritualism was never simply talking to the dead.

Nineteenth-century American Spiritualism frequently intersected with both political and personal issues. Many Spiritualists around the country supported abolition, women's rights, and health reform, and that interest in women's rights has encouraged scholars to examine the gender dynamics of Spiritualism in terms of female agency and middle class manhood.[29] While the field has explored Spiritualism and gender, the intersections of politics, race, and Spiritualism are horribly understudied. Historian John Patrick Deveney's biographical work *Paschal Beverly Randolph: A Nineteenth-Century Black American Spiritualist, Rosicrucian, and Sex Magician* is the only previous book specifically devoted to an African American's practice of nineteenth-century Spiritualism.[30] *A Luminous Brotherhood* is the first text to focus on how racial identity and local society shaped the politics and everyday practice of nineteenth-century Spiritualism and the first text to examine a community of black Spiritualists.[31] The analysis in *A Luminous Brotherhood* shows how those without a white racial advantage envisioned the spirit world. For example, the Cercle Harmonique believed death was an event that released the spirit and left the raced body on earth. Additionally, the spirits communicating with the Cercle Harmonique argued that race was a category devoid of real meaning.

This book also shows that black mainline Christians do not have a monopoly on the intersections of religion, politics, and everyday life.[32] Spiritualism was not a popular religion among African Americans in general, but it strongly resonated with Afro-Creoles in New Orleans. Spiritualism's emphasis on reform, republicanism, and merit spoke to politically active Afro-Creoles. Over the course of the nineteenth century, black New Orleanians witnessed expansions and contractions of their civil and legal rights. Therefore, this book requires close attention to politics. Political personhood, meaning what politically and legally constituted a person, greatly changed over the course of the century. While free blacks possessed some political and legal rights, particularly under colonial New Orleans rule, the 1857 Supreme Court decision in *Dred Scott v. Sandford* declared that African Americans possessed no legal protection under the U.S. Constitution. American slavery formed the base to the country's racial hierarchy, and in various forms, religion both supported and criticized the nationwide commitment to white over black. For many African Americans, religion provided language, spaces, and worldviews that fostered resistance against white political hegemony.[33] Many African American and Afro-Atlantic religions drew from a combination of indigenous culture and Euro-American culture to contest the dominant culture.[34] In the case of the Cercle Harmonique, these Afro-Creoles used a tradition typically associated with white, liberal Protestants in the northeast to criticize a form of American tyranny—the white supremacist, southern, slaveholding oligarchy.

The racial hierarchy in New Orleans increasingly solidified on a white/black binary over the course of the nineteenth century. Within this social environment, the Afro-Creole population was a fluid and complicated one that cannot be limited by any one characteristic but rather developed in a historically contingent matrix of political, cultural, social, and legal vectors. *A Luminous Brotherhood* shows how religion allowed Afro-Creoles to navigate the changes following the Civil War. North and South, winners and losers, blacks and whites, all found themselves in a different world following the war. Following the Confederacy's loss, many white southerners developed the "Lost Cause": the continuing belief that the South's reasons and way of life were righteous, despite their defeat. With their arguments for human rights and republicanism and their focus on the dead, the Cercle Harmonique offers an interesting counterpoint and complement to the Lost Cause. In both cases deceased heroes lent insight, significance, and cultural resonance from beyond the grave and grounded everyday life in a politically and religiously rich world.

Though some Creoles tried to define their social category as solely white in the late nineteenth century, the Afro-Creole population was as old as the larger Creole world that surrounded them. Many scholars of New Orleans and Louisiana define "Creole" as a person born in the colonial new world with any racial or ethnic background, and for colonists, this was a means to distinguish between those born in the New World and those born in the old (either Europe or, in the case of slaves, Africa). This definition becomes less helpful after the late colonial period as more and more Louisianans were born in the New World.[35] After 1803, French or Spanish colonial ancestry and culture increasingly signified Creole identity in New Orleans. Creoles across the racial spectrum found their social and political identities changing much over the nineteenth century. The historian Shirley Elizabeth Thompson defined New Orleans's Afro-Creoles as "an in-between people exiled from the comfortable confines of racial solidarity and national citizenship" and who thus served as "convenient prisms, refracting and reshaping competing ideas about race and belonging."[36] Unfortunately, primary sources revealing the everyday life of nineteenth-century New Orleans Afro-Creoles are in short supply. The lives of some members of this population were well documented, while most others largely have been lost to history. The everyday lives of Cercle Harmonique members are difficult to reconstruct; some of their identities are fuzzy and, while others may be clearer, full biographies are impossible. However, the group's séance records provide an invaluable window into their religious, political, and social ideas.

Ideas about race frequently changed in the nineteenth century causing the social, legal, and racial identity of Afro-Creoles to be in flux. With the Civil War and Reconstruction, the tenure of the Cercle Harmonique's practice was a time of conflict and change. Emancipation was clear progress, but it also meant learned, free black and mixed-race New Orleanians were collapsed into the same legal category as recently freed African Americans. While the séance records of the Cercle Harmonique reflect a commitment to egalitarianism, members of the group came from privileged backgrounds. These privileged backgrounds allowed for their practice; without them, Cercle Harmonique members would not have been educated and conversant in politics and world history. In particular, the Cercle Harmonique's knowledge of French revolutionary thought was vital to the spirits' Idea of egalitarian republicanism.

Egalitarian Republicanism and the Atlantic World

The Enlightenment and the political revolutions of the Atlantic world helped mold the Cercle Harmonique's Idea. The impact of the Enlightenment on Western politics, society, religion, and education cannot be overstated. While studies of the Enlightenment in America typically focus on the long eighteenth century, its "lingering force," as the historian Leigh Schmidt has explored, was felt across nineteenth-century American culture.[37] Discussions of religion and the Enlightenment often center on the growth of deism, its contrasts to Evangelicalism, or the appeal of Scottish common sense to various forms of Protestantism.[38] Additionally, those studies typically focus on white men, but the influence of the Enlightenment extended beyond those religious and racial circles. Because the Cercle Harmonique communicated with an invisible spirit world, outsiders typically viewed them as spiritually misguided and duped. But, according to the spiritual guides of the Cercle Harmonique, Spiritualism was an enlightened religion that fostered progress. The circle's spiritual guides frequently instructed them to throw off old "superstitions" and modes of authority. One spirit connected the Cercle Harmonique to a "great philosophical chain" of thinkers, all linked by a common goal: "to undermine errors; superstition, political or religious despotic governments" and instead "to work for the progress of the generous and refreshing Idea!"[39] Afro-Creole Spiritualists, then, were politically, socially, and religiously enlightened beings.

In the wake of the Enlightenment, many thinkers applied the new evaluative models of science to social and political systems, and the result of this significantly changed Western society and politics. For example, the French Revolution signaled a clear rupture in the current trajectory of social, political, and intellectual ideas. It forced a "reconstitution of the legal, religious, educational, cultural, and political formations of French society."[40] In particular, the creation of France's Declaration of the Rights of Man and of the Citizen in 1789 was a watershed moment in political history. The French *philosophes* and other Enlightenment thinkers influenced the idea of modern republicanism. The rhetoric and success of the French Revolution inspired the Haitian Revolution, and it helped shape the development of party politics in the early U.S. republic. Its influence reverberated beyond the early nineteenth century, and members of the Cercle Harmonique admired those ideas and the men who articulated them. In the United States, the Enlightenment helped shape ideas about the individual, society, science, and government. It influenced how Americans, Creoles, and other actors in the Atlantic world conceptualized race and natural rights. European and American cultures formed discourses about natural rights as they denied those rights to Africans and their descendants. The Enlightenment, largely through its emphasis on natural rights and its influence on the Atlantic revolutions, also shaped Western ideas on republicanism, including the American "affirmation that 'all men are created equal,' in that all possess 'unalienable rights.'"[41] In the wake of the Civil War, the Cercle Harmonique, among millions of other African Americans, hoped the United States would finally fulfill that promise for all her citizens.

The New Orleans Afro-Creoles of the Cercle Harmonique did not participate in any event associated with the Atlantic age of revolutions, but their séance records were loaded with revolutionary rhetoric. With the fall of the Confederacy, they hoped to mimic the overthrow of the French ancien régime, minus the violence. Cercle Harmonique members and their spiritual guides trusted that the end of slavery in America would be a pivotal moment like the French Revolution and bring the material world closer to its destiny—egalitarian republicanism. With great hope, they predicted that America would uphold the goodness and virtue of democracy. The spirits taught that all people had value and dignity regardless of sex, race, class, or nationality, and they supported individualism, freedom, democracy, and equality. Like the Declaration of the Rights of Man, the Constitution and the Bill of Rights promised freedom that was supposed to allow all Americans to enjoy liberty and strive for self-improvement. Neither prejudice nor greed had a proper place in the Cercle Harmonique's vision for America's destiny. Intolerance and materialism bred injustice. In contrast, justice, equality, and democracy ruled the spirit world. That was what made it a spiritual republic and that was why it should be emulated on earth. The Cercle Harmonique looked forward to a material world that would replace the southern ancien régime of a slaveholding white oligarchy with a perfect egalitarian and democratic republic.

While the Cercle Harmonique was in direct conversation with the Atlantic world's age of revolutions through their spiritual guides, American Spiritualism typically is studied as a religion with national boundaries. This is an inaccurate framework. The United States' formal borders have never bound American religions, and the practice of the Cercle Harmonique demonstrates the porousness of religion in American history. Ideas, peoples, practices, and spirits crossed the nation's boundaries again and again. Any sense of a divide between the local and the global is imprecise; however, the transnational elements of American Spiritualism have not been fully considered.[42] This book opens up this conversation by situating the Cercle Harmonique in the Atlantic world. Through their remembrance of French revolutionary history and culture and with their spiritual-genealogical ties with French and Caribbean culture, the Cercle Harmonique's practice extends American Spiritualism beyond U.S. political borders. In this way, *A Luminous Brotherhood* also adds a new element to the study of African American religions. Most studies of African American religious history and the Atlantic world focus on either

African diasporic religions or the physical movement of bodies. Instead, this book elucidates the intellectual and political influences from both the local and the global on Afro-Creole religious practice.

This transatlantic aspect of Afro-Creole Spiritualism also emphasizes the importance of context, locale, and networks in the study of New Orleans religion instead of New Orleans exceptionalism.[43] Rather than identify New Orleans as exceptional or as an outlier in American cultural history, this book views it as a city where a variety of European and African peoples forged relationships and exchanged ideas.[44] New Orleans was not an exceptional place or the foil to other geographic regions of the nineteenth-century United States, but instead it is another "siting" for telling American religious history.[45] While Afro-Creole Spiritualism had a transatlantic element, it was also similar to the Spiritualism practiced farther north in its spiritual republicanism. The Afro-Creoles did not take all their religious cues from France. For example, messages recorded in Rey's séance books identified American Spiritualism as superior to French Spiritism. However, absent in northern Spiritualism was the influence of the city's Afro-Creole Catholic culture. New Orleans provides historians with a rich history of black Catholicism, and as demonstrated in this book, Catholicism helped shape the ideas and practice of the Cercle Harmonique.

The New Orleans Cercle Harmonique

The desire for political agency permeated the messages recorded in the Cercle Harmonique's séance records. Thus, their practice illuminates the intersections of race, authority, and politics in American religion. The messages they received argued the meaninglessness of race in a world built on racial difference. The spirits denied the validity of institutionalized authority in religious and political circles, while many in New Orleans and the United States sought to keep power in old hands. Rey and the rest of the Cercle Harmonique offered an alternative and egalitarian political model for the post–Civil War United States. While a few scholars have touched upon the Cercle Harmonique, none has brought all these threads together in their full vivid color and texture.[46] One scholar who began this process was the historian Caryn Cossé Bell in *Revolution, Romanticism, and the Afro-Creole Protest Tradition in Louisiana, 1718–1868* (1997), a text that examined the political radicalism, egalitarian ideals, and outspoken protest of Afro-Creoles in New Orleans. Bell focused one chapter on Spiritualism, but the Cercle Harmonique received less than ten pages of attention because of her periodization and the book's endpoint in 1868. One of the other scholars to examine the Cercle Harmonique is Robert Cox in *Body and Soul: A Sympathetic History of American Spiritualism* (2003). Cox's emphasis on the sympathetic highlighted Spiritualism's interrelated ideas regarding human nature, time, the natural world, and the social world, but he only spent one chapter in New Orleans. The Cercle Harmonique is, thus, a blind spot in the study of American Spiritualism, African American religions, and American religious history more broadly. New Orleans was a rich contact zone of racial politics, Catholicism, social changes, and Spiritualism, making it a prime location for communication between the spiritual world and the material world and a premier place to study nineteenth-century American religion.

The argument proposed here begins with a close reading of the group's séance records as kept by Rey. After Rey's death, his friend and fellow Cercle Harmonique leader François "Petit" Dubuclet kept the records, which he later gave to his son-in-law René Grandjean, a French émigré and Spiritualist himself. Grandjean later donated the séance records, along with numerous other documents, to the University of New Orleans. The Cercle Harmonique's archive spans twenty years and thirty-five large register books, which amounts to over seven thousand handwritten pages. I spent extensive time with the Cercle Harmonique's records and transcribed and translated from the original French over a thousand pages of spirit messages.[47] I paid particular attention to significant dates, spirits, and recurring themes, and I was careful to transcribe and translate a wide sampling of randomly selected messages to ensure a fair appraisal.

Focusing on the content of the spirit communications, the identities of the spirits themselves, and the context in which the messages were received, *A Luminous Brotherhood* presents a multilayered analysis of the Cercle Harmonique's practice. Equally important here are the spiritual genealogy in which they imagined themselves, the political and theological nature of the spirit messages, and the messages' and spirits' relationship to the wider world. As such, this book considers the interplay between the messages' contact, the messages' content, and the messages' context. Spirit, message, and context together reveal the business of Afro-Creole Spiritualism, and that business's product was a reimagined post–Civil War America that honored her founding claim of equality. Additionally, the received messages did not arrive randomly to the Cercle Harmonique but rather from a spiritual genealogy purposefully curated by the Cercle Harmonique in which the members imagined themselves. It was the spirits of Abraham Lincoln, Voltaire, and Jesus who relayed their vision for Reconstruction society.

The Cercle Harmonique stitched together local, national, global, and cosmological communities and conversations. This book unstitches their encounters, looks at the pieces, and asks where they came from, how they got there, and what they meant in those moments. *A Luminous Brotherhood* is organized as a series of concentric circles extending out from the Cercle Harmonique, tracing their interactions with the material world and spirit world around them. Chapter 1 introduces the Cercle Harmonique in terms of leaders and members, Rey's initiation to Spiritualism, the details of the circle's practices, and the spirits who communicated with them. This chapter sets the stage for the following pages by providing the reader a primer for understanding the Cercle Harmonique. The Afro-Creole Spiritualists held much in common doctrinally with their northern Spiritualist comrades and their neighboring local, white, French Creole, and émigré mediums. The spirits visiting the Cercle Harmonique emphasized unity and harmony, and their communications denoted a level of personal connection between the community of spirits and the Spiritualists at the table. Part of the reason for the personal flavor of Afro-Creole Spiritualism was the number of Cercle Harmonique family members who advised their loved ones from the spirit world. This chapter presents an overview of the spirits in the spiritual republic, who ranged from political celebrities to deceased parents. Rey's own conversion to Spiritualism, the structure of the Cercle Harmonique meetings, and the spirits who appeared at their table unveil much about Spiritualism's appeal to the Afro-Creoles. Egalitarian in its focus and its actions, the spirit of French nobleman and philosopher Constantin François de Chassebœuf, better known as the Comte de Volney, described "the harmonic circle" as a collective that desired "communion together to help each other in research."[48] The chapter concludes with a section describing and reconstructing the spirits' Idea—that principal concept of egalitarian republicanism.

Chapter 2 moves beyond the immediate séance table and begins to situate the Cercle Harmonique in their local environment: New Orleans. This chapter depicts the spirits' views on local politics, violence, and vice. Materialism was at the root of what the spirits considered the city's problems, which included prostitution, street violence, gambling, political corruption, and economic and racial inequality. The city's materialism worked against the spirits' Idea of egalitarian republicanism and instead fostered prejudice. These prejudices could spur violence, and Reconstruction was a complicated and bloody epoch in Louisiana history. It was also a time of political promise, and Afro-Creole interests in politics intersected with messages received by the Cercle Harmonique. The spirits took note of New Orleans politics and advised how to make the city a more egalitarian place, but this process was not easy. New Orleans was home to some of the worst Reconstruction violence. Martyrs of the 1866 Mechanics' Institute Riot, a massacre of primarily black Republican delegates, offered guidance and assurance from the spirit world. Street violence erupted again in 1874's Battle of Liberty Place when white supremacists took control of New Orleans, and the Cercle Harmonique's spiritual guides continued to encourage Rey and others to keep their courage and confidence in the Idea. The day following the Battle of Liberty Place, the spirit of Saint Vincent de Paul assured them that "you will see the civil rights of each one proclaimed and they will be maintained!"[49] Even when everyday life indicated otherwise, the spirits saw progress.

The next chapter remains in the local concentric circle of New Orleans and examines Afro-Creole Spiritualism over and against Catholicism, its religious neighbor. I focus on the relationship between the Cercle Harmonique and Catholicism by investigating the Spiritualists' religious genealogy and examining their ideas about religious authority. The members of the Cercle Harmonique pushed against Catholicism to carve out a space for their own religious identity. Yet at the same time, resonances of Catholicism echoed in the Cercle Harmonique's practice in the form of advisement from Catholic spirits and reverberations of a few Catholic ideas. These Afro-Creoles left the church pews, but Catholicism did not leave them. Though their practice included Catholic ideas and prominent Catholic spirits, they also received numerous anticlerical messages demonstrating their negative perspective on religious despotism, tyranny, and exploitation. The spirits and members of the Cercle Harmonique regarded the revealed knowledge of Spiritualism as a more legitimate form of religious power than Catholicism's formal authority. Priests were greedy, corrupt, and undeserving of the laity's reverence. In a spirit message from the French monk Rabelais, the priest received a particularly vitriolic depiction as "the enemy" and an "intruder who wants to be your master." While a shepherd shears his sheep "to the skin," a priest "shears his sheep to the bone."[50] Criticizing Catholicism illustrated the group's ideas regarding materialism, greed, and corruption and simultaneously underlined Spiritualism's egalitarianism.

Chapter 4 moves to the next concentric circle encapsulating the Cercle Harmonique and describes the Spiritualists' and the spirits' hopes for the postwar United States by highlighting their love of republicanism and simultaneous criticism of slavery, the Confederacy, and political corruption. In contrast to the southern oligarchy and its white supremacy, the spirits endorsed republicanism and celebrated democratic ideas. Afro-Creole Spiritualism's emphasis on progress, republicanism, equality, and spiritual perfection resonated with the political aspirations of the Afro-Creoles seated at the séance table. The spirits' messages on slavery and the Civil War affirmed the Cercle Harmonique's belief that the country should regenerate itself with equality and liberty as its foundation. The Idea stood with the Union, with civil and legal rights, and with racial equality. The spirits rejected the categories of race and nation because they did not exist in the spiritual spheres, and this spiritual deconstruction inherently criticized America's white-over-black racial hierarchy. Additionally, the presence of various American celebrity spirits, most notably Abraham Lincoln and John Brown, solidified the circle's imagined place in the progress of egalitarianism and liberty. "The Republic is marching on," the spirit of John Brown proclaimed, "with gigantic steps, towards the Union of the Races."[51] If the United States followed the spirits' instructions, the American republic could become more like the ideal world of the spirits—the perfect spiritual republic.

Also present in the group's practice were the ideas of and major players in the French Revolution and the broader Atlantic age of revolutions. Thus, chapter 5 situates the Cercle Harmonique in an Atlantic world where France, the Caribbean, and New Orleans were the main nodes. The Cercle Harmonique reinvigorated the French revolutionary motto "Liberté, Egalité, Fraternité" to convey the group's political ideology and their understanding of the spirit world. The way in which the Cercle Harmonique remembered the French Revolution and, to a lesser extent, the Haitian Revolution emphasizes their dedication to particular revolutionary ideals. Republican governments, Robespierre's spirit taught, offered "people . . . the immense advantage of the right of discussion, of religious liberty." Indeed, "the republic is the people marching towards progress."[52] Spirits and ideas from the French Revolution and the Haitian Revolution frequently appear in the séance records and express the circle's attraction to republicanism and aversion to despotism. This adds a transnational element to nineteenth-century American Spiritualism. The Atlantic world's revolutions continued in New Orleans through the Cercle Harmonique and their envisioned spiritual republic. Parallel to the French Revolution's overturn of the ancien régime, the Cercle Harmonique was interested in the demise of another oligarchy—namely southern slave-holders and their white supremacist heirs.

Finally, *A Luminous Brotherhood*'s conclusion examines endings. It describes the Cercle Harmonique's view of death, or what was simply the end of life in the material world. Death was not to be feared, for it meant the escape of the spirit from the material, raced body and the spirit's entrance into the higher spheres. The spirits' assessment of death is followed by remarks on the end of the Cercle Harmonique and the end of Rey's individual practice. When Reconstruction failed to rebuild the South with equal civil or legal rights for African Americans, this was not the only failure. The rise of Jim Crow laws illuminated the collapse of the spirits' vision too. The material world still looked nothing like the spiritual republic. The conclusion also provides a final overview of the social and political changes in lower Louisiana from the Haitian Revolution to the end of Reconstruction and recaps the significance of the Cercle Harmonique's practice in this context. The book closes with a short postscript regarding the last dated message recorded in the Cercle Harmonique's register books. The final messages transcribed in the séance books bring us back to the beginning—an intimate conversation with spirits at a simple séance table in a private home.

CHAPTER ONE

The Creation of the Cercle Harmonique

Many excellent mediums were found among the colored population, one of whom, a French creole named Dr. Valmour, attained a high and deserved celebrity as a healing medium.

—Emma Hardinge Britten, *Modern American Spiritualism: A Twenty Years' Record of the Communion Between Earth and the World of the Spirits*

The advice of the wise is always beneficial for those who put forward his reason as his guide.

—Spirit of Mesmer to the Cercle Harmonique, 19 November 1865

Come to the table in order to become just, wise, and to elevate yourselves by your soul.

—Spirit of a Brother to the Cercle Harmonique, 18 March 1873

In late 1859, Emma Hardinge Britten delivered a series of lectures on Spiritualism in New Orleans hosted at fraternal lodges.[1] During one of these lectures at the Odd Fellows' Hall she began to tire while performing her Spiritualist demonstrations. At the same time, a local black Creole blacksmith popularly known as J. B. Valmour (John B. Aversin) was walking by the building when suddenly he was "seized" by a "spiritual influence" and entered the auditorium. Britten immediately recognized a spiritual affinity with Valmour and exclaimed, "Let that Brother come up here to me, to give me strength to speak, he is full of electricity." Valmour went on stage and sat there for the next two hours, during which Britten was able to continue her demonstrations and keep the audience "charmed."[2] In her later writings, Britten noted how "either the noble Creoles [in New Orleans] are determined to take Spiritualism by storm, or the spirits are determined to take them."[3] The "noble Creoles" she referenced were likely Valmour and his friends Henri Louis Rey and "Sister Louise." Britten was a popular practitioner and fervent defender of Spiritualism. Her book *Modern American Spiritualism: A Twenty Years' Record of the Communion between Earth and the World of the Spirits* was an encyclopedic account of Spiritualism in the United States. During another trip to New Orleans, one of her friends reported meeting a powerful African

American named Tom Jenkins who would channel the spirit of a Mississippi River boatman named Big Ben and make "magic." Jenkins reportedly "became entranced, took off his shoes and stockings, rolled up his pantaloons to his knees, and entered the pine wood fire, literally standing in it as it blazed upon the hearth, long enough to repeat in a solemn and impressive manner the 23rd, 24th, and 25th verses of the third chapter of Daniel."[4] While most nineteenth-century Americans who practiced Spiritualism were white, middle class northerners, black southerners also communicated with the world of the spirits.

Before the inception of the Cercle Harmonique, other Creole New Orleanians communicated with the spirit world. The first community of Spiritualists in the city was led by white French émigré Joseph Barthet in mid-nineteenth-century New Orleans. Meeting with Barthet were a few Afro-Creole men, such as Valmour, who would later develop the Cercle Harmonique. Spiritualism's northern origins, support for abolition and equality, and calls for progressive liberal politics found allies and enemies in the South. Britten was threatened with lynching during one of her southern tours, and Alabama law made Spiritualist demonstrations illegal and subject to a $500 fine. The message of Spiritualism could threaten the status quo of the South, and thus, those desirous of social and political change found in Spiritualism a religious orientation that interlaced with their goals. The world of spirits located a receptive audience in the free blacks in New Orleans who suffered increasingly restrictive laws and then met with violent resistance to suffrage and racial equality after the Civil War.

This chapter offers a primer to the Cercle Harmonique. The spirits wanted to help humanity better itself, and advising the New Orleans Spiritualists was a clear way to achieve this goal. Rey's conversion to Spiritualism, the spirits who communicated with the group, and the egalitarian focus of many of their messages all indicate the spirits' investment in the material world's progress. The spirits who communicated with the Cercle Harmonique ranged from former U.S. presidents to religious leaders to the mediums' deceased family members. The spiritual republic frequently emphasized harmony and equality—and humanity's need for them. In particular, the spirits referenced "the Idea," a concept that meant equality and brotherhood. The Idea should shape the material world, and as later chapters will demonstrate, the Cercle Harmonique believed the Idea could justly rebuild and reconstruct the United States in the wake of the Civil War. For the Afro-Creole Spiritualists, their social and political aspirations found a spiritual medium.

"Parlez-leur, ils vous répondront": French Spiritualism in New Orleans

Metaphysical religious thought began gaining popularity in New Orleans in 1845, though some in New Orleans had accepted mesmerism before. Throughout the 1840s, references to mesmerist meetings and lectures and negative exposé pieces about mesmerism became common in the local newspapers. The *New Orleans Daily Picayune* (*Daily Picayune*) informed readers of the "awful" effects of mesmerism, as well as the "wonderful effects."[5] Newspapers advertised local lectures and reported on the medicinal and therapeutic value of the practice but also lightheartedly referred to the "wags" mesmerists had at the expense of others.[6] Joseph Barthet organized the city's first metaphysical religion organization, the Société du Magnétisme de la Nouvelle-Orléans, in April 1845. The Société planned lectures, staged public demonstrations, developed a library, and attracted a sizable number of French émigrés.[7] One local observer explained the appeal of Spiritualism to the city's Catholic Creole population in this way: "Spiritualism has made much more rapid progress among the creole and Catholic portions of our population than the Protestant; first, because most of them have more time for investigation than the rushing hurrying, money-making American, and secondly, the creed of the Catholic Church does not deny the possibility of spirit communication."[8]

Initially the Société met little opposition from the local Catholic Church. In fact, Abbé (Father) Malavergne was a member, and he and other priests would refer ill congregants to mesmerists for help.[9] However, the church's official periodical, *Le Propagateur Catholique,* and its editor (and later New Orleans archbishop) Abbé Napoleon Joseph Perché began to criticize and denounce mesmerism and later Spiritualism. The paper formed in November 1842 and supported both local Bishop Antoine Blanc and Catholic Romanization of the diocese. For example, the paper criticized the St. Louis Cathedral *marguilliers* (trustees) and heralded the *marguilliers'* waning control of the cathedral. *Le Propagateur Catholique* and Perché sought to maintain proper hierarchical authority in the church, which meant adherence to doctrine and dogma and complete recognition of religious authorities. The leniency and fluidity of late eighteenth- and early nineteenth-century New Orleans Catholicism under the leadership of Antonio de Sedella and Aloysius Leopold Moni, two earlier pastors of New Orleans's St. Louis Cathedral, were over. Sedella and Moni were beloved by Creole Catholics of all

skin colors for their openness to freemasons and mesmerists and their support for the Creole laity. Despite Catholicism's long history in Louisiana,
some members of the hierarchy, Perché and Blanc included, felt that religious ignorance and immoral indulgence were problems in the city, which *Le
Propagateur Catholique* was to address and correct.[10] In addition to mesmerism, adherents to Spiritualism became targets in Perché's editorials.

Shortly after news of the Rochester rappings swept the country, Barthet
became a believer in and practitioner of Spiritualism. In 1852, Barthet published a Spiritualism manual, the *ABC des communications spirituelles*, and
when the periodical *Le Spiritualiste de la Nouvelle-Orléans* debuted five years
later, the communications received by Barthet's circle often dominated the
pages.[11] The tagline for *Le Spiritualiste* was "Ils ne sont pas morts. Parlez-leur,
ils vous répondront."[12] "The doctrine of Christ has been disfigured," the periodical contended, and Spiritualism concerned itself with "the restoring of
its purity."[13] The Catholic Church, its dogma, and its hierarchy received harsh
criticism from the spirits who frequented the séance tables of Barthet and
the Cercle Harmonique. The periodical also printed responses to critics
of Spiritualism, often citing the editorials of Perché in *Le Propagateur
Catholique*.[14] In response to its Catholic critics, *Le Spiritualiste* explained the
differences between Spiritualism and Catholicism. The periodical's editors
argued that Catholicism told people to believe everything it asserted, even if
it seemed contradictory. The laity had to take Catholicism's claims on faith
alone. However, Spiritualism encouraged believers to "see, think, question,
study." Barthet described Spiritualism, unlike Catholicism, as a directly revealed, more hands-on religion, in which believers personally engaged spirits
and experienced communication with the spirit world.[15] When the Cercle
Harmonique began communicating with the spirits a few years later, they
received similar messages critical of Catholicism. Though some New Orleanians embraced Spiritualism, others were more cynical and skeptical. Throughout the 1850s, advertisements ran in the local newspapers for lectures on
Spiritualism, corresponding reporters sent articles about Spiritualist circles
in the Northeast, and exposé-style pieces were published. In the local press
both Spiritualists and their beliefs were often called "humbugs."[16]

Charles Testut, another French émigré, also became a Spiritualist during
the 1850s and distributed the results of some of his séances in a publication
called *Manifestations spirituelles*. Testut's dedication to the ideals of the French
Revolution, his abolitionist stance, and his belief in the brotherhood of man
manifested in his séance records, in his 1858 novel, *Le Vieux Salomon: ou, Une*

Famille d'esclaves au XIX siècle (*Old Solomon: or, A Slave Family in the Nineteenth Century*), and in his short-lived 1871 newspaper, *L'Equité*. For example, his characters in *Le Vieux Salomon* belonged to a revolutionary secret society called Les Frères de la Croyance Universelle (The Brothers of the Universal Faith), a group that transcended racial and gender lines. Testut described the beliefs of the society as including "fraternity, charity, freedom, happiness, the present, the future, the greatness of man on earth and his pleasure in heaven; the equality possible in the social order."[17] This belief system possessed similarities with the Spiritualism of the Cercle Harmonique in its emphases on fraternity, charity, and equality on earth and in heaven.[18] Barthet, Testut, and those interested in Spiritualism and mesmerism were not only white Creoles or French émigrés. Black Creoles also read Testut's novel, his 1871 newspaper, and possibly *Manifestations spirituelles*.[19] And the séances that Barthet headed were multiracial and attracted some Afro-Creoles. A few of these Spiritualists would emerge as the early leaders of the Cercle Harmonique.

"Always follow your path"[20]:
Formation of the Cercle Harmonique

One New Orleanian medium Barthet held in high esteem was Valmour. Barthet compared him to Jesus and noted how Valmour's home residence reminded him of the humble birthplace of "the great Nazarene."[21] Local blacksmith and respected healer Valmour, a man highly regarded for "the laying on of hands and in the transmission of spiritual messages," was one of the most renowned black Creoles interested in metaphysical religion.[22] He was also an early member of the Cercle Harmonique. Valmour's home was both his blacksmith shop and a séance meeting place. Locals would also come to see Valmour for his curative abilities, but not all in the city supported him. The police disrupted a séance meeting at Valmour's house in fall of 1858 under suspicion of practicing Voudou.[23] Grandjean recorded in his notes various cures of Valmour and others affiliated with the Cercle Harmonique. Grandjean also reported some of their healing successes. For example, Valmour cured a bishop from Italy who had visited "prominent doctors" in Europe and the United States, but none could restore the bishop's lost voice. During the bishop's visit to New Orleans Valmour cured him with just "a few impositions of his hands."[24]

The Afro-Creole population that Valmour, Henri Louis Rey, François "Petit" Dubuclet, and others of the Cercle Harmonique came from was a racial, ethnic, and cultural group that differed from whites and other blacks. It was no one characteristic that differentiated Afro-Creoles from non-Creole blacks but rather a complex network of identity vectors. Much of the city's Afro-Creole population came from families who were freed during the colonial or antebellum era, were Catholic, were often mixed-race or of lighter skin color, were French-speaking or bilingual, were educated, and were often wealthier than their black non-Creole neighbors. Before the Civil War, much of the Afro-Creole population occupied a racial and social space somewhere between slave and white, but following emancipation, their special status as free black now described all blacks. In response to the city's changing racial stratification, many Afro-Creoles argued for full civil and legal rights for all races. Others drew attention to their community's unique history and heritage.[25] The Cercle Harmonique sought advisement from the spirits on how to properly remake society and fix politics.

The most active mediums and leaders of the group were first Valmour and Louise, and later Rey and Petit. Valmour and Louise died before the circle entered its most active years (1871–74). Rey remained a key leader for the circle's entire tenure. In the group's earlier years under the leadership of Valmour and Louise, Joanni Questy, Nelson Desbrosses, Adolphe Duhart, Paulin Durel, and Charles Veque also met for séances.[26] Questy, Desbrosses, and Duhart were esteemed local black Creole scholars and poets, active in the publication of *L'Album littéraire: Journal des jeunes gens, amateurs de littérature* (*The Literary Album: A Journal of Young Men, Lovers of Literature*) and *Les Cenelles*. *Les Cenelles* was a sizable book of poems by seventeen Afro-Creole male poets that locals of all racial and social classes regarded as a literary triumph, and accordingly, these men were seen as leaders in Afro-Creole culture.[27] However, the vast majority of the séance records that have survived come from the late 1860s and into the mid-1870s under a different core group, though Questy and Desbrosses would remain with Rey's circle as spiritual advisors from beyond.[28]

In addition to Rey, the other two primary mediums of the Cercle Harmonique were Petit and Victor Lavigne. One spirit identified Rey, Petit, and Lavigne as the "blessed trio" who should "be happy" with their "Union." Lavigne was a healer, medium, and cigar maker who owned a small cigar shop. Other members included Desbrosses, Emilien Planchard, Emile Luscy,

Donatien Déruisé, Maitre Brion, Joseph Alexis, Romain, Jules Mallet, and Lucien Lavigne. Mondays and Fridays were the primary meeting days for the circle, and some members usually attended on a set day (either Monday or Friday). Typically seven members met for each meeting of the Cercle Harmonique. The size of the circle was not as important as the quality of spiritual work achieved at a meeting. According to the spirits, three solid mediums could achieve "much more than the assembled masses with incoherent ideas." The harmony of a circle was "due to the wisdom of those who come to join the search" rather than the size, social status, or race of its members. The strength of a circle came from the members' "work," not their backgrounds. After his death, the spirit of Valmour instructed the group to "unite" and "not abandon anyone" of the "Cercle harmonique."[29] Unity and integrity trumped social rank.

Notes from the circle's first archivist, René Grandjean, indicate that the permanent members of the circle were all men, with occasional black Creole women in attendance, such as Rey's wife. The overwhelming majority of spirit communications were from male spirits to a male circle, but messages occasionally were addressed to brothers and sisters.[30] The respected medium Louise is the only definite example of a female Afro-Creole regularly practicing Spiritualism with Rey's group. Many of Rey's early séance records (those from the late 1850s) came from meetings held at Louise's home, and she returned in spirit form to the Cercle Harmonique. "Thousands of spirits" greeted her upon her arrival to the spiritual spheres and her reward was "grand and magnificent." A main reason for her spiritual success was her rejection of materialism. While "Louise the Medium was enchanted Matter; Louise the Spirit revolves about eternal perfumed Spheres." Though women were not the main leaders of the Cercle Harmonique, female spirits occasionally visited the circle, and some spirits spoke of gender equality and proper gender dynamics while others covered similar ground as their male counterparts. A message from "a devoted sister" echoed the advice in many other messages—work for harmony, aspire for spiritual progression, and recognize the happiness of those spirits in the spiritual world.[31]

The spirits periodically celebrated the skills and character of the Cercle Harmonique's members. For example, a spirit identified as Alpha described Romain as "quiet" and "modest"; Mallet was a "young child in study" but possessed "a prepared mind"; Victor Lavigne was an "Apostle"; and the "wisdom of Petit" was something to be admired. Another spirit described Tillius as "a child who has received the light." An anonymous spirit spoke of Mallet's "Light," Petit's "confidence," and the "stability" that Lavigne provided the Cercle Harmonique. Another unidentified spirit marveled at the "extraordinary" development of Mallet, Petit, and Rey. A spirit identified as Lunel also described the work of the "dedicated" brothers Petit and Rey as "beautiful" and "beneficial," which was exceptionally admirable considering that they were "working in the midst of corruption." Petit was "a pillar of confidence and abnegation," while Rey's "confidence, his dedication, his prodigious strength of humanitarian love, and his great dedication" were esteemed.[32] High praise like this coming from the spiritual spheres helped motivate the Cercle Harmonique even if much of the New Orleans society disagreed with their religion or politics.

Though the spirits affirmed the importance of all members of the Cercle Harmonique, Rey acted as the group's primary leader. Rey was well educated and a "bright mulatto"[33] born into one of the Tremé's most successful Afro-Creole families on 20 February 1831. After his father's death in 1852, Rey's life drastically changed in material and spiritual ways. Just one hour after his father's passing, Rey fleetingly saw the spirit of his father, but when he went to embrace him, the spirit disappeared. Though it would be a handful of years before Rey joined a Spiritualist circle, the experience remained with him. Spirits also noted the significance of this event in Rey's development as a Spiritualist "Apostle" and medium. An 1858 message from his father, Barthélemy, noted how Rey recognized his voice during that early Spiritualist experience but disregarded it as imagined.[34] In 1857, the same year Rey began to experiment with Spiritualism, he married Adèle Crocker, the daughter of Rose and Pierre Crocker. With his marriage to Adèle, Rey became part of a family with a wide range of religious relationships. Pierre Crocker's cousin was Henriette Delille, the lead foundress of the Afro-Creole *Sœurs de la Sainte Famille*, who were the second order of black nuns in the United States.[35] Additionally, Pierre Crocker was involved in a *plaçage* (mistress) relationship with Marie Heloïse Euchariste Glapion, daughter of famous Voudou priestess Marie Laveau and sometimes known as Marie Laveau II.[36]

The Rey family was an active and respected one in the city's Afro-Creole Catholic community. Rey's parents, Barthélemy and Rose Sacriste Rey, were free Afro-Creole émigrés from Saint-Domingue who left following the Haitian Revolution. Barthélemy Rey was a member of a private organization called La Société Catholique pour l'Instruction des Orphelins dans l'Indigence, which used a donation from ex-African slave Marie Couvent to open L'Institution Catholique des Orphelins Indigents in 1848. L'Institution

Catholique was a school that offered affordable or free education for local black children. Barthélemy also served as the school's director for the year leading up to his death. In her will, Marie Couvent declared that her land and estate were to support a school for black orphans. Though she died in 1837 her land, money, and plan sat idle for years. The city's anxiety regarding black education delayed her wishes for a time. With city ordinances prohibiting the creation of free schools for black children, estate executor Henry Fletcher could do little. It would take a large group of well-connected Afro-Creole men to fulfill Couvent's wishes.

In April 1847 Barthélemy Rey, François Lacroix, Nelson Fouché, Maximilien Bruslé, Adolphe Duhart, and Armand Lanusse organized themselves into La Société Catholique pour l'Instruction des Orphelins dans l'Indigence and worked toward the proper execution of Couvent's will. The school opened the following year, and they augmented the estate through donations. Black orphans were admitted free of charge and others were asked for a modest tuition. Students who could not afford textbooks were given supplies as well.[37] The school offered lessons in grammar and writing (both English and French), rhetoric, geography, history, music, algebra, geometry, and even hygiene.[38] Barthélemy Rey served on the school board until his death. La Société Catholique member François Lacroix, along with the wealthy Afro-Creole philanthropists Aristride Mary and Thomy Lafon, supplied additional funds for the school. The city's most educated and respected Afro-Creoles served as teachers and administrators, including Joanni Questy and Paul Trévigne (who later served as editor for the *New Orleans L'Union* [*L'Union*] and the *New Orleans Tribune* [*Tribune*], local Afro-Creole newspapers). Historians Joseph Logsdon and Donald DeVore identified the school as "the nursery for revolution in Louisiana."[39] Former board members from La Société Catholique were common spirit guides; the spirits of Questy, Lanusse, Duhart, and Barthélemy later communicated to the Cercle Harmonique.

Though his father, Barthélemy, was a high profile local Catholic, Rey became an active Spiritualist shortly following his formal introduction to it, though not immediately. Rey wrote that about three or four months after he heard of Spiritualism for the first time, he tried to levitate a table "out of curiosity" and succeeded. However, this was not yet enough to convince him. On 19 April 1857, Rey attended a séance and "laughed" at what he called "the madness of some people," but after putting his hand on a chair at the séance table and proclaiming himself to be a medium—in a mocking fashion—he felt his hand shake violently. He identified the spirit in the room as Pierre Crocker, his deceased father-in-law, and asked him questions to confirm this.[40] Later that month, Rey attended a séance at the Tremé home of Afro-Creole and accomplished medium "Sœur Louise."[41] During the séance, he was invited to try receiving messages. His hand began to scribble across the page, writing with a power foreign to Rey's material body.[42] He could hear the voices of spirits, and as he grew fatigued, his father instructed him to keep writing, telling him "you are not tired." From this point onward, Rey would often see the manifestations of various spirits. One afternoon he saw the spirits of a "pretty young lady" and a "big man" on his front porch. He also thought he was a possible clairvoyant.[43] Rey's wife, Adèle, converted to Spiritualism, but not immediately after Rey. Rey reported that Adèle frequently saw the spirit of her father following his death, an experience that often brought her to laughter or tears but not enough emotion to inspire a conversion. However, one night "at midnight we saw our room lit up like a thousand candles," which prompted Rey to turn to his wife and ask, "Do you believe in Spiritualism now?" Another time Rey asked a spirit "to hit" (but in a "positive way") during the night, and he and his wife were awakened about midnight by the sound of a fist punching the back of their bed. Tests and experiments like this further convinced Rey and then Adèle that Spiritualism was real.[44]

Henri was not the only Rey who possessed the abilities of a medium. Rey recorded a long essay about his family's interactions with Spiritualism in one of his early register books. His sister, Alphonsine, and his brother, Octave, both could access the spirits.[45] Octave was a police captain for the Metropolitan Police in the 1870s, and the spirit of "some poor urchin thirsty for revenge" attacked him one day while he patrolled the Tremé neighborhood.[46] In the following years, many spirits would lament how Octave ignored and denied his abilities.[47] Rey reported in his family's Spiritualism history that even his father, Barthélemy, saw the spirit of a grocer three days following his death. At least one of Rey's children, his daughter Lucia, attended a Cercle Harmonique meeting. In November 1871 she requested the spirit of recently deceased politician O. J. Dunn (an African American politician who briefly served as lieutenant governor for Louisiana) to come to the table.[48]

Rey's first register book begins shortly after his first session at Louise's house. Some of the messages he recorded were marked with the word "Seul," indicating that Rey practiced Spiritualism alone sometimes early in his career as a medium. This first book spans four years, the longest period of time for one book. Its entries stop in April 1860, interrupted by Louisiana's involvement in the Civil War, and resume in May 1863 after Rey's military discharge. Rey served as a captain in the Louisiana Native Guards when they volunteered for the Confederacy, and he and others surrendered the city and offered to enlist in the Union Army when General Butler occupied New Orleans.[49] The Native Guards, who saw no active combat while on the Confederate side, were ordered to leave the city as the Union approached. However, they disobeyed Confederate orders, remaining in their city, and a committee of four, including Rey and his brother, Octave, surrendered their weapons to the Union Army.[50] Rey served at the level of captain in the Native Guards when they mustered for the Union, though he was discharged due to disease before the siege at Port Hudson, the battle that claimed the life of his friend Captain André Cailloux.[51]

In addition to serving in the Civil War, Rey also wrote poetry during the war years. Just months after northern troops took the city, French-speaking black Creoles in New Orleans launched *L'Union*, a newspaper dedicated to the interests of the black community. The 1862 inaugural issue printed a poem by Rey entitled *"L'Ignorance."* Ignorance, he wrote, "suppresses Liberty" and victimizes all "apostles of truth," including Jesus, Joan of Arc, Christopher Columbus, and Swedenborg. Though contemporary politics, society, and religious institutions seemed to enthrone ignorance, Rey wrote that truth would bring "Liberty, universal peace, Human happiness, fraternity!"[52] The themes of liberty, progress, peace, and fraternity—so frequently seen in the Cercle Harmonique records—were important to Rey at and beyond the séance table. His Spiritualist orientation molded his understanding of history's progress and the world's latent victimization of truth. He also served in local politics. In 1868 Rey was elected to the Louisiana House of Representatives, and he even received a message from Valmour while at the chamber house in February 1869. He was a strong supporter of Article 135, Title VII of the 1868 Louisiana Constitution, which prohibited segregated public schools. He also served as chairman for the Committee on Constitution in 1870. In the 1870s Rey served as New Orleans Third District assessor and was appointed as a member of the Orleans Parish School Board.[53]

François "Petit" Dubuclet was another leader of the Cercle Harmonique. Petit's father, Antoine Dubuclet, served as Louisiana state treasurer (on the Republican ticket) from 1868 until 1878. Antoine Dubuclet appointed his two sons, Petit and Auguste, as his assistants. Antoine and his first wife, Claire Pollard Dubuclet (Petit and Auguste's mother), were highly regarded among the Afro-Creole *gens de couleur libres*. Both of Petit's parents brought land and slaves to the marriage. In fact, between his assets and the profit from his sugar plantation, Antoine Dubuclet was one of Louisiana's wealthiest free men of color during the antebellum era. Antoine and Claire's civil union in New Orleans in the 1830s was followed by a proper Catholic marriage in France.[54] Claire died in 1852. Later when she manifested at the Cercle Harmonique's séance table, she signed off using her maiden name, Claire Pollard, likely to distinguish between herself and Petit's deceased sister Claire. Starting in 1865 the Dubuclet brothers practiced Spiritualism with their friend Rey, though it seems only Petit would continue into the 1870s.

Though he was always there in spirit, Valmour's material life ended before the Cercle Harmonique's prime. The beloved medium remained close to his friends and fellow Spiritualists as one of their most vocal spirit advisors after leaving the material world. Valmour died on 6 February 1869, at four in the morning. On the eighth of the previous month, Rey and Petit received a message that Valmour identified as the announcement of his impending death. In it, the spirits of Nelson Desbrosses and others spoke highly of Valmour's character and abilities as a medium and healer. The spirits told the circle, "dear and loving friend of suffering humanity, we are here waiting with the patience of those who have to share eternity! At your coming here, your friends will have a great procession." On the day Valmour died, Saint Vincent de Paul visited the Cercle Harmonique to comfort them. He assured them that Valmour's spirit was among them and had "conquered his place at the top of the luminous mountain of progress and the goodness of God." Furthermore, God was "happy and content with the one who was called." The remaining members of the Cercle Harmonique were instructed not only to follow Valmour's example but also to care for his widow and children. Saint Vincent de Paul was not alone in his high regard for Valmour. When the spirit of French priest Hugues-Felicité Robert de Lamennais[55] complimented Andrew Jackson Davis for being "learned and luminous," he also noted that "[Charles H.] Foster, [Emma] Hardinge, and Valmour" were further "proof of our existence that speaks to the mind and soul of all." Another spirit noted Andrew Jackson Davis for his "love and charity," Valmour for his charity, and Sister Louise for her hard work.[56]

Valmour would frequently return to the séance table from the other side as a spirit. He reaffirmed his status as a mesmeric healer when he recounted how "Providence" blessed him with the ability "to throw the regenerative fluid." Though outsiders accused him of "charlatanism," he remained confident in himself and encouraged his devoted brothers to continue in the face of their critics. In a rare message recorded in English, Valmour seems to forgive Rey (calling him by name, "Henri") for any of Rey's offenses. This suggests that there may have been some tension early in the circle between the two powerful mediums. However, as a spirit and now "more than a man," Valmour did not worry about such things. Instead, he came to the table to express his love and respect for the Cercle Harmonique and their work. Though Valmour, like other spirits, instructed Afro-Creole Spiritualists not to be attached to things and persons on the earth, in one communication he admitted that he missed Petit. Interestingly enough, in light of the message in which he forgave Rey for his past offenses, he did not mention missing Rey.[57]

One reason for the tension between Rey and Valmour was their disagreement on how public the séances should be, and in death Valmour seemed to have moved closer to Rey's desire to restrict strangers. Though it was good for the circle to be accepting, Valmour's spirit warned that they should not allow vagabonds with "disorderly manners" who might taint the circle's harmony and effectiveness. It was good to be "generous," he admitted, "but, the animal that is infected by a contagious disease must be separated from the flock by the good shepherd." In the end, the unity of the circle must be preserved, especially because the circle had many critics. A "systematic opposition" was "at work in order to hamper the ascending march of Truth!"[58] They did not need to add to their challenges by allowing troublemakers at the séance table. Though Valmour and Rey disagreed on earth, when Rey received messages from Valmour, the spirit of his former mentor now agreed with him.

The Cercle Harmonique's primary aims can be summed up by the "Spiritual Invocation" they inscribed in their records at one point, likely in May 1871. It reads much like an everyday prayer. It opens with thanks to the "Eternal and infinitely Good Father" for their place on the earth, followed by a statement of purpose: uniting their "hearts in search of Truth, to illuminate our souls with the Good, Love and Charity." They asked "the spirits of Peace and Light" to guide them, put them "on the path of eternal progression," and "drive away the darkness." With the "strength to break with error, ignorance and superstition of all false doctrine," the Cercle Harmonique sought the "Light" of the spirits' "Wisdom" to "enlighten[ ] our minds, console our hearts" and "render a brilliant and solemn Path that leads to your holy and eternal abodes, to be received with honor and glory, for the purification and sanctification of our souls."[59] Spiritual elevation and progress went hand in hand.

Cercle Harmonique Séance Records and Séance Meetings

Valmour's spirit described the Cercle Harmonique as "the light that shines within." A fully harmonic séance would occur only if "each member" participated; in this way, their session would and "must shine." The spirit of French nobleman Volney (Constantin François de Chassebœuf, the Comte de Volney) described "the harmonic circle" as a collective that desired "communion together to help each other in research." Egalitarian in its focus and its actions, a Cercle Harmonique séance meeting had multiple pleasant effects on circle members. In fact, after a meeting, one could feel the effects of the achieved harmony "for three days." The "happy influence" of that "harmony of souls" could make a soul feel "so full of grand emotions and ineffable joys."[60]

The Cercle Harmonique recorded the messages their mediums received, and messages would be read and reflected on in later meetings.[61] A key reason the Spiritualists kept good records of their séances was that the spirits told them to do so. Simply put, the communications the Cercle Harmonique received were "for instruction." Transcribing the spirits' "thinking" helped illuminate the "Road" of humanity's progress. The spirits encouraged the Cercle Harmonique to "keep all these writings and especially reread what we give you." Reading previous messages could strengthen a circle. Or, in the words of another spirit, the pages should be "constantly reread" in order to "develop many Truths." Similarly, Saint Vincent de Paul explained how the pages of the séance records should be read at the beginning of each session "to prepare you." The spirits also occasionally referenced earlier messages, further signaling that the communications were read from the books again and again.[62] Other mediums affiliated with the Cercle Harmonique also kept records of séances. Unfortunately Valmour's books were misplaced and lost after his death, as were the books from Louise's leadership.[63]

The spirits told them to write, and write they did. The Cercle Harmonique's séance records are extensive. Rey's practice and record keeping bordered on graphomania. While Spiritualism is typically described by both practitioners and scholars as a religion focused on the spiritual and the nonmaterial, the copious records of the Cercle Harmonique indicate the importance of putting to paper—and, thus, making material—the spirits' messages. The act of transcribing the messages they received from the spirit world legitimated the perfect, egalitarian world of the spirits and justified the republican outlook of the Cercle Harmonique. Simply put, the idealized spiritual world was not really real until it was written down. Once the words of the spirits became tangible, they became truth.

The Cercle Harmonique was able to keep such extensive records because, like many of the city's Afro-Creoles, the group's members were privileged and, thus, educated. Some Afro-Creole men were sent to schools in France, Spain, Haiti, or the North. Many worked as private tutors for wealthy white families and some opened private schools in the downtown area of the city. Others were composers, poets, and dramatists. The publication of *L'Album littéraire* in 1843 and *Les Cenelles* in 1845 demonstrates the rich literary tradition of the city's Afro-Creoles. In addition to printing *L'Album littéraire* and *Les Cenelles*, Afro-Creoles also published news periodicals. *L'Union*, an Afro-Creole newspaper, operated from 1862 to 1864 and was replaced by the *Tribune* in 1864, a newspaper that would play a key role in the founding of the Republican Party in Louisiana. Many of those affiliated with *L'Union* and the *Tribune* also contributed to *L'Album littéraire* and *Les Cenelles*. The *Tribune's* publication of poems like "*Le 13 Avril*" about the death of Abraham Lincoln and "*Ode aux Martyrs*" about the victims of the Mechanics' Institute Riot of 1866 reflected the continued tradition of Afro-Creole political writing long after *L'Album littéraire* and *Les Cenelles*.[64] Rey's séance records provide another example of the continuation of Afro-Creoles' political writing, though in this case the content was believed to have come from the world of the spirits.

The spirits instructed the Afro-Creole Spiritualists to arrive at meetings "with abnegation, charity, good will, and love of humanity at heart." More precise regulations for the séances were put to paper on a later day. In spring of 1872, the Cercle Harmonique wrote some rules for their séances in one of Rey's register books. They explained that the purpose of the séance meetings was "to accelerate the development of the faithful believers," who, additionally, were "required to be punctual." The séance was to begin with a "lecture on some spiritual communication" to organize the group in "good harmony," and to "avoid any interruption, the door should be kept closed while the lecture lasts." When the lecturer concluded, everyone was to calmly take his "habitual" seat at the table, and no one was to be admitted to the séance once it began. The spirits prohibited any "conversation either political or otherwise . . . before or during the séance." Despite these rules and their inclusion of punctuality, someone must have arrived late shortly thereafter. The first message to arrive after the recording of these rules came from Claire Pollard, who began her message stating, "It is understood, my brothers, that the belated ones, arriving after their lecture, would take their places at the table with respect and in a deep meditation so as not to disturb the harmony already established among the present ones. A minute in one's life seems a trifle but often is of consequence, carries its weight. Thus, come to the table of spirits as soon as it is possible for you to be there." One can safely assume that the latecomer felt duly shamed; as Pollard's spirit said on another occasion, "Listen to your mother." It was important to arrive before the meeting and be present for the opening lecture. Lunel explained that reading previous messages at the "Table of Truth" could chase away "the worldly thoughts" and focus the group on higher ideals.[65]

As with any human endeavor, meetings of the Cercle Harmonique were not perfect. Even one unfocused member could "produce unfortunate influences." A message from the spirit Lunel in April 1872 explained why the previous evening's séance failed. Though there was more than one reason the meeting was unsuccessful, the primary reason in this case was the "disposition of several brothers who had the idea to go somewhere else" but chose to attend the séance anyway "in fear of losing their rights and privileges to attend the meeting on Monday." Monday was the main meeting of the Cercle Harmonique; in his notes Grandjean described Friday as the meeting of the "ordinary circle." Distractions, apparently due to "material interests" in this case, disrupted the harmony of the séance and rendered the meeting tedious, ineffective, and unfulfilling. In another message, "the Unknown" (an anonymous spirit) scolded Planchard for not meeting his full spiritual potential. Opening the lines of communication between the spiritual world and the earthly world was not always easy. Thinking "holy and pure things" facilitated "moral and elevated manifestations" of the séance. Distracted thoughts would disrupt the harmony. It was difficult, a spirit explained, for spirits to manifest to the circle if "the necessary currents" were not established between them. On an evening where the séance must not have been overly successful, the spirit of politician Daniel Webster comforted the circle, telling them not to be "discouraged" and advising them forward.[66]

Because spiritual work was difficult, the spirits needed "energetic and dedicated" mediums. The relationship between spirit and medium was an emotional, personal, and sensory connection; on one occasion, Rey described the hand of Voltaire as "very energetic." According to Saint Vincent de Paul, the spirits sought "in perfect harmony . . . to control" the bodies of the mediums or use clairvoyance "to make them reach certain levels." On another occasion, a spirit named Paul described a medium as "the true agent," "he who is in charge of activating the sacred fire of the Philosophy of love and charity," and "the apostle giving voice to an evangelical and angelic gospel." Indeed, being "the intermediary between Heaven and Earth" was no small task. According to Swedenborg's spirit, a medium was "an apostle who receives and gives the word of truth" and like a "physician who soothes but does not send the [bill] Collector"—someone truthful, generous, and selfless. Swedenborg's affinity for metaphor continued, describing the medium as "the wire that transmits to Humanity the results of discoveries of Spiritual Science and the principles derived from it." A medium became more advanced the more selflessly he acted. "Mediumistic powers" were "natural," but "he who is advanced in this work by the state of his soul can enlighten you and cause the beneficent force of your faculties to increase."[67]

After the group established their harmony, the spirits who manifested at meetings were the ones who initiated communication. Though Rey's daughter had requested the spirit of O. J. Dunn to the table on one occasion, this was rare. In fact, a spirit named Sophia instructed the circle to "never call any Spirit" by name for "often he cannot come, and another then could take his name." Therefore, the circle should always "weigh" each message by "Reason" and make sure it is accurate and comes from a good spirit. Cercle Harmonique meetings typically occurred in the evenings, but sometimes the spirits arrived on their own time. For example, the spirit of John Jones manifested at 3:25 one afternoon, and though Jones noted that the time was "strange to me," he did not think too much of it since "the truth shines everywhere" and at all times.[68]

The spirits who appeared during the séances were a varied group. Political, social, and religious heroes of the Cercle Harmonique advised them from beyond and extended the membership of the circle. Though their meetings typically were small, Saint Vincent de Paul suggested that the Cercle Harmonique was larger than they knew. Deceased circle members and other spirits in the spiritual world worked with them, as well as "many workers [on earth] who do not have a brave enough soul to admit the Truth." More significantly, the spirits who came to the mediums greatly expanded the size of the circle. The spirits ranged from family members, friends, and local priests to Enlightenment thinkers and even American celebrities, such as U.S. presidents and Pocahontas. Many spirits offered advice on how to fix the material world, while others came to identify themselves and wish they could communicate directly with their own families. Some spirits affirmed the authenticity of Spiritualism. For example, in death, even a self-described "rabid, fanatic Baptist" recognized the truth of Spiritualism. Others expressed regret for their earthly lives and the choices they had made.[69] And many spirits communicated their political opinions.

The identities of the spirits who came to the Cercle Harmonique sometimes disclose more about the group and their practice than the content of the spirit messages. The spirit guides in the séance records indicate whom the Cercle Harmonique wanted to support them and whom they wanted in their spiritual genealogy. In addition to French revolutionary thinkers and leaders like Maximilien de Robespierre, metaphysical theologians like Swedenborg, and republican American martyrs like John Brown, the Afro-Creole Spiritualists included certain Catholic voices like Saint Vincent de Paul in their spiritual network. From family members and locals to world celebrities, the spiritual advisors guiding the Cercle Harmonique indicate whom the Afro-Creoles admired and wanted on their side.

Major figures in Spiritualism's own history came to the Cercle Harmonique's table. Mesmer encouraged them to remain steadfast to Spiritualism even if they achieved only "mediocre success." Progress still would be on the way and Mesmer and other spirits "will always be ready to assist in your development and the success of your noble enterprise." Swedenborg too assured them that the spirits' messages, which came "from Heaven," were the "intellectual seeds" of humanity's progress. It was also common for spirits to sign off in the plural. Swedenborg concluded this particular message with "we will return," suggesting that though one spirit might deliver the communication, a large contingent of spirits stood behind the message. The ideas of religious leaders like Swedenborg and Mesmer were also present among Rey's table. A spirit simply identified as "Curious" described how both material bodies and the spirits could make use of "electro-magnetic fluid." Swedenborg noted the effectiveness of magnetism, and another message explained how "magnetism" was "evidence of the superiority of the mind." Mesmer too encouraged medium-healers not to be discouraged if all of their cures by "fluids" were unsuccessful. Even the spirit of Confucius[70] recognized the power of fluids.[71]

Deceased family members of circle attendees frequented Cercle Harmonique meetings. In American Spiritualism, communicating with the spirits of deceased family members typically signified part of a family's mourning process and, more broadly, reflected Victorian America's keen interest in death. The burden of mourning could be borne more easily by communicating with the dead and receiving assurance from loved ones that they were happy in the spiritual world.[72] This does not seem to be the same impetus behind messages from Cercle Harmonique deceased family members. Messages often came years after a father's, mother's, sister's, or other family member's death and were not directly intended for grieving loved ones, though some messages from deceased parents might have been part of an indirect form of mourning. Now part of the spiritual republic, the dead were in a better place, and by encouraging their loved ones in their spiritual work, they ensured a happy reunion in the spirit world. Claire Pollard frequently manifested, particularly if her son Petit was the medium, and she primarily delivered messages of encouragement. One December day her son's hand wrote, "be patient, gentle, and kind. Redouble your courage." She often assured her son and his fellow Spiritualists that she and other spirits surrounded them as "your Invisible protectors!" Rey's father, Barthélemy, often came with messages for his son and his circle. Another spirit reported that Barthélemy cried with "the immense joy of a victorious father" because he watched his "victorious child in the struggle." Another member's father validated the circle's practice, telling the Spiritualists, "Today I am in the spiritual world" and now "I see the Truth."[73]

Cercle Harmonique member Victor Lavigne's sister, Henriette Lavigne, apologized on Christmas 1865 for not visiting sooner but explained that she had been unable to manifest to the Cercle Harmonique due to the "crowds" of more advanced spirits that frequently enveloped the table. The spirit of Joseph Rey, Henri's grandfather, had progressed much in the years since 1857 by following "the circle of Louise and Valmour" and hearing the messages of the "Invisibles who visited." Rey's maternal ancestors, the Sacristes, appeared to the circle from time to time. Adèle Crocker Rey's mother and father also appeared at the séance table. In one message her father described his apparent suicide, explaining that he "succumbed to a weakness that made me take my life." He was "afraid to face the world" and now awaited "the hour of deliverance." It is possible that this message was also an apology for the *plaçage* relationship that he kept with Marie Laveau's daughter Marie Heloïse Euchariste Glapion. Adèle's mother, Rose, regretted that she was not able to see her children practice Spiritualism during her time on earth. Emilien Planchard's brother Charles came to the table with some regularity, often with a message of encouragement. Charles also reported that because he watched his brother's work, he too was "progressing" in the spiritual world. Emile Luscy's father encouraged his son to continue practicing Spiritualism and keep his place at the Cercle Harmonique's table for it gave him "Truth."[74]

The primary members of the Cercle Harmonique were male, with the exception of the early leadership of Sister Louise and the occasional attendance of one of Rey or Petit's family members. During a séance with Petit's younger half sister Joséphine Dubuclet present, Joséphine's deceased husband, Antoine Décuir, appeared despite having not believed in Spiritualism during his life. He came to encourage Joséphine to continue her spiritual lessons. In another message, Décuir apologized to Joséphine for his faults as a husband and father. During one of Petit's first séances, his sister Rosalie Dubuclet manifested through a medium who had fallen asleep at the séance table. Upon waking, the medium had no memory of the communication. Georges Bally Dubuclet, another Dubuclet family member, also visited the Cercle Harmonique. He was raised in France and came to the United States, but upon arrival in Louisiana was disgusted with slavery and left for Tampico, Mexico. Petit's deceased younger sister Claire Dubuclet also manifested to the Afro-Creole circle.[75] Altogether, Claire Pollard and Barthélemy Rey were the most frequent family members to visit the table.

Major revolutionaries from France also delivered messages, including Montesquieu, Robespierre, and Lamennais. French monk and writer François Rabelais also appeared somewhat regularly. Saint Vincent de Paul visited the table frequently, as well as the spirits of other Catholics. Other famous figures who visited the circle's table include Confucius, Lorenzo Dow, Montezuma, and Pocahontas. For example, Pocahontas reported that she was happy in the spirit world though she was a "Poor Indian" in the material world. A spirit identified as Cagliostro, likely a reference to Count Alessandro di Cagliostro, the alias of Italian occultist Giuseppe Balsamo, delivered a brief message in September 1877 to Rey, instructing him to continue meeting and uniting with his brothers. Some spirits, like John Wilkes Booth and Robert E. Lee, came to apologize for their past offenses, particularly those related to slavery, violence, and politics. A number of Rey's fellow soldiers from the Louisiana Native Guards, most notably famed locals André Cailloux and John Crowder, appeared to the Cercle Harmonique. Cailloux in particular cared for the Cercle Harmonique in a "brotherly" fashion after death, though he avoided Spiritualism in life.[76] Victims and "martyrs" also frequently manifested to the Afro-Creole Spiritualists, particularly Abraham Lincoln, John Brown, and the victims of the local 1866 Mechanics' Institute Riot.

Former local Spiritualists visited the Cercle Harmonique, including Cercle Harmonique member Jules Mallet, who died in 1875. Beloved local Afro-Creole writer Nelson Debrosses also communicated with the Cercle

Harmonique from beyond the grave, encouraging his former circle mates to continue their struggle and prepare for the spiritual spheres he now inhabited. After his death, local Afro-Creole writer Joanni Questy communicated with the Cercle Harmonique and helped deliver the messages of spirits not yet able to communicate on their own. He encouraged the Spiritualists to "come to the Table of Truth" and never leave it. Though his Spiritualist brethren respected and admired Questy, his spirit did not claim perfection in the spiritual world. He regretted that he "hesitated" and "sat there lazily" during his earthly life. He complimented Rey and others for their efforts and predicted that they would "reach the perfectible Regions" and "walk in triumph." In one message Joseph Barthet, the former leader of the French émigré Spiritualist group, lamented how little most circles persisted and succeeded in their spiritual work. As a spirit, Louise, the medium who first advised and taught Rey, received a "grand and magnificent" reward for her spiritual work on earth. Though she encouraged the circle to look forward to the spiritual world where she now was, she had not forgotten the challenges of the material life. "I see you, my poor brothers and sisters, in your world of miseries and disappointments," she acknowledged. Indeed, "the heart grieves, working for a Future which is not yours" and feeling the "fatigue of material life." Though life may seem bitter, the Cercle Harmonique should have "courage and patience" for "there will be happiness for you." She also promised them that their hard work would be rewarded in the spiritual world and that "the spirit of Louise" would always be there to guide them.[77]

It is possible that the Cercle Harmonique believed that they also could communicate with the spirits of the living. A spirit named Adolphe Duhart, who described himself as intelligent, lamented that he, like other "poor devils," believed he received "absolution" but had been going to Catholic Mass and confession out of "fear of mortal sin."[78] Adolphe Duhart also was the name of a local dramatist and instructor at L'Institution Catholique des Orphelins Indigents, the school operated by La Société Catholique pour l'Instruction des Orphelins dans l'Indigence. Additionally, he was a medium who practiced Spiritualism with Valmour and Rey in their earlier years and held séances at his home in the late 1850s. Born a free man of color in New Orleans in the late 1830s, he was educated in France. Under the pseudonym Lélia he published poetry in the *Tribune* in the 1860s, and his play *Lélia ou la victime du préjugé* (*Lélia or the victim of prejudice*) was performed at the Théâtre Orléans in June 1866.[79] It is not a far leap to conclude that the Cercle Harmonique believed the poet and dramatist was the spirit behind the message, given that Duhart traveled in similar social circles as members of the Cercle Harmonique, taught at L'Institution Catholique, and was a medium.

Other New Orleanian locals also delivered messages to the Cercle Harmonique, often to affirm the truth of Spiritualism.[80] Local District Court judge Charles Leaumont, who seemed to have been a Spiritualist himself, also appears a few times in the Cercle Harmonique's records.[81] Paul Bertus, who briefly served New Orleans as mayor in 1838 and again in 1843, was an occasional visitor to the table to speak of the dangers of materialism and the glories of Spiritualism. Rey's former employer Eugene Hacker, who owned the Tremé hardware store where Rey worked as a young man, also appeared. Additionally, a spirit identified as Charles Laveau encouraged forgiveness in February 1872.[82] Charles Laveau was the name of famed Voudou priestess Marie Laveau's French Creole father but, with a common last name, could be a reference to another Laveau. However, considering the rise in popularity of Voudou in the 1870s, particularly its coverage in the local press, it is quite possible that it is a reference to the priestess's father.

Under Valmour's leadership, the séances were often public, with strangers and newcomers at every meeting. These visitors typically asked for proof of Spiritualism or for messages from their deceased family. This was a point of contention with Rey, who argued that visitors often inhibited the circle's progress. Following Valmour's death, strangers were rare at the séance table though some family or friends would attend periodically. One periodic visitor sitting at the Cercle Harmonique's table was the wife of deceased Louisiana lieutenant governor O. J. Dunn. For example, on 3 June 1874, Dunn appeared at the table at the request of his wife. He relayed his happiness and gratitude for their beneficent influence on his wife, Fanny, and her subsequent "development."[83]

Learning from the Spirits

The spirits taught the Cercle Harmonique that there was much work to be done on earth, and the séance table was a school where the spirits taught social and political values. The "dear children of progress," as Saint Vincent de Paul once called the Cercle Harmonique, should "always be vigilant about the state of your heart, you have to work to purify [your heart] day after day, to be worthy of the One who created you." Thus, he warned them not to "drag" their spirits "through the mud"—the mud being corruption and greed.[84] According to the spirits, freedom was humanity's natural state. Many of the messages centered on equality, egalitarianism, brotherhood and harmony. The success of these ideals would propel the progress of humanity.

Though the progress of humanity might have seemed slow, the spiritual republic assured the Cercle Harmonique that it would continue and, like the proverbial tortoise, win the race in the end. Centuries might pass before the universal acceptance of "the spiritual philosophies," but the work of "Voltaire . . . Volney, [Denis] Diderot, and '93 [the French Revolution]" had shown that "truth" and "Freedom of Thought" would shine. Many spirits spoke of humanity's progress and "the Triumph of the Idea." Though the Idea was never defined in any spirit message, its meaning was rooted in the ideals of the French Revolution and its well-known cry: Liberté! Egalité! Fraternité! Through the Idea the Cercle Harmonique memorialized the legacy of the French Revolution and its impact in the wider Atlantic age of revolutions. The Idea was equality; it was harmony; it was brotherhood. "Universal love" was the tool that would secure "brotherly union." Principles like liberty, equality, fraternity, peace, harmony, justice, and equity were often cited together. Spiritualism was "the key" that opened "the soul" to fairness, justice, universal brotherhood, and solidarity. The spirit of Montesquieu described Spiritualists as freethinkers and philosophers carrying "the torch of truth." They would break the "barriers that hindered its [the torch of truth's] Route."[85]

As taught by the spirits, the triumph of the Idea meant humanity's progress. Lamennais's spirit promised that the "progressive march" of humanity would succeed and the "Human Rights" of each person were "guaranteed." As members of the Cercle Harmonique climbed the political ladder, he encouraged them to maintain the "purity" of their hearts and work for "all your brothers." In another message Lamennais taught that "generous and beneficent ideas" were the source of the "social regeneration" of the country and "the forward march of the great social body" to moral improvement. Saint Vincent de Paul agreed because "social improvement" would come from attention to "moral issues" and questions of "a general humanitarian purpose." Sympathy and harmony ruled the spiritual spheres. Justice and equality were the main forces of humanity, and that could not be changed. "Justice, Equity, Love, and charity" were the "natural laws."[86] If these laws were implemented in the material world to guide governments and structure legal systems, humanity's progress would be eased and quickened. If they were ignored, the material world would be corrupt.

The harmonious Idea appealed to Afro-Creoles during the Civil War and into Reconstruction. The city's political instability, its social hierarchy, and the beginning of Jim Crow confirmed the city's need for harmony. The spiritual realm was a harmonious union "more and more cemented by the immense grandeur of the noble and admirable thoughts which dwell incessantly there and fill each heart devoted one to the other." The spirits lauded harmony as "the supreme law of a perfect union"; in contrast, hatred had no place in a Spiritualist's heart. A "fraternal union," another spirit explained, was built upon "universal love." One should endeavor to augment the "beautiful fraternal chain" and unite "all people" with love and charity. Then, the laws of justice and equity would reign. When Ambroise explained the progress of spirits, he referred to the union of true Spiritualists in the celestial world as a "harmonious concert."[87] Indeed, the spirit world was one to look forward to joining and one to aspire to become a part of during séances and then permanently after physical death. Unfortunately for members of the Cercle Harmonique, their environment was hardly harmonious. Inequality, slavery, war, political jockeying, and Reconstruction violence hampered the realization of the spirits' promise of harmony, but nonetheless that suggestion of harmony offered an attractive goal for the republican Cercle Harmonique.

Impeding harmony was injustice, and from the perspective of Afro-Creoles and the spirits, injustice could be found easily in American politics and society. Slavery and white supremacy were two key examples. Fighting injustice was an active practice and a necessary struggle at the séance table and in everyday life. Saint Vincent de Paul rallied the circle to "fight against human errors and prejudices." Charity, he said, was "the balm" that would heal "social wounds because it teaches Justice towards all." The spirit of French poet Pierre-Jean de Béranger explained how his life had been dedicated to defending "the rights of the children of God" because it was "so sweet to relieve those who suffer." Those on earth, particularly Spiritualists like Cercle Harmonique members, should try to alleviate the suffering of others. The "soul of a True Spiritualist" possessed "exquisite sensitivity to the misfortunes of his brother." Those who did not have a roof over their heads or food to eat needed and deserved others' support. Instead of seeking money, Spiritualists should devote themselves to the "betterment of Humanity," for this would lead to "eternal riches." Greed yielded only "distrust."[88]

A chief reason the spirit world was a far superior place in comparison to earth was that the spirits submitted "to the laws of harmony and love." Recognition of the superiority of spirit over matter led to the acknowledgement of equality. Communicating with the spirit world helped implant "egalitarian principles" in the minds and hearts of Spiritualists. The higher ideals of spirits were built on the fundamentals of democracy and liberality. Béranger's spirit believed that Spiritualism provided "the solution to all questions of justice and Equity." Ideally the world of politics should imitate the world of Spiritualism: motivated by mutual enlightenment and structured on the equal exchange of thoughts and ideas. As "a strong and recognized fraternity," Spiritualism provided a useful model for society and government. Additionally, one spirit reported that it was good to listen to ideas "opposed to what you believe" for it could help enlighten one even more.[89] Then the Idea could prosper on earth.

Letting all have a voice, including disagreeable ones, was a necessary component of a liberal and equal society because it promoted harmony. Harmony was a "powerful weapon" against injustice. Those on earth should "love each other" and "be informed of the truth [in order] to live in harmony." Indeed, Jesus's spirit felt joy when people acknowledged the "Solidarity between you and all Beings." One was part of the universal and spiritual brotherhood if one lived in accordance with the Idea and encouraged harmony. The spirits promised that fighters for humanity and its progress would "come with us to the glory" and be rewarded in the spirit world. Unfortunately, working for egalitarianism was neither simple nor easy, and spirits like Volney knew that "few" of the "workers" would persist. Spiritualism could help to keep them "faithful" to liberalizing and democratizing work, but the spirits could not promise a perfect material world. If members of the Cercle Harmonique continued with their labors, though, spirits such as the Comte de Volney would show them "glories." However, the spirit of Voltaire recognized that some "sages" who tried to bring society "into the path of Truth" were soon persecuted.[90] Despite that danger, the Cercle Harmonique and all Spiritualists were encouraged to continue the struggle in the face of adversity.

One force that retarded humanity's progress and worked against the Idea was prejudice. Prejudice belonged to the vain and obstructed justice. The spirit of Rabelais characterized prejudice as "a ridiculous ghost" that maintained "foolish pride." Volney taught that prejudices were "born of ignorance" and belonged to "fools." Prejudices "born from crazy assumptions" worked against justice and equity. Intolerance was "foolish" and "the greatest sign" of a government's, a religious institution's, or a person's "weakness." Good Spiritualist brothers listened to others "with respect" and understanding, while intolerance rendered one deaf. Prejudice obstructed the ability to recognize truth, and this explained why some people failed to appreciate and observe the equal rights of others. The removal of prejudice meant the elevation of "Reason" and, as a result, the recognition of rights. To combat prejudice, Spiritualism dissuaded people from thinking negative thoughts about others. It instructed people to "forgive" the "injustice and selfishness" of others.[91]

Spiritualism's great value came from the significance and importance of spiritual work, work that would bring the Idea to the material world. Spiritual work was achieved by conversing with the spirits, contemplating their messages, and changing the world based on the spirits' wisdom. Spiritual work was putting the Idea into action. For example, Confucius explained that the spiritual work done by the Cercle Harmonique during their earthly lives bestowed upon them more stars "shining in your bright sky." They would be rewarded for their effort. The "immense advantages" of Spiritualist gatherings came from spiritual labor. The spirits offered "happiness and peace" as the reward of successful spiritual work and elevated thinking. The Cercle Harmonique's spiritual guides also spoke often of light. With the help of the spirits, the Cercle Harmonique's work would ascend "the luminous mountain of Progress and Truth." Additionally, the presence of a good spirit surrounded the Cercle Harmonique "with his protective fluid like a luminous circle."[92] This helped ensure quality spiritual work would be achieved.

Solid spiritual work was the measure of a good Spiritualist, not the amount of time spent in practice. One spirit explained how a Spiritualist's worth came from "not the number of years passed at a table," but rather one's value depended on the purity and sanctity of the soul. A spirit simply identified as "a brother" argued that there was "a great difference between the one who comes to sit at a table to listen only to the word of the Spirit and the one who struggles persistently against Evil." Indeed, listening to the spirits was not enough. Proper action was necessary. The courage to recognize one's mistakes was regarded highly by the spirits as the mark of a quality Spiritualist. The spirit of Jean-Jacques Rousseau lamented that many lacked "the courage to admit their weaknesses and mistakes," and "this is why many suffer." Those who avoided "the teachings of true Light" were cowards and should be "ashamed." Bravery was determined not by fighting but rather through the ability to "conquer" one's "passions and be true to all men."[93]

The spiritual republic effectively governed the spirit world because of the spirits' harmony, and if those on earth could replicate the spirits' unity, a true republic could be possible in the material world too. To achieve harmony, the spirits advised a focus on charity. To describe humanity's "high destiny," Saint Vincent de Paul explained that: "Charity is the Pillar. Universal love is Law. The Search for Truth is one of its joys." Valmour described the "soldiers" of "progression" as those carrying three "flags": the flags of "peace and love and especially Charity." On another occasion Saint Vincent de Paul's spirit explained that charity should be "the basis of all religions." The Spiritualists were to make charity their "sacred duty" and, thus, "contribute to the happiness of your brothers teaching them moral Truth." Harmony, universal love, truth, progress, charity, and equality were frequent topics for the spirits. For humanity to reach its goal, the spirit of Jesus taught, "Charity" would need to be the guide along with "Justice." Père Ambroise explained that the spiritual world was organized "by the most perfect harmony." The spirits worked together to help elevate each other and progress to higher "spheres," and this should be replicated on earth. The spirit described "your world" as "the glimpse of God's Creation" and "ours" as "the complement of his work."[94]

The spiritual world was a higher, more perfect, and more godly place than the earthly world. Thus, those on earth should try to emulate the world of the spirits—an idea clearly expressed in the spirits' views on politics through their focus on equality. The luminous brotherhood of spirits was harmonious because the spirits had been purified of prejudice and intolerance, either through their actions in the material world or through a purgatory-like period in the spirit world called retribution (see chapter 3). A "vulgar spirit" was weighed down and moved about "with difficulty," while a purified spirit existed more freely and enjoyed a "luminous appearance." In this sense, spirits reaped what they sowed. Any "spirit who is unhappy here [spirit world]" owed "it solely to what condition in which he has placed his mind and soul." A true Spiritualist appeared "magnificent and beautiful by the soul" and would "shine like us [the spirit guides]," but "when passions and cowardice have soiled" one's soul, he appeared "surrounded by darkness, in spite of the light which shines by us!" He who spent his life struggling for "Good" was welcomed in the spiritual world "by our joyous cheers, because he has atoned for his shameful past in liberating himself from Materialism and in spreading Light."[95]

Spiritualism would shepherd them in their future endeavors, but the spirits did not want to constrain the Cercle Harmonique. A person's free will allowed Spiritualists to accept the spirits as their guides on their own accord. One should come to Spiritualism willingly, but then should "place yourself at the disposal of the Spirit." However, the spirits never wanted to force any-one; they criticized Catholicism for that offense. Instead they wanted people to listen to them and accept the spiritual teachings by their own judgment, though the spirit guides certainly hoped people would listen to them. Those in the spirit world had the advantage of *true* knowledge, which was why they advised the Cercle Harmonique. The spirits knew it would be difficult to achieve the Idea in a corrupt material world. The spirit called Lunel en-couraged them to "not be discouraged" for they "will be rewarded" for their "work" and "diligence." In another message, Lunel told the circle, "those who want to know the Truth must look for it, unite themselves and work in harmony in order to develop it." Indeed, work was a key element of Lunel's message: the necessity of it, the need to continue it, and the group effort it would require of the circle. Claire Pollard also encouraged hard work—"firm and resolute." But members of the Cercle Harmonique were not on their own. Pollard assured them that "Valmour, Vincent de Paul, and millions of happy spirits are watching over you." Confucius also assured the Cercle Harmonique that they were not alone. Rather, he and other spirits will "take care of you and will always be ready to constantly speak to you." Jesus too came to the table to speak of courage and preparation for the future. He came to the table "with delight," for he approved of the Spiritualists' cour-age and hard work. "March! Fear not! . . . Do not tremble!" he encouraged them. Their work at the séance table prepared them for any troubles that may lie ahead.[96] And life in New Orleans held many challenges for members of the Cercle Harmonique.

CHAPTER TWO

The Disharmony of New Orleans City Life

To these countless attractive sights and seductive external influences I was not
insensible. But the horrible personations of vagrancy and distress which I daily
saw—appealing as they did to my constitutional sensitiveness and disposition
to sympathize with the suffering—eclipsed all the glories and neutralized many
of the temporary pleasures of my city life.

—Andrew Jackson Davis, *The Magic Staff: An Autobiography of
Andrew Jackson Davis*

Dividing a house is ruinous to all. For the sake of harmony, and for the
freedom of all, don't shatter to pieces the great Work already done.
United we stand, divided we fall!

—Spirit of Oscar J. Dunn, New Orleans Republican politician and Louisiana
lieutenant governor, to the Cercle Harmonique, 8 December 1871

Our blood flooded the streets of the Bloody City [New Orleans]. Your blood . . .
that of the martyrs has not been shed in vain. Because of the tragedy Congress
had responded to the atrocity.

—Spirit of Victor Lacroix, martyr of the Mechanics' Institute Riot, to the
Cercle Harmonique, 21 February 1869

In early 1875, William Weeks, a leader in the city's Republican Party, died in
a brutal fight with George E. Paris, another Republican, at the New Orleans
Republican Club. Governor William P. Kellogg appointed Paris as harbor-
master, and when Paris alleged "that Weeks had interfered to defeat him,"
Weeks responded by calling Paris a "dirty liar." This quickly devolved into a
fistfight. Weeks pulled out a gun while Paris armed himself with a large knife,
and by the end of the fight, Paris had stabbed Weeks multiple times.[1] A few
days following his death Weeks appeared before the Cercle Harmonique and
instructed them to "forgive the unhappy men who sent me here suddenly,"
as he was "bound to forgive George."[2] A victim of both Paris's knife and his
own quest for power, Weeks's spirit recognized that there could be no harmony without forgiveness, and the Idea—the spirits' promise of egalitarian
republicanism—could not succeed in local politics without harmony.

If the Afro-Creole Spiritualists wanted to reform the material world and render it more like the spirit world, their own immediate surroundings were a fitting place to start. The Cercle Harmonique and their spiritual advisors were not alone in thinking that the city and city life needed a cleanup. In the extended introduction to his edited volume *Gods of the City*, religious studies scholar Robert Orsi explores how the city was "rendered as the site of moral depravity, lascivious allure, and the terrain of necessary Christian intervention" throughout nineteenth-century America.[3] Primarily in the North, many Protestant reformers believed the city needed physical and spiritual order. The spirits guiding the Cercle Harmonique held a similar perspective and advised Rey and others to combat the violence, vice, and disharmony of their city. New Orleanians needed to get their heads out of the political and moral gutter and focus on what mattered: equality and harmony. Greed and materialism held back the city and rendered it a socially and politically turbulent, and sometimes brutal, place. New Orleans was a racially and ethnically diverse city and a center of cultural exchange, and it was a violent place and had been home to the Deep South's largest slave market. The spirits recognized this and praised the Cercle Harmonique for "working in the midst of corruption to produce a beneficial result."[4]

New Orleans city life shaped the everyday lives of Cercle Harmonique members and their séance records. The material world was corrupt, and this included the Cercle Harmonique's material home. According to the spirits, many of the city's problems came from greed and inequality. The city's racial hierarchy, its "loose morals," and, at times, violent politics prompted the spirits' criticism. Gambling, prostitution, white supremacist violence, and political dishonesty all demonstrated the city's need for the spirits' guidance. Moving beyond the séance table in the private home, this chapter explores the spirit messages received by the Cercle Harmonique in relationship to the city of New Orleans, with particular attention to what the spirits saw as the city's disharmony. The spirits and the Cercle Harmonique wanted to reform the city. Some of their attempts were successful while others ended in mass bloodshed. Afro-Creoles who desired political and social reform put themselves in danger and could be killed by a white mob, as in the case of the 1866 Mechanics' Institute Riot, or by the hands of armed members of the White League as in 1874's Battle of Liberty Place. In either case, the spirits' egalitarian vision for New Orleans could and would come at a price.

Much of New Orleans's perceived disharmony stemmed from its racial hierarchy. With the city's quick adoption of slavery and its frontier location,

New Orleans developed a diverse racial hierarchy founded on the supremacy of whiteness. This racial hierarchy informed many of the séance messages recorded in the Cercle Harmonique's books. Opposed to hierarchy or oligarchy, the spirits spoke fondly of "the Great Principles of Fraternal Equality and Liberty."[5] Society should be based on equality, not prejudice and greed. But slavery and privileged whiteness were part of New Orleans everyday life and had been from the city's early years. The lax manumission process in colonial New Orleans led to a thriving population of *gens de couleur libres*, but the Louisiana *Code Noir* regulated their lives.[6] For example, the law harshly punished free blacks for aiding slaves. The fine for concealing a slave was three times more for a free black than a white perpetrator, and if the free black was unable to pay the fine, the punishment was enslavement.[7] One of the most famous laws passed on the *gens de couleur libres* was the requirement for mixed-race women to bind their hair with a handkerchief called a tignon and the ban on wearing plumes or jewelry in their hair.[8] While a hair scarf may seem an innocuous rule, it reflected a more deep-seated racial anxiety. The free Afro-Creole population possessed some social and financial power and they occupied a racially ambivalent space; thus, a requirement for a simpler appearance drew clearer lines between the white and black classes.

During the antebellum period, free blacks in Louisiana experienced simultaneous privilege and discrimination. They could own property and write wills, they paid taxes, they could enter legal contracts, and they could serve as witnesses in court cases involving whites. Through owning slaves, businesses, and real estate, free Afro-Creoles amassed wealth in the city and surrounding areas. Petit's wealthy family owned over one hundred slaves and Rey's father owned a few slaves too, though neither Petit nor Rey personally owned slaves. However, free blacks were hardly at the same level as whites. Most notably, the government denied them the right to vote. As Louisiana grew more powerful and valuable to the United States, it also became uneasy and nervous with its racial middle caste.[9] The new Louisiana Black Code of 1806 officially prohibited free black men from other states to enter the territory, and laws in the 1830s built upon this earlier one. In 1818, the short-lived rights of free blacks to "own" whites had become too uncomfortable for Louisiana whites, and the state forbade free blacks from owning white "redemptioners" (indentured servants). A slave uprising scare in 1829 just forty miles from New Orleans influenced some of the laws passed in 1830, including one that limited the right of free blacks to work with slaves. In 1830, the Louisiana legislature also passed a law against writing or publishing any document that could cause discontent among the black population; doing so was now punishable by life imprisonment or death. These laws, passed in the antebellum period, and those that followed leading up to the Civil War restricted free black rights and affirmed white supremacy.

Starting in 1830, it was a criminal offense for an inn or tavern keeper to house any person of color who had entered the state illegally. The state also denied permission for free blacks to return to Louisiana, even if the state was their former home. In 1850, the Louisiana legislature passed an amendment that denied free blacks the right to organize religious groups or secret associations such as freemasonry.[10] In other words, Rey's early séance meetings were illegal. In 1855, this prohibition was extended to include scientific, literary, and charitable societies. The law allowed those groups already established to remain, but no new groups were permitted to organize. In 1848 a regulation in Claiborne Parish forced free blacks to pay a bond of $500 to the state as a show of good faith and "good behaviour" if they wanted to remain in Louisiana.[11] In 1859, the state legislature passed "An Act to Permit Free Persons of African Descent to Select Their Masters and Become Slaves for Life," which encouraged all free blacks to choose self-enslavement.[12] The city increasingly regulated Afro-Creole life, and in reply the spirits encouraged listeners against such prejudice. As explained by one spirit guide, it was better to be at the bottom of the racial hierarchy than be its enforcer. Reminiscent of Napoleon's lament, recounted in the introduction, a spirit named X warned that only "a time of shame" awaited "the Oppressor."[13]

Reconstructing New Orleans

Communication with the spirits grounded the Cercle Harmonique during the local turbulence of Reconstruction. While political drama thrived in post–Civil War New Orleans as the local parties exchanged insults and gunfire, the spirits were the Cercle Harmonique's port in the storm. The historian James Hogue identified Reconstruction Louisiana as "a unique epicenter of violent politics."[14] The Union occupation of the city from May 1862 onward fostered antagonism among Confederate sympathizers and white supremacists and promoted hope among much of the city's black and mixed-race population. Following slavery's abolition and the Union victory in the Civil War, many Afro-Creoles hoped that legal and civil equality would be possible. Spirit message after spirit message recorded by the Cercle Harmonique imagined the possibilities.

Free blacks in New Orleans had long sought full civil and legal rights, and before the war's end, Union and Unionist clubs formed en masse to organize the push for black rights.[15] Two prominent, wealthy Afro-Creoles sought an audience with Lincoln in early spring of 1864 but continued to find discussions of their suffrage at a stalemate.[16] When the constitutional convention met in 1864 to amend the Louisiana Constitution of 1852, the question of emancipation produced a lively debate among the delegates, many of whom were former slave owners. While the ordinance to formally abolish slavery passed fairly easily (despite some naysayers), the question of black suffrage was met with almost complete disapproval.[17] Many delegates who were supportive of immediate emancipation did not believe any nonwhites were entitled to the vote. One delegate even proposed an amendment to the constitution to officially deny free blacks the right to vote or the right to move to Louisiana.[18] In the coming months, many former slaveholders and Confederate sympathizers and veterans quickly gained political power and seats in the legislature through the activity of political clubs. Amid all this political maneuvering and change, the city's racial and ethnic composition changed too. Not only did the end of the war bring a large number of newly freed African Americans into the city, but a large influx of German and Italian immigrants also added to the ethnic complexity and conflict.

The *Tribune*, heir of wartime newspaper *L'Union* and managed by the same Afro-Creole men, proved to be one of the most outspoken forums for black rights.[19] During a séance in February 1872, the spirit of John Brown recognized the political activism of the *Tribune* as the "Blackman" defending himself with "the pen in hand."[20] The newspaper developed into a powerful center for advocates of black rights, and their opponents even sought legislation to shut down the newspaper in late 1865.[21] The newspaper organized a "Convention of Colored Men of Louisiana" in early 1865 to discuss the struggle for civil and legal rights, and this was but the start of many conventions organized in part by the *Tribune*. In June 1865, the paper called for "The Friends of Universal Suffrage" to meet and later organized a Universal Suffrage Convention in September, during which the delegates declared themselves to be the "Convention of the Republican Party."[22] The Republican Party of Louisiana's proclaimed focus was universal male suffrage and the "equality of all men before the law."[23] These conventions were attended by not just black and mixed-race Louisianans, but their white allies as well, many of whom were criticized as "carpetbaggers." The most famous of these conventions was held in July 1866 at the Mechanics' Institute, re-convened to amend the 1864 Louisiana Constitution and extend suffrage to black men.

Until the Reconstruction Acts of 1867, the main topics of debate and conversation at these conventions were the need for equal rights before the law for all men, an investigation into validity of the Constitution of 1864, and the dispatch of delegations to Washington to voice the attendees' opinions. Two men attending these conventions who later would serve in gubernatorial capacities were Henry Clay Warmoth, a white Missourian and Union officer who arrived to New Orleans in early 1864, and Oscar James "O. J." Dunn, a non-Creole, African American local whose spirit later advised the Cercle Harmonique. Warmoth in particular attacked the legitimacy of the Constitution of 1864 on the grounds that it was not ratified by a majority vote of the people and that many people were denied the vote. He gained popularity with his outspoken nature. In 1865, concurrent to this Republican growth, the Democratic Party of Louisiana called a state convention in which the delegates, mostly former Confederate soldiers and sympathizers, expressed their support for President Johnson's proposal for unaggressive Reconstruction and—citing the *Dred Scott* case decision—declared that the state government should be "a Government of White People, made and to be perpetuated for the exclusive political benefit of the White Race."[24] During the 1866 session of the Louisiana legislature, now dominated by former Confederates, a new form of the Black Codes passed, though vetoed by Governor Wells. It was in this charged political climate between state Republicans and Democrats that the Mechanics' Institute Riot on 30 July 1866 occurred. The riot, which began as a Republican convention to discuss the 1864 Louisiana Constitution, claimed the lives of approximately forty black and three white Republicans in some of the country's worst Reconstruction violence.

The spirits used Reconstruction bloodshed and fighting, like the Mechanics' Institute Riot, as examples of the material world's corruption and racism. The violence of New Orleans Reconstruction brought many local opportunities to become a martyr for black equality, and the spirits claimed these martyrs as fighters for the Idea. According to the spirits, "the martyrs of July 30 surround the song of victory," and those hopeful martyred spirits came to the Cercle Harmonique's séance table.[25] The convention that would become the riot had a hopeful beginning even as some local periodicals wrote negatively of the proposed convention, calling the Friends of Universal Suffrage "the small minority of the fractional rump."[26] White Democrats met at Lafayette Square just before, on 24 July, to discuss their opposition to Republican plans.

The Mechanics' Institute convention began its preliminary meeting Friday evening (27 July) before an audience of former *gens de couleur libres* and whites. Some of the white delegates in attendance, such as John Henderson, were outspoken supporters of black suffrage, but white men such as Henderson, who spent much of the Civil War in an insane asylum in Mississippi for his antislavery views, were the exception rather than the rule.[27] The call to reconvene the 1864 convention largely generated bitterness and anger among the local white population.[28] Regardless, the meeting was well attended, and local blacks surrounded the building in hopes of hearing the conversations inside. An opening address at the convention declared: "As President Lincoln and the Union Army were unable to restore the Union until the colored men came to their aid, so the Union men of this State feel that they cannot maintain the principles of the union of the States without the aid of the patriotic colored men."[29] This revolutionary fervor for racial equality, however, had unintended and unfortunate consequences.

As if foreshadowing the violence to come, records indicate that local white dentist A. P. Dostie (often referred to as Doctor Dostie) advised blacks to arrive armed on the thirtieth in order to protect themselves. According to an eyewitness unsympathetic to black suffrage, Dostie told those assembled, "The very stones of the streets of New Orleans cry for the blood of these traitors, these rebels. We shall have a meeting here on Monday, in this hall in the second story, come armed; we want no cowards; come armed; if any white man molest you, knock him down."[30] Others reported that while Dostie endorsed self-defense, his speech did not propose violence. Whatever Dostie's words, they were reported in the white press as inflammatory and extreme, and the report was taken as fact. The previous year white Democrats had nicknamed Dostie the "Robespierre of the Union party in New Orleans," equating him with revolutionary rhetoric and violence.[31] After the meeting that Friday night, Dostie led a large torchlight procession down to the Henry Clay Statue at the corner of Canal and St. Charles, singing: "John Brown's body lies a-mouldering in the grave, but his soul is marching on."[32] The police confronted Dostie's group and arrested ten of them. In the process, four policemen were wounded and two blacks were killed. Despite this, hopes were high if not a bit resigned before the convention's official opening on Monday.[33]

Monday, 30 July, began triumphant for local blacks, but the day quickly turned sour. With drum and fife, they marched to the meeting and were joined by more on the way, but local whites stopped a parade of participants and observers of the convention just before noon. Whites shot at those en route to the convention and one black was arrested, but many eventually arrived at the Mechanics' Institute. Unfortunately, they were followed by a developing mob. Rioters began shooting into the building, and with the help of local white police and firemen, they forcefully entered the building and opened fire on the delegates. Some of those assembled for the convention tried to fight back, but they had few weapons among them. Many were shot or clubbed. Some jumped out the windows to escape the mob's gunfire. By the time federal troops arrived to stop the riot, approximately forty-four people had died and two hundred were wounded. Most of the casualties were black. Three white delegates and one white riot agitator died.[34]

The white victims were Dostie, Henderson, and convention chaplain Reverend Jotham Horton. The mob shot Horton twice and fractured his skull with clubs. They clubbed, shot, stabbed, and dragged Dostie downstairs to street level by his hair. His body was taken to a local police station with one policeman sitting on his head during transport. He died the following week.[35] The damage to black bodies was no less gruesome. The rioters mutilated and even looted the dead. Victor Lacroix, a wealthy Afro-Creole and Union veteran, was found dead and disfigured, missing his watch and wallet. According to former governor Michael Hahn's testimony after the event, "The hall was all bloody and strewn with dead, and the chairs and railings were broken to pieces, and there were bullet-holes all over the walls. I staid, perhaps, a few seconds looking at it: The floor was covered with blood, and in walking down the stairs the blood splashed under the soles of my boots."[36] Some of those fleeing the Mechanics' Institute were pursued by white police officers and shot. A black man selling watermelons a few blocks away was seized and shot. Reports claimed that a black carpenter walking home with his tools was attacked and struck in the back of the head with his own hatchet. Local whites raided the homes of local blacks and seized their weapons. Many of the city's outspoken black population temporarily went into hiding.

The U.S. Congress convened a federal committee after the riot that interviewed witnesses and compiled a gruesome report on the event. Early in the report, the committee declared:

> It is in evidence that men who were in the hall, terrified by the merciless attacks of the armed police, sought safety by jumping from the windows, a distance of twenty feet, to the ground, and as they jumped were shot by police or citizens. Some, disfigured by wounds, fought their way down stairs to the street, to be shot or beaten to death on the pavement. Colored persons, at distant points in the city, peaceably pursuing their lawful business, were attacked by the police, shot, and cruelly beaten. Men of character and position, some of whom were members and some spectators of the convention, escaped from the hall covered with wounds and blood, were preserved almost by miracle from death. Scores of colored citizens bear frightful scars more numerous than many soldiers of a dozen well-fought fields can show . . . men were shot while waving handkerchiefs in token of surrender and submission; white and black with arms uplifted praying for life, were answered by shot and blow from knife and club; the bodies of some were 'pounded to a jelly'; a colored man was dragged from under a street-crossing, and killed in a blow; men concealed in outhouses and among piles of lumber were eagerly sought for and slaughtered or maimed without remorse; the dead bodies upon the street were violated by shot, kick, and stab; the face of a man 'just breathing his last' was gashed by a knife or razor in the hands of a woman.[37]

The federal government and the Cercle Harmonique put to paper the horror of that day. It seemed Rey and other members remained home on 30 July, but they still had direct access to the events of the Mechanics' Institute Riot through communication with the spirits of its martyrs.

The spirits of those who died in the 1866 Mechanics' Institute Riot were quite vocal about matters relating to the politics surrounding their deaths. Though his body was dead, the spirit of self-identified Mechanics' Institute Riot martyr W. R. Meadows stated, "Progress cannot be stopped." The "hour of reward" had "struck for the suffering blacks" and now the "paramount" human rights denied to some were available for all. Slavery was detrimental to slaves and it spiritually enslaved and hindered the "human rights" of slave owners and slavery supporters too. Those who believed themselves to be "giants" should recognize that they deserved punishment for their obstructions to "the law of Justice." Though justice would be rendered to all, Meadows knew it would not come quickly or all at once. In a similar message, Victor Lacroix's spirit came to his fellow Afro-Creoles to assure them "nothing can obscure the road to Progress." Lacroix identified the Mechanics' Institute Riot as a "massacre of innocents." The African American's and Afro-Creole's "only crime was being black." Because of this crime: "Our blood flooded the streets of the Bloody City [New Orleans]. Your blood . . . that of the martyrs has not been shed in vain. Because of the tragedy Congress had responded to the atrocity." It is worth noting that Lacroix had a personal connection to Rey's family. François Lacroix, Victor's father, was a member of the Société Catholique pour l'Instruction des Orphelins dans l'Indigence along with Rey's father, and François Lacroix might have occasionally attended meetings of the Cercle Harmonique.[38]

Spirits of those who died in the Mechanics' Institute Riot did not lament their deaths. In October 1869, some of the event's martyrs appeared in succession. First, Dostie assured the Cercle Harmonique that his murderers, who killed him like "a dog," would pay for their deeds. He gave a message warning those who opposed black rights: "I am alive and I am awaiting your arrival in the Land of Justice and Equity! God is to be your judge, but Dostie will be the one who will ask him forgiveness for your great Sin." Though viciously tortured on 30 July, Dostie harbored no resentment for his attackers and magnanimously would help their spirits when they crossed over. Following Dostie's spirit, Lacroix instructed the Cercle Harmonique not to "weep for your martyrs." The spirit of Telesphere Auguste, another spirit who identified as a Mechanics' Institute Riot martyr, also appeared that day. He too was murdered "like a dog" for fighting "the monstrous tyranny that enslaved my brothers." Now his spirit, like the spirits of all martyrs, continued to fight "relentlessly by all possible means that God puts at my disposal." Lincoln and a group of "martyrs of the war" rounded out the day and explained that while a man could be killed, the Idea would not die. The martyrs of war described themselves and all martyrs as "champions of truth and justice."[39] The martyrs of the Mechanics' Institute Riot had joined a larger group in the spiritual world, led by their beloved, martyred president.

A couple years later, the spirit of John Henderson visited the table with one of the Cercle Harmonique's rare English messages. He saw the silver lining of the Mechanics' Institute Riot and proclaimed, "the 30th of July has been satisfied by our blood as the day of Independence of the Black men of Louisiana!" Though his death was gruesome and he was "killed as a mad dog

A recorded message from Dr. A. P. Dostie, 12 February 1872. While most messages were recorded in French, this is an example of a rare English message. Courtesy of the René Grandjean Collection, Louisiana and Special Collections Department, Earl K. Long Library, University of New Orleans.

by a furious mob," his martyrdom for republican progress paved the way for a lovely afterlife in the spiritual world. Henderson was "satisfied to have been a victim of the cruelty of fanatical enemies of Human Rights; for it has given me Light, and I am going forever towards Eternal Progress!" In the spirit world, he worked to "inspire many to faith against prejudices" and hoped that these prejudices he fought "will soon disappear as an evidence of the strength of the Power of Justice to all mankind." He and the rest of the "Invisible army will help you and will carry the Day, and Victory will be inscribed upon your Banner, oh! friends!"[40] He promised that one day racial prejudices no longer would be a problem, but only if members of the Cercle Harmonique, along with other Spiritualists across the country, continued the fight. A lofty goal to be sure, but certainly one the Afro-Creoles at the séance table thought worth pursuing.

Similar to martyrs in Catholic narratives, these spirits did not shy away from identifying the violence of their deaths.[41] The spirits of multiple Mechanics' Institute Riot martyrs referenced dying "like a dog," and this phrasing pointed to the miserable nature of their deaths. The Mechanics' Institute Riot was certainly horrific. However, the martyrs' deaths were not shameful

for the victims. Rather, the spirit messages from the martyrs and other spirits cited the unfairness of their deaths and the cowardice of their killers. To
die for the Idea was to die a meaningful and courageous death. Martyrs of
the Mechanics' Institute Riot hoped their deaths ushered in a new political
age for the United States. For example, the spirit of Reverend Horton identified the actions on 30 July as the "cruelty of human beings" and the consequence of "the miseries of the human heart . . . developed . . . to their fullest
extent." However, his death was not in vain, for "the blood of the friends of
freedom is not to be lost to the sacred cause of Justice." Because he "died in
glory" his spirit now existed in glory too. He and "Dostie, Zanno, Lacroix,
Auguste, and millions of spirits" were "watching like angels and good spirits
do" over the Cercle Harmonique.[42]

Not surprising, the Mechanics' Institute Riot became a watershed date in
the Cercle Harmonique's and the spirits' timeline of black civil rights. In a
brief message a few years after the 1866 violence, Saint Augustine came to
the circle to say, "July Thirtieth? Fratricide. Fourth of July? Freedom." Lacroix also identified 30 July as Louisiana's Fourth of July. The spirit of Dostie
told the Cercle Harmonique to: "Remember the 30th of July! The blood
of those who fell teaches and commands you to be united as a solid phalanx."
Those who died in the violence sometimes appeared on the anniversary of
the Mechanics' Institute Riot. In a group message on the sixth anniversary
of the violence, the spirits of Lacroix, Dostie, Henderson, and "others" informed the circle that their blood, the blood of martyrs, fortified the earth
and humanity's progress. Referring to the white slave-owning patriarchs and
leaders of the old South as members of an oligarchy, the spirits reassured the
circle that "the idea is a blazing torch which is there, luminous!" On the
ninth anniversary, Telesphere Auguste encouraged the Afro-Creole Spiritualists to progress "forward" with "glory." He also reminded them that he
and other victims of the violence forgave their murderers. Other martyred
spirits of the Mechanics' Institute Riot spoke of forgiveness from time to
time. On another occasion, Lacroix recognized that "for many" he was
known as a "Victim of the 30th of July 1866." As a spirit, though, he arose
"with happiness" not only because of his martyr status but also because
he forgave all on earth, even those responsible for his death. The spirit of
Dostie appeared on the eleventh anniversary of the Mechanics' Institute
Riot to assure the Cercle Harmonique that his spirit was still "battling
[those] against human rights!" He also reminded them that those "who
have acted like wolves" will have to face the consequences of their actions in

the spirit world. He warned that all "will be called to account for your wrong deeds!"[43]

In addition to such victims, other spirits noted the anniversary of the Mechanics' Institute Riot. A couple days before the fourth anniversary, a spirit identified as DuBuys drew attention to that "terrible massacre." The slaughter was the work of "proud and miserable assassins" who wanted "to prevent the conquest of political rights" and deny blacks the right to vote. But because of their "cruel fanaticism" and their "innocent blood-soaked hands," the march of rights progressed "faster." DuBuys believed that the blood of martyrs sped the Idea's advancement, but it is unclear whether martyrs' blood was powerful because it was supernatural or because its power derived from its ability to garner support for the black cause; after all, nothing drew attention to a political issue quite like a massacre. Either way, DuBuys's spirit confirmed that the Cercle Harmonique should commend the martyrs for their sacrifice. According to another spirit, the deaths of the Mechanics' Institute Riot martyrs marked the proclamation of rights. If the Mechanics' Institute Riot was a landmark on the Idea's timeline, then the deaths of martyrs helped move that timeline forward. When a martyr died, the spirit of Lacroix told the Cercle Harmonique, "the disinherited of the earth rise." Immediately after Lacroix delivered this one-line message, Dostie appeared and said, "We died, but principles never, nor the soul!"[44] The continuation of Dostie's and other martyrs' principles marked humanity's progress.

Motivated in part by racial violence like the Mechanics' Institute Riot, the Republican Party triumphed in many of the 1866 elections, and though the impeachment of President Johnson failed, a new brand of Reconstruction politics was set in motion. Major General P. H. Sheridan became the military governor of Louisiana and Texas, and he readjusted the New Orleans City Council, appointing several men of color (former free blacks and often those with military experience) to various posts, including O. J. Dunn. The Constitutional Convention of 1867–68, nicknamed the "Black and Tan Convention" for its racially mixed delegates, reconfigured much of the state's law and rule.[45] The Democratic delegates hotly contested those articles related to black rights, and local newspapers lamented various articles of "the Black Crook Constitution" that sought to put the state "under the control of negroes."[46] The black delegates at the convention were a fairly unified group, both in voting and in background: mainly Louisiana born, of higher social ranking, and from Afro-Creole backgrounds. Integrated public education and universal adult male suffrage were key points for black delegates and remained so for black legislators. The spirits visiting the Cercle Harmonique agreed. The "social and moral improvement of mankind" was the goal, and this would come with "Fraternal Union" and schooling. Meadows's spirit stated that mixed-race schools would come and "the sooner the better."[47] Education continued as a focal point of many black legislators, and throughout Reconstruction black legislators were most visible on education committees, while whites chaired and filled the key business and financial committees (such as House Ways and Means and Senate Finance).[48]

"Unite in solid phalanx!"[49]: The Beginning and End of New Orleans Reconstruction

The fracture of New Orleans Republican politics began soon after its beginning. Many of the same delegates serving in the constitutional convention also oversaw the Republican Party's convention later in 1867 and prepared the party's ticket for the state's general election. Following the Mechanics' Institute Riot the party divided between the more radical Republicans led by the *New Orleans Tribune* and the more conservative Republicans initially led in part by Henry Clay Warmoth. When the convention voted, it selected Warmoth as the gubernatorial nominee with Dunn as his running mate. Warmouth won the election, and the first state legislature following the constitutional convention possessed a strong Republican majority, including some black representatives who were allowed to take their seats after the ratification of the Fourteenth Amendment. These victories did not come easy or without voting intimidation at the polls. In parishes near New Orleans, black Republicans were beaten and even shot. At some polls white Democrats gave certificates to African Americans who voted for their ticket so that other white Democrats could "be friendly to those who befriended us."[50] Local political groups in New Orleans too asserted authority through acts of violence.

Warmoth's time as governor was never calm. Rumors of Warmoth's corruption and turncoat ways spread from the beginning of his tenure as governor.[51] Soon after he took office, he began to court his rivals' supporters to develop a wide backing. Warmoth also gained command over a vast array of Louisiana offices, including the state militia, the city's interracial Metropolitan Police, the returning board, and the registrar of voters office. But this did not mean he easily made friends. Instead, he was at the center of the Louisiana Republican Party's division. An 1868 civil rights bill called the Isabelle

Bill (for its author, black representative Robert Isabelle) sought to guarantee "equal rights and privileges" with regard to travel and business licenses to all persons "without regard to race, color or previous condition," and furthermore the bill would make segregation a criminal offense.[52] Though it passed the Louisiana House and Senate, Warmoth vetoed it, fearful that it would add kindling to the fire of racial tension. He denied a similar bill in 1870. Actions such as these alienated him from some of his black supporters, and following the suspension of the *New Orleans Tribune*, other Republican voices, both black and white, began to speak louder. Near the end of 1870, the spirits even warned that not all members of the Republican Party should be trusted for party affiliation alone, and the "mouths" of some "might deceive your fellow citizens."[53]

Warmoth's earliest Republican dissenters were the Custom House faction, overseen by the federal employees of the New Orleans Custom House including President Grant's brother-in-law James B. Casey. Some wanted to eclipse the young governor's power, but most felt wronged by Warmoth's corruption and dishonesty. During this time Dunn began to stray from Warmoth and focused more strongly on guaranteeing black suffrage. Frustrated with Warmoth, Dunn joined the Custom House faction and brought many black Republicans with him. Evening meetings at various ward political clubs grew heated, and members of the rival Republican factions often tried to sabotage each other. With this divide in the Republican Party, it was unclear who had blacks' best interest at heart. Some of the city's Afro-Creoles went with Dunn, while others remained loyal to Warmoth. Possibly among those who remained in Warmoth's camp was Rey's brother, Octave, who served as a captain in Warmoth's Metropolitan Police.

In the midst of Dunn's accusations that Warmoth wanted to sacrifice the interests of blacks for Democrat support, Dunn briefly oversaw the governor's office while Warmoth recovered from an injury. During this time the Republican State Committee called for a state convention and elected Dunn to oversee it. Warmoth hurried back to New Orleans to try to take over the August 1871 convention. When he was unsuccessful, he and P. B. S. Pinchback (a black northerner who came to New Orleans in 1862) set up a rival convention. At the outset of the convention, a run-in between federal troops loyal to the Custom House and some of the Metropolitan Police nearly escalated into a street fight over control of the official convention's location.[54] Later that fall, during the gubernatorial and presidential campaigns, Dunn quickly took ill and passed away on 22 November 1871. His death proved to be a scandal, and though doctors determined congestion of the brain and lungs as the official cause, rumors of poisoning persisted for years. A procession of several thousand people took part in Dunn's funeral. Three former governors served as pallbearers and even Confederate generals participated in the procession. In one of his early 1872 speeches supporting the Civil Rights Bill, Charles Sumner memorialized Dunn as "an example of integrity" who upheld duty over riches.[55] Dunn immediately became a prime example of black political honor for Sumner as well as the Cercle Harmonique.[56]

The day following Dunn's death, a spirit named Oscar Bellevue, who claimed to have died for political reasons, advised the circle. Bellevue's spirit was trying to achieve "a spiritual life full of Progress towards Him" but found himself still "attached a little to Earth." This attachment came from his desire "to protect Octave [Rey], [P. B. S.] Pinchback, and a host of true and tried friends I left." Bellevue lamented that these friends were "seeking only material favors" rather than looking to "spiritual interests." The death of Dunn— "who now belongs to our Broad party of spirits"—should prompt reflection on "the small weight of what is attached to material life." It was naïve to depend heavily upon the main political figures and hope that a "big fellow" like Dunn "would preside over their good fortune." Political inaction and reliance solely on leaders would result in getting "their necks broken like Oscar got his."[57] Obvious in Bellevue's message is a plea for more political action. Hoping black politicians like Dunn would secure rights was not enough. All who wanted rights would have to work for them or else certain death loomed. What is unclear is whether Bellevue's lament regarding Octave and Pinchback was due to their Warmoth affiliation, because they denied Spiritualism, or both. His message was likely an expression of the Cercle Harmonique's frustration with their political party's drama. Reconstruction politics were messy, and it was difficult for locals to find a port in that political storm. For the Cercle Harmonique, the spirits grounded them during such violent and tumultuous politics.

Two and a half weeks following his death, Dunn made his first appearance at Rey's séance table, and he seemed to speak directly to the tension among the city's black and Republican population. His message seemed simple: "For the sake of harmony, and for the freedom of all, don't shatter to pieces the great Work already done . . . Dividing a house is ruinous to all . . . United we stand, divided we fall!" This message came with much emotion and force, concluding that "as this pencil—broken by my will—so you are to be, if divided you are." The following day, the spirit of Mechanics' Institute Riot martyr Dostie commanded Louisiana Republicans to unite. Only then could they muster "the Power to secure victory" for their party and their ideals. Later that month Dunn appeared again; his spirit echoed Dostie and encouraged the Republican Party to remain unified. All Republicans would need to harmonize into "a solid phalanx, to be able to vanquish your real political enemies." Dunn felt responsible for some of the party's division and apologized for it. "I did not want to divide our ranks," he said, "I was wrong." He would not take all the blame though, and his words suggested a criticism of Warmoth. Others continued to pit the party members against each other, and Dunn had a warning for these "deceivers": Their "plot" would be discovered.[58] The black New Orleanians' real political enemies were Democrats not fellow Republicans. Now as a spirit guide, Dunn viewed the conflict among the city's Republicans as far less important ideologically and detrimental to the party's professed, common goal.

Dunn's successor as lieutenant governor was Pinchback, who later became the state's first black governor following Warmoth's impeachment. Leading up to Warmoth's impeachment trial, the Louisiana legislature was in disarray. The Custom House ring arrested Warmoth, Pinchback, some of the city police, and a few Warmoth-loyal legislators in early January. This put into motion a political power standoff that ended the following week with the shooting of a Warmoth-loyal Republican and the setup of a rival legislature. While the official House of Representatives functioned in the State House chambers, a shadow house of representatives run by the anti-Warmoth Custom House group openly defied Warmoth from the Gem Saloon on Royal Street. When rumors spread that Warmoth planned to remove some of the black anti-Warmoth representatives from the chambers at the statehouse, a Custom House handbill announced a rally for "LIBERTY OR DEATH."[59] Warmoth, with the backing of Metropolitan policemen and the state militia, quieted the rabblerousing of the Custom House ring by the end of the month.

The political muddle was not limited to the Republican Party. Following the war, the main Mardi Gras Carnival krewes (Rex, Comus, and the new Twelfth Night Revelers) consisted of former Confederates who celebrated white supremacy, but even they failed to work together. Rival parades during the 1872 Carnival season between Rex and Comus kept Democrats from capitalizing on the turmoil internal to the rival party.[60] This did not mean that the streets were safe for Republicans or blacks. In February 1872, a spirit identified himself as one who suffered and was killed, and he described "political crimes" as the acts of "cowardly oppressors" who wanted to hold onto their undeserved power. The spirit's own "miserable persecutors" were "shivering with fear" when they killed him, while he remained courageous. The spirit identified himself as "François Sénateur," a man who Grandjean noted was from New Iberia, Louisiana, and assassinated "at the beginning of the republican regime by democrats."[61]

To make matters more complicated, there were five political parties by the general election in November 1872. The two main contenders for governor were Republican nominee William P. Kellogg, a former Union cavalry colonel, and Democratic nominee John McEnery, a former Confederate colonel.[62] The campaign and election were particularly partisan, bitter, and even violent. In October the Ku Klux Klan burned a Carroll Parish Republican newspaper's printing press. Voter intimidation on behalf of various Democrat-affiliated organizations and social clubs was widespread, especially in the more rural parishes. Employers threatened to fire black employees if they voted Republican, and the locations of polls in predominately black areas often were not advertised or published.[63] During the campaign, Dunn's spirit encouraged the Cercle Harmonique to remain confident and hopeful in their political outlook. They should not "despair of the political aspect" of their situation.[64]

Amid this volatile election culture and around the one-year anniversary of his death, Dunn again came to the table with a message of black unity. Dunn instructed those working to secure "the salvation of your Sacred Rights" to keep pushing forward. "Tell the boys! Do not Despair! Hold on together. I am in the light." It was important that they keep together "in rank" and "Unite in solid phalanx!"[65] The spirits encouraged hope regardless of the political divisions.

The results of the 1872 gubernatorial election were fiercely contested, and the outcome was dual governments, one headed by Kellogg and the other by McEnery. Both held inauguration ceremonies on 14 January and installed governments, Kellogg's Republicans at the Mechanics' Institute and McEnery's supporters at Lafayette Square. The state returning boards were divided. As acting governor, Warmoth claimed McEnery the winner, which led to accusations of election stealing and to Warmoth's impeachment. As acting governor, Pinchback declared Kellogg the winner.

Republican Senator Oliver H. P. Morton from Indiana was brought in to investigate the election results and determine the rightful victor, a role he would repeat for the election of 1874. Both times he backed the Republican candidate. This made him an ally, and after his death in 1877, the spirit of Dunn assured Rey that "Morton" joined him and others in "the happy land" and was met by "old friends and late foes."[66] In the end President Grant agreed with Morton and in 1873 seated Kellogg as governor with federal support. This did not stop McEnery's rival government or its influence, and the Democrats' dissent manifested in public culture. The 1873 Carnival theme for the Mistick Krewe of Comus was "The Missing Links to Darwin's Origin of Species." While many costume designs were of animals, both fanciful and real, others carried a clear political bite. Some animal designs were meant to be specific figures. For example, the "Ass" was depicted as Charles Darwin, both in the design image and in the parade. The Hyena was General Butler, the Tobacco Grub was styled as President Grant, and the Rattlesnake was Warmoth. The "Negro" was portrayed as Darwin's missing link personified.[67] The only animals identified as contemporary figures were those identified as people with political and social views that opposed the Mistick Krewe's social apparatus. In short, they were the butt of the parade's joke.

Violence was another element to the dual government tension. The so-called First Battle of the Cabildo in March 1873 was McEnery's first attempt to overrun the police at the Cabildo near Jackson Square with his own militia headed by former Confederate officer Frederick N. Ogden.[68] The Colfax Massacre in Grant Parish on Easter Sunday in April 1873, identified by the historian Eric Foner as the "bloodiest single instance of racial carnage in the Reconstruction era," began as a conflict between rivals who both claimed a local office in Grant Parish.[69] What began as a localized result of the competing McEnery and Kellogg legislatures ended with the slaughter of much of the district's black militia at the hands of whites. This incident was not unique; similar events transpired in St. Martinsville and later in Coushatta in August 1873. The most successful rebellious act of McEnery's Democrats happened in late summer 1874 in New Orleans, and it was an event that gained the full attention of the spiritual republic.

The terror dispensed by groups like the Ku Klux Klan was not absent in Louisiana. The development of White Leagues illustrated the popularity of militant white supremacy. Chapters of the White League formed across Louisiana, starting first in St. Landry Parish in April 1874 and then developing into a military-style campaign for white conservative "Redeeming" Democrats. The New Orleans branch, overseen by Ogden, formed in the wake of a fear-mongering and false story published in the *Daily Picayune* about a pending outbreak of black-on-white violence by local "Black Leagues" planned for 4 July. The story warned that these men would "fire and kill" those in their way and then "supported by the other colored people who would rally to their support . . . kill all the men and keep all the women."[70] Ogden led the New Orleans White Leaguers in an attack in September 1874, which resulted in the brief rule of a rogue Democrat government for three days until federal intervention removed them. McEnery loyalists, most of whom were aligned with the newly formed White League, exchanged gunfire with the racially integrated Metropolitan Police and temporarily took over the city. Locals named this street violence the Battle of Liberty Place. In the days leading up to the September violence and during the ensuing White League rule, the White League's pro-white agenda clearly manifested in its supporters' words and actions. In response, the spirits advising the Cercle Harmonique noted the event and encouraged the Afro-Creoles to remain confident in their rights and progress.

Late on Saturday, 12 September 1874, the steamer *Mississippi* arrived to the port of New Orleans, and its cargo included guns and ammunition for the city's White League members. Anticipating that the Republican mayor would confiscate their weapons, the White League prepared for a confrontation. During the preceding weeks, local police seized many of the White Leaguers' weapons in raids sanctioned by the local Republican administration. White Leaguer J. Dickson Bruns wrote a proclamation published in the Sunday, 13 September issue of the *New Orleans Daily Picayune* lamenting and decrying the violation of the White Leaguers' Second Amendment rights. Similar to rhetoric used by the Afro-Creole periodicals *L'Union* and *Tribune*, Bruns's piece asserted, "Declare that you are, of right out to be, and mean to be free."[71] The White League also distributed a handbill throughout downtown to announce a meeting that Monday morning at eleven at the Henry Clay Statue that would feature prominent city leaders. Former Confederates and White League leaders, such as the lead defense attorney for the Colfax Massacre perpetrators, delivered fiery speeches and at one point had the crowd chanting "Hang Kellogg!"[72] With a large crowd turning into a mob on their side, leaders of the White League began to make their way toward the guns aboard the docked *Mississippi*. In the meantime other White Leaguers strategically placed barricades throughout downtown.

When word of this mass meeting reached the Metropolitan Police, forces were dispatched to the Clay statue, where the White League now assembled with upward of three thousand armed men.[73] Crossfire between the two groups devolved into disorganized charges and bloodshed. White League snipers took out the Metropolitan officers operating howitzers, and within an hour, the White League outnumbered and overpowered the racially integrated police and Louisiana State Militia units. Sixteen White Leaguers died, along with thirteen killed or mortally wounded policemen. Six bystanders also died, one young man mortally wounded while crossing the street. The following morning, the Metropolitan Police and militia surrendered the police station and state arsenal to the White League. The result was the creation of a temporary government controlled by Democrats and Confederate veterans until federal forces restored Republican rule a few days later. McEnery was out of town during the melee, and so former Confederate colonel D. B. Penn was installed as acting governor in his place. Penn asked those assembled to go to church and thank God for their victory and ask for his continued favor and protection. After seizing Kellogg's office, one White Leaguer wrote a note for his wife late on the night of 14 September: "I never have seen so complete an uprising of the people and their faces indicated the reaction a change of government must produce. The citizen troops were received with a complete ovation."[74]

Members of the Cercle Harmonique publicly remained quiet during the upheaval, and the spirits did not advocate fighting back. On 15 September, the spirit of a devoted sister warned that hatred only "begets . . . bad feelings" and "evil." During the Democrats' occupation of the city, Saint Vincent de Paul comforted the circle, telling them not to worry "about the Political unrest taking place right now." They should "stand firm" in their "liberal views" and, if anything, further dedicate themselves to "Rights for all." In short, all supporters of republicanism in the city should remain confident throughout the White League's rule because the spirits would take care of them.[75] Despite de Paul's urging for hope and confidence, Rey was no doubt concerned for his brother, Octave, who served in the Metropolitan Police.

Governor Kellogg remained safe during the violence on 14 September and the resulting White League rule, barricaded at the local Custom House under the protection of a small band of federal troops. The White League's actions immediately angered President Grant, who swore he would go to New Orleans and personally "clean them out" if necessary.[76] He sent General William H. Emory to head the federal troops tasked with restoring order to the city. Emory arrived the evening of 16 September on the same train as McEnery, who was making his way to New Orleans to join Penn and the White League. Knowing they would be overpowered, McEnery and Penn surrendered to federal troops the following day, and Kellogg was restored as rightful governor four days after what local white New Orleanians dubbed the Battle of Liberty Place.[77]

Saint Vincent de Paul offered the Cercle Harmonique encouragement more than once in the wake of the violence. The day following the Battle of Liberty Place he lamented, "The blood shed yesterday demonstrates how much hatred there is in the hearts of those men who seek to enthrall their brothers." But he assured them, "You will see the civil rights of each one proclaimed and they will be maintained!" He and other spirits would take care of the righteous dead and "martyrs." Those still in the material fight on earth should remain positive because this was only "the passing of some accumulated clouds, but which will let appear the clear sky of the Future!" He recognized that his words were "written at the time of the apparent triumph of the oligarchy," but he classified them differently. His message was meant to reiterate "the certainty that you will realize the full conquest of your proclaimed and maintained rights." He encouraged them to preserve their courage, as "you have been the victims, the unfortunate ones slaughtered by barbarian brothers who were blindfolded by their hatred, envy, and the prostitutions in their thought." But the Cercle Harmonique should "fear nothing: the sun of realization is rising beautiful and magnificent . . . Oh, my children! Forward! And wait with expectancy for what your guides promise to you." Later that week, another spirit echoed the saint's sentiment and used similar language too. "You will be victorious," he told them, "for you, your rights acquired, proclaimed, and maintained, notwithstanding any contrary appearance." This current "turbulence of the oligarchy [the White League and the heirs of slaveholding white power] will cause its fall which will be apparent to everyone" including "its own hideous and repulsive face!" Though confident, the spirit's message also recognized the uncertainty and fear of those times. He assured them, "We are watching over you! Have confidence in us."[78]

The day following the firefight between the White League and the Metropolitan Police and state militia was a spiritually active one. Following de Paul's message, the spirit of Alexander Lanna appeared. Lanna sought to comfort and embolden the Cercle Harmonique. "Do not weep for those who were violently released from the material in the discharge of Duty," Lanna stated. He then differentiated between the spirits of those who died for the Idea and the spirits of oppressors. While the spirit of "the martyr of a just and sacred cause" and the spirit of one blinded by "hatred and anger" held different views in the material world, everyone in the spirit world affirmed "natural Rights."[79] God intended all to have equal rights, though the oligarchies on earth would try to deny civil rights to blacks. Any spirit, even of a slave owner or a French monarch, could not argue against human rights. It was distressing that political rights were not universally established in the material world, but the spirits had hopes for the material world's future even in the face of racial violence.

The spirit of C. W. Culbertson, a second lieutenant in the Confederate Louisiana infantry, also appeared on 15 September to report that he was crying and moaning after entering the spirit world. His spirit suffered because he had "ignored these great and noble thoughts of Freedom and Equality for all beings" and instead had wanted to protect the ideas of "the proud oligarchy of race." The day following the Battle of Liberty Place was an auspicious time for a Confederate spirit to grieve for his past ideology and actions. Now surrounded by the wisdom of the spirit world, he recognized the universal truth of rights and equality, just as all white supremacists would after their deaths. Following Culbertson, a spirit identified as André reminded the Cercle Harmonique that spirits might arrive to the spiritual world "imbued with their Prejudice," but he promised that these spirits would encounter Truth and then "work for the good."[80]

In the days that followed the Battle of Liberty Place, temporary White League rule, and the restoration of the Republican administration, the spirits tried to reassure Rey and others. A "devoted brother" encouraged them to remain focused on universal "solidarity" as their guiding "principle." It was quite possible that some members of the Cercle Harmonique or their family wanted revenge on the White League since this spirit discouraged them from retaliating against someone "because he oppressed you." All needed to "respect the laws" and let the legal system rectify injustice, rather than take matters into their own hands. "The law must be equal for all," the brother lectured, because all were equal before God.[81] Indeed, violence was not the answer according to the spirits; rather, peace should be the modus operandi for change.

As order was restored in New Orleans following the Battle of Liberty Place, the spirit of Saint Vincent de Paul reflected on martyrs, violence, the Mechanics' Institute Riot, and the recent unrest. He assured them that a "large amount of spirits" rallied around them, including the "martyrs" who had "fallen to the fatal bullet of the Infamous Oligarchy." Despite the apparent power this white supremacist oligarchy wielded, members of the Cercle Harmonique were not to worry because "the Sun of Liberty" shined "brightly" on them with the promise of "redemption." Even if they felt despondent, they were not hated "outcasts" or "pariahs on this arid land." Black civil rights were "proclaimed and maintained" despite the "Blood Pact" that had been "signed to destroy you" and the "hungry pack of carnage" that came for them on "14 September 1874." The Cercle Harmonique also had the "hearts of martyrs" on their side. The spirit of the Afro-Creoles' favorite saint then referenced "the massacre of July 30, 1866," as a step in their "redemption" and that it was connected to the affirmation of their "Civil Rights" on "September 14, 1874." Though these days were soaked in violence, de Paul and all the spirits assured them that "the Table will not be stained with blood." Rather, the spirit guides "are with you, we know your pain, your expectations, and we talk and proclaim your arrival with dignity recognizing your Civil Rights."[82] This repeated reference to their rights—proclaimed and maintained—offered hope in the wake of such instability and violence.

The spirits' immediate response to the unrest of mid-September 1874, like the presence of Mechanics' Institute Riot martyrs and references to that 1866 day, reflected the Cercle Harmonique's hope that egalitarian republicanism could remake the material world. However, as Reconstruction wore on, that hopeful vision slipped further and further away. While the spirit of Saint Vincent de Paul referenced the Battle of Liberty Place in the event's immediate aftermath and noted that the "martyrs of July 30, 1866" looked out for the group and were "fighting for your spiritualist victories," spirits did not reference the Battle of Liberty Place during the Cercle Harmonique's final years.[83] The city's Republican Party more generally and black Republicans specifically bounced back from the horror of the Mechanics' Institute Riot and achieved a certain amount of political power, but the White League's takeover of the city in 1874 revealed how vulnerable they were.

In the wake of the Battle of Liberty Place and similar white terrorism, Afro-Creoles continued to support the Republican government and party. Voter fraud and intimidation were rampant in the election of fall 1874. Signs printed with "2 × 6," indicative of the dimensions of a grave, along with the image of a skull and crossbones, were posted across New Orleans on election day with the intent to scare black voters.[84] In some cases, armed white Democrats stood near the polls. To incite fear of black political power a New Orleans newspaper reported that the city's "Radical Africans" roamed the streets and attacked blacks who they believed voted Democrat.[85] While the Republican Party initially seemed successful in elections for seats in the state legislature, the Wheeler Adjustment reclaimed some of those seats for Democrats. This compromise, overseen by William A. Wheeler, came after another gun-toting standoff in front of the statehouse in early January 1875. Fistfights erupted inside between Republican and Democrat representatives. Compounding the loss of seats, even fewer of the black politicians remaining in the legislature served on committees in the coming months.[86] Though Kellogg won the governor's seat again in this election, only the federal presence in the state kept the office his.

As the political situation for the black Republicans in Louisiana worsened, some members left the Cercle Harmonique in late 1875. For most of 1876 and 1877, Rey appears to have practiced Spiritualism alone or with only one or two others. The spirits remained hopeful though. In November 1875, Dunn reported he was now "pursuing a course of studies" that would enable him "to act in a better state of knowledge, as a missionary of Peace and Harmony through the Land and for the good, for the Elevation of a part of the citizens who are yet held in a state of bondage, for the want of humanity, by the enslavement of unhappy Brothers under the yoke of their past ideas of Rights." All in all, he was pleased to have watched the changes in "the unworthy tendencies of a part of the citizens of the Republic." Fighters for freedom should not despair, for he and other spirits were still there to help "the success of the Good Cause—the triumph of Liberty over Slaveocracy." Those on earth would "vanquish the foes," and if they remained "true to the principles of Justice and Equity," those ideals would "run high in your Land of Liberty and Freedom."[87]

While the Republican Party maintained control of the governor's seat through the end of 1876, Kellogg would prove to be the end of the line. The successful "redemption" of neighboring Mississippi threw fuel on the fire of the Louisiana White League. When impeaching Kellogg did not work, the White League's focus turned to the upcoming 1876 election, which pitted Marshal Stephen B. Packard of the Republican Custom House faction against Democrat candidate General Francis Nicholls of Confederate army fame. Both candidates claimed victory. Like Kellogg and McEnery years earlier, each held an inauguration ceremony and installed a government—Packard's behind federal guards and closed doors and Nicholls's across town near Lafayette Square with public fanfare. The following day, entire regiments of White Leaguers surrounded the Packard statehouse and staged a bloodless coup. The Compromise of 1877 solidified Nicholls's victory.[88] Despite all the spirits' encouragement and hope, Republican Reconstruction was over. But political unrest and violence were not the only New Orleans problems the spirits criticized. The material world was a bloody, unequal, and disharmonious place because of materialism—the source of all violence, political strife and inequality, selfish behavior, and vice.

"The vanities of this world are ephemeral"[89]: Materialism and Local Vice

Antebellum visitors to New Orleans frequently found the city's morality wanting and wrote about the city's problems with vice. Writing in 1836, northern Presbyterian minister James Davidson called New Orleans the "great Southern Babylon—the mighty receptacle of wealth, depravity and misery."[90] It was largely the Creole population and its racial spectrum that Davidson found intriguing but also disgusting, and he was not alone in this conclusion. After the Louisiana Purchase, many incoming Americans viewed the Creole population as their foil in numerous ways, including religious practice, sexual liaisons, racial purity, education, political competency, and class. Anglo-Americans believed these deficiencies in civilization and God's—meaning Protestant—law had allowed for the city's "depravity." Prostitution, concubinage, and social drinking were common in New Orleans across all social boundaries. Various sorts of entertainment could be easily found in the city long into the early hours of Sunday, including gambling, quadroon balls, cockfighting, and horse racing. In 1860 one northerner observed "rum shops on almost every corner." In addition to describing such moral laxity, others observed how freely money was spent in the city on luxuries of all kinds.[91] People made money in the slave markets and the cotton exchange, and New Orleans's location on the Mississippi River meant that merchants and shop owners quickly moved money and goods. Wealth and depravity seemed to go hand in hand in the city, as profits accrued by locals or travelers supported New Orleans vice. Like some of New Orleans's visitors, the spirits too could be critical of the urban greed in the Cercle Harmonique's city.

The Cercle Harmonique's spiritual guides were quite concerned about humanity's proclivity for materialism. They used materialism to describe greed for possessions and power or for an overwhelming focus on the temporary material world. Materialism caused men to desire authority over others, desire women's bodies, and desire money. All these cravings had negative consequences for a person's spirit and for society. According to one spirit, materialism "enveloped" people "in darkness." Materialism was the "vile" source of "antagonism" and angling for "supremacy" in society. It created "selfishness, pride, and vanity." The greed for material possessions was linked frequently to greed for power. The spirit of J. Olivier lamented how materialism often led people "astray from the path of the Just." In contrast, Spiritualism "rejects materialism completely." Thus, selflessness was a desirable Spiritualist trait. The spirit of Valmour described "abnegation" as "necessary" because material interests not only distracted people but could disrupt a séance. A spirit's "triumph" in the spiritual world, such as Valmour's, was "due to his abnegation." Though a "humble blacksmith," he now fulfilled "the grand role of Spiritualist Apostle" because of his admirable "love and charity."[92]

Materialism cultivated injustice, ordered social hierarchies, and encouraged economic disparity, and these were the main reasons the spirits taught against it. Materialism fostered a kind of ignorance and egotism that retarded one's spiritual development on earth. Lamennais warned that it was the "thousand headed hydra which vomits the egotism" humanity used to "nourish" itself. Ingesting this materialism as nourishment was unwise. A person's time on earth was fleeting, and it was foolish to devote it to materialistic ends. A spirit named Fisk lectured that "the power of men" lasted but "a moment," and therefore it was wise to use any social power "for the general benefit of every man" and not for personal gain. Greed worked against the Idea and against harmony. One's money, and certainly one's social status, did not define a person. Rather, wisdom did. The spirit of U.S. senator Daniel Webster warned that one "must never forget the poor" because wealth was fickle. According to the spirit of Lincoln, "the ant, as well as the lion, deserve the attention of men." Social status did not dictate a person's importance, and so the Cercle Harmonique was encouraged to "console those whom society rejects."[93]

The spirits taught that materialism supported unfair class divisions and racial hierarchies because egotism and wealth bred injustice. Selfishness and "personal interest" divided humanity and fostered hatred. The privileged classes, "indifferent to the misfortune of their fellow creatures," worked against "the solidarity of all beings!" Sitting atop the hierarchy cultivated apathy toward the rest of humanity. Those who thought themselves high and mighty on earth—"the proud and vainglorious"—remained isolated in the spirit world, "bewildered in the midst of the darkness of ignorance." Additionally, those who oppressed others, laughed at charity, and obstructed "Brotherhood" came to regret those decisions. After entering the spiritual world, they realized that their decisions furthered unfair social divisions. Living a life of leisure, especially if supported by slavery, impeded spiritual growth. It was far better to "experience the product of your work" as opposed to profiting from "the sweat of others."[94]

According to the spirits, society could be broken down into two main camps: the rich and the poor. The poor frequently were forced "to work at any price" and to allow others to take advantage of them. Anyone who believed himself "superior" to those "poorer than himself" was foolish. Unfortunately, the wealthy often felt they possessed "intellectual superiority" too. Thus, the spirits taught, the rich did not accept their social duty to "reach out to those who suffer" and "relieve" them. The "struggle between the righteous and the wicked," or, put another way, "the oppressed and the oppressor," was a chief concern of the spirits. Another spirit related the conflict between "evil and good" to the struggle between "the oppressor and the oppressed." And these were conflicts that spanned history. A spirit named Assitha described society as the continual "struggle of the oppressed who wants to break the chains that surround him and the oppressor who wants to keep his iron foot on the heart of his victim to prevent him from fighting." The spirits lauded the Cercle Harmonique for their courage in the face of "oppression" and the powerful who tried to break them.[95]

Though materialism and money promised happiness, it made people miserable. The "bitter fruit" of materialism unfortunately kept people captive to greed. For example, materialism fueled gambling, which slowly destroyed one's soul. "Unhappy" were those who spent their time in the "infamous gambling dens." A man who frequented the "gambling dens" subjected himself to a "degrading torture." According to the spirits, "gambling and debauchery" were two "infamous vices." Additionally, gambling and prostitution were two corruptions that reinforced each other. One spirit admitted he neglected his familial duties, and instead of caring for his wife and children, he served material pleasures, likely drinking or gambling. The spirits of some former card players remained riveted to those gambling dens they frequented during their earthly lives, which slowed their spiritual progress.[96]

Materialism fostered vices like gambling and encouraged people to focus on the "ephemeral" and material "vanities of this world." One should "despise the Goods of the Earth" and instead "work with Courage" to receive "the bread of the soul." On one occasion, Rey's father, Barthélemy, lectured those who wanted "earthly riches." They would not be able to carry their material fortune, or anything for that matter, into the spiritual world with them. Everything material would be left behind on the earth. To overcome materialism was a "triumph" in a person's spiritual progression. Materialism and greed weighed down a spirit, and so people must "fight" against their "passions." A soul could "sink in an abyss of darkness more and more gloomy," or if that soul were "elevated by right-doing, it will ascend in light, illuming its peaceful route ad infinitum!"[97] Rather than focusing on the material, the Afro-Creoles should focus on the spiritual.

Though the Cercle Harmonique appears to have been primarily male, they were not blind to how urban vice supported gender inequality and unfairness toward women in their city. The spirits were critical of prostitution and sexual exploitation, both of which were problems in nineteenth-century New Orleans. Materialism sparked in men the "craving for money, for the carnal possession of women, for luxury, for excess, for immoderation in everything." Because of materialism, men ignored the body's ephemerality, which led them to "condemn and reject from your society the virginal maid" and instead "entertain with respect the prostitute." A spirit identified as C. Boudreau criticized men who "extol vice" and revel in materialistic pursuits. Their "shameless" natures were "increasing prostitution" and forcing "your sisters" into positions where they became "more and more degraded by your coward and infamous calculations."[98]

The spirits blamed male greed and the unequal power balance between men and women for prostitution. One of Petit's female relatives noted how a man's actions could ruin a woman. She chastised those men who, instead of offering charity to "the poor woman who suffers with her children," chose actions that furthered her demise into "the abyss of your immorality." She was harsh toward libertines "sowing children everywhere," for those fatherless sons likely would follow suit. Without a male role model, they would grow up "with the most horrible opinion on the virtue of women." Indeed, for some men, Jean-Jacques Rousseau's spirit lamented, a woman was "a hobby," perhaps "a doll they like to dress nice" but ultimately abandoned like "a toy." Though they strove to greatness, it is possible that members of the Cercle Harmonique did not always treat women as they should have. In a message addressed to "my dear son," the father of circle regular Maitre Brion explained, "An hour here [at the Spiritualist table] pays more than hours of caresses of a woman."[99] If he had to remind his son to value spiritual work over the touch of a woman, perhaps Brion's focus had been elsewhere.

Prostitution, *plaçage*, and sexual exploitation of black and mixed-race women have a long history in New Orleans. Though Storyville, the city's most famous legal prostitution district, was not formed until the very end of the nineteenth century, prostitution, particularly of black bodies, was common long before. Female slaves between ages fifteen and twenty-nine comprised a substantial percentage of slaves sold in the New Orleans slave market. The market of "fancy girls," light-skinned female slaves primarily sold for sexual exploitation, was a lucrative business particularly after the 1790s with the rise of the domestic slave trade.[100] *Plaçage*, or the keeping of a free black mistress, though not commonplace was not unheard of in colonial and antebellum New Orleans. Described by one scholar as "a ritualized system of prostitution," *plaçage* offered free women of color access to furniture, nicer homes, and often a monetary allowance.[101] *Plaçage* presented opportunity but at a price.

Many Afro-Creole men were critical of *plaçage* and its destructive effects on free black women. The Afro-Creole writer (and later spirit guide after his death) Armand Lanusse wrote a multi-issue tragic story published in the Afro-Creole journal *L'Album littéraire* about a young quadroon woman, and this piece was indicative of the periodical's critical tone toward the city's racial status quo. The character became a mistress, or *placée*, but her partner abandoned her when he married a white woman. In despair the quadroon woman threw herself under the wheels of his carriage.[102] The second Afro-Creole literary publication, *Les Cenelles*, also included stories and poems critical of the *plaçage* system. For these authors, *plaçage* represented the immorality, inequality, and ignominy of the city's racial dynamics. To provide for themselves and their families, these women entered relationships with no chance of legal marriage and every possibility of heartbreak.[103] For Lanusse and others, the *placée* was nothing more than a sexual object for her partner and was then discarded.

The Cercle Harmonique's and the spirits' condemnation of prostitution was a social commentary on the sexual politics of their city. Like the essays and poems before them in *L'Album littéraire* and *Les Cenelles* about the dangers of *plaçage*, the Cercle Harmonique's séance records identified the corruption of sexual exploitation as a hindrance to local harmony and humanity's progress. While their status was regrettable, prostitutes should not simply be scorned and blamed for their plight. Society was culpable, not the women. A spirit identified as "a woman who suffered" instructed the Cercle Harmonique never to judge a "loose" woman. This particular spirit had turned to prostitution to provide for herself. Society's injustices "compelled" her to seek such a "dishonest" living. Though she came from a wealthy family and inherited, she married a greedy man who became the "master" of her fortune and then abandoned her. If she wanted food and shelter, she had no choice but to sell her body. Only death put a stop to her suffering. She told the circle to learn from Jesus's example when he "comforted and consoled" Mary Magdalene.[104]

According to the spirits, the natural occupation for a woman was motherhood. A message from Valmour compared these two contrary identities of women: prostitute and mother. There was the woman "adorned with attires and jewels, . . . the ardent and lascivious Woman, easy to be accosted and covered with precious stones . . . the Courtesan riding in a splendid team, displaying herself." In contrast there was "the one who is wise, reserved, modest, and virtuous . . . the Housewife addicted to her maternal duties and to her tender solicitude for her husband." These two options, mother or prostitute, left little in between. True mothers were selfless, and because abnegation was a frequently lauded trait, some spirits found women superior to men. One male spirit concluded that his transition to the spirit world was eased because his wife was "so just" and "so pure." A spirit identified as Paul Trevigne Sr., likely related to the *L'Union* and *Tribune* editor, stated that mothers were more "solemn" than fathers. Everyone should "always respect the poor mother and have pity on her." Many "poor" mothers—though rich in love— were in their economic state because men took advantage of them. In many cases it was a father who drank away the money his family desperately needed. Spirits guilty of this apologized from beyond the grave. A spirit identified as John Sweet regretted that he got "drunk" and would "beat" his wife; he now "stood with remorse and shame."[105]

Though gender equality and the treatment of women were not primary emphases of the Cercle Harmonique, the spirits' comments on these topics reiterated the group's dedication to the ideals of liberty and egalitarianism (Valmour's iteration of the "Madonna-whore complex"[106] notwithstanding). Men who defended women and tried to combat male gender prejudices were admirable. A joint message from Valmour and Saint Vincent de Paul instructed the male Spiritualists to "consider women your equal in everything." Righteous men fought for women and their rights, while immoral men drove women into prostitution and then reveled in their bodies. A romantic pair that featured a woman not afraid to challenge her husband on intellectual or spiritual matters was made stronger and more stable by it.[107] If the wife was willing and encouraged to speak her mind, the pair were on equal footing. Power dynamics should be equal in every regard, including gender and race relations.

The materialism of New Orleans prompted the spirits to teach about the dangers of prostitution, gambling, racial inequality, and economic disparity. Materialism sparked in men a carnal desire for women; it supported the wealthy and encouraged them to take advantage of the poor; it encouraged men to seek unjust political authority; it fueled racial violence and white supremacy. In short, materialism was the root cause of all power disparities and injustices in New Orleans. The Cercle Harmonique's spiritual guides hoped the Afro-Creoles could and would clean up their city, and this included cleaning up religious institutions, namely the Catholic Church. One of the spirits' main issues with the Catholic Church was its materialism: the greed of the hierarchy, the lies of priests, and the opulent buildings, even though poverty beleaguered so many parishioners.

CHAPTER THREE

Spiritualism and Catholicism

They [Catholic priests] believed that they themselves were the designed apostles of this great faith; and they taught their followers to consider them as the instruments to perpetuate apostolic power, prophetic wisdom, and heavenly teaching. Hence they claimed the power to cure diseased persons, and to be authorized to make believers, if not by preaching, yet by the sword, the stake, the rack, or in a more honorable way, their sacred inquisitions!
—Andrew Jackson Davis, *The Principles of Nature, Her Divine Revelations, and A Voice to Mankind*

The path you have followed, all of you, at this table, who have been raised up as Roman Catholics, show to you the succession of years required to bring yourselves to a good result.
—Spirit of Edmond Capdeville to the Cercle Harmonique, 18 December 1872

Think maturely and discard your mistakes that Catholicism provided you.
—Spirit of Léonine to the Cercle Harmonique, 26 December 1865

While Rey's writings indicate that his wife, Adèle, also believed in Spiritualism and that at least his daughter Lucia was no stranger to the séance table, an October 1872 message from Lamennais suggests that Adèle wanted their children to be raised as Catholics. Lamennais reassured Rey, reminding him that he had heard Rey's son "laugh and force his mother to laugh at the absurdities" that Adèle wanted "to stuff in his head" in order to "make him a Roman Catholic." Not to worry, Lamennais told Rey; reason would shine through and the child would recognize the "absurdities of a Roman catechism before him."[1] Despite Adèle's wishes, Rey tried his best to keep Catholicism out of his home. In January 1873, Rey turned away a Jesuit priest who knocked on his door, and the spirits praised him for it: "Oh! be satisfied, brother Rey, of having today, met face to face one of them who presented to you the little prayer written on a piece of paper—a disguised way to beg." He continued, "Be happy of your moral courage for having avowed frankly to him your belief and that you are opposed to such oppressions on the masses." The spirit, Ambroise (a former Capuchin priest himself),[2] also noted the haste with which the priest left "as soon as he understood that there was nothing to reap from you." It was better that the priest left, for contact with a Jesuit was "unhealthy."[3] Ambroise would not be the only spirit to criticize the Jesuit order in particular, and priests in general, as exploitative manipulators who took advantage of the vulnerable. Though the wealthy seemed to be the priests' primary targets, they would prey upon anyone in order to satiate their greed for material riches. However, this disapproval is not to say that the Afro-Creoles of the Cercle Harmonique left their Catholic pasts.

Rey and fellow members looked outside the church's sacraments and living clergy for support, but communicating with deceased priests and saints kept the Spiritualists connected to their larger community's Catholic past. Though Catholic priests were targets of criticism among the spirits, spirits of former Catholics also communicated with the circle and led the Cercle Harmonique along their spiritual progression. Afro-Creole Spiritualism was grounded in the religious history of New Orleans. Thus, resonances of Afro-Creole Catholicism and anti-Catholic sentiments manifested in the Cercle Harmonique. The Cercle Harmonique's relationship with Catholicism helped shape their view on the role of religious institutions in society, a view depicted in the spirits' criticisms of the Catholic Church and its priests.

The resonances of Catholicism in the Afro-Creole Spiritualist circle are not surprising, given the members' own religious upbringings within the larger context of the New Orleans religious milieu. Unlike many of the nineteenth-century Spiritualists other historians have investigated, the Cercle Harmonique did not come from white, liberal, Protestant communities in the Northeast. Though the historian Bret Carroll has identified similarities between the Catholic priestly authority and a "Catholic cosmos" of spirits, the Catholic influence upon American Spiritualists largely remains unstudied.[4] The practice of the Cercle Harmonique reflects a multivalent relationship with Catholicism. Spiritualism was superior to Catholicism in all ways, but some of the circle's closest advisors had been Catholics, even clerics, during their earthly lives. The Afro-Creoles at the séance table pulled from their Catholic pasts even as they defined themselves sharply against the Catholic institution. The strong Afro-Creole Catholic culture of New Orleans was not left behind when Rey and others sat at the séance table.

Identifying resonances of Catholicism, either in the form of Catholic ideas or Catholic spirits, illuminates how the Cercle Harmonique's engagement with Spiritualism fit with the members' own religious pasts and contemporary

New Orleans context. A key way the Afro-Creole Spiritualists carved out their religious identity was by pushing off from others, mainly Catholics. Calling attention to the differences between Catholicism and Spiritualism illuminated the boundary between the two and the preeminence of Spiritualism. According to the séance records of the Cercle Harmonique, Spiritualist enlightenment was a much superior form of religious intelligence in comparison with Catholic dogma. The revealed knowledge of Spiritualism was a more legitimate realm of authority than Catholicism and its imposed domination. The Cercle Harmonique argued that a cleric claimed authority based on the power invested in him from a human hierarchy and corrupt institution on earth. Spiritualists gained insight from spirits, and it was this spiritual wisdom that endowed them with power. Numerous spirit messages described Catholic priests as exploitative authoritarians who took advantage of the unfortunate. Priests—at least according to how the spirits described them—were no better than slave owners or white Redeemer Democrats: All fed on undeserved power and all represented the kind of politics the circle denounced. Even as the Cercle Harmonique pushed off Catholicism to shape their own religious and social identity, they used Catholicism to do so. Catholic language, ideas, and, most notably, Catholic spirits remained with them even after leaving parish pews. The Catholics who loved them in life continued to love them in death.

A Catholic Spiritual Network

Spirits who were Catholic during their earthly lives appear frequently in the Cercle Harmonique's séance records. With its French colonial origins, New Orleans was a Catholic stronghold in early American history.[5] Colonial Louisiana's *Code Noir* required slave owners to see to the baptism and religious education of their slaves in the Catholic Church. In addition to the *Code Noir*'s requirement to baptize all slaves, the law allowed only Catholicism to be the religion practiced in the Louisiana colony. Those who practiced any other religion would be punished as disobedient rebels.[6] Jesuit and Capuchin priests and Ursuline nuns supported the colony's Catholic population by preaching and sharing a universal message of Catholic salvation. This Catholic universalism offered salvation to all regardless of gender, class, or race, and due to its spiritual egalitarianism, it was a welcoming and inviting message for slaves and free blacks in Louisiana. Rather than dividing people based on their skin color, the Catholic Church categorized Louisianans as saints or sinners before black or white. However, this equality before God's eyes did not easily translate into everyday life.

While the spirit and rhetoric of universalism in the Catholic tradition made Catholicism an attractive religious orientation for slaves and free blacks, this universalism did not underpin all social interactions. The nuns and other religious orders, such as the Jesuits, owned slaves and, thus, were complicit in the stratification of the city's racial and social hierarchy.[7] In fact, upon Spanish ownership of Louisiana, the Catholic Church was the colony's single largest slaveholder.[8] While Catholic colonists and priests preached a theology of universalism to their slaves, the reality of the power dynamic between them should not be overlooked. The *Code Noir* provided the base for the city's racial stratification and religious flavor. Slaves could be punished severely for various infractions, and these punishments violently displayed the racial hierarchy. But they also were to be cared for both materially and spiritually. A result of this fraught relationship between Catholicism and slavery was a strong Afro-Creole Catholic culture in New Orleans.[9]

Catholicism provided a strong foundation for the religious cultures of both Afro-Creoles and white Creoles. The historian Caryn Cossé Bell has identified the influence of the Capuchin order as part of the Catholic influence on New Orleans's Afro-Creole population.[10] The Capuchins are a branch of the Franciscan order known for simplicity in their sermons and lifestyle. After Louisiana was ceded to Spain in 1763, the French Capuchins left and were replaced by Spanish Capuchins in 1772, and seventeen of those twenty-one Capuchins left Louisiana following the 1803 American purchase. One of the remaining Spanish Capuchins, Antonio de Sedella, affectionately called Père Antoine by much of the laity, was one of the Cercle Harmonique's occasional spiritual advisors. Though many of the Spanish Capuchins left Louisiana, Sedella chose to stay and ministered in New Orleans from the late eighteenth century until his death in 1829. One reason for Sedella's popularity among the Afro-Creole population was his disregard for civic and religious prohibitions that hampered Afro-Creole spiritual growth. Sedella administered the sacraments to the illegitimate children of interracial relationships and their parents, despite the contrary regulations laid out in the *Code Noir*.[11]

Though Sedella was to be relocated to Spain following the Louisiana Purchase and initially agreed to the move, he changed his mind, remained in New Orleans, and continued as pastor at St. Louis Cathedral until his death.[12] Sedella's support of the city's black population, his involvement in local court cases testifying for the city's free blacks and slaves, and his frequent godparenting of nonwhite children endeared him to black New Orleanians.[13] It was the tenure of Sedella especially, and his successor, Father Aloysius Leopold Moni, that constituted what historians identify as the golden era of Catholic universalism in New Orleans.[14] While the spirit of Catholic universalism should and can be interpreted only in the context of a very prevalent slave system, it does point to some of Catholicism's and Sedella's and Moni's appeal to black New Orleanians. Mixed-race congregations, godparents across the racial divide, and celebrating a Catholic Church who loved all her parishioners equally—at least in principle—appealed to free and enslaved black Creoles. But, according to the spirit guides of the Cercle Harmonique, it was Spiritualism that delivered the universalism that Catholicism promised.

Sedella's spirit messages were signed either Père Antoine or simply Antoine. In Rey's early years as a Spiritualist, Père Antoine was one of the most frequent spirits to visit. A number of his messages contained encouragement for the circle or explanations of truth. For example, Sedella promised that those who sought the truth would find it and that "we [the spirits] are with those who are with us." Pére Antoine described a benevolent Creator of "magnificent works" whose "infinite wisdom" created the world and its laws. In contrast, the God of non-Spiritualists was the result of human materialism projected onto a deity and, thus, an "unjust and cruel" God. Only Spiritualists had a proper and correct understanding of a wise, loving, and republican God.[15]

Many of the spirits communicated messages that criticized materialism, and Sedella was no different. Warning against falling victim to greed, he encouraged them to keep their souls "pure of defilement." Additionally, members of the Cercle Harmonique proved themselves to be "charitable" through their "good deeds." In another message, he told the medium that no one should complain about his or her "unfortunate" status, nor should anyone desire wealth. Greed would beget only more greed, as "the king is on his throne, surrounded by the prestige and glory of human vanities, wants more than the beggar." Indeed, like most spirits, Sedella admonished those who were too attached to the material world. "Material wealth," he explained, was only a mirage. He taught the Cercle Harmonique that their "moral enfranchisement" came from "the energy of your soul" and their rejection of materialism. In this particular message, he also chastised Napoleon Bonaparte, who for all his ambition and power could carry only "the remembrances of his crimes" into the spirit world.[16] Ambition and materialism would bring a person only to greed and corruption. It was better to focus on the soul and spiritual progression.

With his death Sedella had recognized where truth resided—Spiritualism rather than Catholicism—and he came to the Cercle Harmonique to share this knowledge and guide them to truth. As a former priest, Pére Antoine's spirit recognized that his messages that spoke negatively of Catholicism might puzzle listeners. He told the Cercle Harmonique to "not be surprised" by the spirits' "repeated blows against the colossal power that obstructs the progress of humanity." With its "erroneous dogmas," the institutional Catholic power of Rome "falsifies the truth, and in the name of divine justice, exterminates men and bloodies their clothes." Sedella admitted his own "crimes" and how he had "worked to consolidate this power." During his time on earth, he "ignored my mission" and "helped establish greater ignorance to ensure [Catholicism's] domination." But, in the spirit world, he confessed his sins and dedicated himself to a new mission: to reveal the truth and support Spiritualists everywhere. With his help, and the help of other spirits too, "Satan will be recognized under the hypocritical mask" and "Rome will be regenerated." On another occasion he reminded the Cercle Harmonique that he often came to the "circle of Louise" to "undermine prejudice and tradition" and show the ugliness of "Religious Domination"—a mission he continued for the Cercle Harmonique.[17]

Father Aloysius Leopold Moni was Sedella's successor and pastor of St. Louis Cathedral from Sedella's death until his own in August 1842. He was also beloved by the local laity, in part because he continued Sedella's fight to maintain the power of the lay *marguilliers* (trustees). Like Sedella's, Moni's spirit visited the Cercle Harmonique and did so frequently. He spoke of the eternal struggle between good and evil and how people were responsible for their actions in this world and the next because of free will. Though Moni encouraged the Spiritualists to make their own decisions, he also instructed them to "drive from your soul anything that might corrupt and stain." Instead, he told the group, "charity must be your guide." Moni and Sedella also delivered messages with political edges. Sedella encouraged them to try to understand the political perspective of others. Moni was pleased to see the passage of the Fifteenth Amendment but was even happier to reside in an environment where such man-made laws were not necessary to ensure justice and fair governance.[18]

Despite being a former priest, Moni endorsed Spiritualism as the best religion, stating "Spiritualism produces beautiful and noble sentiments; it inspires justice and charity for all." Like Sedella, in the time since his death Moni discovered that religious truth was found outside the walls of his former institution. In another message Moni likened the power of priests to "the despotic pressure of cockroaches" keeping "three-quarters of humanity groaning under a monstrous clerical yoke." But hope existed for those still on earth since "the truth must shine in all its splendor" and truth would fight "the clerical yoke." Instead of praising clerics, Moni extolled the virtues and abilities of the circle's former medium Valmour. "Afraid of nothing," Valmour was "triumphant" in the spirit world. Moni instructed the circle to "continue to fight injustice, error, and superstition, and you'll have the satisfaction of the heart; and as Valmour, you will leave without fear and without reproach" and reach the invisible world.[19] Moni was not the only spirit who celebrated Valmour, but his identity as a former priest made his positive appraisal of Valmour particularly noteworthy. Rather than admire and praise Catholics, this priest complimented a local black Creole medium.

Moni also told the circle to "not be astonished at the Spirit speaking incessantly and relentlessly of your soul" because the soul's purification and sanctification would lead to its "elevation and glory." The Catholic sacraments did not cleanse a spirit of defilement. Rather, a soul was prepared for "elevation" through Spiritualist progression, by work done at the séance table, and from supporting the Idea. Moni assured them that the spirits and the Creator desired to see all of them "cleansed from defilement, enlightened and with the soul of the true believer."[20] And a believer in truth would be a Spiritualist, not a Catholic. The spirits of the two beloved former priests, Moni and Sedella—priests supportive of the black and white Creole Catholic laity—recognized this and shared their wisdom with the Spiritualist circles. Indeed, who better to endorse Spiritualism over Catholicism than former clerics? Even with this criticism of the church, the visits by the formerly Catholic spirits and their guidance connected the Cercle Harmonique to their Catholic heritage and past. The pastors' support of the masons and *marguilliers* would have resonated with the liberal affiliations of the circle members. Communicating with Sedella and Moni allowed the Cercle Harmonique to express their approval for those priests' pro-laity and pro-Creole actions without contradicting the spirits' anticlerical messages. Beloved pastors remained so even after their death.

In addition to spirits of former local pastors, spirits of deceased family members also spoke about Catholicism. In a communication from early in Rey's involvement with Spiritualism, his father, Barthélemy, lamented how the Rey family had believed "the absurdities of the Roman Church." Petit's mother, Claire Pollard, also regretted how her adherence to Catholicism blinded her. When she arrived to the spirit world, she realized that she was in "a different paradise," not the one taught by Catholicism. She appreciated how the spirit world was the best conceivable place once she stopped "believing in the fairy tales that had adorned my imagination." Petit's younger sister Claire was sent to France for her education as a child and possibly joined, at least for a time, a convent. In one of her messages she cried for "the poor child who isolates him/herself within the walls of a cloister." Reminiscent of *The Abominations of Maria Monk* and other nineteenth-century nun captivity narratives, she wept for her own past and the "orgies that had soiled me, the mire that had reached my virginal dress . . . I believed a Devil, what Error!" Near the end of the message she chastised those "Religious" who thought only of their own souls and forgot their family and "the most sacred duties."[21] In regretting the Catholicism of their past, trusted family members and former local priests supported the Cercle Harmonique's choice to practice Spiritualism. By communicating with the spirits of former Catholics, members of the Cercle Harmonique did not abandon their local and familial religious heritage.

Both Bernard and Marie Couvent came to the Afro-Creoles' table. The Couvents were beloved in the Afro-Creole community, and the money left behind by the widow Marie supported the work of the Société Catholique pour l'Instruction des Orphelins dans l'Indigence and its school, which offered affordable or free education for local black children. As a spirit, Bernard taught that if a person "nobly fulfilled his mission," he was welcomed into the spiritual world. He also endorsed the work done at the séance table, in part for the pleasure it brought his spirit. Bernard, like many others who were Catholic in life, regretted his previous religious orientation in death. Calling Catholicism "such nonsense," "foolish belief," and "errors which I accepted as infallible dogmas," he was happy to be enlightened. Marie congratulated the Cercle Harmonique for their persistence because the work they did was for both "your soul" and "the good of all." Though a devoted Catholic during her earthly life, Marie's spirit attested that Spiritualism provided the best route for "Good and Progress."[22] Communicating with Bernard and Marie Couvent kept the Cercle Harmonique connected to the charitable work of the Société Catholique pour l'Instruction des Orphelins dans l'Indigence without having to remain attached to Catholic theology or the hierarchy.

The spirits in the Cercle Harmonique's network continued the Afro-Creoles' relationship to the Catholic Church, and the spirit of Saint Vincent de Paul, one of the circle's most loquacious spiritual advisors, represented the circle's link to Catholicism on a more global scale. Lamennais even referred to de Paul as "the top Apostle" in one of his messages. The inclusion of this saint along with Sedella and Moni strengthened the Cercle Harmonique's spiritual bond with their Catholic pasts. Like many other Spiritualists around the country, they communicated with Mesmer and Swedenborg too, but their frequent interactions with Catholic-turned-Spiritualist spirits set them apart from other séance groups. Though a Catholic saint, de Paul did not extol the virtues of other Catholics. In fact, much like Moni, he often complimented former Cercle Harmonique member, leader, and medium Valmour. "Valmour has been elevated magnificently," he assured the circle. The "love and charity" of his "splendid" soul ensured him a happy existence in the spirit world. The saint was not short on praise for the medium. Valmour was also "noble and sublime"; his soul possessed a "brilliant light"; and he was a revealer of "eternal illuminations." Others should emulate Valmour, particularly those who felt called to be mediums.[23]

The saint's dedication to service and the poor identified him as an ally to humanity's harmonious progress—the cause of the Cercle Harmonique. Saint Vincent de Paul's popularity rose after his canonization in the early eighteenth century and again in the 1830s with the founding of the Society of Saint Vincent de Paul in Paris. The Saint Vincent de Paul Society, as it was called in the United States, was organized in New Orleans in the early 1850s. In the late 1850s and early 1860s, announcements for local masses in honor of the saint's feast day were printed in the local newspapers.[24] More significantly, interest in Saint Vincent de Paul increased among the city's black and mixed-race population when *L'Union* published a biographical series on the saint called "*Le Pasteur de Peuple*" ("The Pastor of the People") over the course of 1862 and 1863.[25] This biography came from popular French author Clémence Robert, and it emphasized de Paul's dedication to Catholic reform, an "intense mystical piety," "Catholic charity and Christian universalism."[26] Robert's work and the series in *L'Union* championed the saint and focused on his tireless work for poor and vulnerable populations. "*Le Pasteur de Peuple*" lauded de Paul for his "fierce piety" and called him "the eldest son of charity."[27] Indeed, in mid-nineteenth-century New Orleans "the Vincentian ideal of a new-model Catholic leader animated by selfless service in humanitarian works carried particular force." "And for some," according to historian Caryn Cossé Bell, the saint's "mystical piety, fraternal charity, and egalitarian spirituality proved an irresistible model."[28] The saint's general association with charity and compassion, combined with his life experience with slavery and his desire to evangelize, made him an attractive patron saint for the Cercle Harmonique.

Many of de Paul's messages to the Cercle Harmonique focused on the virtues of charity, courage, and equality. All three were connected by a love for humanity. Like the spirit of Père Antoine, de Paul also instructed the circle against the dangers of materialism, because greed greatly damaged one's soul. "You are a spirit in a material body," but in the spirit world, you will "be relative to the state of your soul." In other words, one's economic, racial, or class status in the material world did nothing to guarantee a spirit's state in the spiritual spheres. Materialism was only one type of greed de Paul referenced. He also denounced society's desire for domination and instead endorsed equality. He must have realized that all the struggles for egalitarianism and equality he encouraged were not easy, for he also spoke frequently of courage. Courage would be necessary for progress. The Spiritualists would need to "fight with courage against evil and prevent its spread, for it is the scourge which has slowed the Progression."[29]

Indeed, the success of the Cercle Harmonique depended on their perseverance in the face of adversity. Courage against greed and materialism supported the cause of justice and brotherhood. Shortly after the Civil War, he reassured them: "Courage, therefore, my children, with the support that we are always eager to give you, no doubt you will succeed." The following week, de Paul told the Cercle Harmonique "courage, my dear children, you have gained your freedom with blood." It is unclear whether this was with the blood of black soldiers, the blood of slaves, or the blood of Union supporters in general, but the freedom that is alluded to is clear. This message came on the heels of a communication from "your brother and friend, Abraham Lincoln." Although the members of the Cercle Harmonique had been freed long before the war, the freedom of the message likely meant either freedom from slavery or from the Confederacy. The Afro-Creole Spiritualists would need courage during the long road of postwar Reconstruction, and the spirits' support helped impart the necessary courage. "We take care of all your ups and downs," de Paul told them. "We will defend you . . . as we are for just cause—Liberty." De Paul also advised against revenge and rather instructed them not to let "any hatred accumulate against you through your own fault; do not sow in the soul of your brothers and sisters a sad thought." In the world to come, their enemies would be forced to deal with their mistakes. Instead, "with courage," the Afro-Creoles should "labor . . . for good."[30]

De Paul encouraged the circle to persevere despite how disappointing and difficult postwar New Orleans could be. He assured them that they would later "discover that you have gained [much] through our help and you will be happy, Courage and Patience, my brothers."[31] The Spiritualist group led by French émigré Joseph Barthet in the mid-1850s received some spirit messages that referred to courage as well, specifically the courage to recognize one's mistakes or the courage to make decisions in an honest and thorough manner. Another spirit reported to Barthet's group that the happiest person was one with "courage in adversity."[32] In the messages from Barthet's mixed but primarily white Creole circle, courage was an admirable trait. This was true for Rey's Cercle Harmonique as well, but the spirits who visited his table also spoke of courage as a necessity. In particular, de Paul encouraged them to maintain their courage and use it to face prejudice. Courage was not simply a respectable quality for Afro-Creole Spiritualists in the tumultuous and volatile years of the 1860s and 1870s; it was essential.

Courage was not the only virtue de Paul encouraged among the circle. He spoke much about charity too. Providence watched over everyone with love, he told them, and so it was good to possess "charitable hearts." Just "as Jesus said 'Forgive them, father, for they know not what they do,'" humanity too should be forgiving—a trait best cultivated by charity. The saint explained, "charity must reside in your heart, because it is that which saves [a human] Being." He concluded another message by instructing the table to be "full of charity and devotion to the work that will accomplish the redemption of many souls." "Abnegation, love and charity" were three necessary traits for the "spiritualist heart" because one should be "more than a mere believer." Charity was no abstract idea; right action, too, was necessary. The Cercle Harmonique members should not just learn the lessons of Spiritualism but also "endeavor to practice them." Benevolent deeds cultivated within a soul "love and charity" and helped elevate it. If a soul were instead "under the unfortunate pressure of Evil," it would "sink in an abyss of darkness" and become "more and more gloomy." However, if one elevated his soul "by right-doing," the soul "would ascend in light." In three consecutive messages received in June 1871, de Paul continued to encourage all these good traits and good works. "The peace of a man's heart" came from knowing that he did his duty while on earth and left with a clear conscience. Therefore, "keep your soul healthy from defilement."[33] Charity was materialism's foe.

The Catholic saint-turned-Spiritualist also spoke of the forward spiritual progress of humanity and the triumph of the Idea, both of which required charity, courage, and equality. Progress meant the success of egalitarianism. "Enlightened philosophies" would extinguish "social prejudices." Now residing in the spirit realm, he was hard at this work "to purge the numerous errors that impede its [humanity's] progress towards the Good." It seems a saint's work was never done. Spiritualist brothers on earth, the "sentinels of civilization," needed to do their part too. With Spiritualists working on earth and spirits like de Paul in the spiritual spheres, "generous ideas and truth can only triumph in the struggle." Therefore, there should be "no doubt" in "the triumphant march of good over evil." Though he was certain of eventual triumph in some messages, he still needed both those on earth and the spirits above to do their part.[34]

De Paul and all the spirits taught that the egalitarian triumph of humanity would need republican ideals. He knew that the oligarchy of old white southern power would eventually complete its fall from social power. A communication the Cercle Harmonique received from him in April 1869 began, "The noisy clamors caused by the expiring oligarchy under the terrible blows given by the invincible chief (Grant) with his sword, must, little by little, cease." Everywhere, the saint praised, "the chains of slavery are falling under the voice of Reason and Logic." He chastised Spain and Portugal which still "bore the burning stigma of the Slave Trade," and described these two countries in particular as "branded with the seal of infamy for having the last, preserved human slavery." Later in the same message he told the circle "to extinguish moral Slavery, under any form it presents itself, in order to liberate Humanity of all chains." If Spiritualists could end moral slavery, then they would "spread the greatest quantity of happiness possible among Earth's children, in destroying all power tending to control thought, action, and conscience." Both the slave trade and moral enslavement came from the same inspiration: materialism and selfish desire. But the "diverse social revolutions which take place among you and your neighbors" were symbolic of the "march of Progress." The United States had a significant role in this progress, for here "you owe refuge to the oppressed of the Earth, without distinction of races, religions, nationalities." He instructed them to "invite everyone to come and partake with you of the benefits of the rights of the press, of thought, and religious liberty."[35] De Paul's instructions to "extinguish moral slavery," his chastisements of white domination, and his support for humanity's triumph are significant parts of the circle's understanding of politics and society, and receiving these messages from a saint rendered a degree of authority to the Cercle Harmonique. While the Afro-Creole Spiritualists and their guides criticized Catholicism and the hierarchy, they had Saint Vincent de Paul on their side. He was still their saint.

Catholic Terminology and Ideas

Though former priests and others criticized certain elements of Catholic dogma, they also used terminology from Catholicism and seemingly Catholic ideas in their messages. However, this occasional use of Catholic-sounding terminology did not mean an acceptance of Catholic ideas. According to Edmond Capdeville,[36] the "most stubborn" spirits to accept the truth of Spiritualism were former Roman Catholics. After a lifetime in the church, their free will had been so "subjected to the ecclesiastical iron hand" that they had lost their ability "to reason," and, he continued, "we do not want the blind acceptance of anything." Rather than an expression of assent, spirits typically used Catholic terminology to better explain themselves to those still stuck in the material world. Spirits who told the circle that they were in hell did so in order "to make you know their position" because they knew that the use of hell "would carry the best explanation to your understanding." Likewise, "there have been spirits who have employed the word 'Paradise' to make you comprehend how happy they were!" According to Saint Vincent de Paul, those often called "angels" were really spirit guides. Capdeville echoed this idea and equated the notion of a "guardian angel" to the guiding spirits. "Some of our brothers here have felt obligated to use the word," he explained, in order to use a term recognizable to those still on earth. Catholic terminology was used only to render their messages more intelligible.[37]

The language of the sacrament of the Eucharist also was adopted by some of the spirits. Jesus's spirit referred to Cercle Harmonique meetings as the "bread of the soul" or "Communion." The act of communicating with the spirits was "a holy duty" that contributed to the "gospel of peace, love, and charity." The spirit of Volney referred to the "Word of the spirit" as "the daily bread of the soul." Saint Vincent de Paul instructed them to "work to earn the daily bread that must relieve your body," and while he did not define what that daily bread was, it came from charitable work rather than the Catholic Mass. The Afro-Creole Spiritualists needed "spiritual food," gained from working for charity and justice. One obtained "his daily spiritual bread" from work at the séance table. The frequent spirit guide Lunel, a non-Catholic allowed to live in French colonial Louisiana,[38] compared the "metamorphosis" of a soul under spiritual guidance to "Holy Communion," for both were thought to purify and sanctify.[39]

Rather than absolving sin and becoming reconciled with God through Catholic sacraments, those with "pure hearts," as Moni informed the circle, would be afforded the rewards of the invisible world. For some, though, "penance" of a sort would be necessary. "Terrible punishment" awaited "for the vain glorious one who believed himself privileged, and did not understand that his clothing of flesh [the material and raced body] was merely a gross and perishable envelope, a food, or a prey for myriads of insects more disgusting the ones than the others." Though "terrible punishment" might make it seem as though Moni was referring to a kind of hell, most American Spiritualists did not believe in hell.[40] Moni described a state of "darkness" awaiting those who unjustly oppressed others. Their spirits roamed "about like shadows" as a result of their cruel actions on earth. The spirits spoke of a period after death in the physical world called "retribution" that seemed similar to purgatory. According to Moni, it would be after "penance is accomplished" that each spirit enjoyed "happiness." The period of retribution was necessary for spirits because "each fault bears its own penalty."[41]

The use of the term "penance" in conjunction with the waiting period of retribution parallels the temporary punishment in and purification from Catholic purgatory. Retribution kept one's spirit accountable for his or her actions in the material world, much like how purgatory allowed Catholics to purify themselves of their sins instead of directly going to hell. Upon entering the spirit world, spirits underwent retribution, during which they would be spiritually cleansed of their past injustices, biases, and superstitions. Recognizing their spiritual neglect during their earthly lives, realizing their own prejudices, and seeing their sinful ways, spirits policed their own atoning period. Observing themselves in the "mirror of Truth," the spirits of the dead recognized their offenses, found themselves "hideous," and were "horrified" of their "ideas," their "past," and their "false appreciations." Unlike someone in any kind of Christian hell, the individual spirit, not anyone else, regulated his or her own retribution period. "Everyone here," the spirit of former New Orleans mayor Paul Bertus explained, "will be his own judge." Retribution allowed spirits to learn the lessons they missed in life and punish themselves accordingly. A spirit identified as André warned the table that retribution would show them, "by its mirror of Truth, what you are! Oh! then, you will behold yourselves hideous, and you will be horrified of what you are by your ideas, your past, your false appreciations." A person was better prepared for retribution by keeping the soul "pure of defilement" on Earth and committing "good deeds." Additionally, retribution readied a soul for entrance to the high spiritual spheres. The truly "penitent" was burdened with "paying his debt." While a spirit might weep for the past during retribution, afterward he would rise "educated and blessed" and then travel to "splendid regions" with a "sublime soul." During this time, the spirit viewed himself "reflected by the mirror of Truth with his weaknesses, his cowardice. The flesh is no more there to obstruct his reason." Some spirits would be "unhappy and stubborn for a long time" in the spiritual world "owing to the action of Evil having its force upon them."[42] Ill prepared for the spiritual spheres, these spirits would experience quite a jolt.

Not all would make the transition to the spirit world smoothly. While it seems most spirits willingly underwent retribution, a few were "antagonistic" toward it. These spirits, not understanding the truth and often thinking themselves "condemned for eternity," unfortunately still were "inclined to vengeance." This was a main reason circle members needed to be cautious and avoid communication with those spirits. A spirit named Robert warned them that certain spirits, those "unhappy," "stubborn," and "gloomy" brothers, were "opposed to Humanity's progress." These spirits were "lurking" and "anxious to break the luminous circle." However, these bitter and malcontent spirits must have been rare, for in the spiritual spheres no one was really "safe from the punishment of his wrongs" because all experienced "the shame of seeing that everyone can read" in one's thoughts any "committed wrongs." The spirit of Emile Bertrand taught them that nothing could save someone from "the judgment you will pass yourself on all your actions."[43]

Spiritualism's understanding of the world beyond this one pushed against the theology of Catholicism in other ways too. While retribution seemed akin to purgatory, the Cercle Harmonique abandoned the concept of hell. Though terror of hellfire had been a common theological and rhetorical spur for Catholic evangelizers of Native Americans, such as the Jesuits during the earlier colonial era, such imagery was on the wane in the nineteenth century.[44] This does not mean that theological discussions of the horrors of hell dropped from Catholic communities, but they did lessen during the nineteenth century among both American and French Catholics.[45] As the spirits came to the Cercle Harmonique to discuss the happiness of good spirits in the invisible world, the church's sermons on the joys of heaven and the love of God replaced the earlier fearsome homilies in the United States and France. The spirits' positive messages of encouragement, progress, and the constructive self-cleansing of retribution were at odds with earlier Catholicism's exploitative fear of hell.[46] Moni condemned the Catholic Church for its teachings on the afterlife, including hell. Catholic priests tried "to scare" the laity with the threatening image of an "eternal fire!" In contrast, Spiritualism taught "eternal happiness!" Moni used this difference of afterlife theology to compare Catholicism with Spiritualism: "One seeks to frighten mankind in order to dominate, the other to comfort him by showing the Truth to be everyone's judge."[47]

The spirit of Lamennais agreed with criticisms of hell and affirmed that eternal punishment was neither rational nor just. Thus, a noble God could not condone it. Voltaire too pitied those "poor beings who spend their lives in this terrible hell of the fear of an imaginary hell." Another spirit described hell as a "horrible invention" of the "black robes in order to dominate." Moni described many former priests—whom he called "Minister[s] of Lucifer"— aimlessly wandering in the spirit world, seeking answers in their former churches "where they used to harass the . . . conscience with false precepts" like hell. A "devoted brother" chimed in: "the idea of a hell preached in the material world has caused nearly all those unfortunates to believe in the eternity of their punishments." In contrast to "the eternity of suffering preached by some bigots," Spiritualism taught that the immortal spirit moved toward "perfectibility in its eternal progress."[48] This could be a criticism of Catholicism or more orthodox Christianity in general, but considering how priests were typically identified as those who intimidated with threats of hell, the spirit likely was referencing Catholicism.

Ambroise was disappointed in how the "religious oligarchy" manipulated people and squelched free thought. Those in monasteries, safely guarded from "prying eyes" with their "high walls," offered indulgences for those who hoped to escape "imaginary hell." Though he and other spirits taught that hell as the church described it did not exist, Ambroise also seemed to use the ideas of Catholicism even in his rebuke of Catholicism. He stated that "the Lord will have mercy" on the innocent, but "ravening wolves" would "be punished like me. May you see your error!" Though he did not identify his punisher, Ambroise used passive voice, indicating that his punishment came from someone other than himself. This is another example of how the ideas of Catholicism, in this case the judgment by God, echoed in the messages of the Cercle Harmonique, even though in the process this message reproached and warned priests like himself. This appropriation of some Catholic theology and respect for those who transcended the Catholic institution demonstrate a continued relationship between the Cercle Harmonique and Catholicism. The Afro-Creole Spiritualists maintained various connections to their Catholic pasts, but the Catholic Church clearly did not teach the right understanding of the world beyond the material or even a full understanding of sin. Reconciliation and confession did not save one's spirit after passing from the material world, and according to former clergy, the deadly sins preached by the Catholic Church were not the most egregious. Rather, it was cruelty toward others and prejudice that impeded spiritual progress and harmed one's spirit. Salvation came from proper knowledge and understanding of the spiritual world and spiritual progress. And so, the institution of the church was not to be trusted.

"They blessed the Confederate flags"[49]: Anti-Catholicism in the Cercle Harmonique

Barthélemy Rey, Henri's father, was an active Catholic when alive, and like many members of the Cercle Harmonique, Rey was raised in a Catholic home. His parents, Barthélemy and Rose Rey, were first-generation, free, black émigrés from Saint-Domingue who left following the Haitian Revolution. The Rey family was an active and respected one in the city's Afro-Creole community.[50] Rey's father was part of the Société Catholique pour l'Instruction des Orphelins dans l'Indigence and served as director of the school for the year leading up to his death. When Barthélemy Rey died, his funeral at Annunciation Church was lavish, included board members and instructors of the school, and was quite expensive. Though a devoted Catholic in life, Barthélemy proved a harsh critic in death. His spirit shared with Rey that he was suspicious of Father Morisot, the family's priest at Annunciation Church, and that he watched in horror as the priest and the family were "haggling" over money for the funeral arrangements. The priest asked the family for "your whole fortune." Barthélemy lamented how "the next day [after the funeral], there wasn't a penny to feed the large family" because "you [Rose] gave him [Morisot] everything." Witnessing this display of "avarice" and greed, in combination with living now among the harmonious spirits of the invisible world, Barthélemy finally learned the spiritual truth. "I realized that their [priests'] dogmas did not exist," he told his son, for "a just God could not want unfortunate orphans to be robbed of everything."[51]

Though resonances of Catholic ideas like purgatory echoed in the circle's messages and former priests appeared in the séance record books, the spirits' messages also demonstrated anti-Catholic sentiments from a variety of spirits. In a message on the importance of religious freedom, Swedenborg explained that Catholicism was easy for the spirits to attack because it was "the religion with the least harmony."[52] The institution of Catholicism and its priestly representatives were frequent targets for spiritual critique. This was not a trait singular to New Orleanian Spiritualists. Many Spiritualists across the country disapproved of the Catholic priesthood and criticized the perceived undemocratic nature of the institutional church.[53] In the Cercle Harmonique's séance records some of the spirits' criticisms were based on New Orleans Creole Catholicism and the actions of the archdiocese, particularly its support of the Confederacy. According to the spirits at the Cercle Harmonique's table, the Catholic Church and its priests sought domination and power and were corrupted by greed and materialism. Catholics and dioceses across the South supported the Confederacy and the racial status quo, and the local archdiocese's backing of the Confederacy certainly did not help keep the city's Afro-Creoles in its pews.[54]

Early during the war, New Orleans archbishop Jean-Marie Odin[55] wrote in a pastoral letter that "our country . . . has become involved in a bloody war," though "justice is on our side." He continued, "let us fervently beseech the Lord that he may be pleased to shield them [Confederate soldiers] with his powerful arm, protect our rights, and to preserve our liberties untouched."[56] Even during the Union occupation of New Orleans, the archdiocese officially continued to support the Confederacy. Blessing ceremonies for Confederate flags, Confederate troops, and the Confederate cause persisted through the war and afterward.[57] The religion of the Lost Cause, as the historian Charles Reagan Wilson described it, was present in New Orleans, though in a more muted fashion than elsewhere in the South.[58] In the years following the Civil War and into Reconstruction, former Confederate soldiers who were Catholic remained bonded over the common experience of war and wore their Confederate uniforms proudly during funeral processions.[59] Archbishop Napoleon Perché ordered all parishes to celebrate the official end of Reconstruction by singing a *Te Deum* in "thanksgiving to God for the pacification of Louisiana which, reinstated in its legitimate rights and governed by a man of its own choice, will henceforth see all its children, without distinction, united in a spirit and one sentiment."[60]

The church's support for the Confederacy was so ubiquitous in New Orleans that a pro-Union, abolitionist priest was unique and scandalous for the archdiocese. French-born Father Paschal Maistre was not always a priest with the best reputation (he was twice accused of sexual impropriety), and he moved frequently around the Midwest during his initial years in the United States. When he was transferred to the New Orleans diocese, he came with a warning: His former bishop warned New Orleans archbishop Antoine Blanc that Maistre "behaved well" but suffered from "the mania to make money."[61] However, it was his open and unapologetic support for the Union and aboli-tion that marked him as a local renegade. This also made him a popular reli-gious leader for the city's black populations, as he was a priest who spoke for racial equality despite his institutional leaders' reproach.[62] Maistre's radical behavior included serving black Union troops near his parish at Camp Strong who were denied an official chaplain.[63] In April 1863 he offered a high mass in thanksgiving for the Emancipation Proclamation, and his sermon cele-brated freedom. He identified the Emancipation Proclamation as the hard first step in the triumph of righteousness.[64] Pro-Confederate New Orleani-ans began to threaten Maistre, including a fellow priest who alluded to lynching him by his stole, according to the *L'Union* staff (though they hoped they misheard).[65] For his support of the Union and abolition, the arch-bishop revoked Maistre's clerical faculties and in May 1863 shut down Mais-tre's parish under penalty of excommunication until further notice. Yet Maistre and a group of parishioners continued to celebrate at the parish while building a new, and completely schismatic, parish nearby.[66] Continuing to criticize the Confederacy and the region's complicity in slavery, the renegade priest officiated a funeral service at the rogue parish in honor of radical abo-litionist John Brown on the anniversary of Brown's death in December 1867.[67] Maistre's story stands in contrast to the pervasive acceptance and support of the Confederacy by the local Catholic Church and its hierarchy. While many black Catholics remained in their parishes' pews, it is not surprising that some left the church for the spiritual republicanism of Spiritualism.

The spirits saw the church's support for the Confederacy as part of the in-stitution's thirst for power and proclivity for material success. Indeed, spirits came to the table to criticize the church for its support of the Confederacy, and this included a former priest who had endorsed segregation. In 1871, the spirit of New Orleans priest Father Gabriel Chalon came to regret how the institutional church thought it needed "so much," including information. Echoing other priests, Chalon noted that he had sought the secrets of the laity and their money. "Confess!" he had shouted, "We're curious." Seeking not just information, the church wanted money too. Though "the Negro" was forced to the back of the church, his "greenbacks" (money) were seen as "white" and welcome. Chalon and other priests would "bless" any and all "greenbacks." Blessing not just money, he and others "blessed the Confederate flags."[68] During his time in New Orleans, Chalon oversaw mass at St. Mary's Church, and in 1863 he began segregating the pews in a city well-known for its integrated parishes. Antebellum visitors to New Orleans frequently commented on interracial Catholic worship.[69] Under Chalon's direction at St. Mary's, whites sat in the front of the parish, blacks in the rear, and the mixed-race occupied the middle pews.[70] Coming to the Cercle Harmonique indicated that in death Chalon recognized his errors, or that at least the medium felt he should. The spirit of Lamennais also reproached the church for its support of the Confederate cause:

> My children, we did see them, during the last war, preaching the sanctity of the horrible institution of slavery; we did see them, blessing banners of the battalions which were forging new and stronger chains for their brothers, black as well as white; we did see them, flattering the vanity of those who relegated to the last pews in their temples their poor brothers, their children; we did see them, girding the sword, marching to battles, praying God for the extermination of the children of Progression, and for the enslavement of poor forlorn creatures, who were feeding them and their children, by the sweat of their brow, with their manual labor; we did see them—these unworthy disciples of Jesus— lie with effrontery to his beautiful principles.[71]

In addition to criticizing the enslavement of Africans and African descendants, Lamennais seemed to criticize the general social power of upper class whites.

Many spirits who were Catholic clerics in life expressed harsh judgment upon Catholicism in their messages. Among the former priests who expressed shame for their past errors was none other than Father Morisot, the priest Barthélemy's spirit accused of swindling the Rey family out of their money. Morisot admitted that his "black robe . . . hid" his "weaknesses," but he felt "ashamed" now and "bowed my head before my infamy." His past experiences as a priest made him even more aware of "the dangers of the power of these mercenaries [priests], who, like me, are ravening the purity of those who are entrusted to them." The people would be better off without priests.

Ambroise likened revolutions that brought "Freedom of conscience" to ones that freed the people from "any clerical yoke." This spirit, Ambroise, frequented the table of the Cercle Harmonique and occasionally identified himself as an "ex-Capuchin," thus joining Moni, Morisot, and Sedella as former priests who came to the group. Accordingly, his disapproval of Catholicism could be trusted. He knew well "that cohort of demons, because I was one of their leaders." Equating freedom from Catholicism with escaping from hell, he admitted that he "paralyzed the progress of humanity." Additionally, like many others, he pointed out how all of Catholicism's material wealth, such as the church bells and organ, was at the expense of the laity. And this greed was regrettable since "the rings of the Bishops, [if] sold and distributed to the poor of the earth, could relieve much misery." Ambroise also delivered his criticism with attitude. "They," meaning Catholic powers, "build splendid residences and Theatres . . . pardon, churches, at your expense." The spirit of French Renaissance writer and monk François Rabelais also apologized for his former status as a Catholic cleric. Though he was an "abbot," he now "confesses to you [the Cercle Harmonique]." Wearing the vestments of a priest did not make one special since "the clothes do not make the man."[72] Rather, everyone was responsible for his or her actions regardless of status.

Spirits sometimes found comparisons between Spiritualism and Catholicism to be helpful. On one occasion, Rabelais provided a glossary of Catholic and Spiritualist ideas, and the message largely targeted the exploitative nature of Catholicism. He described baptism as the imposition of beliefs on someone "who does not think or understand anything yet"; confession was "a demon laughing at the naïveté" of others; a choir boy was a child "learning to be a hypocrite"; a church was "the religious theatre"; purgatory was a place that depended on "the rise or fall of indulgences"; and the devil was "the bogeyman for devotees." The priest received a particularly vitriolic depiction as "the enemy" and an "intruder who wants to be your master." While a shepherd shears his sheep "to the skin," a priest "shears his sheep to the bone." In another message Rabelais compared priests to "ravenous wolves," demanding money even from "beggars." While the "black Robes" still on earth would identify spirits like Rabelais as "demons," it was they who were the agents of "deception." He, in contrast, was happy to be free from Catholicism's "insolent dogmas" that "commanded obedience" and to be free from "intolerance."[73]

The spirits identified the various theological ideas taught by the Catholic Church as backward, misleading, and just plain wrong. The idea that "a kneeling posture" while "muttering prayers" could "obtain forgiveness" was pre-posterous to the spirits. To be deserving of the spirit world and its glory, one should actively "struggle against Evil" in order to "vanquish it" and should not rely on asking for forgiveness later. Simply praying could not right someone's past wrongdoings. Instead, one needed to possess "the moral courage" to do the right thing simply because it was right and not out of fear. Additionally, the "mysteries" preached by Catholic clerics were intellectual "barriers" for the poor believer. Voltaire called the act of hiding behind an ex-ploitative religion "pathetic, really!" But those who held power and demanded "religious subservience" were being "weakened" by the "march of humanity's enlightenment."[74]

The "pomp and apparatus" of the Catholic tradition also brought criticism. Shortly after a grand ceremony honoring Archbishop Napoleon Perché, a spirit came to the table to lament the ceremony. Perché had just returned from a seven-month stay in Rome, and his return was heralded by a great pro-cession through the city, followed by a service at the cathedral.[75] The whole ceremony was, according to the spirit of Pierre Méllo, a "great demonstra-tion for a man who represents error, lies, and hypocrisy." Méllo asked: "More than twenty thousand people attended to see what?" He then answered his own question: "to receive a blessing" from a man "who only thinks of wealth at the expense of the poor and orphans." Perché gained some local notoriety for being a harsh critic of Spiritualism and mesmerism, for denying the black *Sœurs de la Sainte-Famille* (Sisters of the Holy Family) the right to wear a habit, and for his general condemnation of liberal and revolutionary thought. Thus, it comes as no surprise that the spirits were critical of him. Méllo's criticism of Perché's celebration and its splendor was not the only such critique. The spirit of Armand Desdunes explained that the materiality and pageantry of the Catholic Mass distracted worshippers from what truth did reside in Cath-olic teachings. In contrast, the simpler practice of Spiritualism kept the fo-cus of practitioners on their practice. The practice of the Cercle Harmonique was good because of "the simplicity of your table." Their humble practice en-sured that their "work" had "harmony."[76]

According to Voltaire, a true Spiritualist was nothing like "those great pomps for a God" and the Cercle Harmonique should keep from the table those who claim to be Spiritualists but who have "lowered themselves to the level of those extinguishers of thought, who have organs, songs, and theatri-cal auxiliaries and apparel." Those men soon would "want to institute churchly ceremonies" and turn Spiritualism into a scripted affair that would overshadow Spiritualism's real point. The spirit of Robespierre understood the church to be opposed to republican egalitarianism. Whereas "Galileo saw himself thrown into prison," Robespierre's spirit contended that republics "produced great men, who have been able to unfold their theories and put them into practice, without any fear from the revengeful hostility of the church." Catholic authorities not only subdued intellectual progress, they also quelled the progress of humanity. His comparison continued, "[the] Republic—it is the People marching towards Progress; the Monarchy—it is the Church, the Power striving to hoodwink the People, to gag, to lead it, to retard its march, denying it light."[77]

The Afro-Creole Spiritualists fought Catholicism beyond the séance table as well. Some stories about Rey and others in New Orleans were recorded by Grandjean from conversations with Petit (his father-in-law) and glued into one of the register books. One story recounted a popular, local, French healer named Madame Charles Thomas who maintained a good relationship with the city's metaphysicals and Catholics. When a priest approached her and suggested they work together to provide physical and spiritual guidance to locals for a price, she rebuked him; since she received the help of the spirits for free, her services would be free as well. Only a selfish person would use spiritual power for personal and material benefit. On another occasion, a priest from Bayou Lafourche named Thibodeaux approached Rey with a similar plan—padding their "pockets." The priest also invited Rey to his home to discuss Spiritualism over "two bottles of wine." Rey turned him down. Another local priest, a Father Subilo at St. Augustine parish, one day asked a local spiritual healer named Madame Jourdain why she no longer attended church. When she responded that she had given up Catholicism for Spiritualism, the priest admitted that he agreed with her. When she pressed why he continued to "teach error," he explained that "the world is not prepared to accept" Spiritualism. By keeping quiet about the truth (Spiritualism), she retorted, "the world would never be prepared." A final story recounted when the priest in Iberville, Father Dupuis, chided Petit for not attending confession. Petit responded that he would confess his wrongdoings only to those who cared about him, like his mother or father, and not "a stranger indifferent to what happens to me."[78]

The spirits periodically admired other critics of Catholicism, such as Calvin and Luther, for their willingness to speak out. Joining their ranks were the former priests who now criticized the institution of the church, including two former popes. The spirit of Clement XIV repeatedly likened priests to "vampires" since they "sucked" power from everyone—men, women, children, kings, and beggars. On another occasion, a spirit identified as Boniface lamented how "Fraternity and Charity" suffered due to humanity's "imperious Selfishness." According to the spirit, most religions were "born of interest" rather than "the Truth" and favored the material over real salvation. He further explained that this selfishness contributed "to the squandering of the Church of Rome, who, forgetting the Great Humanitarian and Fraternal Principles of Jesus," instead focused on strengthening its own "power" and "domination." Rather than seek truth, the Catholic Church desired power and control over all. To achieve this domination, Jesuits, as Boniface described them, were "the smaller soldiers with black robes in [a] humble village [who] work to accomplish these wishes!"[79] This reference to Jesuit priests characterized them as workers in the Catholic institution's plan to dominate the world. Additionally, it is indicative of the spirits' dislike of Jesuits, whom they described as greedy men who exploited and stole money from rich and poor alike. Even if the poor had little money to give, the Jesuits wanted it all and would not shy from taking advantage of every, to use Boniface's phrase, "humble village." Thus, the hierarchal institution of the Catholic Church and the spirit of republicanism were at odds, in large part because of assumed authority of priests.

"Shun the Priest!"[80]: Anticlericalism and Religious Authority

The disillusion with the Catholic hierarchy, as expressed early in Barthélemy Rey's disapproval of Father Morisot, continued throughout the circle's tenure. Even the spirit of Jesus recognized "the infamous role of the Black Robe among his flock." In their final days, the séance records contained denouncements of the "religious oligarchy"—meaning the "monstrous power" of Catholic priests. Spiritualists could avoid the "religious subservience" demanded by priests. Instead of giving power to clerics, Spiritualists held religious knowledge and truth in their own hands and in their table's records. The "freethinkers" at the table should "delight" in their knowledge and superiority over Catholic priests and their followers. "Triumph" and "progress" came from Spiritualism, not a hierarchical religious system. The "Religious Oligarchy" had ordered many to "Close your Eyes!" to keep them from seeing the truth. Another spirit likened the power of clerics to "the devouring wolf that watches and subsists on its victim's blood." This "clerical power," the spirit taught, combated the enlightenment of nations and the path of liberty, for "tyrants are anointed by it [clerical power], because they are its minions and associates, in order to deceive the People." Rabelais also told the Cercle Harmonique about the corruption of priests, their lust for both money and secrets. Rabelais warned that the priest wanted to be their "master" and "know all their family secrets."[81] Money or secrets— priests would exploit the laity for both.

In addition to their materialism, priests were criticized for their assumed and undeserved authority and how they used it to exploit the masses. "The evil caused by the religious oligarchy will be known to you here," a spirit assured the circle. Without the obstruction of the physical body, Cercle Harmonique members would be able to survey the earth and see for themselves "the perversity and the terrible immoral calamity which prevail inside of the so-called holy places." This moment would confirm all the spirits' warnings about the Jesuits, for they too will "shudder to behold the lugubrious history of the priest's heart" and see the horror of "the unfortunate who has submitted to the black robed priest's manacles." The priest used his authority over the laity to exploit their vulnerabilities. Thus, in the spirit world there were "no priests" because each spirit was a child of God "who has in his bosom a spark which will illumine his thought, will expand his intelligence, will elevate his soul toward Him, will teach to himself the eternal principles of justice for all."[82] The Spiritualists had a different understanding of the origin of religious authority and believed their understanding was a more just and fair one.

The Jesuits in particular were frequent targets of the spirits. On one occasion the spirit of Saint Vincent de Paul associated the Jesuits with slavery. "Their command is an extreme one," he argued, "and has marched from century to century, dominating the masses." He called Jesuit priests "those cruel enemies of all liberties, who are posing as dictators of conscience." He further described them as those "who, hypocritically come with their flattering voice demonstrating a false humility." There was a time "when the simple sight of their robes caused one to tremble and shudder; today they see with hate and anger how their robes cause laughter." Though de Paul never clearly identified the "they" in the message, it was the Jesuits. At first glance, with its references to abolitionism, particularly with the exclamation "the chains of slavery have been broken," this message seems to be discussing the enslavement of Africans and their descendants. Furthermore, arriving in 1869, the message's allusion to fear-inducing robes seems a reference to the Ku Klux Klan. However, as he continued it became clear that the "they" were Jesuits propagating moral slavery to Catholic dogma. In this message, de Paul also suggested that their power was diminishing: "The times are gone when Kings were trembling before them, when a papal bull was making a man, a reprobate; an object of refuse, or scorns." Another spirit likened the "black robed men" to "mercenaries."[83] Desiring power and money, mercenary seemed an apt comparison.

Priests were the subject of a particularly harsh critique in a long message from an unknown spirit. The spirit lamented how "this fatal black army . . . fetters humanity" and attacked the idea of indulgences because they favored the wealthy. The "gates" of purgatory were "heavy for the small purses, but light for the full and round ones." In other words, money could save a person from the priests' "dreadful theories of an eternal hell." The strong censure of priests and money continued as the unknown spirit noted how the quality of a mass, be it "pompous or shabby," depended upon "the number of coins thrown into the big pocket of your robe." Even worse, the priests taught "error" and "superstition." Then, to really highlight the corruption of priests, the spirit began a long comparison of the behavior and dogma of priests with Jesus:

Your divine master used to preach Charity and was generous to the poor; you, you despoil them!

Your temples overflow with riches!

Jesus surrounded himself with the unfortunates of society; you, you associate with royalty; your pope wants to dictate to the whole world.

Jesus died between two robbers!

Jesus carried his cross; you, you gild and worship it!

Jesus used to comfort the afflicted; you, you dishearten them by your cruel theories!

"It is as difficult for a rich man to reach Heaven, as it is for a camel to pass through the eyes of a needle" has said Jesus.

The gates of Purgatory are wide open for money at the sound of the cacophony of your choristers!

You imprisoned Galileo; science would be put under a cover if you could!

You bless the flats of despots; Jesus blessed the people!

Jesus died for humanity; you, you live off it in torturing it!

Girded with a crown of olives, Jesus rode on a donkey; you, you preach war; in your palaces you collect the tithe. The pope receives seated on his throne and presents his big toe to be kissed!

Jesus charged twelve apostles with the mission to propagate his doctrine by speech to spread truth; you, to maintain yourselves you need the assistance of foreign soldiers, of bayonets, of cannons![84]

In the eyes of this spirit, who preferred to sign as "*L'Inconnu*" (the Unknown), priests corrupted the message of Jesus and contradicted his behavior in every way. These men hardly were worthy of being spiritual leaders and mentors. Rather, they should be avoided.

No matter how successful a priest might be in his earthly life, his life in the spirit world definitely would not be pleasant. This chapter opened with Rey's rejection of a Jesuit priest at his door seeking monetary donations, an action that brought cheering from the spirit Ambroise because acquaintance with these "black robed men" should be avoided. They tricked men and women into following their incorrect theology and then swindled them of their money. "Oh! pity them," Ambroise told the circle, "for, here, they will moan, will have to pass years at work, in order to redeem the evil they will have done by their lies, said to hide their aim of speculation." One of their main sins was their love of materialism, clearly seen in their greed for money. The Spiritualist's soul was far superior, for it was "freed from Matter and from Materialism, purified and sanctified, perfectible, but also full of Love and Charity."[85]

One of the spirits' primary issues with priests was their undeserved authority. "Religious power," Ambroise believed, was "the most odious system." It was also "a myth" or a moot system because real spiritual power permeated throughout the world, and so there was "no need for Temples or ministers." Religious authority was made even worse when it was paired with a political system, for it allowed men as greedy as "vampires" to seek "exclusive control." Spiritualism, or "true belief," would abolish "Religious Despotism," just as "perfect government" would destroy "Political Despotism." Former priests expressed their remorse, and the spirits of deceased lay people recognized that Catholic clerics had mistreated them in life. The spirit of Dr. Blanchard regretted that he "got into trouble" during his time on earth because "black robes had very much dominated me and filled me with errors." He regretted that he gave "credence to such nonsense" and allowed himself to be "governed as a child, without reason." Another spirit lamented how s/he lived his/her life "under the rule of the black robes" and "suffered" as ignorance kept him/her "in the darkness." "Unfortunate" was the one who lived "under the domination of the Priest."[86]

Desire for power was not the only deplorable trait of Catholic clerics. When referencing priests, spirits always censured them for their materialism and their greed. "The priest in Louisiana as everywhere else," the spirit of Orfila disdainfully reported, "always lives luxuriously and amidst abundance." A spirit named Eugene Sue noted how "the masses suffer," were "clad in rags," and ate "stale bread, while the strolling players of the religious theatres [priests], who hawk about and retail God throughout the world, under the form of indulgences, etc, are overflowing with gold." Again, it was the perceived materialism of the priests that the spirits attacked in particular. These priests, who were "clad with sumptuous garments, stroll about with a gilded Christ studded with precious stones! Bow low, coward people, and worship the golden calf." The Spiritualists should be comforted because they would be vindicated when the spirits of the priests entered the spiritual realm and faced Jesus, "the worthy and great philosopher." At this, former priests would recognize their own past sins. Jesus observed the "error" and "infamy of those who call themselves apostles," and he wept "over this great social plague which shall be heralded one day, however! And the vermin who caused it, shall also disappear!"[87] The identity of the spirit who delivered this message also was indicative of the Cercle Harmonique's critical view of Catholicism and priests. The spirit who signed as Eugene Sue likely was early nineteenth-century French novelist Joseph Marie Eugène Sue, known for his anti-Catholic writing.[88]

To discuss clerics and materialism, one spirit found that a comparison of a priest with a doctor was an instructive exercise. "Both know that society considers them as superior beings to be respected," the spirit stated, "especially the priest." Furthermore, they each have a "profitable trade, especially that of the priest." Both also "live at the expense of those who listen to them" and "acknowledge Truth in their heart, but deny it publicly." Additionally, both were captives to materialism. However, for this spirit, one was clearly less necessary and more "dangerous": the priest. People needed doctors for their health, but priests only poisoned minds. The priest was also a coward.

The spirit ended the message with exclamations: "Shun the Priest! Flee from him! But study with the physician, and study him personally also."[89] There was nothing to be gained from an association with a priest, although there was some benefit from a doctor. One could learn about medicine and health from a physician. Additionally, since the doctor was seen as less threatening, he was a good example for comparative analysis of how not to live. To "study him personally" likely meant to survey his habits, to scrutinize them, and to see the materialist error of his ways. Through critical observation, one could better identify the proper way to live.

In addition to spirits who were lay Catholics during their material lives, the spirits of former priests also had critical remarks for the clergy, including former New Orleanian priests like Chalon. On another occasion, a spirit chose to introduce himself as "a brother, ex-priest," perhaps to distinguish between his earthly life and new life in the spiritual world. Moni explained that he and others attacked "the gentlemen with the robes" because, though priests "teach a pure morality . . . their actions are contrary to the moral they teach." And those corrupt actions invalidated the "beautiful morality" of their teachings. In contrast, Moni's spirit believed that a Spiritualist's "first principle" was "charity," both in word and deed. Not only were priests criticized by the circle for their corruption, the pope was too. Haitian Revolutionary leader Toussaint Louverture defined despotism for the Cercle Harmonique as "a heavy chain that weighs the soul" and prevents a moral and reflective man to reach "Truth." Expanding on this, Louverture described "religious despotism" as something that will "torture Consciousness." He then identified two despots—the king and the pope. In fact, the pope was worse, for he was both a political and religious despot.[90]

Louverture was hardly the only one who reprimanded the pope. Another spirit particularly critical of the Catholic Church's leader was Voltaire. On one occasion Voltaire delivered a particularly condemning message regarding the pope as a greedy man seated on "his tottering throne." Using "soldiers" and the threat of "the gallows," the pope, Voltaire charged, sought to "represent himself as God." He and other priests took advantage of confession—"the infamous raid of the conscience"—to learn "family secrets," not to help the laity but to support their own religious power. To get a priest's help one had to pay upfront and in full. Voltaire pointed to the "high" price of indulgences and the offer of a votive mass in exchange for money. "Oh Pope," he lamented "you are far from being a son of God, you are the son of Error, you are the enemy of Progression." The spirit of Rabelais agreed, and using similar language, Rabelais contended that the collapse of "the throne of the Pope" would benefit humanity.[91]

This was not the only time Voltaire or his spirit criticized the pope, and the 1870s were an auspicious time to do so. During the 1870s, many American Catholics were looking toward Rome uneasy about the "Roman Question," defined by the historian Peter D'Agostino as "the abnormal status of the pope as a prisoner of Liberal Italy without a territorial sovereignty to guarantee his spiritual autonomy."[92] With the dissolution of the Papal States on 20 September 1870, the pope began to live in internal exile within the Vatican, but Catholics around the world remained committed to their Holy Father and expressed their solidarity with him. Many American Catholics were apprehensive about liberalism because of the new unified Italian Republic and its treatment of the Pope. Liberalism was a threat to their religion and, consequently, some American Catholics categorized the creation of a unified Italian Republic as "an evil and monstrous injustice."[93] In contrast, the Afro-Creole Spiritualists saw this downgrade of the pope's temporal sovereignty as a positive move that stripped an unworthy man of undeserved political power.

In June 1871, just months after the end of the Papal States, Voltaire responded to a spirit message from "a believer" regarding the pope. The believer spoke in favor of the pope, stating that he was "God on Earth," "the master of intelligence," and a "representative of God on earth." Thus, "everything must belong to him." Additionally, "his army in black robes is sacred and must be respected." Not surprisingly, Voltaire offered a "response" to this message that the Cercle Harmonique recorded immediately under it. Across the world, people "felt his [the pope's] yoke." The pope created "hatred and pain" beyond the "Inquisition" and the "Crusades." Everyday people from all corners of the earth "were impoverished and lived under his sweat and toil." His wretched army of priests caroused about "plundering society," "lying brazenly," and "hiding their saturnalia of the Night." Indeed, Voltaire concluded, if Lucifer existed he would be "at home" and "with many companions" in Rome. Voltaire was happy to see the end of the Papal States and the pope's territorial sovereignty, though he may have gotten a bit ahead of himself likening it to the "fall of the Papacy." "As a huge roar," he and others "proclaim the fall of the Papacy which held humanity for so long in a cruel and merciless yoke." Catholicism was like a "bogeyman" keeping people leashed to the pope. But finally, this "giant" (the Papacy) was losing power, and Voltaire shouted "Hosanna!" for "humanity will be liberated from an error and

Despotism." Similarly, Ambroise called Rome a "modern Sodom" because of its "rampant corruption." In a joint message from Montesquieu and Ambroise, they hoped for the release of humanity from "the bloody sword of kings and princes, and the infamous and shameless hypocrite successors of Peter!" A spirit identified as Jacques Dellile [*sic*], likely French poet and scholar Jacques Delille, also lambasted the pope for enslaving "thousands" under his "hypocrite yoke."[94]

The spirits of French thinkers were not alone in their opinion on the pope. Beloved, local black soldier John H. Crowder, a young second lieutenant in the Louisiana Native Guards who died during the Civil War's Battle of Port Hudson, frequently came to the séance table to discuss his happiness for dying for freedom. Criticizing Catholicism was an occasional spiritual hobby as well. On 16 June 1871, he hoped to see "Men of Progress" be "more careful and not go and give a certain moral support to the Ceremonies that are to take place tomorrow in favor of the Pope." Crowder identified this as the Roman Catholic Church's "last struggle to retain a power in their hands." And Crowder was not afraid to express his frustration with the church. Humanity should not be "controlled by a set of impudent impostors trying to command as masters of your intellectual powers which they want to limit in order to be masters of your mind." Crowder hated watching his old friends succumb to the exploitative power of the Holy See in Rome and the pope, and so he was happy to watch the power of Rome "dying" and humanity set "free" of the Catholic oligarchy.[95] The "Ceremonies" in question were likely Pope Pius IX's silver jubilee anniversary, an event made more significant due to his lack of political or temporal power. During the month of June, the New Orleans press printed short news dispatches from across the globe regarding masses and other ceremonies in his honor.[96] Around the same time as Crowder's negative message, the circle received other critical communications regarding Catholic clerics. Voltaire likened a priest to "a vampire in chase," a reference to priests' perceived greed. An anonymous spirit echoed this the following day, noting "the corruption of the clergy" and how clerics enslaved the people and, thus, were able to manipulate using the horrors of the Inquisition.[97]

An important difference between the religious authority of a priest and of a Spiritualist medium was the origin of that authority. Whereas a priest's authority came from the institution of the church, a medium's authority originated from the spirits and his/her own individual abilities. For Catholicism, religious authority came from ecclesiastical institutions and human hierarchies. In contrast, the spirits and the mediums who could access them were the source of Spiritualism's authority. Rightful Spiritualists became mediums by their own "free will," a term the spirits used to compare the behavior and beliefs of Spiritualists and their Catholic neighbors. In contrast to the greed, corruption, and immorality that the spirits identified with Jesuits and other priests, the spirits encouraged Spiritualists, in particular mediums, to emulate Valmour. "He has set, for healing mediums," a brother told the circle, "the example to be followed" and thus "has received his reward." Therefore, mediums should "imitate his abnegation." A medium's heart was troubled only when he was surrounded by the materialism of others, while Catholic priests seemed nearly synonymous with materialism in the spirits' messages. The Catholic sacraments administered by priests did not lead one to heaven either. Rather, the spirits guided people through their teachings "in order to open for you from the Earth a road to the Happy Land of good Spirits."[98]

Unlike the priest, a true and successful medium could not be a corrupt person. "The state of the soul" was a determining factor in who could be a medium. Furthermore, mediums were required to cultivate their talents further through practice and purification of the spirit. But Spiritualists were to be aware, the same spirit warned, that there were mediums "scattered here and there" who did not care about good spiritual work. These mediums were more like priests and should be avoided. "A luminous brother" told the circle that the "sublime societies" of spirits in the invisible world helped advance humanity toward "perfectibility," and this was why they "control you as a medium." In response, the medium would receive "a glimpse, a very feeble glimpse of what there is beyond your world." A medium also could replace the priest's role of confessor for the dead. The spirit of Napoleon was very grateful for the medium who received and transcribed his messages, and Napoleon "was somewhat relieved in imploring compassion, and exposing my regrets of my past conduct."[99] His spirit found solace in Spiritualism and its mediums, not the Catholicism of his youth.

The religious culture of Catholicism and its materialism, seen most clearly in priests, gave the spirits much to criticize. The greed of the church was hardly the Cercle Harmonique's only problem. Like Catholicism, U.S. politics suffered from a lack of harmony and egalitarianism. Corrupt priests were like corrupt politicians: Both took advantage of others. According to the spirits, the U.S. republic's destiny was to become the system of government on earth most akin to the spiritual republic. The founding documents pledged equality for all men, but the country had failed to deliver on this promise because of greed and materialism. In the material world, freedom was not universal, and American liberty was not catholic. Slavery and a racial system premised on white supremacy kept American republicanism from reaching its full potential, but the spirits were hopeful that the Idea would rule American religion, American politics, and American society.

CHAPTER FOUR

The Spiritual Republic and America's Destiny

A general Republic, the stepping-stone to Freedom, Association,
Justice, Accord, and . . . Unity.
—Andrew Jackson Davis, *The Magic Staff*

Praise Jesus and Lincoln: one will regenerate humanity, the other the
U.S. Republic.
—Spirit of Lamennais to the Cercle Harmonique, 25 March 1869

Sympathy, Harmony: these are our laws.
—Spirit of a brother to the Cercle Harmonique, 17 March 1873

On 27 May 1863, the Union, supporters of abolition, and particularly African
Americans acquired a beloved and famous martyr. Captain André Cailloux
was an officer in Company E of the Louisiana Native Guards, the first black
regiment in the Union Army to see action in a major battle. His death was
mourned by Union supporters, and his company's attack on Confederate
Port Hudson convinced many skeptics of black soldiers' abilities and effectiveness. His funeral nearly two months later, on 29 July, was well-attended
by New Orleans's black and white populations. His memory was eulogized
beyond the funeral, and local and northern newspapers printed poems
celebrating his bravery and courage in the siege of Port Hudson.[1] Even in
death, Cailloux's presence could be felt. More than felt, it also was heard
by the Cercle Harmonique. A couple weeks before the funeral, he began
to deliver messages to Rey, his Afro-Creole friend and fellow soldier. Captain
Cailloux, the self-identified "brave soldier of Progress," would prove to be a
frequent spirit visitor at the table. Though the Confederate army destroyed
his body, his soul lived on. He fought for freedom in "your world," but
achieved freedom "in the invisible world." Truly, "God has rewarded me."
"Man falls! Principle Lives!" he told Rey's circle later that year. Cailloux's
messages identified him as a fighter for freedom, a key element in the Cercle
Harmonique's view of republicanism. The "Principle" he referenced was
that of liberty and human progress. Though the message was simply those
four words, it came on the heels of a brief communication from George

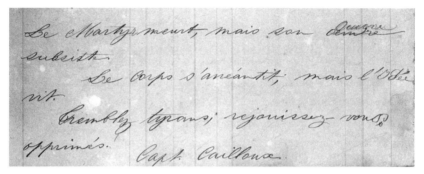

Conclusion of a recorded message from Captain André Cailloux, 12 February 1872. Courtesy of the René Grandjean Collection, Louisiana and Special Collections Department, Earl K. Long Library, University of New Orleans.

Washington celebrating the conclusion of the Confederate rebellion and one from radical abolitionist John Brown praising the end of slavery in America. Shortly after Cailloux's message, the spirit of Andrew Jackson endorsed the Union. Thus, the cause of the Union—though a glorified understanding of it—and its relationship to the cry of freedom were attractive messages for those arguing for civil and political rights in postwar New Orleans. Though Cailloux "the martyr" died, "the Idea lived."[2]

The séance records of the Cercle Harmonique illustrate an Afro-Creole understanding of religion, race, and nation. If the United States remade itself with egalitarian republicanism at its core, the postwar country finally would live up to its Declaration of Independence promise that "all men are created equal." With the assistance of their large spiritual network, the Cercle Harmonique wrote America's destiny in their séance records. In the historian Laurie Maffly-Kipp's *Setting Down the Sacred Past: African-American Race Histories*, she examined how Protestant African Americans in the nineteenth and early twentieth centuries constructed sacred histories of their racial, religious, and national pasts. They were "communal narratives," which, Maffly-Kipp stated, "are never simply texts." Rather the communal narratives were "the artifacts— and the sculptors—of particular collective experiences and desires." Resisting the dominant Anglo-American understandings of religion and race, these histories offered new narratives that undermined the definitions imposed by white Americans. The process of writing was a spiritual and intellectual practice that formed a "collective self-awareness."[3] The communal narrative created by the Cercle Harmonique's séance records focused on themes different than the race histories examined by Maffly-Kipp, but in both cases the authors created an alternative to a white Anglo-American imperial under-standing of race and nation. Rather than using biblical stories, particularly the story of the exodus, the Afro-Creole Spiritualists reworked memories of Atlantic world revolutions and American republicanism.[4]

Racial violence inspired by white supremacy was part of southern culture during Reconstruction, and according to the spirits, it quelled the progress of American republicanism.[5] In addition to inciting physical violence against nonwhite bodies, the emerging American nationalism also enacted ideolog-ical violence. While much of the United States rallied "around a newly ro-bust white Christian identity" during Reconstruction, the spirits visiting the Cercle Harmonique offered a different religio-racial vision for the nation.[6] Historians Joshua Paddison and Edward J. Blum have excavated how the "white republic," to use Blum's term, was remade after the Civil War by powerful white Americans. This new national vision was gendered male, ra-cially white, and theologically Protestant, and it was seen as progress after the Civil War. Those who did not fit this "robust" image were left behind. In con-trast, the spirits and the Cercle Harmonique offered a vision of American democracy and republicanism that affirmed the value and equality of all persons.

This chapter extends further from the Cercle Harmonique's immediate surroundings of New Orleans and considers the circle, their spirit guides, and their séance recordings in the context of the larger U.S. republic. The spirits' emphasis on egalitarian republicanism shaped the Cercle Harmonique's understandings of race and nation, both of which were empty signifiers. A person's soul mattered, not his or her raced body. The Civil War and Re-construction politics shaped the messages from the spirits and the Cercle Harmonique's spiritual network. The spirits continued to be critical of slav-ery and the Confederacy throughout the tenure of the Cercle Harmonique, indicating that liberty and the Union were on the side of progress and the Idea. Though war was regrettable, American society now could be re-made more like the spiritual republic. The world of politics in New Orleans, Louisiana, and the United States following the Civil War was complicated and unstable, and the messages received by the Cercle Harmonique offered a positive message of republicanism. Celebrity spirits also visited the Cercle Harmonique, and their participation and messages revealed knowledge about the country's past and destiny. The war offered the United States the ability to "regenerate" itself, and the spirits hoped to see that happen with liberty and equality as the guiding forces.

"Forward march, humanitarian soldier"[7]:
American Slavery and the Civil War

Slavery and the white-over-black racial hierarchy it reinforced were part of everyday life in New Orleans and in the South. The city's racial stratification was underpinned and reinforced by pervasive slavery. The importation of African slaves led to colonial Louisiana's adoption of the *Code Noir* in 1724, which both provided for and punished slaves. Owners were expected to provide for their slaves' physical and religious (Catholic) needs, but the *Code Noir* also plainly stated that slaves were to be regarded as property, not people, and that their duty was to their owner.[8] The *Code Noir* controlled slave behavior and detailed the punishments for infractions. White citizens were allowed to stop free or enslaved blacks on the city streets and demand to see their emancipation papers or their passes from their masters. Both protecting and penalizing slaves, the *Code Noir* reinforced the racial hierarchy, a necessity for whites, especially in the city's earlier decades.

During the nineteenth century, New Orleans became one of the centers for the selling and purchasing of slaves, and it was the largest such center in the lower South.[9] Writing in his journal in 1836, a northern traveler called the slave market "the Soul of New Orleans."[10] This booming slave market saw high traffic until the Union capture of the city in May 1862, and its high volume activity made it akin to a tourist attraction.[11] The quadroon offspring of owners and their female slaves or any other concubinage relationships were known for their beauty and grace and thus were another New Orleans racial attraction and curiosity.[12] Shortly before secession, the Louisiana Legislature passed "An Act to Permit Free Persons of African Descent to Select Their Masters and Become Slaves for Life" (1859). Though it encouraged rather than forced free blacks to self-enslavement, it was part of a wider culture of antagonism toward the city's free black community.[13]

Slavery was part of the lives of Cercle Harmonique leaders too. Rey's father, Barthélemy, owned eight slaves between the ages of two months and fifty years in 1850.[14] Petit's grandfather owned a plantation and Petit's father, Antoine Dubuclet, would have been active in running and maintaining the property. After Antoine Dubuclet married Claire Pollard (Petit's mother), who also came from a wealthy Creole family, the couple's combined estate was valued at almost one hundred thousand dollars, which included over one hundred slaves.[15] Needless to say, Petit was raised in an environment dependent upon slavery, and this was not uncommon. Free men of color owned some of the largest plantations during Louisiana's antebellum years. Owning slaves was common among the New Orleans *gens de couleur libres*, though in some cases it was for the purpose of securing family members' freedom. In 1830 in New Orleans, 11,301 free persons of color owned a total of 753 slaves.[16]

Though some of their mediums' families owned slaves, the spirits spoke harshly of slavery. What the ancien régime was to French Revolutionaries, the slaveholding southern oligarchy was to the spirits advising the Cercle Harmonique, but with the guidance of Divine Providence. "Human Slavery shall disappear little by little on this continent." Those who fought for "Progress" and "Truth" would happily march "towards Heaven." The spirit of French priest Hugues-Félicité Robert de Lamennais explained that in the post–Civil War era the "generous principle" of "'Liberty for all' has conquered and vanquished" the enemy that had "inscribed on its banner: 'Moral and Physical Slavery.'" Though the "Oligarchy will fight again," it would not defeat justice and progress. The spirits were happy that the war had ended the "social plague" of physical slavery, but the abolition of slavery did not mean that society was healed from its effects. The "sore" that remained still needed to be "cauterized."[17]

The spirits argued that slavery impeded humanity's progress, and in this way they had a similar view of slavery as famous escaped slave Frederick Douglass. Douglass expressed love for religion that "is based upon the glorious principle, of love to God and love to man; which makes its followers do unto others as they themselves would be done by. If you demand liberty to yourself, it says, grant it to your neighbors."[18] The "glorious principle" referenced by Douglass was akin to the spirits' Idea. The end of human slavery and the anticipated end of "moral slavery" were linked with the Idea. According to the spirit of Ambroise, slavery's abolition "threw a great disturbance in the ideas of backwards minds [proslavery Americans]" who could not understand their own prejudices. An unsigned message asked if the circle could "hear the shrieks" that came from "the slave" who cried during his "degrading punishment." The unknown spirit asked for "Pardon," admitting, "I was blind" and "I was weak!" The identity of the spirit is unclear, but considering his need for pardon, the spirit likely engaged in the behavior he lamented— the lashing of enslaved, black bodies. For many former slavery supporters, death revealed the immorality of "riveting chains." Instead they now spoke of Liberty.

The ownership of people solidified the southern oligarchy's power and the dominance of white supremacy. Expressing their disgust for this, some spirits used the mediums of the Cercle Harmonique to deliver general messages for humanity and reprimand its materialism, materialism that caused slavery. The spirit of former New Orleans mayor Paul Bertus asked: "Why do you reject those unfortunate brothers whom you held so long under a degrading yoke?" The "you" of the question could be the federal government, Confederate supporters, all slave owners, or New Orleans society. The censure from the spirit did not end with the rhetorical question. Bertus continued and focused on slavery. He rebuked the "you" for chaining those unfortunate brothers "as beast[s] of burden," denying them "their most sacred rights," withholding intellectual advancement, and keeping them at "the level of brutes." Bertus warned listeners about those who wanted another war in order to bring back southern, pre–Civil War society. Instead of promoting war, he encouraged peace and equality. Listeners should heed his words, for if they knew "like us . . . the chastisement to be the lot of those who, like you, are committing injustices over injustices, how quickly would you change!" Rather than hearing "the voice of Reason," those men were "dominated" by "a foolish pride."[19]

In communicating with the Cercle Harmonique, former statesman Daniel Webster found an avenue for apology for his complicity in American slavery. He encouraged members of the circle to forgive ignorant men, admitting that he was ignorant during his "earthly life." Though he held a position of power, he "had been led to believe, through the many errors of this earthly world, that I was superior to a certain class of my brethren. But what a sudden change I met with, when I was debarrassed [sic] of my material envelope." This regret could be a reference to his support for the Compromise of 1850 or he simply apologized for not endorsing abolition. Webster returned a week later to continue his message for the circle and spoke again on why he was inclined to forgive "those of my brothers whose ambition has led them to spread so many evils through this earthly world." He explained that even a very "learned man" could develop a Napoleon complex and "begin to think himself above all his fellow brothers . . . [and] positively believe that he is a king on earth." Men such as these had "very bitter regrets hereafter," no doubt painfully realizing the errors of their ways. Indeed, the spiritual lives of those guilty of "vile and base actions" in their earthly lives were "gloomy."[20] In other words, former slave owners were ill poised for the spirit world.

The spirits of both former slave owners and slaves recognized the horrors of slavery. A deceased slave came to the Cercle Harmonique and was followed by a Confederate officer. The slave, John Jones, noted how the register book the Spiritualists used to record messages was originally purchased in 1822 while "slavery was the curse inflicted upon an age of enlightenment, of Progress." The "lash" forced people to work, treating them like "brutes." Slave owners mistook themselves for masters and "forgot that a Master of all men" would hold them accountable for their actions.[21] Jones was merely "a poor slave of man" on earth, but he was now "a pure Spirit of God." He was happy to see the spread of liberty during Reconstruction. The spirits of slaves did not wish vengeance on their former owners; instead Jones and others "let C. D. Dreux first fulfill the other page [of the book] to show how Great we are in our forgiveness." The spirit whose message followed Jones was "weeping like a child" at his "Past of shame." Though slavery "was dead," he continued to feel "ashamed" of his participation in and support of the system. He hoped others would come to the spirit world "not as slaves of prejudices but as Exponents of Light."[22] This spirit belonged to Lieutenant Colonel Charles D. Dreux, a native of New Orleans who served in the Confederate army. He was the first Louisianan killed in the war (July 1861), and his funeral was a well-attended event in New Orleans.[23] Dreux was popular in the higher social circles of New Orleans and served as a district attorney and a representative in the Louisiana State Legislature.[24] An apology from such a high profile figure confirmed that the physical victors of the Civil War were also the moral victors.

The spirit of John Jones came to the Cercle Harmonique again the following year. In the material world he suffered "under the yoke of a barbarian master" who worked him from dawn until sunset. Though Jones was a slave, he possessed an intelligence "superior" to that of his owner, which roused "petty jealousy" and physical punishment. From then on, Jones kept his head down and tried not to draw the attention of his owner. Others also recognized and lamented the violence of slavery. The spirit of Joanni Questy, a local Creole of color, writer, and former medium, was disappointed with the recent past's "slave chains" and "Black Code."[25] The violence of slavery and white supremacy retarded humanity's progress and the United States' progress. Only good individuals could make a good and egalitarian nation. If citizens allowed themselves to be ruled by personal greed and materialism, the country would follow. And this could have violent ramifications; the relationship between materialism and U.S. slavery was a good example.

Since slavery was antithetical to humanity's progress, it comes as little surprise that the séance records of the Cercle Harmonique contain numerous messages that celebrate President Lincoln and many messages from the assassinated president himself. Lincoln's spirit criticized the wealth and power the white upper classes reaped from the slave labor in their fields. "King Cotton was a myth," he proclaimed, "he had an imaginary crown, but Liberty shelters under its aegis thousands of citizens who helped to disperse the last remnants of a huge army." According to a joint message from Ambroise and Saint Vincent de Paul, Lincoln's Emancipation Proclamation was "magnificent" and struck slavery in its "disdainful face"—a task finished by Grant's sword. Lincoln reported that he was "happy" in the spirit world because "my Emancipation Proclamation" shortened his period of retribution. In other words, ordering the freedom of southern slaves gave Lincoln an immediate spiritual promotion at his death. Upon entering the spiritual realm, he was recognized as "a martyr for a just cause." The spirits knew that the recently emancipated would "rise despite the obstacles," such as those who pined for slavery's reign. "Political affairs" would and should work in favor of those "formerly crushed" under slavery's "degrading yoke."[26]

John Brown's spirit found it unfortunate that Jefferson Davis still lived, but the end of slavery was cause enough to celebrate. The spirits viewed the Confederacy as the side that fought for slavery and, thus, against the Idea. A spirit identified as B. explained that "the materialism of the Confederacy" had "armed" John Wilkes Booth, but "spirituality" had broken "the materialism of the privileged." While violence should be avoided, the Civil War had guaranteed freedom for citizens who had been denied "the most sacred rights and domestic affections." The denial of their rights had been for the benefit of a group of "autocrats" who had "forgotten the creed of Liberty" and had scorned "the beautiful teachings of true Republicanism." The struggle against slavery took "too long," but adverse ideas and teachings were difficult to erase from "the heart of the nation." The Confederacy, much like France's ancien régime, was fueled by the "insolence" of an "oligarchic power" adhering to "antiquated ideas."[27] Some northerners contemporary to the Cercle Harmonique saw secession and the Confederacy as an evil and cast Satan as the "first secessionist."[28] For the spirits and others, the Confederacy's downfall was both inevitable and part of humanity's progress.

When Louisiana joined the Confederate States of America, many among the city's Afro-Creole population volunteered to fight for the Confederacy in the Louisiana Native Guards (a black regiment). Though certainly some might have felt obligated or forced to join on behalf of the Confederacy, the city's Afro-Creole soldiers and militia possessed a history of supporting their local government. The city's free black militia helped quell the 1811 slave re-

Conclusion of Abraham Lincoln's "King Cotton was a myth" message, 25 October 1869. Courtesy of the René Grandjean Collection, Louisiana and Special Collections Department, Earl K. Long Library, University of New Orleans.

volt along the German coast of the Mississippi River (just upriver from the city and dangerously close to New Orleans), and Afro-Creoles proudly recalled defending their city during the War of 1812 in the Battle of New Orleans.[29] Thus, part of Afro-Creole identity was providing military support for the local government. Rey and his brother, Octave, mustered for the Native Guards first for the Confederacy and then the Union.

When the white Confederate forces cleared out of New Orleans, many white, pro-Confederate residents felt abandoned and despondent. "Poor New Orleans," one local woman wrote in her journal. "What has become of your promised greatness?"[30] The Louisiana Native Guards were ordered out of the city, but they refused to leave their home unattended. After the Union took New Orleans in May 1862, these men offered their services to General Butler. Along with two other black Creole men, the Rey brothers presented their guns and their dedication to Butler. Butler's General Order No. 63 called for the enlistment of black soldiers for the Union and was met with much enthusiasm.[31] Not all black New Orleanians supported the Union though. In 1863 the Provost Court fined a woman named Emma Walden three dollars for singing a rebel song that began, "Jeff Davis is a gentleman."[32] Later that year a group of whites and free blacks performed a Voudou ceremony to ensure a Confederate victory. In court a slave girl testified that she saw free women of color perform spells to return local power back to the Confederacy and keep slaves in a position subordinate to the free black class.[33] While some locals hoped the supernatural world would help the Confederacy, the Cercle

Harmonique and their guiding spirits supported the Union. On 31 August 1864, the spirit of Father Antonio de Sedella let the circle know that they had a role to play in "the current revolution." He also assured them that they would "fight" and "defeat" their enemy.[34]

While at Union Army Camp Strong in New Orleans on 20 October 1862, Rey received a message from Lamennais that he later recorded in one of his séance books. In it, Lamennais shamed those who believed themselves superior to others; rather, all were "sons of the same father." Indeed, all "men" were "created by the same Master" and, thus, "worthy to participate as you [likely meant to be pro-Confederates] in the benefits of civilization." It was a "shame" that in 1862 "a prejudice of caste" still ruled the nation. Defending "the oppressed" was a "noble cause" of justice and woe to those who fought against liberty. Lamennais encouraged supporters of slavery to imagine their own children when they saw mothers and children separated by slavery. And though soldiers in 1862 could not be sure which way the Civil War would end, Lamennais assured Rey and others at Camp Strong that "no barrier can obstruct the march of good over evil." Those who "committed the crime" and "chained your brothers" would regret their offenses after the "social and political rise" of the black race.[35] Rey was honorably discharged from the Native Guards before the Battle of Port Hudson, which would claim the life of his friend and later spirit guide Captain André Cailloux.

Cailloux was a hero of New Orleans. He was one of the men who volunteered for both sides, as a Confederate lieutenant and later captain of the Union 1st Regiment, Louisiana Native Guards. Cailloux's death in the unsuccessful Union attack on Confederate Port Hudson (outside Baton Rouge) was lamented nationally, and he became one of the first black Union heroes. Eyewitnesses heralded Cailloux's bravery. Leading the charge, he was seen "with his left arm dangling by his side,—for a ball had broken it above the elbow,—while his right hand held his unsheathed sword gleaming in the rays of the sun."[36] Local newspapers, *Harper's Weekly*, the *New York Times*, and the *New York Herald* all covered his funeral, which was both a solemn affair and a social one, for thousands watched or participated in the procession to the cemetery.[37] A local periodical reported that with the death of Cailloux, "the cause of the Union and freedom has lost a valuable friend."[38] *Harper's Weekly*'s coverage even included an image of Cailloux's funeral procession. In New Orleans, the American flag was kept at half-staff for thirty days in honor of Cailloux.[39] The celebration of Cailloux's life and his elevation as a national black military hero offered black New Orleanians a rally point to argue for black rights and equality. Though Cailloux had fallen, his spirit knew the cause for which he died continued forward.[40]

In addition to Cailloux, the spirits of other Civil War casualties visited the Cercle Harmonique's table. A spirit named Crowder assured them that he and other spirits were "preparing for you a better world, where Progress will be your Motto." This spirit was young Lieutenant John H. Crowder of the Union Louisiana Native Guards. He was among many fallen black Civil War soldiers whose spirits appeared one April day in 1870. Crowder reported he was pleased to have "died for Liberty." A spirit named Anselme of the 1st Louisiana Native Guards now resided in a world surrounded by "millions of free citizens." The spirit of J. Handsborough, who identified himself as a corporal in the Louisiana Native Guards, had been perplexed by harsh cruelties of war and violent conflict. He now advised the circle that it was noble to fight for a principle but not to kill for it. Jack Thompson affirmed that when he "shouldered the musket, it was to battle for human rights." Though he died in the war, he rejoiced because "my brothers are free!" Other spirits chimed in too, including President Andrew Jackson. "The union," a spirit identified as A. Jackson stated, "must and shall be preserved!" Later during the same meeting, Jackson's spirit exclaimed: "1814 and 1815! 62 Grant 1869!" likely referring to the Battle of New Orleans, the fall of Confederate New Orleans, and President Grant's inauguration.[41]

All the spirits were happy to see the war end and the Union win. The storm of war had run its course and now the "calm" had "returned." The "hydra," John Brown proclaimed, was "defeated." The spirit of Brown taught the circle that liberty and equality went together because "Liberty creates Equality; and Equality shows the power of Right over Evil." The "power of Right" always defeated "Evil" because "the law of God" dictated that "Justice and Progress always come out the victors in the end, when Evil, in order to maintain itself, provokes a conflict." Part of this message's larger goal was to celebrate the victory of the Union over the Confederacy and emancipation over slavery, and thus, it was very likely that Brown considered the Confederacy and enslavement of blacks as part of "Evil." The spirit of Albert Sidney Johnston, the vice president of the Confederacy, described the Civil War as a "terrible time." His spirit was happy that the side of "freedom" won the war, and he rejoiced in the end of slavery. "Long live Freedom! but for everyone," he signed off. "Unite brothers, and remember the lesson." The lesson—egalitarianism and the error of slavery—was one that Johnston's spirit only recently had learned. Johnston appeared at the table again on

Bastille Day 1872 and echoed the sentiments of many other spirits on the ephemerality of life on earth.[42] It was better to accept the truth of universal equality while on earth than wait until entering the spirit world.

In addition to Johnston, other former Confederate soldiers came to the Cercle Harmonique. The spirit of Colonel Dreux lamented how he and other Confederates "fought for nothing!" In reply, Cailloux affirmed that he and others who mustered for the Union "fought for something!" Even the spirit of Robert E. Lee came to the table of the Cercle Harmonique once. He identified himself as a representative of "those thousands" affected by "the cruel war that desolated this country." He was pleased to see that the rights of all were now observed. All the spirits, including him, desired harmony on earth. He wanted those who participated in the "fratricidal struggle" to "forget your foolish pretentions" and recognize the rightful solidarity of all. Supporters of the Confederacy and slavery needed to realize their past errors in order to grow. Rather than "live in the illusion of the Past," they must accept "the Truth of the [present] situation." "Do not dream of chains for slavery" he ordered. Instead, "talk of Freedom" and "Justice ... Shout ... Long live Liberty. Long live the Union of beings, that of Friends!" Humanity must recognize the "right of everyone." His voice on matters of struggle, conflict, and rights carried extra weight because he was the leader of the Confederate Army and one "who commanded the respect of his political enemy."[43] Lee was a great hero of the South's "Lost Cause" and a saint of its theological pantheon, so hearing the spirit of Lee lament the Civil War and the southern way of life proved that the cause of the Union was right. Just as other spirits found comfort in apologizing and admitting their past errors to the Cercle Harmonique's mediums, Lee found solace in chastising the white southern oligarchy and his wartime defense of it.

Though the victory of the Union was celebrated, war itself was not an inherent good. Lamennais lamented the number of dead from the "terrible and bloody war," not to mention the assassination of the "apostle Lincoln." Still, though war was "a scourge," it was worth it in this case because slavery was "an abomination." But in general, the spirits dissuaded war. Saint Vincent de Paul encouraged listeners to walk with "the olive branch in one hand and light in the other" because "those who want war will be paralyzed or destroyed." War was not the spirits' aim. Humanity was "not created to make war against his brother." Rather, humanity's purpose was "to unite" and "to love." The "sword" did not create "Freedom," nor did "blood" fortify "the tree of Liberty." Ideas did these things. In contrast to warring peoples, the spirits lived together in harmony. Though the Cercle Harmonique hoped the Civil War had changed a society of injustice to one of justice, physical fighting was not the only way—nor was it the preferred way—to catalyze change. Rey's friend in the spirit world, Crowder, partook in the "changes of war" with Rey and others and "was sent to the spiritual life by our foes." Rey, however, did not perish in war. He was appointed "to accomplish another work" and "went to the legislature."[44] Now that the Louisiana Native Guards had helped the Union win freedom for the United States, the political sphere was the new realm of action for Afro-Creoles.

"The same rights as you"[45]: American Republicanism

According to historian Justin Nystrom, both black and white southerners during Reconstruction chose a political party affiliation "largely on self-interest, racial fear, or in the case of some Republicans, high-minded ideals."[46] Afro-Creole members of the Cercle Harmonique fell primarily in the third category. Following the end of slavery and the Confederacy, the spirits and the Cercle Harmonique hoped the Idea of republican egalitarianism would shape U.S. politics and society. It comes as no surprise that the spirits supported republicanism and wanted the United States to model its postwar self on the spiritual republic of their world. In the wake of the Confederacy's fall and nationwide emancipation, the spirits and the Cercle Harmonique believed republicanism was liberty's best bet. References to republican politics and liberal politics frequent the séance records as the best option for making the material world a more equal and harmonious place. The spirits taught that if the U.S. could properly embody the ideals of republicanism, freedom and equality were possible. With the figure of Lincoln and antislavery politicians at the helm, the Republican Party seemed the likeliest to achieve this goal both during and after the war.[47] The spirits taught that the whole country needed to become more republican, not just the former Confederacy. The "invisible army" of human progress knew neither South nor North but rather stood for "humanity and one flag for all and every one." The flag of the Union "must" include "Harmony," for "the stars and stripes must and will protect all the citizens of the Great Republic."[48]

The spirits unequivocally supported republicanism. "Universal Brotherhood" would be the culmination of effective spiritual work and political work for equality.[49] And brotherhood was best fostered by a republican outlook. According to another spirit, a government's strength came from "the morality, the honesty, and the liberal, political, and moral education of the inhabitants." And this would be a two-way street, for "more advanced citizens" were found in countries with "solid, liberal, and generous" governments. A "wise" and "solid, liberal, and generous" government sought to lessen "the burden of taxes" and supported the "liberal" populace by encouraging a "progressive march in sciences, arts, etc."[50] This way, humanity as a whole could move forward. If people and politicians sustained this "progressive" type of government and society, "the evils caused to the people by the political corruption of the parties" would cease because political parties would become extinct. Honest discussions would render political parties unnecessary, and all would be working for the perfection of society.[51]

Republicanism was synonymous with the common good. For the spirits, the common good meant supporting not only the common people but all classes. This was reflected in the spirits who came to the Cercle Harmonique's séance table, which included kings, presidents, soldiers, and slaves. The spirit guides of the Cercle Harmonique lived out the saying "no respecter of persons." Representing all humanity and supporting the common good was the true expression of republicanism. Egalitarian republicanism, the spirits' Idea, was more than just equal legal rights, legislation, and suffrage. While these were important, American democracy needed to be more. It needed to be embedded in social interactions and political leadership. While equality and the Idea were natural and what God and the spirits wanted for the material world, equality would not fully develop in the United States unless it was encouraged and nurtured.

Since the spirit world required both mutual respect and a democratic spirit, the American republic should imitate it. "Harmony" was the foundation of the spiritual spheres, and each spirit acknowledged that all had the right to their own opinion. Respecting the diversity of opinions was necessary for both harmony and liberty. After listening to and respecting the opinions of all, the spirits then would follow the wishes of the majority. Thus, the world of spirits was a democracy, where, though majority opinion ruled, even those in the minority were offered a voice. To deny representation to the minority was "a monstrosity" both in the spiritual world and on earth. A society could move toward progress only if all were allowed to vote. All had representation in the decision-making process in the spirit world, and so the spirits disapproved of earthly societies that allowed those in power to "misuse" their authority. The shared desire "to further the advancement of each and all through Perfectibility" structured the sublime government of the spirits.[52] To make the government of the United States more like that of the spirits, emancipation and universal male suffrage would need to be secured first.

In a republican government, the people would have the power and ability to elect fair leaders. John Brown's spirit believed that the people should be the "King of the Earth," rather than the monarchs he observed around the world. Those leaders were "slaves to selfishness." The power struggle he watched between "Justice" and "absolutism" would end eventually, and "Despotism" would lose to the "triumphant march of the Idea." Quality leaders could be ensured through election "by popular voice . . . with the guarantees for the purity of the ballot, and the purity of the elected." As long as a candidate was willing to produce a signed disclosure of his political philosophy, any man should be allowed to enter the preliminary elections. The general election then would determine who was "the most dignified" to represent "the people." Upon election, "the people's choice" would serve only a "limited term" to avoid tyranny. A nation's leader "ought to be the Father of his brethren" and not act like "the Master of his subjects." Tyranny went hand-in-hand with despotism. Fighting against despotism secured one's status as a "knight defending the cause of the righteous"—an achievement that glorified the Lord.[53]

A republican government was molded by the spirit of fraternity. Père Ambroise called the "Perfect Government" one that focused on "the Happiness of men." A government that repeated antiquated norms and backward laws to hold on to its power worked against "the forward march of the liberal Idea." Those who held on to old, undeserved power were greedy like "vampires." Revolutions and reason could fix this oligarchical hold on authority. Rather than endorsing an authoritarian mode of government, Ambroise echoed the political motto of Alexandre Dumas's *Les Trois Mousquetaires*: "It's all for one and one for all, and all for all and everyone." He continued, "It is brother united to his brother for good and the destruction of evil." The spirit of French novelist Eugène Sue lectured the table on ideal government structures and organization. "Governments will have some stability," the medium wrote, "only when Representation will truly be that of the majority of the nation, and when that majority will work for the general welfare with justice, and especially with integrity and equality." A government's leader should "come from the people," know "their needs and sufferings," and have a "great heart." A leader with wisdom and a good heart would ensure smart policies and keep small the taxes on necessary goods, "agricultural implements," and "all that tends to the amelioration and general welfare." Instead, taxes on "articles of luxury" should bring the most revenue for a government. This way, the people would be deterred from materialism and the rich would bear the tax burden rather than the poor.[54]

Spiritualism also was described as an expression of proper republican politics. The spirit of W. R. Meadows, who died in the Mechanics' Institute Riot, described the spirits in the spiritual spheres as "the invisible army of true Republicanism." As such, the spirits encouraged the circle to include others in their hopes for humanity's salvation and progress. Cercle Harmonique members should be "wise and true" brothers and "give light, light to any one, friend to you or enemy; in darkness, do not leave anybody." Spiritualism was for all and for the progress of all. Those who hampered egalitarian progress were some of the worst spiritual offenders. Paul, "a brother," rebuked those who immigrated to the United States, accepted their own "Political and Civil Rights," and then proceeded to oppress others. This type of oppression was even more repulsive, as the accused enjoyed their own new rights and freedoms while denying those rights to others. Paul warned that when these men arrived to the spiritual world, they would feel much shame for their past offenses.[55]

Racial and economic injustices in the United States meant the Afro-Creole Spiritualists were to be tireless workers and "thinkers." And thinkers should not be afraid to criticize oppressive regimes, laws, and social systems. The spirits admired those who fought against "the infamous powers that want to dominate man as master of his conscience or his personal liberty." Combatting "prejudice . . . bigotry, error, and superstition" cultivated a "noble soul." Despotic leaders were frowned upon, as was greed, especially when that greed was linked to a desire for domination. The spirit of Charles Albert came at the end of 1859 and lamented that, though a new year was about to begin, men would "continue to live in their cruel egoism" and not cease "their rapid strides" in "this immoderate desire they have to dominate the other." Only the "Grand Voice of the People" could succeed in stopping the advance of a tyrant's domination of the people. Those hungry for power and the malicious were not happy in the spirit world. The spirits of those who worked against progress, liberty, and republicanism felt shame. In death, even the spirit of John Wilkes Booth had to admit that nothing could stop the march of progress and "woe to those who want to obstruct the road." On another occasion, a "victim" helped a spirit named Booth seek "forgiveness and your prayers" from the "brethren" of the Cercle Harmonique. Indeed, all were worthy of forgiveness, from John Brown and Abraham Lincoln to Jefferson Davis, John Wilkes Booth, and Jesuit exploiters.[56]

Sometimes it seemed as though the spirits had group conversations that the medium simply observed and recorded as a grouping of short spirit messages. These quick spirit messages happened from time to time, and politics, republicanism, and issues facing American society were common themes. One example of these group conversations began with one spirit naming a government and then describing it. Immediately after one spirit shamed the "two despots" of Napoleon the First and Napoleon the Third, another identified the United States as "the promised land of Liberty!" In contrast, Russia, England, and Ireland were all cold and stagnant places. Another spirit called the Confederate government "a dream." Saint Augustine deemed the thirtieth of July (the day of the Mechanics' Institute Riot) "fratricide" and the Fourth of July "freedom." While "Judge Taney" of *Dred Scott v. Sandford* infamy shouted for "The Past!," both Lincoln and John Brown replied, "The Present." Another spirit identified Lincoln and his achievements as a "moral victory" and Grant and his wartime success as a "physical victory." Finally, Union and Confederate soldiers together exclaimed, "Union forever!"[57]

In another of these multiple-spirit conversations, John Brown began the transcript and expressed happiness that "human slavery has disappeared from the United States of America . . . Moral and Religious Liberty is marching and gaining ground. God be blessed!" Captain Cailloux, Washington, and Napoleon agreed with similar ideas. The spirit of Andrew Jackson seemed to channel Lincoln when he added, "The Union Must and shall be preserved." Another spirit added (echoing the previous group conversation), "The 30th of July is the 4th of July for Black Independence in Louisiana." On another occasion, John Brown stated that "to die for the freedom of his brothers, that is walking towards the Spiritual Life." Jesus appeared immediately after Brown and spoke positively of Brown's courage and abnegation. As if creating a political holy trinity, Lincoln appeared after Jesus and seemed to echo Brown: "He who dies for Humanity teaches the Glory."[58]

Republicanism was the best option because its egalitarian philosophy was based on a divine order and sacred rights instead of the old divine right of kings. Providence's "immutable law," according to a spirit, was "the solidarity of all beings." George Washington taught that the "stability of Government" was based on the wisdom of its laws and of its lawmakers. The result should be universal "Liberty" and "no privileged classes!" Seeking peace and attending to the needs of the masses were critical for fraternity. Equal civil and legal rights for all would be required for liberty, and for this reason, Lincoln and others frequently spoke of rights. Those who disregarded the equal rights of their brothers made "wild assumptions." Lincoln encouraged all to "acknowledge" the "legitimate rights" of their brothers, for those rights were "equal to yours." People should not force the poor and the outcasts to live as slaves. Instead, all should be united. A spirit named Simon reassured the Cercle Harmonique that he and other spirits were still with them working for the "Just Rights" that were "due for all!" Republicanism's promise of rights could help heal the country's wounds of war and slavery. The spirit of Georges Bally Dubuclet lamented the "glaring injustice" of the American slavery system. This Dubuclet was a member of Petit's extended family who moved from France to the United States but then, disgusted by slavery, quickly left the United States for Mexico. His disgust centered on how American "children of the same father" experienced much different lives in this "ungrateful country." The United States ignored some of its citizens' "just rights" and denied them their "enjoyment of the Republic." Remembering how appalled he was at slavery, his heart was "relieved" to see how Republican politics now helped "reduce suffering."[59]

The spirits' calls for republicanism sometimes directly referred to liberal politics or the Republican Party. The spirits wanted all to support the party of the people, and this began with children. Since politics often were learned at home, the children of the North and South needed to be taught republican values. A spirit named A. Dutillet promised the Cercle Harmonique that if parents raised their children "with liberal ideas" and taught them the truth—"the rights of everyone, love and charity for all"—then they would follow "the Route of the Just." The spirit Lunel remarked that a "desire" for "good" inspired a person to be "politically liberal" and "tolerant" of others' beliefs. The spirit of Joanni Questy hoped to see republican youth grow and later thrive in politics. Another spirit noted how a "clash of interests" and differing opinions on justice caused the "antagonism" between Republicans and Democrats. This spirit also differentiated between the "party of Injustice" and "the party much closer to Justice." In this description lies an inherent criticism of the Republican Party that, while better than the Redeemer Democrats, still needed to improve its policies and positions. The spirits encouraged Cercle Harmonique members to be good and true republicans in the United States and France. It was regrettable, the spirit of Virgil explained in 1860, that "selfishness" crippled "the generous efforts of Republicans." More "ardent patriots of the Universal Republic" would surface if it were not for humanity's tendency toward "selfishness and pride." Even if "the Republican Party" and various republican speakers, such as Alphonse de Lamartine and Victor Hugo, were imperfect, they were "better than these servile despots" reducing themselves "to the rank of a slave dominating other slaves." Virgil hoped all children would be "Republican."[60] Whether speaking of the Republicans in the Second Empire of France or of Republicans more globally, this promise of the Republican Party's ability to foster the "Universal Republic" was one that comforted the New Orleans Cercle Harmonique. And in a true "Universal Republic," categories like race finally would be seen as meaningless.

Race and Nation in the *New* American Republic

Unlike American politics and society, which based their hierarchies in part on racial difference, the spirits denied the ontology of race. Additionally, while the Cercle Harmonique's messages pointed to a race-less spirit world, many of their Spiritualist contemporaries believed that one's race remained with a person in the spiritual spheres.[61] Some American Spiritualists believed in white racial superiority too.[62] The racial hierarchy and racism of New Orleans and the United States illuminate why the Afro-Creole Spiritualists believed that when a spirit left its material body it also left its racial identity behind. In response to American white supremacy, the spirits taught that one's worth resided in his/her spirit and not the material, raced body. By looking forward to a spiritual world without race, the Cercle Harmonique revealed their views on racial identities. They believed that, in theory, a person's race had no real value, and this idea formed in a city and country where race defined and dictated one's status and experiences.

Both blacks and whites would be luminous in the spirit world because, in spirit form and before God, there were only "equal beings." One spirit noted that if Jesus had possessed a "black envelope [body]" and was "capped with wooly or crisped hair," he would have been "disowned by many." His race should not matter, but the spirits knew that in the material world it would have. Those still on earth had no idea what race Jesus was—whether he was "black, yellow, or white." Race marked one's material body but not one's spirit or soul. After death, when one left the material body, the spirit entered a race-less world. The spirit guides noted that race meant little in the spiritual spheres and, therefore, should hold little significance on earth. Antoine Dubuclet, likely the spirit of Petit's grandfather, explained that though his hair "looked black" on earth, his spirit manifested as his "real Being" in the spirit world. Confucius affirmed that there were "no different races" because all were "children of the same father." The "great lesson" of death was recognizing equality and solidarity. The "flags" of nations should be replaced with "the universal flag" of humanity. Lamennais agreed and explained that Spiritualism disregarded categories like "race" or "nationality."[63]

Though the spirits deemed race irrelevant, they were aware of the racial realities of the material world and the consequences of raced bodies. A martyr of the 1866 Mechanics' Institute Riot in New Orleans, Victor Lacroix, lamented how American society forced "the blacks, sons of the Republic" to "work as a flock of sheep in the fields." Those in power had decided to refuse their black brothers full rights and force them into "human bondage," but their "only crime was being black." Despite the dehumanizing aspect of slavery, African Americans had fought back "valiantly like lions." Fortunately, with emancipation a "new route" had emerged in American political and social culture that was granting "all the rights" to these "new citizens." The United States should provide "all the privileges" of a republic to each of "its children." The spirits encouraged New Orleanians to support fellow citizens of all racial backgrounds, but particularly those with darker skin. A message from R. Preaux Jr. concluded with the instructions, "Extend your hand to your black brother; do not reject him. He belongs to God the same as you. He is entitled to the same rights as you. Render justice to him, and fear that future one [God of Judgment?] which shall show to you your hatred and egotism."[64] Preaux instructed all to offer justice to blacks because the United States systematically denied it to them, both socially and culturally.

Though American culture and society denied racial equality, the spirits noted with joy the possibility of political egalitarianism and interracial solidarity. The spirit of Louisiana plantation owner Bernard de Marigny was happy to report, "The Black is on the rise!"—quite the exclamation for a former slave owner. He was not alone in his hopes for racial harmony. A spirit identified as "a black man, once" recited a poem to a Cercle Harmonique medium on a particularly busy day in October 1870. Though he was "Black in the land of America," his "hands" were "pure in the spirit-land." He implored the "White men of America" to put race aside and "Join the sons of Africa" in "love." He and other spirits endorsed racial unity as a step toward true republicanism and the progress of the Idea. According to Joseph Rey, the value of a Spiritualist came from her/his dedication to the Idea and justice, "despite the burden of the flesh he wears."[65] The world of the spirits was void of races and thus free of racism. The spirits and the Cercle Harmonique hoped the material world would come to imitate the spirit world's racial vacuum and its resulting solidarity.

The spirit of a slave named Jean Pierre explained that he was someone's "property" and was forced to call that someone "my master" because he possessed a "black envelope [body]." Pierre was harshly whipped and suffered. He "dreamed of hatred and vengeance" toward his master. Though angry during his life as a slave, he noted that upon his death—a death caused by the whip—all his "hatred" remained with his physical body. He saw "another myself," one "bright and shiny." Pierre was free and no longer known as "the slave Jean Pierre" but was now called "the Sublime One." He forgave the slave owner who whipped him to death. He knew that one day he would see the spirit of his former owner and promised that when the slave owner saw the "noble and sublime" spirit of his slave, he would feel shame. Pierre's message was followed by a spirit who lamented the crude manner in which Pierre's body had been laid to rest. His "funeral oration" was the complaint of his owner: "What is this body? Is this the dog negro? Bury it now!" Comparing black bodies with animals, this attitude was the "hideous face" of New Orleans before the Civil War.[66] But Pierre had escaped the racism of the material world when he left his black envelope behind.

The South's racial prejudices hardly ended with emancipation. While the spirit world rejoiced and "rang [bells] to announce to the world that human slavery disappeared from the [U.S.] Republic," many white Louisianans romantically began to reimagine and whitewash their pasts.[67] For some Creoles this consisted of a nostalgic overemphasis of *white* Creole importance throughout the antebellum period. In the wake of the Civil War, clarifying the boundary between black and white became more significant, making it impossible to accommodate "a pan-racial creolism."[68] The power of white supremacy even influenced white Creoles to redefine Creole identity. In the summer of 1873, the local French periodical *Le Moniteur* neatly and clearly stated the new identity binary in the city: "The moment has come for the sons of Louisiana to declare themselves. It is imperative that everyone choose to be either white or black. Two races are here: one superior, the other inferior . . . their separation is ABSOLUTELY necessary. Let us separate then, from this day forward, into two well-defined groups: the white group and the black group. The position will then be clear: White Louisiana or Black Louisiana."[69]

After the close of the Cercle Harmonique, the white Creole historian and former president of the Louisiana Historical Society Charles Gayarré began a campaign for Creole to be designated a white-only ethnic category.[70] To protect the sanctity of whiteness, he and others emphasized racial difference. And this was effective. In the mid-1880s, a German traveler observed that the color line was "sharply drawn" in New Orleans.[71] The Cercle Harmonique developed a racial outlook different than Gayarré and others. The spirits taught that race meant little as an identity marker and instead championed equality in the spirit world and in the material world. However, as the Mechanics' Institute Riot and the Battle of Liberty Place proved, attaining political and social equality in New Orleans was easier said than done.

The races of material bodies no longer existed in the spirit world, and instead the color of spirits typically was described as "bright." As mentioned before, the former slave Jean Pierre noted that while his body was "black," his new self was "bright and shiny." Lamennais explained that spirits possessed "luminous" bodies. The soul gave off a "radiant glow" in the spirit world and this glow illustrated one's "true value." The transformation of a spirit after death happened according to "the state of his soul" rather than according to physical appearance or social status. And one could be held accountable for the "state of his soul," unlike the color of one's skin. The soul appeared in the spiritual spheres "relative" to its spiritual "beauty or ugliness" in the material world. A spirit would manifest "more beautiful" in the higher spheres due to the spirit's dedication to "love," "charity," and "abnegation." This was especially true for a martyr. The victim of a violent and wrongful death arose "a Spirit bright and luminous, grand, and with sublime beauties and glories." In death, black bodies were replaced with bright spirits.[72]

According to the Cercle Harmonique's séance records, this emphasis on a spirit's light and its brightness meant that the spirit world was without race. As spirit guides Confucius and Lamennais taught, race truly meant nothing. However, lightness or brightness would seem to register visually as white. Thus, while the spirits described a race-less spirit world, it might be more accurate to identify the spiritual spheres as a world without a racial hierarchy. Instead of seeing spirits of different races, everyone appeared white. If the spirits' lightness was visually akin to whiteness, then this points to the overwhelming power of whiteness to present itself as neutral. Historians of American religion have begun to scrutinize how whiteness naturalizes itself in American religion and the study of American religious history.[73] However, whether the spirit world was without race as the spirits said or only void of a racial hierarchy, either case stressed the necessity of racial equality and racial solidarity in the material world.

The spirits taught that identity markers like race and nationality were superficial and no hierarchy should be based upon them. Slave owners and white supremacists later would feel shame for "their mistakes and their cruel oppressions against unfortunate beings whose only crime was the color of their skin." The spirits chastised supporters of slavery and segregation for how they "divided men." The spirit of W. R. Meadows proclaimed that he and other spirits would "unite them [all men] in a brotherhood, under a flag which knows not nationality, no race; but men, brothers!"[74] Humanity needed to shed itself of racial prejudice, and tied to this was nationalism and national exceptionalism. The Cercle Harmonique, though they resided in New Orleans, had responsibilities that went far beyond national borders. The following chapter will examine the Cercle Harmonique as part of the Atlantic world's age of revolutions. A Native American spirit named Poloah (whose appearance followed spirits named Pocahontas, Pacoha, and Piloho) was happy to report that the "peace pipe and tomahawk"—mementos "of barbarism"—had been "buried forever." While this message contained a negative view of Native American religions, it also expressed a universalizing sentiment. Poloah and other Native American spirits were now part of the enlightened "spiritual brotherhood" that included themselves, the "Chinese," and the "Hottentots." "Brothers" of all communities worked together under the "Grand Chief," meaning God.[75]

The spirits emphasized a fraternity that did not respect political borders. A person's background did not determine whether he or she would be a good "soldier of humanity," be he or she "a French, an Austrian, or a Russian." One's place of birth did not matter; decisions and actions did. A spirit simply identified as *L'Inconnu* (The Unknown) taught that once Americans extracted all prejudices from their hearts, they would realize that they were "citizens of the world, and not American citizens." They should consider "all children of the Globe" to be their brothers. Even Robert E. Lee instructed all to unite for "the harmony of the races, of the nationalities in this country!"[76] While nationalities and racial differences ceased to exist in the spirit world, they still shaped everyday American life.

"Praise Jesus and Lincoln"[77]: U.S. Celebrities, America's Past, and America's Destiny

Before the end of Reconstruction and while Afro-Creole hopes for a spiritual republic on earth still flourished, certain spirits who could be considered U.S. political celebrities visited the séance table and brought validation to the Cercle Harmonique. Montezuma, Pocahontas, and Lorenzo Dow, as mentioned in chapter 1, were among the famous figures at the séance table. The presence of these and other celebrity spirits, particularly Abraham Lincoln and John Brown, bestowed an air of authority on the spiritual network of the Cercle Harmonique. Other spirits extolled various spiritual celebrities as champions of freedom and the Idea and thus confirmed what the Cercle Harmonique already knew: Their heroes endorsed the same goals. Those figures most often praised by the spirits were Lincoln and Brown, followed by George Washington and various local martyrs. "Washington! Lincoln! Grant!" the spirit of Mechanics' Institute Riot martyr Victor Lacroix shouted in one short message, followed by "Fraternité! Liberté! Egalite!" The spirit of French poet Jacques Delille noted how Lincoln, with the "stroke of a pen," proclaimed freedom; Brown had advanced that freedom with his death; and the "sword of Grant" helped secure victory for the Union. Together John Brown and Jesus worked for the triumph of moral ideas and the progress of equality. Another spirit cited additional lovers of freedom such as Robespierre, Moses, Luther, Calvin, Swedenborg, Diderot, and Volney who stood as "apostles" of the revolution.[78] The invocation of these historical figures reinforced the Cercle Harmonique's emplacement in a prestigious spiritual genealogy.

The chosen celebrities of the Cercle Harmonique worked together for a common goal—the victory of the Idea in the United States. The spirit Ambroise provided descriptions for various political figures that identified their relationship to the Idea. Washington would always be the "high majestic figure representing the march of ideas," and Lincoln would be remembered by humanity as "the victim sacrificed by Error and Rage of the enemies of Justice." Booth, on the other hand, was infamous for "wanting to stop the relentless march of Progress." Brown represented "the faith in God and the good law." Napoleon the First served as the synonym for "despotism and unbridled ambition."[79] Celebrities in the séance records also included American political founders Thomas Jefferson and George Washington, and their presence at the séance table is not surprising. The Cercle Harmonique possessed an affinity with some of America's founders in their thinking on democracy and providence. Bishop James Madison, cousin to the fourth president, wrote of "the divine principles of liberty, equality, and fraternity." Madison believed that the new American republic would be the first "Republic of Virtue" on earth—a real city of God.[80] Similarly, the Cercle Harmonique hoped that their nation would fulfill its promise and destiny and become a place where all were equal.

Lincoln was the most celebrated of all by the spirits, and he continued to work for the nation's best interest after his death. The figure of Lincoln memorialized at the séance table was a glorified version of the president, remembered as a warrior for equality who continued to fight. Lincoln's presence meant the Cercle Harmonique was not alone in their struggle. He "and other workers who, being more enlightened and advanced here, devote themselves to the work of liberating the Great Republic from its shameful stain." While the Afro-Creole Spiritualists on earth were breaking "all chains which tie you to Evil," Lincoln and others were breaking "those chains which have been forged for your political enslavement." A joint message from Ambroise and Saint Vincent de Paul suggests that the Cercle Harmonique celebrated Lincoln's birthday. The message included an explanation for Lincoln's greatness: His soul recognized the horrors of slavery. Additionally, his willingness and courage to speak out, as seen in the Emancipation Proclamation, and his decision to step into "this fratricidal struggle" were admirable. The spirits went as far as to call Lincoln "one of the most brilliant figures in the country," the "Torch of Liberty," and even the "American christ." In contrast to these glowing appellations, Jefferson Davis, as the leader of an "Immoral Republic" with its "cornerstone" of slavery, was the "American Judas." Another spirit explained that just as Jesus showed the world love and charity, Lincoln performed a parallel act and "honored his nation."[81] Indeed, his martyrdom for the cause of freedom was a frequent focus of the spirits.

The spirit of Lamennais also likened Lincoln to Jesus. Both suffered for their progressive perspectives, but righteous "struggles are necessary, be they moral or physical." While Jesus died on the cross "to prove to humanity the power of his teaching," Lincoln succumbed to the bullet of an assassin to show the danger of "pride and lust for domination." Lincoln "sealed with his precious blood, the funeral stone which must cover Human Slavery." Jesus "died for Humanity," while Lincoln "was sacrificed for wishing to liberate the black race, subdued under a degrading yoke by brute force." Thus, Jesus and Lincoln fulfilled analogous roles. Lamennais concluded his message saying,

"Praise Jesus and Lincoln: one will regenerate humanity, the other the U.S. Republic."[82] What Jesus set into motion for humanity—salvation—Lincoln did for the United States, and having the spirit who died for the greater good of the country on their side gave the Cercle Harmonique courage and confirmation in their struggle.

Lincoln was a very active spirit as well, and his messages always referred to slavery, politics, freedom, or a combination of them. Lincoln encouraged the circle to continue despite political and social setbacks. Though "the monstrous oligarchy . . . wanted and still wants to crush out the germ of civil rights for the dark skinned children," the members of that oligarchy later would meditate on "their horrible crimes and their depravity of manners." Similar to how spirits of the French Revolution rebelled against the ancien régime, Lincoln's spirit struggled with an oligarchy, and because he fought slavery, he had a better spiritual existence. Lincoln and other members of the "beautiful, spiritual, liberating army" helped humanity's progress "despite obstacles." For his part in this struggle, Lincoln was "happy" and enjoyed "the reward" of "my Emancipation Proclamation, which freed the new citizens and saved the republic." In addition to fast tracking Lincoln's retribution, the Emancipation Proclamation also saved the soul of the nation. "Inscribe on your banners," the former president commanded, "'Victory is ours'!"[83]

On the national day of Thanksgiving declared by his successor, Andrew Johnson, on 7 December 1865, Lincoln came to the Cercle Harmonique to celebrate freedom. "My brothers," he began, "today is the day of fasting, of prayer, and thanks for the peace and freedom that you have acquired at a price worthy of torture." It was a day to honor the breaking of "the chains of slavery." Though the war had been long, no one should be surprised by the Union victory, as "freedom must reign over all the earth, because it originated in heaven." Lincoln assured them that he would "always be here to defend [freedom]." Part of this message was a criticism of the racialized element of slavery. To make his point, Lincoln, in a style many other spirits used as well, posed a rhetorical question to the circle: "Is it your fault if God created his children with different colors?" Lincoln's message, the séance record reported, was "immediately" followed by the appearance of another spirit who wanted to chime in on the topic. Saint Vincent de Paul wanted his "dear children" to have courage, for they had gained their "freedom with blood."[84]

By embracing Lincoln's spirit as a political guide, the Cercle Harmonique joined many other Americans in memorializing the assassinated president and constructing a Lincoln to fit their needs. Lincoln was both an obvious spirit guide for the Afro-Creoles and a complicated one.[85] While Frederick Douglass continued to see Lincoln as "preeminently the white man's President, entirely devoted to the welfare of white men," the Lincoln of the séance table was the glorified Lincoln after his apotheosis.[86] The Cercle Harmonique's spirit guide known as Abraham Lincoln was shaped by its members' situation and their desire for civil and legal equality. In addition to the Afro-Creole Spiritualists, many African Americans began to see Lincoln as "slavery's enemy" and "America's greatest president."[87] Because of the Emancipation Proclamation and his assassination, in death Lincoln became a beloved martyr remembered as a symbol for the Idea.

The spirits of Lincoln and radical abolitionist John Brown often came to the Cercle Harmonique the same day, almost as if the presence of one called the other. They held similar positions in the circle's spiritual network since both were considered martyrs for the cause of liberty. According to the spirit of Brown, the "freedom of the people" had two main components—"freedom of political and religious powers." The most "perfect" government was built on "the consent of men," "the true faith," and "harmony of mankind." This was how the republic of spirits worked and it was how the material world should operate. Following Brown's message, Lincoln appeared and promised that the "crowns of kings" would fall before "the upward march of humanity." The chains of "physical slavery" had broken and "human progress" continued. The spirits often lauded Brown and Lincoln in tandem as well. The spirit of Joanni Questy praised "the great and sublime figure of Lincoln" and "the majestic form" of Brown. He also asked the country the rhetorical question, "Are you not ashamed of Booth?" Revolutions by those who carried "the spiritual banner," like Brown with his sacrifice or "Grand Lincoln" with the Emancipation Proclamation, brought the Idea into the social and political structures of the earthly world. These were fighters who dreamed of freedom and a world without "chains." According to another spirit, John Brown's choices and actions made him a "noble" man and an "Apostle of Peace and Love." He fought for "the magic word of Freedom!!!!!!!"[88]

The presence of celebrity spirit guide Brown at the Cercle Harmonique séance table coincided with the spirits' view on slavery: that it was an evil to be expunged from the material world. Before his death, Brown reportedly justified his actions at Harper's Ferry with "the Golden Rule," saying, "I pity the poor in bondage that have none to help them: that is why I am here; not to gratify any personal animosity, revenge, or vindictive spirit. It is my sympathy with the oppressed and wronged."[89] His spirit retained this opinion and even praised himself for his beliefs and actions. He reported that "Brown triumphed" for he was willing to tell "the truth," meaning liberty for all. He now resided on a "bright and shining Pedestal" because he supported "the idea of the Freedom Lovers!" Though he was executed for upholding truth in the material world, in the spiritual spheres he was rightfully "recognized" for having "worked for Good and Justice."[90]

Brown was proud to have died for the cause of black liberty. He told the Cercle Harmonique, "I was battling against an evil . . . black brothers were attached to the plow, as beasts of burden." But his fight ended in his death. "I paid, strangled with a rope . . . And I am free from your atrocities; Brown is luminous!" Having made clear his support for political equality and referencing the relationship between the execution of his physical body and black freedom, he told the medium that "this gibbet and this body of a hanged man, it is the Flag of Equality that you have hoisted yourselves to the top of the Mast of Liberty." The message articulated support for the circle, but it was also a rebuke to former Confederates and advocates of white supremacy. "The Republic is marching on," Brown proclaimed, "with gigantic steps, towards the Union of the Races." Violence will not have "the force to stop the progress of the Citizen." Though his message came to the Cercle Harmonique, he warned, "Brown and Lincoln are contemplating the work of God; and you, poor brothers, you are marching in the darkness of your hatred and shame." Shortly thereafter, during the same meeting, beloved Lincoln arrived at the table also with a message directed at white proponents of racial violence: "Like me, thou hast killed him [Brown]; but the Idea has progressed. Beware! Thy hate blinds you; let thee be enlightened by the Idea! A man may disappear! But the Idea never stops advancing."[91] Reconstruction Louisiana was a violent place and created martyrs for the Idea. To sacrifice oneself for egalitarian republicanism, for progress, and for liberty was something to be admired. It was better to die trying to make the United States more like the spiritual republic than live as a coward.

Though many American abolitionists had disagreed with Brown's violent approach, he quickly became "an irresistible symbol in the fight against slavery."[92] His image "transcended immediate political, partisan, self-interested discourse, linking to core conceptions of the nation's values."[93] With his death, he became a martyred hero. According to one story, on his way to the gallows Brown met a black woman holding her child. She blessed Brown, and in return Brown kissed her child. This exchange of affection, mass-produced as a lithograph by Currier and Ives in 1860, became a popular image depicting Brown's love for the black race. However, not all saw Brown as a helpful rallying point, let alone a positive figure. Americans had split opinions of Brown, and so, in memory, his identity was similar to that of Haiti's Toussaint Louverture. He was either a symbol of equality to be lauded or a specter of racial violence to be feared. To some in the South, Brown was "satanic."[94] Conversely, his spirit that advised the Cercle Harmonique was more akin to the Brown of Henry David Thoreau's 1860 piece, "A Plea for Captain John Brown": an admirable and moral fighter of injustice.[95] For both Rey and Thoreau, Brown was a man of just action.

More than national celebrities appeared to Rey and others; regional celebrities appeared too. Beloved local black Civil War soldiers John Crowder and André Cailloux were frequent spirit guides. Cailloux's funeral was glorious, as mentioned previously, and the memory of his bravery lasted after the captain was laid to rest. When the *New Orleans Tribune* sought the establishment of "a permanent delegation of colored men at Washington to advocate the cause of the colored people of this State" in 1865, the publication did so to ensure the legacy and liberties of "the posterity and relatives of Caillou[x], Crowder . . ."[96] On another occasion the *New Orleans Tribune* called upon the memory of Crowder and Cailloux to inspire others to fight for civil and legal rights.[97] Their spirits did the same. The spirit of Crowder reported that he was happy to have "joined the worthy sons of Liberty" and enroll "under the Banner of Freedom." Crowder instructed those on earth to "throw away prejudices" and "be true to your brothers as you must be to God." Spiritualists should fight for "moral and intellectual advancement" and march toward progress with "Light and happiness for all" inscribed on their banners. "Give a man power and money," Crowder warned, and "you will see what a great change" in his actions toward even "his most intimate friends." Prayers and hopes for monetary success indicated the power of materialism and, thus, worried and bothered the spirits. Cailloux's spirit told the Afro-Creole Spiritualists to be "ready" and "faithful to the Post." He assured the Cercle Harmonique that he continued to look after them and care for them in a "very brotherly" manner. He also wished he had been a Spiritualist during his earthy life instead of remaining "sadly indifferent" about the practice. With his spiritual wisdom, Cailloux affirmed that it was "beautiful to fight for the cause of justice." Indeed, he was happy to "die for the holy cause of Liberty" and "break the terrible chains of human slavery." Other spirits also recognized Cailloux's glory. According to a message from John Brown, the

Captain's "great heart" and "great soul" wanted to give pardon to General Robert E. Lee.[98] Though Lee commanded the Confederate army, the wisdom Cailloux gained in his new existence in the spiritual world, along with his compassion, urged him to forgive his former enemies.

The political celebrity spirits who came to the séance table were always figures the Cercle Harmonique considered supporters of liberty, republicanism, and equality. Another spirit at the séance table, J. W. Hutchinson, may have matched a celebrity still alive at the time of the communications.[99] This spirit was most likely either John W. Hutchinson or Jesse Hutchinson of the Hutchinson Family Singers.[100] The Hutchinson family was familiar with both republicanism and Spiritualism, as the older brothers of the family, including both Jesse and John, became Spiritualists.[101] The Hutchinson Family Singers were dedicated to nineteenth-century reform issues, most notably abolition. John edited the *Hutchinson's Republican Songster* in 1860 in honor of, as the title page exclaimed, "Lincoln and Liberty!"[102] The spirit of J. W. Hutchinson communicated one of the few spirit messages recorded in verse, either as a poem or a song. The poetic message celebrates the "Light," and it tells how the spirit delighted in being in the spirit world with God and John Brown.[103] Because of the songster's emphasis on republicanism and Lincoln, it is not a stretch to conclude the Cercle Harmonique was familiar with the *Songster* and, thus, identified the spirit as one of the brothers.[104]

Many of the celebrity spirits who visited the Cercle Harmonique delivered messages about the United States' political destiny. Calls for the United States to live up to its claim that "all men were created equal" frequented the séance table. The spirits taught that United States had a particular destiny to fulfill. In this way, they echoed Frederick Douglass's famous speech "What to a slave is the Fourth of July?" Douglass chastised the country, "America is false to the past, false to the present, and solemnly binds herself to be false to the future."[105] For Douglass, inequality, namely in the form of slavery, was the reason for America's deceit. For the spirits, inequality stood in the way of America reaching her destiny. According to Saint Vincent de Paul, the United States "owe[d] refuge to the oppressed of the Earth, without distinction of races, religions, nationalities." To fulfill the American promise of equality, the United States should strive to become more like the spiritual spheres. The world of the spirits was more perfect than the world of earthly man, which meant it should be emulated on earth. Cailloux affirmed that the Cercle Harmonique's spiritual "brothers" were surrounded by "equality." Similarly, Ambroise taught the circle that "Your world is the glimpse of God's Creation; ours, the complement of his work."[106] Even if the material world could never quite mimic the spirit world, it was the task of Spiritualists like the Cercle Harmonique to try to turn the United States into the perfect republic.

America's future ideally would be one marked by liberty and freedom, like the spirit world. Brown promised that the "Oligarchy of your country will be defeated" and the "Truth of Rights for all" would be universally recognized. He and other "souls of Progress" were working "to bring the triumph of Justice and Equality" to earth. The Cercle Harmonique could "count on us!" Following this message from Brown, the spirit of recently deceased radical Republican leader Charles Sumner appeared. Though his body had died, he was "still living and full of the strength of my Just Cause!" The nation could continue to rely on his efforts. Everyone still would hear him and heed his words, from those living "in the Castle" to those in "the log cabin." He assured the Spiritualists that the spirits continued to fight slavery in its physical and moral forms. On the heels of Sumner's spirit came the spirit of Louisiana celebrity O. J. Dunn, who reported that he united "with others to comply with the Desires of good to see Peace and Harmony within the Land!" He instructed the group not to falter; "triumph is ours." Closing this sequence of politically oriented spirits was one identified as "L'Official," who echoed the previous messages. "Yes! Victory is ours!" Nothing—not the "Dagger, the Pistol, powder, shot canister"—could "prevent the success which will show Human Rights perserving [sic] all along the line."[107] America eventually would fulfill its destiny to be the material complement of the spiritual republic.

To struggle and bring the United States in line with the Idea and its true destiny was noble and honorable work. A group message from three spirits (Cailloux, J. P. Lana, and Anguies Pédéslaux) told the circle to "work with courage" because "the reward will be great for the noble children of Progress, who seek Truth." Thus, "Forward march, humanitarian soldier(s)."[108] A spirit named P. B. reported that "Progress" could extinguish "certain political and social prejudices of the country."[109] This hope for America's republican future and the spirits' call for the Cercle Harmonique to work for that future gave Afro-Creole Spiritualism a postmillennial flavor. Though covering an earlier time period, historian Ruth Bloch's *Visionary Republic: Millennial Themes in American Thought* demonstrated how millennialism "contributed to the formation of revolutionary consciousness" and "provided the main structure of meaning through which contemporary events were linked to an exalted image of an ideal world."[110] Though Bloch and many other historians of millennialism in America focus on the prophecies of the Bible, millennialism was a diffuse force in American culture.

In its clearest iteration, American millennialism presents itself as the anticipation for the thousand-year reign of Christ. While premillennialism, made popular by dispensationalism, teaches that humans will have no role in inaugurating Christ's millennial reign, postmillennialism promotes benevolent causes and work as a way to bring the Kingdom of God on earth. Postmillennialism flourished in the antebellum spiritual hothouse and frequently was linked to reform. For example, many abolitionists saw their cause as a postmillennial one and believed that, by ridding the country of slavery, America would find better favor with God.[111] The Cercle Harmonique looked forward to another kind of millennial future, though instead of inaugurating Christ's millennial reign on earth, the Afro-Creole Spiritualists worked toward making the material world more like the spirit world. To fix the material world, the United States needed to subscribe to egalitarian republicanism and regard all its citizens as equals. Religious and civic order would come about when the material world became a more harmonious place.

At the center of the Cercle Harmonique's quasi-millennial quest was, of course, Spiritualism. The spirit of their "friend" Henry Clay believed that Spiritualism could help the United States and the world reach their destinies. Spiritualism taught him the "love" that was "due to the great human family." The lessons learned by the Cercle Harmonique were not meant for them "in particular, but for all!" Clay's spirit believed that "Man must contribute to the great philosophical work of the Improvement of Humanity" and that the circle's involvement in Spiritualism allowed them to "develop accordingly." He also spoke in support of black political advancement, likely in apology for owning slaves and constructing laws that sustained slavery, such as the Compromise of 1850 and its fugitive slave laws. No one could prevent the "elevation" of blacks and their "ascension to the greatest honorary posts in the country." Clay's spirit supported the political progress of blacks in part because they had earned it; they had brought "together the different parts of the Union with [their] blood which has been spilt in profusion." Not only would African Americans rise politically and gain governmental positions, their "unquestionable rights will command authoritatively" and their "vote will weigh heavily in the seal of the destiny of the nation; and, believe me, it will be appreciated and solicited." Their participation "in everything" would make the United States "greater than ever." Though the polls frequently were sites of race violence in New Orleans and Louisiana, those sitting at Rey's séance table could be certain of their "moral enfranchisement."[112] The guarantee of black rights was part of America's fate.

The spirits lauded President Washington as the "Father of the Country," and therefore, the political and social destiny of the country was wrapped up with his legacy. Washington's spirit also came to the circle. He celebrated the Union victory and the resulting hope for real racial justice. In a séance group conversation where the medium recorded brief back-to-back messages, Washington came to celebrate the Confederate defeat and lament Lincoln's assassination. "Lincoln, the martyr soldier of peace falls. The Sword of tyrant weighed in the balance, the Rebellion is dead." Later, Washington returned and shouted to the medium, "Rejoice!" "Vive l'Égalité!" and "Vive la fraternite!" "Liberty," the former president explained, "is not an empty word" and would triumph along with fraternity, equality, and justice. Though he was the country's first president, Washington chose not to highlight his national pride. He claimed to be "not French nor Prussian, not African nor Italian, but men; brothers. I'm not American, I am of Humanity; Its flag is mine!" While his message did not highlight his status as the nation's first president, the significance of his position was not lost on the Afro-Creole Spiritualists who received his message. Having the support not only of Abraham Lincoln and Andrew Jackson but also of Washington further justified the work and message of the Cercle Harmonique and provided the support and validation denied by many of the circle's peers. Lamennais compared 4 July 1776 to the birth of Jesus, as both began new eras in humanity. He explained, "Jesus engraved the beneficent seal of his beautiful doctrine, in the heart of humanity; and which announced the Luminous Star that Washington made to shine, in order to direct Nations towards the haven of Safety—the Universal Republic."[113]

On George Washington's birthday in 1869 (22 February), Thomas Jefferson appeared at the Cercle Harmonique's table for his only message. Washington's birthday was to be celebrated, as it marked the birth of a man with a God-given "mission to create a new nation and a new government" and "a new people" shaped by his "political ideas." However, this new nation had not yet fulfilled its destiny. It had a dark stain on its history: the "incomprehensible abuse" of the slaveholding class. In perhaps a reference to his own relationship with Sally Hemings, Jefferson lamented how slave owners had treated slave girls as "toys" for their own pleasure. Members of this "aristocracy" did not realize that the harm they caused blacks and "poor whites" hurt

Nouveau Washington, il domi-
nera ses ennemis !

Comme lui, vainqueur des ennemis de son pays, il les forcera
à lui rendre justice et à recon-
naitre que, s'il fut terrible en
guerre, il fut un père pour tous.

Patience, frères, et sachez attendre
L'homme *d'État se dévoilera,
l'homme de guerre disparaitra.
La paix succédera à la guerre,
la tourmente révolutionnaire se
dissipera; les turbulents seront mis
à la raison, et peu à peu le
calme succédera à l'orage,

suscité par les derniers soupirs de
l'oligarchie du sud, qui s'éteindra
bientôt sous l'administration sage
et honnête du Grand Conquérant,
qui a pris pour devise : La Paix !...

Jefferson

Conclusion of the message from Thomas Jefferson, 22 February 1869. Courtesy of the
René Grandjean Collection, Louisiana and Special Collections Department, Earl K.
Long Library, University of New Orleans.

themselves more than it did their victims. However, with the defeat of the Confederacy, "a shining new era for the Young Republic" began. The "tree of domination and injustice" was defeated, and "the darkness" that had "invaded the Republic" was disappearing "before the bright light brought by Justice." Finally, the "last sighs of the oligarchy of the South" were over, and now the United States could be the world's great republic. The country's "new citizens" (freed people) would defend her "with more courage" and ensure that she fulfilled her promise "to shelter the oppressed and disinherited of the earth."[114] According to Jefferson, America's destiny was wrapped up with the Idea, and in a parallel way, a contemporary of the Cercle Harmonique, American writer Walt Whitman, agreed. In *Democratic Vistas* (1871) Whitman referenced "the democratic republican principle," which the United States, above all other nations, would see develop to its full potential.[115] Whether termed the "democratic republican principle" or the Idea, this political philosophy was America's true self and destiny.

The nation's promise of freedom garnered the spirits' interest simultaneously with the nation's dark past with slavery. The Civil War, while regrettable, was an important step to bringing the U.S. republic more in line with the republic of the spirit world. The Cercle Harmonique found comfort in knowing that their racial identity bore no spiritual consequence even though it dictated so much of their lives in the southern United States. America's destiny was to be the most perfect republic on earth, but the spirits advising the Cercle Harmonique did not limit themselves to national borders. The identities of the Afro-Creole Spiritualists' spirit guides reflected an international family who paid close attention to the Atlantic world's age of revolutions. Republicanism and the Idea were global.

CHAPTER FIVE

The Spiritual Republic in the Atlantic Age of Revolutions

The spirit of a universal republicanism, richly impregnated with grand and philanthropic objects, and contemplating in its sweep the universal liberty and happiness of man, is frequently arrested in its flight from heart to heart, surrounded by the soldiers of the king, bound in chains and hurried to the dark retreats of despotic incarceration.

—Andrew Jackson Davis, *The Great Harmonia, Vol. III: The Seers*

Republics have produced great men.

—Spirit of Robespierre to the Cercle Harmonique, 24 February 1869

Spiritualism is the solution of all questions of justice and Equity. With spiritualism, the spirit-world has its raison d'être. Spiritualism is the liberation of the Spirit of the material to the spirit-world, freedom of mind gained.

—Spirit of Pierre-Jean de Béranger to the Cercle Harmonique, 17 January 1872

In May 1872 a spirit named Robert Preaux likened the United States to the "wife I love" and France to the mother he remembered "with delight." Like a mother providing the foundational ideals a child needed to grow, France offered the "bold principles" that supported republics. The "spirit of '93," meaning the French Revolution, shined everywhere, but Preaux thought it seemed to flourish best in "the heart of America . . . amidst a people who have already shown its progress." A Creole born on the island of Guadeloupe, Preaux's spirit proclaimed to now wave a "flag for Humanity."[1] Race, birth, or privilege should not divide people. Rather, brothers across the world were entitled to "the same rights everywhere and in everything." With the spirit of '93 in her heart and Spiritualism as her religion, America could be "the torch" and shine with brilliance.[2] The ideas of the French Revolution were felt in the wider Atlantic world and repeated by the spirits in the séance books of the Cercle Harmonique. Afro-Creoles could hear their social and political goals echo in the messages from the invisible world of the spirits—the call for harmony, desire for progress, the triumph of humanity, the need for moral and just leaders, the fight against despotism, fair political representation, and a voice for the people. The French revolutionary motto "Liberté, Egalité, Fraternité" resonated in the recorded messages. Spirits from the Atlantic age of revolutions appeared at the séance table, and they encouraged religious liberty, freethinking, and progress. The ideals of the French Revolution, though ethereal, were malleable and would be revitalized and reinvigorated by the Cercle Harmonique. The Afro-Creole Spiritualists hoped to bring the French Revolution's promises of universal liberty to their immediate environment—a place that denied Spiritualism's truth of luminous equality. Spiritualism's ability to mediate the memory of the French Revolution and its promises for a republican society offered answers to the politics and violence of postwar New Orleans. Additionally, this memory of the French Revolution's legacy took place in a city that also was part of a wider Atlantic world and Caribbean world.

Examining the Cercle Harmonique in the Atlantic and Caribbean worlds adds a transnational chapter to the story of American Spiritualism. Spiritualism regularly traversed the boundaries between the material and immaterial and the divide between life and death. Afro-Creole Spiritualism added passage over national borders. In American religious history Spiritualism is depicted as a U.S. religion, but in New Orleans it was more than that. The influence of the French Revolution, Haitian Revolution, and spirits from French history and literary culture on the Cercle Harmonique provides another angle on the question of New Orleans's nineteenth-century "Americanization." Generally, the historical paradigm of Louisiana's Americanization process asserts that after the Louisiana Purchase, an Anglo-Protestant worldview assumed power in the city.[3] Situating the Cercle Harmonique in an Atlantic world focused on the nodes of France, Haiti, and New Orleans offers another viewpoint of the city's Americanization process. For Rey and his fellow Spiritualists, the spirit world never would be fully Americanized by an Anglo-Protestant outlook, and the spirits continued to provide perspectives that challenged the material world around them. The principles of liberté, egalité, fraternité, and république gave the Afro-Creole Spiritualists a transnational orientation, and so this chapter takes the Cercle Harmonique into another circle—the global.

The Cercle Harmonique operated within a dual-layered Atlantic frame as part of both Paul Gilroy's black Atlantic and the broader Atlantic age of revolutions. With its "webbed networks" and transnational and intercultural networks, Gilroy's black Atlantic transcended any direct relationships between diasporic homes and the African homeland. The black Atlantic was a fluid and dynamic space, and thus absolute conceptions of national or ethnic identity do not sufficiently theorize the black Atlantic. The black Atlantic's "desire to transcend both the structures of the nation state and the constraints of ethnicity and national particularity" also materialized in the séance records.[4] The Atlantic and Caribbean worlds possessed a racial and ethnic hierarchy that owed much to the slave trade, but it was an ambiguous and fluid hierarchy, particularly during the eighteenth century when the Afro-Creole class or caste first developed. The anti-aristocratic, antimonarchical, pro-popular sovereignty, and pro-natural rights language of the Atlantic age of revolutions in the late eighteenth and early nineteenth century reverberated in the messages from the Cercle Harmonique's spirit guides.[5] New Orleans's location in the Atlantic world cannot be overlooked, as ideas about race, nation, and politics from the Atlantic world continued to develop in the pages of the Cercle Harmonique's séance records.

With this understanding of Atlantic history in mind, this chapter examines Afro-Creole Spiritualism as part of an Atlantic world hinged upon New Orleans, France, and the Caribbean. The Cercle Harmonique's practice included spirits of the French Revolution, European Enlightenment, and Haitian history in their spiritual network, and the presence of these spiritual identities in the Cercle Harmonique's network demonstrates how the local practice of Spiritualism in New Orleans existed in a larger Atlantic world. Though they were not atop the racial hierarchy, Afro-Creoles were not passive in the creation of New Orleans religious cultures; instead they were active in the workings of the Atlantic world and Atlantic world culture.[6] Additionally, they called upon powers from beyond their immediate New Orleans context. By including the spirits of *philosophes* and other revolutionary thinkers like Rousseau, Voltaire, Robespierre, and French priest Lamennais in their spirit network and through their rhetorical work performed in the séances, the Afro-Creole Spiritualists created bonds with their admired revolutionary French and Haitian spirits.[7] The Atlantic world's age of revolutions continued in the practice of the Cercle Harmonique and their creation of a spiritual republic.

"Men are born and remain free and equal in rights"[8]: French Revolutionary Thought

While the Cercle Harmonique did not participate in the French Revolution, the ideas within the revolution affected them deeply, and in their practice they remembered the glory of its intervention in history. That intervention, a reworking of society based on the people rather than the aristocracy, was one the Cercle Harmonique sought for New Orleans and the United States more generally. Messages that echoed the broad scope of republicanism and spirits from the revolutionary era were common throughout the pages of the circle's séance books. The southern aristocracy—white, slave owning, and hungry for power—was the new ancien régime. While they, like France's ancien régime, believed themselves to be on top of a God-given hierarchy, Afro-Creoles, in manners similar to Robespierre and Voltaire, thought otherwise.[9] The continually developing power of white supremacy in Louisiana following the Union occupation of the city and through Reconstruction was the local inheritor and actor of this southern aristocracy. The Cercle Harmonique, with the help of the spirits, saw themselves as fighting for the people against this aristocracy. "Old Societies," the spirit of a white Creole slaveholder told the Cercle Harmonique, would have to "collapse and disappear" in order to make way for those built on harmonious ideas.[10] The spirits wanted all to "unite" for "a common good" rather than be divided over economic, social, or political issues.[11]

Much more than the storming of the Bastille in 1789, the French Revolution sparked a new way of thinking about political systems and the organization of society. The Declaration of the Rights of Man and of the Citizen was adopted in 1789, but it was rooted in older ideas.[12] The politics and social organization of the ancien régime were picked apart by *philosophes*, those writers who used new Enlightenment ideas to question old knowledge and old institutions.[13] Questioning the authority and "reasonableness" of institutions was a significant part of new revolutionary thought.[14] Influential to the revolution were earlier eighteenth-century thinkers, and for good reason: Voltaire criticized the Catholic Church, Montesquieu contrasted despotism with liberty, and Rousseau looked to the natural world to find the foundations of a just society. Voltaire's witticisms, his calls to "crush the infamous," and his historical focus on social forces and culture identified him as a thinker who advocated reform.[15] As a spirit Voltaire taught the Cercle Harmonique that those in positions of undeserved power would tremble in fear of the progress they could "feel" happening around the world.[16]

Montesquieu's *The Spirit of Laws* (1748) was influential to participants in both the French Revolution and the American Revolution. Examining the relationship between types of societies and types of governments, Montesquieu wanted to uncover how governments and societies could best secure liberty. Republican governments, in contrast to monarchies or despotic empires, required "virtue" as a primary principle.[17] Montesquieu contended that to understand a government or nation, one must examine the motivations and workings of its people, religion, economics, and legal system. For Montesquieu, and other founders of modern liberalism such as John Locke, many of society's "political ills" were attributable to "the theological casts of its politics." One of the ultimate goals of the work of Montesquieu and other *philosophes* was "to create peaceful and prosperous regimes in which freedom rather than salvation would be the primary political care."[18] Freedom was not limited to religious beliefs and practices. Additionally, slavery should be abolished. In chapter 15 of Montesquieu's *Spirit of Laws*, he wrote, "the state of slavery is in its own nature bad."

For Montesquieu, there was an essential connection between liberty and republican governments. The spirit of Montesquieu echoed this in communications with the Cercle Harmonique. Montesquieu's spirit taught that recognizing "the rights" of all needed to be "the fundamental basis" for society.[19] Managing liberty was not a simple task though. Democratic republics could be corrupted by the "spirit of inequality" or the "spirit of extreme equality." In the *Spirit of Laws*, he seemed to favor a federative republic over other kinds of political organisms, as long as the spirit of moderation kept the leaders in check.[20] According to the ideas of Montesquieu, despotism had two primary forms: governmental and commercial, or as one scholar has put it, "monarchs and merchants."[21] Both were caused by greed, but one manifested in political systems while the other in self-interest and luxury. These two manifestations of despotism certainly could be interdependent, as seen in the southern oligarchy and the Redeemer Democrats of the late Reconstruction.

The work of Rousseau, an influential figure to Robespierre, was more egalitarian in orientation than Voltaire or Montesquieu.[22] Rousseau's *Discourse on Inequality* (1753) identified private property as the source of moral inequality, wealth, and warfare. He preferred the era of the "savage" or natural man but recognized that a return to this was not feasible or realistic, so in response he offered *The Social Contract* (1762). Though "man is born free," Rousseau lamented, "everywhere he is in chains."[23] His writing on the social contract sought to fix this by emphasizing the need of the community to protect members equally. While John Locke's social contract was established between a government and the governed, Rousseau's was between an individual and the larger collective.[24] Rousseau's appeal to Afro-Creoles included his appraisal of slavery. "From whatever angle one looks at things," he argued, "the right to slavery is null, not only because it is illegitimate, but because it is absurd and meaningless. These words slavery and right are contradictory."[25] Not only was Rousseau radical in his writings, but as a spirit, Rousseau was not shy about responding to the naysayers of the Cercle Harmonique's social and political perspectives. Those who called "the Sublime Idea" nothing more than "Insanity" and equated generosity with "stupidity" were "blind." Only a person who could not properly see and understand humanity would "deny the Light" carried by the Spiritualist brothers.[26]

The influence of Rousseau's social contract between individual and collective can be seen in France's 1789 Declaration of the Rights of Man and of the Citizen. This document proved very influential around the Atlantic world, particularly in Haiti and New Orleans. One spirit visiting the Cercle Harmonique instructed those on earth to let people "speak of rights."[27] The preamble to the Declaration identified "ignorance, neglect, or contempt of the rights of man" to be "the sole cause of public calamities and of corruption of governments." In response, this document's goal was to name the universal rights of all humanity.[28] The first article stated, "men are born and remain free and equal in rights," noting that "social distinctions may only be founded only upon the general good."[29] Secondly, "the aim of all political association is the preservation of the natural and imprescriptible rights of man," and "these rights are liberty, property, security, and resistance to oppression." As if echoing the first article of the Declaration, a spirit explained to the Cercle Harmonique that God did not create "privileged beings."[30] Oligarchies in any form existed against God's will.

The spirits found oligarchy and equality to be mutually exclusive. When the spirits referred to the oligarchy, it could be the French ancien régime, southern slaveholders, or the white supremacists of Reconstruction. Whoever it was, it was a group soaked in greed and desirous of power. The oligarchy worked against the Idea. The march of the Idea, which required "principles" like "equality" and the "solidarity of mankind," fought against an "oligarchy" that only looked out for itself. The oligarchy crafted and enabled prejudices to support its own undeserved political and social power. And it caused the spirits grief. The oligarchy's past offenses and the illusions it spread regarding despotism caused much despair for the spirits. In response to such corruption, the spirit of Montesquieu explained that the struggle for equality also required a dedication to selflessness. "The practice of moral thinking," Montesquieu taught on another occasion, was the best evidence of a worthy person because it indicated a dedication to humanity's progress.[31] Spirits also chastised those who worked against equality.

Thus, those still on earth should "reject the power of the oligarchy." Though the "oligarchy" tried to divide people with prejudices and oppression, the spirits reported that the Idea still worked and still would triumph. Reason inspired brave people to stand up against injustice and unite in harmony as champions "of a Just Cause." The Cercle Harmonique was encouraged to resist the storms of "Hatred" and "the Lust of Domination" all around them. Oligarchical powers used violence to "ensure their domination" while keeping the masses in ignorance. The worst political oligarchies even enjoyed the suffering of the people. The spirit of the priest Ambroise explained how the combination of "political and religious oligarchies" was a primary cause of prejudices. The power held by "archbishops, prelates, popes, kings, or chiefs" was not genuine because it was often undeserved. In other words, it was oligarchical. Furthermore, these types of leaders sought to keep their subjects "blind" and prevented their subjects from recognizing their faux authority. However, while class or race determined one's status on earth, status in the spiritual spheres was based on characteristics like "wit" and charity.[32]

The assurance and guarantee of these rights were significant in French revolutionary thought for both the historical Robespierre and his spirit. Heavily influenced by Rousseau, Robespierre became well-known for his leadership in the Committee of Public Safety and his role in the Terror, but his speeches were also noteworthy. His assertion of the deep connection between morality and politics influenced revolutionary thought long after his death. Constitutional governments aimed "to preserve the Republic," for they were "chiefly concerned with civil liberty," and a "revolutionary government" concerned itself "with public liberty."[33] According to Robespierre, a republic was the best option to ensure the liberty and vitality of a moral people.[34] Anyone advocating something else was a traitor to the people. In February 1794, Robespierre delivered one of his most famous speeches to the National Convention. Highlighting his dedication to virtue, Robespierre described the desires of other Jacobins and himself as a "wish to substitute in our country morality for egotism, probity for a mere sense of honor, principle for habit, duty for etiquette, the empire of reason for the tyranny of custom, contempt for vice for contempt for misfortune, pride for insolence, large-mindedness for vanity, the love of glory for the love of money . . . We wish in a word to fulfill the course of nature, to accomplish the destiny of mankind, to make good the promises of philosophy, to absolve Providence from the long reign of tyranny and crime."[35]

For Robespierre, these wishes came to fruition through virtue, and virtue required the Terror.[36] While his spirit later regretted the Terror, the historical Robespierre saw it as a necessity for humanity's progress. According to the spirits, the triumph of the Idea would happen preferably without violence. In late May 1871, the spirit of French liberal Victor Noir regretted that much "generous blood" had been spilled in "the fratricidal struggle" in France—a physical and moral struggle between "good and evil." The "selfish privileged" took advantage of others, but "the People of 1871, informed by the lessons of the Past," would fight against those who wished to suppress them. The people might be "crushed in the fight," but the "innumerable" spiritual army watched over them and guided them. While the bodies of martyrs like Noir could "succumb" to violence, the ideas of those martyrs would continue.[37] Given the timing of Noir's message, his spirit likely was referring to the Paris Commune and the subsequent "Bloody Week."[38] But in very rare cases, violence was necessary for humanity's triumph. For example, when violent revolutions cleared the road for progress, they were victories for humanity.[39]

However, the Terror and later critiques of the Terror should not overshadow the intellectual influence of the revolution on civil society in France and elsewhere. Significant to political culture during the revolution and in its aftermath was the desire for a unified society focused on the common good.[40] Fraternité, influential in France and New Orleans, emphasized social bonds. It took the form of "divine friendship," as Robespierre called it, and of the spiritual brotherhood described in the Cercle Harmonique's séance records. According to the spirit of Constantin François de Chassebœuf, or the Comte de Volney, a Spiritualist viewed all of humanity as part of a "universal family of which he is a member."[41] Early historian of the French Revolution Jules Michelet believed in a kind of egalitarian religion of humanity that could "provide a real remedy for social disintegration."[42] Michelet identified the revolution as the new religion of France, and this new religion was both the "heir and adversary" of Christianity. While both agreed in "the sentiment of human fraternity," the religion of the revolution found "fraternity in the love of man for man," while Christianity rested upon a "dubious history" of injustice.[43] Similar appeals to the primacy of community and all of humanity and to the need for reform are found in the writings of French revolutionary priest Lamennais, a popular spirit among the Afro-Creole circle.

And not just the spirit of Lamennais, but all the spirits confirmed that Spiritualism provided hope that "Liberty and egalitarianism" not only would enlighten people but also "stop fratricidal struggles."[44]

The French Revolution did not end at the turn of the century; it continued long into the nineteenth century, most notably with the Revolution of 1830, which ended the Bourbon Restoration (1815–30) following Napoleon's stint as emperor, and the Revolution of 1848, which ended the Orleans monarchy. One of the clearest continuations of the French Revolution was in the intellectual and artistic work of people in France and the greater Atlantic world. Social romanticism, defined by one historian as "the semi-religious quest for harmony in social existence, in nature, and in the cosmos," was popular among French writers and thinkers in the mid-nineteenth century.[45] Novelists and writers like Victor Hugo, Joseph Marie Eugène Sue, Lamennais, Béranger, and Michelet are associated with the movement.[46] Saint Vincent de Paul's spirit believed that "liberal philosophy" helped make men "virtuous" and recognize the "suffering" of others.[47] Both romanticism and de Paul's spirit believed that a liberal view connected one to the wider world. The literary works of Hugo, Eugène Sue, and others contained a "fusion" of "heroic idealism associated with the national revolution and the notion of the mystical community with nature."[48] The influence of these men was felt far beyond French borders.

Some New Orleanians expressed support for the French Revolution shortly after it began. When Spain joined the First Coalition against France in 1793, the relations between the Spanish authorities and some of the French Creole population in the city became tense. French patriotism was particularly high in the city after the execution of King Louis XVI. Supporters of the French Republic sang "La Marseillaise" and the Jacobin song "Ça ira" in the New Orleans streets.[49] Both were popular songs of the French Revolution, and the latter's aggressive lyrics encouraged the lynching of clergy and nobility, which caused additional anxiety for the Spanish authorities. Though the Spanish colonials in the city were not the same as the aristocrats, nobles, and clergy whom "Ça ira" sang about hanging from the lampposts, this antagonism toward authority still strained the relationships between those in the city who desired a return to French governance and the Spanish who ruled.[50] The French Revolution influenced Africans and Afro-Creoles in Louisiana as well, as evidenced in the 1791 and 1795 Pointe Coupée slave conspiracies and a 1795 conspiracy and potential uprising involving black militiamen.[51] Contemporary local authorities lamented the influence of

Saint-Domingue's recent rebellion on their own slave and free black populations. According to New Orleans's second mayor, James Pitot, recent events
had "poisoned the populace, who, through imitation, became in general
either partisans of an obnoxious tyranny, or zealous adherents of Robespierre and the disrupting monsters who shared his crimes."[52] French revolutionary rhetoric was attractive to those denied full civil and legal rights in
Spanish Louisiana. When challenged regarding France's dedication to humanity, one of the main black Creole troublemakers of the Point Coupée
conspiracy replied that "the French are just" for "they have conceded men
their rights."[53]

One reason French revolutionary thought, especially that of the Jacobins,
spread quickly was that the new French Republic's government sent Jacobin agents throughout the larger Atlantic world to disseminate Jacobin
and revolutionary thought. Historian Caryn Cossé Bell reported, "At the
same time that French Jacobins plotted to invade Louisiana, they urged
white Creole Louisianans to 'cease being the slaves of a government to which
you were shamefully sold.' "[54] As the nineteenth century progressed, more
French émigrés arrived to the city and brought a fresh supply of French
revolutionary and romantic thought and influence—ideals that helped form
the spirits' Idea.[55]

"Dear France in triumph free"[56]: The Influence of French Literary Culture

French literature and history was influential on the Cercle Harmonique as
seen in the identity of spirits at the séance table, the ideas in their messages,
and the wider Afro-Creole culture around the Spiritualists. The Comte de
Volney was a historian, a politician, and an active spirit during Cercle Harmonique meetings. His work *Les Ruines, ou méditations sur les révolutions des
empires* (*The Ruins, Or, A Survey of the Revolutions of Empires*) was published
in 1791 during the French Revolution. *The Ruins* argued that if humanity
could accept natural religion, then rationality and peace would reign. Volney's writings were popular in the United States, most notably appreciated
by Thomas Jefferson. Volney's conception of natural religion was that God's
laws of the universe would lead all people "without distinction of country or
of sect towards perfection and happiness."[57] It was an understanding of religion he repeated as a spirit and identified by the Cercle Harmonique as
Spiritualism.

The French lyrical poet Pierre-Jean de Béranger, so popular in the nineteenth century, was also a frequent visitor to the Cercle Harmonique's table. His songs were part of the nineteenth-century political and social culture of France and of the whole Atlantic world.[58] Upon the return of the Bourbons, Béranger was reprimanded for his critical poetry. His negative perspective of the Bourbon monarchy caused many to paint him as "a prime mover in the victory of the people" in the Revolution of 1830.[59] In fact, his "Le Vieux Drapeau" was the unofficial anthem of the Revolution of 1830.[60] His songs kept alive the spirit of the French Revolution during the Restoration.[61] His spirit kept alive the memory of the French Revolution among the Cercle Harmonique. "The victory," Béranger's spirit proclaimed in 1870, "is ours; Truth and Justice triumphed."[62]

His love of France and his distaste of tyranny often were demonstrated in his poetic lyrics. One of his most popular songs, "The Coronation of Charles the Simple," a roast of sorts about King Charles X, illustrates the sardonic style crucial to his popularity among the people and his notoriety among royals. Political commentary supplied the core of his writings. In the song "My Republic," he lauds the governmental system:

> For republics I've a taking
> Since of kings I've seen enough;
> One, my own, I'll be a-making
> Give it good laws quantum suf.
> Drink's the only trade that's stable;
> Nought's our judge but Gaiety;
> All my realm is but a table;
> Its device is Liberty.
>
> The noblesses are too aggressive;
> Let your great ancestors rest.
> No more titles even to guests give,
> Who may laugh or drink the best.
> Should a traitor come between us,
> Reaching out for royalty,
> Sink the Caesar in Silenus
> And preserve our Liberty!
> Drink our fair republic's station!
> Settled soon our state shall be:
> But this so pacific nation

Fears e'en now an enemy.
'Tis Lisette, that's us alarming;
In voluptuous bonds are we;
She will reign, for she is charming;
All is up with Liberty![63]

Béranger also was known for anticlericalism. For example, the song "Les Révérends Pères" mocked the Jesuits and criticized them for their greed and harshness toward the laity, an opinion found among the Cercle Harmonique and their spirit guides too.

American literary magazines in the early to mid-nineteenth century referenced Béranger more often than other French poets during that time; Alphonse de Lamartine, another Cercle Harmonique spirit guide, was the runner-up. Many of the references to Béranger appeared in national magazines such as the *American Quarterly Review*, the *North American Review*, and the *Southern Review*. He was depicted as "the French counterpart of the American self-made man" and as "a lover of the people whose feelings he transcribed in his songs."[64] Locals were particularly familiar with his work.[65] According to the *New Orleans Daily Picayune* in the 1840s, "no centre table will be considered graceful (at least in New Orleans) without him."[66] His failing health, his death, and his funeral were newsworthy in the Crescent City.[67] After his death, his influence and his love of liberty did not end. For example, one day in February 1871, the spirit of Béranger arrived simply to say, "Vive la liberté!!"[68]

New Orleanians consumed the works of French writers including poetry, fiction, and nonfiction. Historian Michelet also wrote shorter works popular on both sides of the Atlantic. Michelet's pamphlet *Le Peuple* (1846) sold quickly in France and was translated into English shortly thereafter. In it, he analyzed the effects of France's shift from an agrarian society to an industrial one and the breakdown and interactions between social classes. He trusted that the French people's love for their country and the innate goodness of the people would help humanity's progress. The work reflected Michelet's hope that the French people would unite under the banner of social justice and fraternity and that this movement could spread beyond France itself. The only government that had "devoted itself heart and soul" to the people was the result of the French Revolution.[69] The effects of the "truly human genius of '89" were harmony, liberty, peace, and egalitarianism.[70] Though Michelet's spirit did not visit the Cercle Harmonique, his descriptions of the French Revolution's ideals bore a strong resemblance to the spirits' descriptions of them.

Michelet's work was also well-known in New Orleans. The local newspapers frequently listed book sales featuring his work, and correspondence from Paris printed in *The Daily Picayune* and the *New Orleans Tribune* often raved about his influence in France.[71] Following the historian's death, the local papers reported on his final hours, his funeral, and even the disagreements among his widow and heirs.[72] As he was one of "the greatest and most liberal minded men in Europe," the local press suggested his work to any who wanted to be well-versed in current affairs.[73] Members of the Cercle Harmonique would have been familiar with Michelet's work, and thus, his explanation and analysis of France's history and his hope for the country's liberal future became part of the circle's intellectual, interpretative scaffolding. Like Michelet, New Orleanians knew Montesquieu too. Similar to John Brown, Montesquieu was malleable in memory, and locals used his work to advocate for or dissent from the U.S. Republican Party. The short-lived newspaper, the *Black Republican* (1865) suggested his work if one felt "deficient in political knowledge."[74] *The Times-Picayune*, which was known for criticizing Radical Reconstruction, cited book 12 in the *Spirit of Laws* to support its opposition to "radicalism," claiming that it left hope and freedom impossible.[75]

The intellectual impact of the French Revolution was felt particularly in New Orleans literary circles, among both white and black Creoles and French émigrés. French authors were popular. Many nineteenth-century French romantic writers, such as Hugo and Lamartine, had a tendency to infuse their writings with social and political commentary.[76] For example, while Haitian revolutionary Toussaint Louverture was depicted negatively among white southerners, both Creoles of color and Lamartine described him quite differently. Lamartine's poem "Toussaint Louverture" eulogized him as the "hero of the blacks" and the embodiment of Haiti.[77] Lamartine too was part of the Cercle Harmonique network. The spirit of Lamartine advocated the ideas of Spiritualism and promised "immense happiness" for those who engaged in the "spiritual work of God." He also encouraged the circle along the "Infinite Route of Progress." Lamartine's spirit remarked that "[Victor] Hugo" received revelations of enlightenment and helped bring humanity along the road of progress.[78] Reflecting the ideals of the French Revolution and romanticism in their writings, Hugo and Lamartine made noteworthy spiritual friends.

Free black Creole intellectuals in New Orleans engaged French romantic literature, both in terms of discussion and in the production of new, original work (especially poetry). The year 1843 saw the publication of *L'Album littéraire: Journal des jeunes gens, amateurs de literature* (*The Literary Album: A Journal of Young Men, Lovers of Literature*), a briefly published, biracial literature journal. Black Creoles, including Joanni Questy, Armand Lanusse, Camille Thierry, Mirtil-Ferdinand Liotau, and Michel Saint-Pierre, were frequent contributors to *L'Album*. Social commentary was common in its pages. One lengthy essay published in the journal, "Philosophy of History," described how God's spirit enlightened humanity and led it toward progress. However, a "weakening of spiritual ideals" led to a decline and "the harshest slavery" supplanted "gentile liberty."[79] Other essays criticized the class distinctions in Louisiana society (contrasting the local class system to equality), condemned the practice of *plaçage* (arguing that it made black Creole women akin to prostitutes), and lamented the influence of Anglo ("British") materialism (decrying it for destroying "Louisiana's honor" and Louisiana's youth). The spirits advising the Cercle Harmonique echoed the sentiments and arguments of these essays.

Though *L'Album* did not last beyond a year, many of the same authors published in *Les Cenelles*, an 1845 anthology of black Creole poetry spanning approximately two hundred pages, eighty-five poems, and seventeen authors. Additionally, excerpts from the writings of Hugo, Lamennais, Lamartine, Victor Lemoine, and Louis-Sébastien Mercier also were featured in *Les Cenelles*. Many of the anthology's contributors were educated by French émigrés or in France. The intellectual history of French revolutionary thought and romantic literature influenced the poets as well as their status betwixt black and white and their Catholic backgrounds.[80] This emphasis of their French and Creole heritage reflected their own genealogical-cultural ties to Robespierre, Rousseau, Louverture, and French priest Lamennais.

"If Catholicism were entirely free"[81]: Spiritualism Reimagines French Catholicism

For many thinkers in the French Revolution, political and religious questions were intertwined. Concepts like despotism and tyranny were not limited to politics or religion. They found both the ancien régime and the Catholic Church guilty of oppressing the lower classes and of ethical transgressions against the people. Because of this, the material world needed the principles of justice, liberty, and equality—chief ideas running through the Cercle Harmonique's séance records. Criticism of Catholicism, though, did not mean a complete departure from Catholic ideas and aesthetics. For some French Catholics of the late eighteenth century, to engage the world of spirits was not a far step. In the 1780s, small groups of both men and women in Lyon and Paris began experimenting with new ways to commune with the dead beyond seeking saintly intercession. Using the teachings of Mesmer, members of these groups would enter into trances and communicate with spirits. One group in Lyon was even led by Abbé Jean-Antoine de Castellas, the dean of Saint John's Cathedral. This group, known as *La Concorde*, transcribed the reports of their trance seekers and then privately circulated the reports among "dissidents unhappy with the rigours of Catholic doctrine."[82]

Less popular in New Orleans was the French tradition of Spiritism, a practice similar to American Spiritualism and largely inspired by the fame of the Fox sisters from Rochester, New York. French educator and former Catholic Hippolyte Léon Denizard Rivail, writing under the pseudonym Allan Kardec, is considered the founder of Spiritism. His publication *Le Livre des esprits* (*The Spirits' Book*), first published in 1857, began to systematize and explain Spiritism, and his books were bestsellers in midcentury France. Like Spiritualism, Spiritism centered on communication with the spirits of the dead through mediums and spirit photography. Kardec advocated "individual progress towards perfection" and the advancement of social reform. Messages received by Kardec and his mediums often "described a universe in which equality was a supreme value."[83] Though both French Spiritism and New Orleans Spiritualism looked forward to social regeneration, a big difference between the two was the former's belief in reincarnation. Reincarnation, Spiritism taught, put spirits on a course of spiritual progression toward spiritual enlightenment. The spirits who visited the Cercle Harmonique occasionally referenced Spiritism. The spirit of French revolutionary priest Lamennais described Spiritism as a stepping-stone for Spiritualism and categorized it as "the station that will mark the decay of Materialism and the birth of Spiritualism" and "the first step which shows the Spirit luminous." Lamennais explained that Spiritism could prepare a soul to accept "the blessings of Spiritualism which will safeguard and enlighten it, in order to illuminate it and render it more and more radiant." On another occasion a spirit named Sylvester Weber noted that while a Spiritist was "a believer in Spirits' existence," a Spiritualist was "a believer in the Great Work of

Harmony."[84] Spiritism was better than Catholicism, but the spirits affirmed that the Cercle Harmonique's practice was the pinnacle of religious progression and the core of humanity's spiritual progression.

Revolutionary French priests also visited the Afro-Creole Spiritualists, and like the presence of Sedella and Moni, the participation of these spirits reaffirmed the circle's own Catholic past. Furthermore, the involvement of these spirits in the Cercle Harmonique's spiritual genealogy reiterated the circle's connection to the French revolutionary heritage and Francophone culture in general. The spirit of Lamennais was a frequent guide for the Afro-Creole Spiritualists. His presence at the Cercle Harmonique's table illustrates how Rey and others refashioned the parts of French Catholicism they approved of and integrated them into their practice. As a popular French revolutionary voice, Lamennais made a valuable addition to the spiritual network of the Cercle Harmonique. Though raised in a royalist family, Lamennais increasingly liberalized and sought to combine the church with the spirit of the revolution. Even as he became more radical, he never abandoned the belief that religion provided the only possibility for humanity's salvation, though his views on religion increasingly differentiated from official Catholicism. Lamennais maintained that humanity needed God to preserve order and morality, and though the Catholic Church (meaning the ecclesiastical hierarchy) had been corrupted, Catholicism's God was the true God. As he became increasingly interested in politics, he became more critical of the French church, since it aligned with a hostile regime. Rather, the church should be fighting for the people, reforming society, and advancing justice.[85] His status as a radical and a revolutionary was solidified with his 1834 publication *Paroles d'un Croyant* (*Words of a Believer*), a text that resulted in his official condemnation from the Vatican.[86]

In *Paroles d'un Croyant*, he described three related forces for change: the improvement of the people, the uniting of the people, and God's guidance. *Paroles d'un Croyant* contained poems and aphorisms with the tone of an Old Testament prophet. The work's content ranged from criticism of contemporary religion and politics to hopes for the future and theological explanations of the world. "When those who have abused their power have been swept away before you like mud in streams on a stormy day," he explained in the preface, "then you will understand that only the good endures, and you will fear to sully the air the winds of heaven have purified." Indeed, the preface described a world in "evil times" but promised a return of "Providence" after "the hardships of winter."[87] The "divine seed" of God's word brought to earth at Jesus's birth flowered initially, but "now the earth hath again become dark and cold."[88] Through prophetic parables Lamennais explained the origin of sin and greed among humans, an event he saw when "transported in spirit to the times of old." He identified the serpent (or "Fear") as the cause of greed and despotism, and greed caused men to follow the serpent and become enslaved by it. These men then proclaimed themselves to be kings and "excavated as it were a great cavern and there shut up the whole human family, as beasts are shut up in a stall." This imprisonment of much of humanity was the serpent's "second" conquest over humans, but humanity will have "another birth" that will deliver it from this state.[89] As a spirit visiting the Cercle Harmonique, Lamennais echoed his own writings. Rebuking those who were slaves to materialism—whom he likened to brutes— Lamennais assured the Cercle Harmonique that God wanted justice and equity to be prime forces in the world and offered "the work of harmony" present in even the world's "smallest details" as proof.[90]

Paroles d'un Croyant taught that the enslavement of humanity to self-proclaimed kings was antithetical to what God wanted. Together with "faith and thought," Christ will break "the chains of the people" and emancipate the earth. Equality and liberty were the desires of God, for "God hath made nor small nor great, nor masters, nor slave, nor kinds nor subjects. He hath made all men equal." Liberty was more than simply a word. Rather, "she is a living power which a man feels within himself and round about him; the guardian genius of the domestic hearth, the protector of social rights, and the first of those rights." Tyrants might claim to be supporters of liberty, but only those who defend rights may rightly call themselves champions of liberty. Thus, it comes as little surprise that Lamennais criticized slavery, as all are "sons of the same God, and brethren of the same Christ."[91] Lamennais's writings were read in France and beyond. He was a supporter of the Revolution of 1848 and elected as a deputy for Paris to the Constituent Assembly. During this time, he appeared in the *New Orleans Daily Picayune*'s brief reports on the French Assembly.[92] During the Civil War, the local radical French Afro-Creole newspaper *L'Union* called him one of the "geniuses" of the "noble Republic."[93] Mass production of his work *Paroles d'un Croyant* made his name well-known among those interested in the French Revolution and French culture, and passing references in newspapers attest to local New Orleanians' knowledge of him and his work.[94]

As a spirit, Lamennais argued that "the Fusion of the Races" would advance hand in hand with the march of progress. Racism held back humanity's progress. According to Lamennais those with "Humanitarian Ideas" did not recognize different nationalities but rather focused on humanity as a whole.[95] The revolutionary priest Abbé Henri Grégoire and his spirit agreed with Lamennais. Grégoire was a Jesuit, the first priest to swear the oath of the Civil Constitution of the Clergy, and the author of 1808's *De la Literature des negres*, often translated as *An Enquiry Concerning the Intellectual and Moral Faculties, and Literature of Negroes*. Grégoire's eager willingness to work with the National Assembly and the new French Republic identified him as a revolution-friendly priest.[96] His 1788 work, *Essai sur la régénération physique et morale des Juifs* ("Essay on the physical and moral regeneration of the Jews"), and its support for full legal enfranchisement for French and global Jews reflected Grégoire's support of religious liberty and his interest in minority communities. The 1790 Civil Constitution of the Clergy in many ways placed the French government over the Catholic Church and included the introduction of an electoral process for naming bishops and parish clergy. Like Lamennais, Grégoire was one of the French priests known for his revolutionary sympathies and support of republicanism. This love of republicanism remained with Grégoire in spirit too. The spirit of Grégoire identified and criticized the "social ills" and other evils obstructing "the reign of God." Amid political turmoil between the Republicans and Democrats during Reconstruction, Grégoire's spirit assured the Cercle Harmonique that right would succeed in "the party struggle" because "principles triumph over abuse."[97]

De la Literature des negres was in part a response to arguments regarding race similar to Thomas Jefferson's in *Notes on the State of Virginia*. According to Jefferson, Africans and their descendants were "much inferior" when it came to reason, "and that in imagination they are dull, tasteless, and anomalous." Furthermore, their inferiority was an unchangeable absolute. Whether their skin color came from "the color of blood, the color of bile, or that of some other secretion, the difference is fixed in nature, and is as real as if its seat and cause were better known to us." Though this seems a solely inherent matter, Jefferson took social environment into account, for it was "right to make great allowances for the difference of condition, of education, of conversation, of the sphere in which they move." While Jefferson was not completely clear on how blacks became inferior, he was positive of the racial hierarchy. Whether blacks were created distinct from whites or made that way "by time and circumstance," Jefferson affirmed that they were "inferior to whites in the endowments both of body and mind."[98]

Perhaps God had not created all men equal for Jefferson, but equality was the case for Grégoire. The priest even sent Jefferson a copy of *De la Literature des negres*, for which Jefferson politely thanked him.[99] Grégoire's work deconstructed various justifications for slavery and the racial hierarchy by illuminating and highlighting the accomplishments of the African race. Like Jefferson, Grégoire explained physical racial differences with meteorological climate, but Grégoire argued for the essential universality of humanity and recounted the intellectual and moral achievements of Africans and their descendants around the globe and through history. The prejudgment that Africans were inferior to Europeans and Euro-Americans was predicated on false European assumptions of superiority and, even more so, on European greed. "Africa," the priest wrote, "is not even allowed to breathe when the powers of Europe are combined to tear her to pieces."[100] When it came to the assumed racial hierarchy, blame clearly fell at the feet of those who placed themselves atop it. Grégoire hoped that revolutions would help in the deconstruction of the racial hierarchy and that societies would be rebuilt based on equality and real merit.

The spirit of Grégoire continued this fight for racial equality and world egalitarianism. In one message Grégoire described John Brown as a "patriot" with a "generous heart" and a "sincere friend of all men." Brown's anger at U.S. slavery inspired his attempt "to end the terrible despotism" and break the chains on "the feet of his black brothers." Grégoire was not shy with his high opinion of Brown, a man he called "one of the great figures in American history." This "American Jesus" sought to regenerate the nation. Brown made "sacred to the American people the principles of Liberty." The resurrection of Brown's ideals spurred forward "the great army of the Republic who raised Grant to the Presidential seat." While Jefferson Davis stood for "darkness" and "hate," Brown symbolized "love," "hope," and "freedom."[101] With his combined interests in republicanism and racial equality, Grégoire is not a surprising member of the Cercle Harmonique's spiritual network. Many spirits in the group's spiritual network advocated racial equality and republicanism, perhaps most notably those affiliated with the Haitian Revolution and the resulting republic.

Caribbean Revolutions

The influence of the French Revolution reverberated in the Atlantic and Caribbean worlds almost immediately. In the Euro-Atlantic world the idea of privilege was a main societal organizing principle, and it often had a racial or ethnic component.[102] The rebellion on the island of Saint-Domingue starting in 1790 is the clearest example of the French Revolution's impact on Afro-Creole and Afro-Caribbean culture. Historian Wim Klooster argued that in the Caribbean the message of the French Revolution had a more direct impact on free people of color than on slaves. Because free persons of color sought to gain "full legal equality," they more strongly echoed the Declaration of the Rights of Man and of the Citizen, while slaves focused more on their hoped-for emancipation.[103] The equality promised in the French document offered free people of color in and around the Caribbean, including those in New Orleans, the inspiration to demand full legal and civil rights and a language to do so. In short, the writings and rhetoric of the French Revolution provided "hidden transcripts," or previously unspoken critiques, a ready means of manifestation.[104]

Beginning in 1791, the Haitian Revolution lasted until 1804. Following the 1789 approval of the Declaration of the Rights of Man and of the Citizen, many of the island's free people of color began to argue for their own legal and civil rights. A small group of wealthy free men of color aggressively began to demand voting rights, but it was not until a large group of maroon slaves joined that the revolution gained real speed. With resources supplied by the British and the Spanish and the leadership of former slaves Boukman and Toussaint Louverture, the rebellion expelled European power by the close of the eighteenth century. Louverture declared complete black autonomy for the island. Freedom finally had come for a black contingent in the new world. Decades later, his spirit stated that freedom came from God and was truly found in the spiritual spheres. Communicated by a figure often equated with the fight for black freedom, his contention that "man is not [truly] free" until death carried extra weight for black New Orleanians who experienced the violence and racism of slavery and Reconstruction.[105]

Louverture also proclaimed himself governor-for-life of the island, but this did not last long. Napoleon dispatched a large force to regain control. Though the second and third rounds of fighting with the French also ended in black victories, Louverture was not as successful as his fellow countrymen. Taken prisoner in 1802, he later died in a prison in France, home of the despotic power he fought. Both criticisms and compliments of Louverture in the nineteenth-century United States were political statements. For some his name conjured fear of a black rebellion in the South, while others thought of liberty and justice upon hearing his name. Remembering the Haitian

Revolution was the same; it was good or bad, heroic or horrific. Louverture was a popular figure among African Americans during the Civil War. Black soldiers not only in Louisiana but all across the South sang "La Marseillaise" and exclaimed "To arms!"—a likely homage to the last line of Lamartine's poem about Louverture.[106] In many white circles in the southern United States, however, the name Toussaint Louverture became synonymous with extreme radicalism and violence. During the Civil War and Union occupation of New Orleans, *The Daily Picayune* was woe to report that "the American Jacobins" in the North were gaining speed. The newspaper reporter continued and wrote how abolitionist Wendell Phillips delivered an address at the Cooper Institute in New York that concluded, "A hundred years hence some Tacitus will take Phocion as the noblest model of the Greek and Brutus of the Roman—put Hampden for the glory of England and Lafayette for France—choose Washington as the bright consummate flower of the last generation and John Brown for this, and then dipping his pen in the sunlight, he will write high in the clear blue above them all, the name of the patriot soldier, statesman and martyr—Toussaint L'Ouverture." In response, *The Daily Picayune* lamented how "the bloody wretch who is thus apotheosized, whose name is placed 'high above' that of Washington, massacred with fiendish cruelty about three thousand of the white race."[107] Others reported more kindly on Louverture during the war. Shortly after the war's end the *New Orleans Tribune,* in an article that called John Brown "the Christ of the blacks," celebrated Louverture as a man who put "the general interest of the noble men who had entrusted [to him] their fate" over his own life.[108]

Though less famous in the United States than Louverture, Alexandre Pétion, a mixed-race military leader and first president of the Republic of Haiti, serving from 1807 until his death in 1818, was also a spirit who visited the Cercle Harmonique's séance table. Pétion joined the militia troops and fought alongside Louverture in the initial years of conflict, though he sided with André Rigaud following the revolution and, thus, left for France in exile shortly thereafter. He attended the School for Colonials and the Military College in Paris and then returned to Haiti two years later, in 1802, with General Leclerc (Napoleon's cousin) to retake the island. After Louverture was taken hostage by the French, and rumors of reinstating slavery washed over the island, Pétion joined the black nationals led by Jean-Jacques Dessalines. After black rebels retook control of the island and renamed it Haiti, Pétion moved to the political background until the assassination of Dessalines. Pétion and Henri Christophe both moved for power, Pétion supporting the ideals of republicanism and democracy while Christophe supported a more authoritarian organization. Christophe ruled the Kingdom of Haiti in the north, while Pétion led the Republic of Haiti. As president, Pétion saw to the parsing and giving of land to soldiers who fought for Haitian independence and the creation of public education facilities for children. Pétion also cultivated a relationship with Venezuelan freedom fighter Simón Bolívar. Historical actors and historians alike gave Pétion the title of "the founder of rural democracy" for Haiti because of his decision to fragment large colonial plantations into small farm plots for soldiers.[109]

Pétion's spirit messages complemented this contemporary depiction of him. According to the spirit of Pétion, the "virtuous soul" was one that fought against "tyrannical oppressors," be they political or religious, and fought for "the Freedom of his brothers." Similar to other spirits, he also taught that racial identities and nationalities were constructions of politics and thus had no real meaning. There was only a "common homeland" for all "brothers." Because the place of one's birth was by "chance," all should "unite" despite nationality. Pétion and other spirits instructed the Cercle Harmonique to "reach out your fraternal hand to your brother, whether he is in Asia, Africa, or Europe. They are all men." Spiritualists "should recognize neither nationalities, nor races; all men are brothers and equals." Pétion was not alone in these claims. Swedenborg echoed Pétion and stated that for Spiritualists, there were "neither nationalities, nor races, they are all brothers; the latitude of one's birth is nothing to him [the Spiritualist]."[110] Historians today contend that Pétion's role in Haiti's founding was overemphasized in order to outshine other leaders, such as Dessalines.[111] This might be the case looking back, but the focus on Pétion during the mid-nineteenth century was significant for the practice of the Cercle Harmonique. During the nineteenth century, Pétion was recognized around the Caribbean as a figurehead of freedom.

Following the Haitian Revolution, the island was by no means stable. Historians agree that the real winners of the Haitian Revolution were not the newly freed slaves but rather "the old *mulâtre* land-owning elite (the *anciens libres*) and the new noir generals (the *nouveaux libres*) who seized the state."[112] Members of the mixed-race class, with their lighter skin and higher social status, often were at odds with the newly liberated slaves.[113] Socially, politically, and racially, the island remained diverse and divided.[114] Further rebellions and conflicts were common. The Liberal Revolution of 1843, led by some of the bourgeoisie who wanted to liberalize the country, and the Piquet Rebellion of 1844, led by peasants, demonstrate the instability on the island and the dissent among the peasant class.[115] One mixed-race general who pushed back against the "suffering army"—the name the pike-carrying peasant army gave themselves—was Fabre-Nicolas Geffrard, a man who later would serve as president in 1857. Geffrard's spirit too appeared to the Cercle Harmonique. His message was signed "Jeffrard" and argued that both God and "the sun[light]" prove the "equality of men." He lamented that it took "so much bloodshed" for humanity to "recognize the justice of this Principle."[116] He might have been referring to world history broadly or his own participation in the Piquet Rebellion.

The island's instability was likely the inspiration behind one spirit's prediction. The spirit of Haitian colonel Auguste Brouard prophesized that there would be "no more of these fratricidal struggles" once all of humanity accepted Spiritualism. Humanity no longer would put brothers in chains, and "Freedom" would be for all. There would be no hatred, no struggle. Instead, there would be the flag of only one "universal homeland" as opposed to many flags "soiled with blood." Brouard was part of the Haitian campaign in the 1843–49 Dominican War of Independence, a conflict that created the Dominican Republic. Haitians had taken control of the rest of the island of Saint-Domingue in 1822, and waves of anti-Haitian movements on the eastern side of the island followed. Overlapping with the Liberal Revolution of 1843, the Dominican War of Independence continued even after the new republic drafted its constitution, as Haitian forces continued to try to regain control of the island. On another occasion, Brouard's spirit called "the war," though he did not clarify which one, a "scourge" and "the result of the desire of domination." He likened the "Glories of Earth" to children's toys—simplistic and for the immature. Whether his message was about the recent American Civil War or the war he fought in, Brouard's harsh words about war resonated with other spirits' messages about oppression and oligarchical power. The spirit of Brouard also supported patience and hard work in the face of conflict.[117] For Afro-Creoles hoping for full legal and civil rights during the Reconstruction era, Brouard's encouragement hit close to home.

The Cercle Harmonique's knowledge of the Haitian Revolution primarily came from three sources: stories from some of the members' parents who were born there, contemporary newspaper accounts of current events, and the recent histories of Haiti being published and distributed. The first two volumes of Thomas Madiou's four-volume history of the island, *Histoire d'Haïti*, were published in 1847 and 1848. Madiou's telling of Haitian history highlighted how the world belonged to all people, regardless of race, and observed that world civilization would benefit from a "fusion" of the races.[118] Beaubrun Ardouin's eleven-volume *Etudes sur l'histoire d'Haïti*, published between 1853 and 1860, also celebrated and romanticized Haiti's past. Ardouin wrote history with a purpose and believed that "the past is the regulator of the present as of the future."[119] Thus, knowing Haiti's triumphant history would inspire later generations, like the Cercle Harmonique, to continue propagating the revolutionary and republican ideals of their past.

Ardouin downplayed both Louverture's and Dessalines's roles in Haitian freedom. Joseph Saint-Rémy's mid-nineteenth-century five-volume biography of Pétion reinforced Pétion's celebrated status in Haitian history.[120] Each historian emphasized a lack of racial prejudice in the country's post-revolution history, largely for diplomatic reasons. Furthermore, even with Madiou's talk of racial "fusion," many of the mid-nineteenth-century historians created what contemporary historian David Nicholls called the "mulatto legend," which strengthened the mixed-race upper class's claim to political power.[121] In the accounts of Ardouin and Saint-Rémy, Louverture and Dessalines were not depicted favorably; rather they were despotic, in cahoots with white slave owners, and prejudiced. Pétion and his successor, Jean-Pierre Boyer, emerged as champions of the democratic ideal. Though these particular histories might stress the contribution of mulattos, the common interest of all Haitians and a restrained telling of racial caste prejudice also were emphasized. For example, when Louverture was depicted as a pawn of white power, this was both a negative depiction of black, nonmulatto Haitians and an ideological call to arms for all Haitians to combat colonialism. The *gens de couleur libres*, unlike Louverture, had always led the struggle against colonial oppression. Ardouin and Saint-Rémy's accounts celebrated Pétion as a leader in the fight for Haitian independence and then as the true founder of the republican nation of Haiti. Whether part of this "mulatto legend" or not, these histories of Haiti criticized colonialism and slavery and celebrated the victories of the African race in the new world. And these books were chief sources of Haitian history for members of the Cercle Harmonique. The prevalence of the "mulatto legend" in contemporary nineteenth-century histories of Haiti might explain why Pétion's spirit visited the Cercle Harmonique and Dessalines's spirit did not. Considering Dessalines's more violent plans, such as ordering the massacre of all remaining whites on the island, his absence is not surprising. In contrast, Pétion's characterization as a republican founder made him an expected friend in the spirit world.

The Haitian Revolution influenced politics and cultures around the Atlantic world. While Afro-Creoles sympathized and related with the revolutionaries, many white American Protestants were anxious about Haiti. Both the Catholicism of the island and the violence of the black revolution— for the fear of a rebellious race war haunted Euro-Americans—made many uneasy. Some white American abolitionists posthumously converted Louverture to Protestantism because the specter of a successful rebellion associated with both Catholicism and race violence was incompatible with their views on liberalism and democracy.[122] New Orleans's Afro-Creoles were different in their views on Haiti and the revolution.[123] Sociologist Mimi Sheller argued that a "shared vision of democracy based on the post-slavery ideology of freedom" developed among black Haitians and Jamaicans. This ideology included not just a demand for "full political participation and equal citizenship," but also "an explicit critique of white racial domination and of the unbridled market capitalism that built a world system of slavery."[124] Despite Haiti's struggles and internal conflicts in the following decades, the island and its history was a symbol of black political agency and black republicanism for many Afro-Creoles around the Caribbean.[125]

One of the Haitian Revolution's main points of inspiration for members of the Cercle Harmonique was that race did not dictate the value of a people. As the ideals of the French Revolution taught them, the real value of a person came from the spirit, not status. Afro-Creole Spiritualism agreed. The belief that the "color of the [material] envelope" proved any man's "superiority . . . quickly dissipate[d]" once spirits entered the spiritual world. While bodies were raced by skin color on earth, racist spirits were tainted by "defilement of the soul" in the spiritual spheres. Spirits were "pure and holy" as opposed to colored like their bodily envelopes.[126] The spirit who delivered this message signed as "M. De St. Méry," likely referring to white Creole lawyer and historian Mederic-Louis-Elie Moreau de Saint-Méry from Saint-Domingue. Saint-Mery's *Description topographique, physique, civile, politique et historique de la partie française de l'isle Saint-Domingue* offered a categorical schema for people on the island of Saint-Domingue, a work he finished shortly before the Haitian Revolution. The work recounted the glory days of white supremacy and slavery on the island.[127] Though he celebrated white supremacy while alive, in death his spirit recognized the absurdity of race. While the temporary body was raced, the spirit was not. Because the true value of a person was his or her immaterial and immortal spirit, race should not matter.

Spirits from the Haitian Revolution were not the only Caribbeans to appear at the Cercle Harmonique's table. Rebel efforts on and around Cuba during the late 1840s and early 1850s led by Spanish Creole Narciso López to wrestle control of the island from imperial Spanish power found support among fellow revolutionaries in the Caribbean.[128] As he supported slavery, López's aims were different from those on Saint-Domingue decades earlier.[129] Still, he was primarily known for his revolutionary call and his republicanism. A spirit identified as "Lopez" delivered a message in favor of liberty and critical of despotism in late 1871. He opened the communication calling for "cheers for independence!" Independence was grand because it removed "superstition and error." In contrast, the terror of despotism "grips your consciousness." The people should "lift up and crush [despotism]." Cries of "Long live Liberty!" and "Long live Independence!" emboldened the message with emotion. This spirit was concerned with despotism of both the political and cultural kind. A "barbarous tyrant" was not the only destructive personality for humanity. "A bad son; an enemy of society; an unjust brother or sister; a cruel master," and "a hypocrite minister" were destructive too and would impede the progress of humanity.[130]

New Orleans was both a bastion of pro-López sentiment and a departure point for many of López's expedition ships.[131] In most New Orleans reporting on López's rebellion, "the old desire to save Cuba to the cause of slavery was curiously mixed with a sincere enthusiasm for political liberty."[132] At Rey's séance table, Lamennais proclaimed that López was a worthy spirit whose "blood" and the blood of his compatriots "provoked this spirit of independence which causes the heart of Cuban patriots to beat."[133] Anti-Spanish riots broke out in New Orleans following López's execution, and over $25,000 of damage was done to Spain's consulate in New Orleans and to property belonging to Spanish nationals in the city.[134] Commemorative services for López and the other revolutionaries continued in New Orleans, most notably at the 1854 tribute held at the Mechanics' Institute. J. S. Thrasher, one of the two main speakers, highlighted liberty and freedom in his speech and concluded, "the Union of the Martyrs was the Union of the Races!"[135] By races, Thrasher meant the Iberian race (Spaniards), Anglos, and Spanish Creoles. Not long thereafter, Thrasher's celebration of "the union of the races" echoed at the table of the Cercle Harmonique.

"Better than these servile despots"[136]:
Fighting Despotism and Oppression

The twin forces of despotism and oppression were antithetical to Spiritualism and humanity's progress. The spirits' understanding of despotism was not unlike that of Alexis de Tocqueville in *The Old Regime and the Revolution*. Tocqueville saw despotism and equality as exclusive and despotism as destructive to the "hearts and minds" of people. "Despots acknowledge that liberty is an excellent thing," Tocqueville wrote, "but they want it all for themselves."[137] The spirits agreed that despotism was in opposition to liberty. It was a "noble duty to fight despotism in whatever form it presents itself," the spirit of Saint Vincent de Paul reported. According to Volney, despotism was "the policy of Brutal France" and "distorted" the mind and chained brothers to ignorance. Paired with political despotism, this was what caused the suffering of the French. The savior of France was the revolution and its cry for liberté, egalité, fraternité. Republicanism should replace despotism, not only in France but across the material world. Another spirit encouraged the Cercle Harmonique not to "bend shamefully under the rule" of those who sought to quell thinking or dissent—in other words, they should contest all despots.[138]

The spirits of those who wanted to "dominate the masses and live at their expense" suffered in the spiritual world and felt "shameful and unhappy." For example, Napoleon recognized the error of his ways after his physical death and appeared at the table to warn against pride or else they would end up as he was, "groaning at the foot of the Ladder of Progress." While those who lived for justice celebrated in the spiritual world, he "grieve[d] under the multitude of evils I caused, of the intense grief I had spread." In contrast to a despot, a real leader had "a responsibility for the future" and must guarantee citizens their "free will." Despots in particular, or simply those with excessive and abusive power, garnered heavy criticism from the spirits. Robespierre delivered a joint message with André Chenier—on Bastille Day no less—and exclaimed that "a despot commands and the world is turned upside down." For Robespierre and Chenier, king was another word for despot. "Canons," which were invented "to please the foolish pride of Chiefs, and especially of Despots," should not decide a country's welfare and governmental policies. Chenier and Robespierre connected these ideas to current events. The King of Prussia, then at war with France, was singled out for trying to delay progress. Robespierre and Chenier's condemnation of "tyranny chaining liberty" was similar to the spirits' criticisms of moral slavery. They hoped that the "spirit of '93" would keep kings and despots from triumph. Voltaire too chimed in on the idea of despotism, encouraging the circle to combat "despots of conscience." In contrast to despots, the spirits extolled humility.[139]

In the search for political power, many political despots sought alliance with religious despots, hoping the partnership would "strengthen" their power. Louverture's spirit identified the pope as a religious and political despot and concluded the message, "Death to Tyranny. Long live Freedom." According to the spirit of Lamennais the powerful and greedy left humanity "moaning," stuck "under the political and religious yokes." It was only "the spirit of domination in the heart of man" that "perverted" him to disregard "solidarity" and dream "of chains instead of freedom." The ego was the source of such perversion, which made a man desire power over humanity rather than humanity's "glorious march." While various political powers long survived off "the sufferings of the people," "the march of ideas" pushed against "despots' political prestige." Other political and religious despots armed themselves with the "sword," but weapons could not stop the "march of the Idea." The Idea was a "torch that guided humanity." It was the "moral strength" of Jesus and the "energy" of John Brown; "it was Voltaire, Volney; it was [Victor] Hugo." The Idea and freedom could not be stopped by a despot with a sword. Despotism, whether political or religious, was a "calamity." Securing "freedom of thought" for all was a necessity, the spirit of López taught, especially if the ones obstructing it were the "mercenaries in Black Robes."[140]

Napoleon was not the only former despot or king who appeared to the Cercle Harmonique. Others came to the table to share the knowledge they had gained once joining the spirit world. In the spiritual spheres, despots would and did recognize their past errors, and the proof was in their presence at the Spiritualists' table. The spirit of Louis X, who briefly was king of France in the early fourteenth century, supported the idea of an "Alliance for the common good." A spirit identified as the Duke of Orleans encouraged the Cercle Harmonique and anyone else listening to "be humble of heart." Justice, charity, and self-sacrifice made one "worthy of your Creator." "Human equality" and "universal brotherhood" were key to any properly functioning society.[141]

Indeed, French rulers of the past were not uncommon at the séance table. The spirit of Charles IX, the king who approved the St. Bartholomew's Day Massacre, which saw the mass slaughter of French Huguenots in the sixteenth century, taught that all were equal in the spirit world regardless of the "gold" or "honors" possessed on earth. Furthermore, neither wealth nor social status could keep one from undergoing retribution. Tyrants would appear in the spirit world with their heads lowered and would "howl like me." The spirit of Charles X, the king mocked in Béranger's famous song, had harsh words for those who supported slavery. In one message he asked a long rhetorical question clearly designed to chastise those who favored keeping "under the yoke ... thousands of beings." In response, he explained how a slavery apologist was similar to an "insolent king" with his "head high" and "disdainful" to any who questioned him. The age of slavery and monarchy was dead, as far as the spirit of Charles X was concerned. "The people," he said, were "King." Slavery was wrong because neither one's status nor one's race should dictate one's place in the material or the spirit world. "You talk of races," the medium wrote for Charles X on another occasion, "German, French, Prussian, Parisian, Bavarian or Austrian, Italians." But, the spirit asked, when the body is only dust, what is the value of race then? Or, of what significance is social status? Many of the "greats of Earth" were "very small here."[142] A message denying the meaning of race or nationality carried extra weight coming from a French king who ordered the invasion of Algeria during the Bourbon Restoration. The presence of Charles X and other kings at the table also reaffirmed the possibility of a spirit's redemption in the spirit world. Though in error during their earthly material lives, these spirits wanted to share the knowledge they had gained in the spiritual spheres with those still on earth.

Despotism was not the only form of oppression people encountered. In addition to the political, the primary forms of oppression that most interested the spirits were economic, racial, and social. Lamennais reported that there was truth to the saying "it is difficult for the rich to get through the gates of heaven." On another occasion Lamennais described materialism as one of the primary causes of "social inequalities." Ambroise rebuked many of the world's "captains of industry" for "the exploitation of the masses." While the economically disadvantaged often had nothing but "suffering persecution" on earth, the spirit world promised them "sympathy, love, and charity." The spirit of "a former peasant" criticized those who disowned their parents out of shame and pride. Claiming a rich and powerful biological lineage was not the way to accumulate political or social capital. Status should come from merit, not one's bloodline. Furthermore, coming from a noble or rich family could hinder one's spiritual progression, as a childhood of privilege encouraged a naturalized sense of entitlement. Those in "privileged classes" forgot that the people they considered "their inferiors" were in fact "children of the same Father, who created all equal." Regrettably, a "love of domination," Montesquieu and Ambroise taught together, seemed natural to many people. According to Mesmer's spirit, those who felt superior to others typically were the ones who neglected their spiritual education. Lamennais explained that Spiritualists were to "practice humility" because Jesus preached humility to combat "indifference" and "Human Pride." Thus, the Afro-Creole Spiritualists were instructed to "help break the natural or legal chains" that tied people, often "the poor" and "dispossessed," to "the pariahs of the earth." If humanity could destroy prejudice, Béranger believed, then "the hydra of physical and moral domination" would be crushed.[143]

Gendered oppression was another subject occasionally discussed. One particular spirit spoke on multiple occasions about proper gender dynamics, the cultural elevation of men, and societal oppression of women. Though the spirit of Marie de Rabutin-Chantal admitted that women were physically the weaker sex, men should always treat women with respect. In particular, a mother—the "sister of charity"—deserved admiration from all. Fathers, on the other hand, did not inherently deserve such deference. Her spirit was not alone in this conclusion; a spirit identified as "Mrs. Washington," likely wife of the first U.S. president, stated that "Ladies" would "play a great role in the Progress of humanity."[144]

Marie de Rabutin-Chantal, the marquise de Sévigné, was a French noblewoman remembered for the letters she wrote her daughter during the late seventeenth century. The sentimentality in her writings prompted one historian to compare her to Rousseau.[145] Her outspoken protest against the inferior level of education received by women in her day and her criticism of a legal system that favored men and often placed women at the mercy of the men in their family rendered her noteworthy. Her wit ensured that her letters would be read for centuries. In her letters she frequently wrote of divine will and divine causation, and her reverence toward nature reads as a kind of proto-romanticism.[146] Her famous letters were bound and published in the eighteenth century and reissued again and again.[147] A mention of how she signed her letters in a news/opinion story in *The Daily Picayune* indicates a local familiarity with her and her letters.[148] The preface of a nineteenth-century edition of her letters described de Sévigné as "a woman who lived in and for others."[149] This particular edition's editor lauded de Sévigné as an exemplar of womanhood and motherhood: knowledgeable, graceful, and thoughtful. Her depiction as a feminist, however, has been called into question. The French historian Michèle Longino Farrell argued that people accepted and embraced her letters because "she absorbed and represented the code governing appropriate generic behavior for women at her time."[150] During the nineteenth century, though, she was seen as a model woman and, thus, was a sensible spirit to guide the Cercle Harmonique on the treatment of women and proper gender dynamics.

The spirit of de Sévigné spoke frequently about how men should treat women. A man who spent his time in "infamous gambling dens" and left his wife—"the poor, virtuous woman"—exposed with no support deserved to be shamed. The spirit also ridiculed any man who viewed his wife "as a servant" to attend "to his whims." Even those men seated at the séance table who listened to her words and thought, "I'm not being that infamous," should take an honest look at themselves, for no man was "entirely free from blame." So many "gentlemen" believed themselves to be "superior to the woman." De Sévigné rhetorically asked them why and then berated them for making "the laws to your advantage." "You [men] made injustices for us [women]." The spirit longed for the day when "all social prejudices," such as male superiority, would disappear. De Sévigné also endorsed the idea of "fair and equitable rights" for both sexes. Her spirit criticized how men created laws that they expected women to follow yet did not allow any input from women when drafting them.[151] Republicanism should include all.

"I am he who believed that France could still be saved by becoming a Republic!"[152]

The spirits taught that republicanism secured the rights of all and ensured that all would be free. According to the spirit D'Apremont, the "work of the Spirit" was felt in struggles for freedom, and a person's happiness depended on "political independence." This political independence was best cultivated in a republican society. Montesquieu's spirit believed that only a government run by "moral and industrious people, with honest views" could function properly. Those who accepted bribes did not deserve respect, and an administration full of dishonest politicians would "crumble" like "an old building" with a faulty foundation. Additionally, a power-hungry political party could not promise a just government. Despots did not accompany republicanism. Power rightfully belonged with those dedicated to honesty, justice, and fairness. Dishonesty and greed fueled injustice, but a republic that followed the ideals of the French Revolution would be egalitarian. Volney described the origin of "antagonism in society" as "the pride" of those who believe themselves "superior" to others and want "to make distinctions" based on those false beliefs. The biggest supporter of a "powerful oligarchy" was "selfishness." In the United States, the social antagonism was not as bad as it had been during slavery because "prejudices" had become "less severe," but social prejudice was certainly still a problem. The ideals of Spiritualism, if adopted by a wide audience, could help remedy the country's social ills. This focus on antagonism as the origin of social ills was not confined to Volney. A spirit identified as "Oscar, a devoted friend," agreed that the "antagonism" among people often revealed itself in "unjust claims and unfair prejudice." Indeed, members of the Cercle Harmonique should "stay united," even if "amid antagonisms."[153] The answer to antagonism was republicanism.

Another famous French republican and martyr who conversed with the Cercle Harmonique was Victor Noir, a journalist shot by Prince Pierre Bonaparte in January 1870. His spirit affirmed that he "labored for liberty, for republican government, because I have understood that, without this last, man dabbles, or a part of humanity dominates the other to the detriment of it." Put quite simply, he "loved the Republic because it creates free men!" As Robespierre and Chenier had criticized the Prussian king, Noir censured Prime Minister Otto von Bismarck, a man known for political conservatism and the religious oppression of Catholics. During the Franco-Prussian War, multiple spirits took note of the political climate in Europe. Ambroise referenced how many European nations were confused and made unwise political decisions. Though war was lamentable, it also could be necessary in order to revolutionize old systems and give the power to the people. Ambroise argued that France's successes during the eighteenth and nineteenth century were due to "her warlike and adventurous spirit." But war led to better days, and from the chaos sprang "the march of the Republican Idea . . . more than ever."[154] The social and political progress sought by these figures echoed in the republican ethos that filled the pages of Rey's séance books.

Republicanism also combated human and moral slavery, as enslavement robbed people of their liberties. According to the spirit of Pierre Soulé, he left his homeland of France for America because he "wanted freedom, Freedom!" However, though he arrived in New Orleans with his heart "beating for freedom," his pride and ambition overpowered him. He forgot his "holy inspirations," and after he "sacrificed my republicanism on the altar of slavery" he began to worship "the golden calf." During this time he "suffered the yoke of slavery" and became a "traitor" to conscience and reason. For these past transgressions, he now asked for pardon.[155] Whether Soulé meant participation in the enslavement of Africans or slavery to materialism is not clear. Regardless, republicanism fought against both of these kinds of slavery. The revolutionary cries of "Liberté! Egalité! Fraternité!" as echoed in the messages of the Cercle Harmonique had no room for greed, oppression, or prejudice.

Not surprisingly, the virtues of a republican government were extolled by the spirit of Robespierre. In a republic, "thought is not muzzled" and the general populace was encouraged to consider moral, political, and religious questions. As such, a republican society was distinguished by a "generosity towards suffering nationalities" and "an acknowledgement of the rights of each human being." Indeed, "the republic is the people marching towards progress." Republican governments, Robespierre taught, offered "people . . . the immense advantage of the right of discussion, of religious liberty." Additionally, the freedom of the press allowed "even the peasant" to know of government happenings. The qualities of a nation's leader were important for sustaining a proper republic. While an immoral and unjust "supreme chief" spread "injustice," "an honest chief, firm and just" conveyed the feeling of responsibility to his people.[156]

In many circles of New Orleans society during the antebellum period, the Civil War, and Reconstruction, the name Robespierre typically denoted immoral and despotic political ideas, perhaps even as a wolf in sheep's clothing. Correspondence from Boston published in *The Daily Picayune* called the words of William Lloyd Garrison and other "ultra-abolitionists . . . in speech what Robespierre, Danton, Marat, and Barrere were in action."[157] During the Revolution of 1848 *The Daily Picayune* used the name of Robespierre as a stand-in for the idea of a violent and unworthy republic.[158] Early in the Civil War, local periodicals increasingly referenced Robespierre as a symbol for unruly extremism and evoked the specter of the guillotine. A historical retrospective on his character called him "so cruel, so cold, so ambitious, so vain, and so cowardly," "the perfection of human infamy," and "a traitor."[159] During Reconstruction, the horrors of radicalism and the "destructive and corrupt career of the Radical party" were likened to "the Jacobins of France, and Marat, Danton and Robespierre."[160] For his role in the Terror, Robespierre possessed a negative reputation among many, but he remained a potent symbol of the French Revolution for the Cercle Harmonique. On one occasion Robespierre apologized for his actions during the Terror. "In our anger," his spirit communicated, "we spread terror" and "swam in pools of blood." But this was to a positive end; with their "axe" (guillotine) the revolutionaries ended the reign of a king who unjustly ruled. Robespierre's spirit expressed shame for his role in the guillotine's bloodlust, but it was as if his ideals excused his violent behavior. Even with its "bloody cortège," the French Revolution "was necessary."[161] The rhetoric and ideals of the movement made it worthwhile.

As the inheritors of French revolutionary culture and the republicanism it inspired, Rey and fellow Afro-Creole Spiritualists saw themselves as the successors of Robespierre's, Lamennais's, Montesquieu's, Grégoire's, and Louverture's visions. Their own local ancien régime was the white supremacists and former slaveholders of the South. Armed with republican ideas and bolstered by their spiritual mentors, they criticized the oligarchy around them. As New Orleans became increasingly volatile and violent in the post–Civil War era, Spiritualism continued to keep the Afro-Creole members of the Cercle Harmonique politically grounded and focused on what really mattered—the progress of the Idea. But the Idea never came to fruition during the Cercle Harmonique's tenure. Materialism and oligarchy continued, and instead of the decline of the white southern oligarchy, the close of Reconstruction in New Orleans saw only the end of Afro-Creole Spiritualism.

Conclusion
Endings

Death is but a Door which opens into new and more perfect existence. It is a Triumphal Arch through which man's immortal spirit passes at the moment of leaving the outer world to depart for a higher, a sublime, and a more magnificent country.

—Andrew Jackson Davis, *The Great Harmonia: Being a Philosophical Revelation of the Natural, Spiritual, and Celestial Universe*

Patience for your brothers! Courage for yourself. Continuing to work. Forward to us.

—Spirit of Saint Vincent de Paul to the Cercle Harmonique, 18 November 1877

Dear Petit, Dear Assitha

My heart is filled with good feelings for you. I am the one who loves you above all.

—Spirit of Mme. Dubuclet to François "Petit" Dubuclet and his daughter Assitha Dubuclet, 2 December 1906

Going beyond New Orleans, the United States, and the Atlantic world, there was one final concentric circle that enclosed the Cercle Harmonique: the world of the spirits. Separating the material world from the spirit world was an immaterial boundary that the spirits regularly crossed via communication and that the Afro-Creole Spiritualists would cross after death. The Cercle Harmonique's spiritual guides taught that death was only the departure of the spirit from the corrupt material world. Thus, death was not sad. In particular, martyrs, or any who had died for the cause of the Idea, saw their deaths as steps forward. Leaving their bodies behind, the spirits of martyrs were at home in the spiritual spheres; there, they united with fellow republicans who also recognized the beauty of equality and brotherhood. The material body of Captain Cailloux "fought" and "succumbed" in the material world, but his soul, now in the spirit world, knew that "true freedom" always won. The spirit of Cailloux encouraged those on earth to continue fighting because "God wants freedom." To fall in the fight was not the end; rather, "victims" were necessary. In death, he and other martyrs took the "first steps" to freedom and would lead others to the "temple of equality."[1] In the preceding five chapters *A Luminous Brotherhood* illustrated how the Cercle Harmonique resided within a local, national, and global environment. The Afro-Creole Spiritualists believed a cosmological barrier separated them and the spirit world and that they would cross it when they died. The end of life in the material world was the beginning of life in the spirit world. Therefore, *A Luminous Brotherhood*'s conclusion focuses on endings: first, the end of material life and then, the end of the Cercle Harmonique.

"Freed from matter"[2]: Death and the Material World

Though to die a martyr for the Idea was the most glorious and respectable way to die, death was a fortunate release for all. "To die," according to the spirit of John Brown, was "to be born." After leaving the "material envelope" or body behind, the spirit underwent a "glorious transformation." One should not fear death, because material life was a "painful struggle" and the arrival of the soul to the spiritual spheres was a "glorious birth." Now completely "free of materialism," spirits finally could be truly "free." Death was also the great leveler; rich or poor, no one could escape it. Though death was a reward, it should not be forced or sought after. Suicide was "an insult to God." One who committed suicide "failed in his mission." And for him, "death is a terrible awakening."[3] The spirits told the Cercle Harmonique to "not fear death" but also not to "hurry" it. Important lessons could be learned on earth, and there was much work to be done. Even still, it was vital to recognize the brevity of life on earth. The "material body" was the property of earth, while the "soul" belonged to "the spirit Land."[4] One's existence in the spiritual spheres was eternal. The material world and the material envelope were both temporary, and release from both meant the progress of a spirit.

The spirits compared the spiritual spheres and the spiritual body with the material world. When one died and left the material world, that person entered a superior space. The material existence was "short-lived," while the spiritual life was "eternal." In the material world, there were "tears," while in the spirit world there was "unspeakable joy." "Corruption" and "conflict" filled the material world, but "sharing" governed the world of the spirits. Truly, when compared to the spiritual, the "material" had "little value." The soul's immaterial immortality was the reward for struggling through the material world and being burdened by a material body. The body was mortal, human, and tainted. The body held the spirit back, so to be "separated from matter" was "good fortune." Materialism caused "the corruption of the [material] envelope," and this corruption was remedied completely when the spirit left the material world behind. Mind and spirit remained and would "emerge triumphant" after leaving the body. Once a spirit entered the spiritual world, it was as if a veil contingent on the material existence of the body disappeared and the spirit could see more clearly the error of materialism and its effects, like racism and greed. It was also the material envelope, or body, that dictated one's race. Thus, spirits told the Cercle Harmonique to take comfort in the forthcoming "destruction" of the material. Those rid of the material envelope should consider themselves "blessed."[5] As such, the spirits told the circle not to fear death because death was regeneration in a race-less, egalitarian world.

Beyond the material world and the material body, real harmony and equality might be achieved. The spirits taught that the body was a material envelope, simply matter the spirit manipulated and maneuvered. Rey's father reported that he did not fully understand that his body was merely a temporary covering until his death. A variety of spirits repeated the description of the body as a temporary, material envelope, from deceased family members to anonymous brothers to Abraham Lincoln. Confucius defined the "death of the material envelope" as a spirit's "disappearance into the Great Whole." The material envelope presented "defects" that limited the "development of the Spirit." A spirit would find "more happiness" once "freed from the material envelope and from materialism." Leaving behind the material envelope would be a "relief" from the "pain" caused by enslavement to "excess of passion." Volney told his Cercle Harmonique brothers that once they left the material behind, they could truly "be on the chariot of Progress." After leaving the material world, the spirit underwent glorious "transformations" showing the spirit's magnificence and beauty. Valmour explained that after he left his material envelope, he felt "happy and relieved." While his body was "dead," his spirit was "bright."[6] The spirit was better off without a body because matter bound and limited the spirit.

The ending of one's material life was a spiritual upgrade, but to get there, one first had to survive a material world ruled by greed, corruption, and prejudice. The Cercle Harmonique saw slow progress and the continued strengthening of white supremacy in Reconstruction New Orleans, and increasingly the spirit world might have seemed more and more like a pie in the sky, an elusive dream, or an immaterial fantasy with no bearing on the material world. At the time of their deaths, perhaps only one or two members of the Cercle Harmonique still believed in the spiritual republic. The egalitarian promise in spirits' messages remained intangible, and in 1877 Reconstruction came to an official close though the South had not really been rebuilt. In the words of the historian Eric Foner, it was a "failure."[7] Congress's vision failed as did the spirits' plan for the United States. Rey's séance records end in late 1877.

"I tell you, my children, it depends on you"[8]

By 1877 Rey was the only remaining member of the Afro-Creole Spiritualist circle. Other members of the Cercle Harmonique had died, moved away, or simply ceased their participation. Why some members stopped attending the meetings is not always clear in the records, but perhaps some lost their faith in Spiritualism. The progress of the Idea was slow, particularly when compared with the resurgence of white supremacy and the Democrats' "Redemption" of the South. The spirit of Cercle Harmonique member Jules Mallet apologized for his later indifference during his material life, and in 1875 his spirit acknowledged that Victor Lavigne and Rey were right to keep the practice going. Mallet's spirit admitted he had begun to doubt the effectiveness and truth of the practice of Spiritualism, but in death, he recognized his uncertainties were wrong.[9] Emilien Planchard continued to practice with Rey until November 1875, when he lost his job and possibly left town. It is unclear when and why Petit and Lavigne left Rey's table. In early December 1875, Rey lost his home in a great fire, further disrupting what remained of the circle's practice. Rey's home insurance had expired two days before the fire, and the fire spread quickly, leaving him little time to rescue his "precious objects." René Grandjean does not report in his notes if Rey sacrificed other belongings to save the séance record books or if the books had been in the care of a friend, such as Petit or Lavigne, at the time of the fire.[10]

For most of the final two years of the séance records (1876 and 1877), Rey recorded the spirit messages on sheets of loose-leaf paper later bound together. Though Rey was alone, the spirits of "many" told him not to be "discouraged." He owed it to his family and to all his brothers to continue to "carry" the "light" within him "as the one who can enlighten all!" Other spirits affirmed that Rey must "hold your position" of "fraternal respect." Rey's devoted spiritual advisor Saint Vincent de Paul remained with him through the end. Through "the midst" of Rey's "worldly pain," de Paul comforted Rey and reminded him of his many guides "who are constantly supporting and guiding you to your happiness." In Rey's final recorded message on 24 November 1877, a spirit identified simply as "Friend!" encouraged him: "Ah! Today, how your heart is full of hope, confidence, and assurance of ultimate success. Remember that we are with you, always." Rey joined his spiritual friends and guides seventeen years later on 19 April 1894, at the age of sixty-three.[11] It is unknown if Rey continued to believe in Spiritualism beyond November 1877, but it is no small coincidence that Rey's séance books end in 1877 as Republican Reconstruction in the South came to a close. It seems likely that Rey lost his faith in the possibility of racial harmony in the material world. The spirits' Idea had not delivered its republican promise.

From 1791, the year the Haitian Revolution began, to Reconstruction's end in 1877, the lives of Afro-Creoles in New Orleans changed greatly. They saw both a rise and then a fall in their civil and legal rights. Starting as a French colony, the Francophone base to New Orleans society, politics, culture, and religion was diluted over the years, but it never dissipated. The free black population pulled much cultural influence from the French and developing Creole culture, and this included religion. Unlike most urban centers in the early American colonies and early republic, New Orleans's dominant religion was Catholicism, and many Afro-Creoles had Catholic backgrounds. French and Spanish Catholicism preached a message of universal salvation, welcomed into the church both slave and free, and baptized children of all races and from interracial, unwed relationships. The city's connections to the Atlantic and Caribbean worlds added to this Catholic influence, and the city developed a strong black Catholic population. Not only Catholic but revolutionary ideas also crossed the Atlantic and found a receptive audience among the Afro-Creoles on the island of Saint-Domingue and in Louisiana.

During the years of Spanish colonial rule, the regulations on slave manumissions were more lax and the population of the *gens de couleur libres* grew. Further buttressing the role of the *gens de couleur libres* through the early years of American rule was the arrival and influence of refugees from Saint-Domingue, such as Rey's parents. But with U.S. rule also came stricter regulations on the free black population. It was harder to become "free" in Louisiana and that freedom became increasingly limited. City ordinances reduced the number of business and career possibilities for free blacks, and it became more difficult for additional free blacks to enter Louisiana. Afro-Creoles also watched their opportunities to create social clubs and benevolent societies dwindle. Though they might have owned a significant amount of New Orleans's wealth, particularly among the Creole population, their social visibility became more blurred and hidden. Even if an Afro-Creole was not a slave, the harsh reality of slavery and the racial hierarchy it supported shaped one's everyday life.

Emerging in tandem with these limitations on the *gens de couleur libres* was the city's increasing religious and ethnic diversity. The developing beliefs and practices of Voudou offered some of the city's Afro-Creoles, both slave and free, a religious alternative to the churches of their white owners or neighbors. Additionally, the influx of Italian and German immigrants along with the arrivals from the northern United States expanded the city's cultural milieu far beyond its earlier French, Spanish, and African influences. Mesmerism and Spiritualism gained popularity among the city's Creole populations, too. The French Catholic dominance of the city remained but gradually was punctured with pockets of other ethnic Catholics and Protestants. At the same time, authority in the parishes shifted from a trustee system to a more centralized hierarchy. Racial, social, and cultural friction was on the rise as Louisiana seceded and the Civil War reached New Orleans.

Once the Union took New Orleans, the Afro-Creoles' status began to climb again. Afro-Creoles served in the army and hoped that in return for their service they would be awarded full civil and legal rights. This would be a hard fight, and it was not until after one of the country's bloodiest postwar days, 30 July 1866, that male black suffrage was federally guaranteed. Radical Reconstruction was a hopeful time for the country's black population, but the Mechanics' Institute Riot proved an inauspicious beginning. Black New Orleanians voted and participated in the government, from local city committees to lieutenant governor. However, this hopeful time was temporary and not without political tension or corruption within the Republican Party. Additionally, though the Confederates were defeated, white supremacy was not. Negative reports in the local newspapers denigrated black politics and demonized alternative black religious cultures. The creation of the White League in New Orleans demonstrated the continued strength of old white southern power. Another bloody day followed in September 1874, when the White League overtook the city and for a brief time removed the lawful Republican government from power. Though the federal government restored Republican rule, it was clear that the political and social climates of the city, state, and region were changing again. The end of Reconstruction and the Democrats' "Redemption" of Louisiana came as no surprise a few years after the Battle of Liberty Place.

It was during the promising but temporary period between the Civil War and the end of Reconstruction that the Cercle Harmonique held their most productive and active meetings. Spiritualism provided the Afro-Creoles at the séance table with a new medium to express their political, social, spiritual, and racial goals. They looked to and listened to the spirit world, governed by egalitarian republicanism. The Cercle Harmonique hoped that humanity would progress as the spirits foretold and promised. Harmony would replace social friction, charity would replace materialism, pure spiritual leaders would replace corrupt priests, republicanism would replace despotism, egalitarianism would replace oligarchic rule, "bright" spirits would replace material bodies, and death would release the spirit from the corrupt material world into the higher spiritual spheres. The dream of equality would become reality. Ideally, political power and religious authority were to be equal among the people, and if any system were to dictate authority, it should be a meritocracy of charity and service. The French revolutionary motto "Liberté, Egalité, Fraternité" was revitalized by the Cercle Harmonique to convey the group's political ideology. Communication with the spirits provided the Afro-Creoles a forum to express their political protests, to identify injustices, and to celebrate republicanism. The world of the spirits was the ultimate republic, and the Cercle Harmonique hoped it could be imitated on earth.

Spiritualism mediated the political, social, and religious turbulence of the late antebellum period through Reconstruction. The rich literary culture of Afro-Creole men was sublimated into the Cercle Harmonique's practice, visible in how their Spiritualism emphasized concerns similar to those published in *Les Cenelles*, *L'Union*, and the *New Orleans Tribune*. Society's stereotypes and racial oppression held back progress. The participants in the Afro-Creole literary and educational circles often appeared in the practice of the Cercle Harmonique as spirits, as seated séance participants, or sometimes as both. The presence of Catholic spirits and Catholic ideas allowed the circle to remain connected to their Afro-Creole religious heritage, while the spirits' criticisms of priestly power enabled the Cercle Harmonique to separate themselves from the institutional church's corrupted ideas of religious authority and its support for the Confederacy. No priests, no tyrants—the people should be king.

Spirits of the French Revolution and Haitian Revolution echoed their worldly agendas in their spirit messages by decrying despotism, slavery, inequality, and oligarchy. The "spirit of '93" unleashed the Idea in the world, and the Afro-Creole members of the Cercle Harmonique wanted egalitarian republicanism to mold the post–Civil War United States. The world of the spirits was harsh toward slavery and the Confederacy, and the spirit guides identified white supremacy as the new oligarchy in need of defeat. America's destiny was to fulfill the republican promise it made to *all* her people. The spirits recognized that this would not be an easy process and celebrated martyrdom for the cause of black liberty. The Idea's martyrs, especially Lincoln, Brown, and those who died in the Mechanics' Institute Riot, appeared to the Afro-Creole Spiritualists and reaffirmed the meaning of their deaths. Death itself was not to be feared because it meant release from a material and raced body. After death one could enlist fully in the spiritual republic.

A close examination of the Afro-Creoles' séance records provides a clearer depiction of their lives. The Afro-Creole men (and occasional women) seated at the table engaged in a dynamic religious culture that connected them to a deep spiritual genealogy curated through their practice. Members of the Cercle Harmonique did not abandon religion when they left the Catholic Church. Resonances of Catholicism reverberated through the practice, but it was also a significant religious change from a church they saw as disconnected from the people. And the people were who mattered. The political nature of so many messages illustrated the Cercle Harmonique's democratic and republican hopes for the immediate world. The spirits spoke directly to the needs and the situation of members of the circle and those like them—a population who first watched their little social prestige fade and then felt optimism for a truly harmonious world. Members of the Cercle Harmonique worked out their frustrations and voiced their hopes through Spiritualism as their social status wavered and their political rights developed in fits and starts. They looked forward to humanity's progress and felt vindicated by the spirits' promise that it was on the horizon. But members of the Cercle Harmonique seemed to slowly lose their faith in racial harmony and shrank to one medium by the close of Reconstruction.

Postscript

Though 24 November 1877 marks Rey's final entry in his séance books, it is not the spirit message with the latest date. René Grandjean, Petit's son-in-law, was a French émigré who arrived in New Orleans in 1911 by way of Cuba and Haiti. Grandjean married Assitha Dubuclet in 1913 and later became the caretaker of Rey's séance books. In addition to his role as Cercle Harmonique archivist, he was a Spiritualist and an amateur historian who shared notes with local Afro-Creole historian Rodolphe Lucien Desdunes, author of 1911's *Nos Hommes et Notre Historie,* the first scholarly look at the Afro-Creole community. Based on his conversations with Petit, Grandjean made historical notes in the pages of the register books and occasionally recorded brief reflections on the content in the margins. Of Rey's passing, Grandjean wrote: "Rey . . . the dedicated worker, the noble Apostle went to the world of spirits to find the apostles that had preceded him and with whom he had communicated their instructions to all."[12]

Grandjean also copied eight short spirit messages from 1906 in the end pages of one register book. These messages predate Grandjean's arrival in New Orleans and were addressed to "François," "Petit," "Dear child," "My daughter," or "Assitha." With the exception of one message from "V. de Paule," the recorded messages were signed "Mme. Dubuclet" or "sa mère" (your mother).[13] From where Grandjean copied these messages is unknown, but they indicate that even if Petit left Rey alone in the final years of Rey's practice, Petit did not cease believing in Spiritualism and even introduced his daughter Assitha to the practice. The messages are ones of love, family, and encouragement, revealing the spirit of a loving mother and wife who continued to look after her family. But these final messages lack the political potency of the Cercle Harmonique. Gone were the days of Voltaire, O. J. Dunn, John Brown, Abraham Lincoln, Robespierre, and A. P. Dostie. The political nature of the earlier messages depended on those seated at the table.

Notes

Introduction

1. Those "suffering spirits" frequently believed "themselves to be in Hell, and forever!" This spirit continued that it was a kind of hell, though one of their own making. René Grandjean Collection, Register (Reg.) 85-51, 17 March 1873, message from "another devoted brother."

2. Grandjean Collection, Reg. 85-32, 18 February 1869.

3. Though the name Cercle Harmonique may not have been officially adopted until after the Civil War, Rey began practicing Spiritualism regularly with other Afro-Creoles shortly after his conversion.

4. The term "spiritual republic" comes from the writings of nineteenth-century American Spiritualist Andrew Jackson Davis in *Beyond the Valley*, 323–26.

5. Grandjean Collection, Reg. 85-31, 12 February 1869.

6. Pension records describe Rey in this manner, quoted in Daggett, "Henry Louis Rey," 33.

7. Because the Cercle Harmonique was primarily male, I used masculine pronouns when quoting or paraphrasing spirit messages.

8. Occasionally a message was transcribed in English, indicating that Cercle Harmonique members were likely bilingual. When this happened, it was almost always from an American spirit (John Brown or Daniel Webster), though these particular spirits did not always communicate in English. For example, Brown's messages came in both languages. Thus, choosing what language the message was transcribed in may have been the call of that meeting's scribe. Regardless, messages in English were rare, limiting the circle to French and bilingual speakers.

9. Modern, *Secularism in Antebellum America*, 41.

10. To put this another way, the Cercle Harmonique created what social theorist Michael Warner called a counterpublic, a response or alternative to the public, formed "against the background of the public sphere." Counterpublics are "formed by their conflict with the norms and contexts of their cultural environment." Similar to the subaltern, a counterpublic creates subjectivities in response to the authoritative culture as outsiders or subordinates to the larger public. Warner, *Publics and Counterpublics*, 56–63.

11. Throughout this text, when Republican is capitalized, it is in reference to the political party affiliation. When republican is lowercase, it refers to general republicanism. Democrat and democratic are treated similarly.

12. Kucich, *Ghostly Communion*, xii.

13. Butler, *Awash in a Sea of Faith*. Ann Braude concurs with this appraisal in an earlier rendition of Butler's work in *Radical Spirits*. Also see Carroll, *Spiritualism in Antebellum America*, 4; Cox, *Body and Soul,* 16. Catherine Albanese agrees with Butler to an extent, but ultimately finds metaphysical religion (or the occult, as Butler referenced it) central to the story of American religious history, an idea she argued in *A Republic of Mind and Spirit*. Albanese also dates the origins of American Spiritualism before the Fox sisters by looking at Native American religions.

14. Braude, "News from the Spirit World"; Nartonis, "The Rise of 19th-century American Spiritualism."

15. Bell, *Revolution, Romanticism, and the Afro-Creole Protest Tradition in Louisiana*, 197–201.

16. Britten, *Modern American Spiritualism*, 22.

17. Andrew Jackson Davis, *The Principles of Nature*, 323.

18. Albanese, "On the Matter of Spirit," 4.

19. Andrew Jackson Davis, *Beyond the Valley*, 323.

20. Carroll, *Spiritualism in Antebellum America*, 37.

21. Hare, *Lecture on Spiritualism*, 14.

22. Cadwallader, "Spirit Photography and the Victorian Culture of Mourning"; Kaplan, "Where the Paranoid Meets the Paranormal"; Stolow, "The Spiritual Nervous System"; Walker, "The Humbug in American Religion"; Hazen, *The Village Enlightenment in America*, 65–112.

23. Andrew Jackson Davis, *The Present Age and Inner Life*, 68.

24. Braude, *Radical Spirits*; Morita, "Unseen (and Unappreciated) Matters"; Prothero, "From Spiritualism to Theosophy."

25. Modern, *Secularism in Antebellum America*, 18.

26. Braude's pivotal text *Radical Spirits* was one of the first books on Spiritualism to have popular appeal in the subfield of American religious history and American history more generally. Like *Radical Spirits*, *A Luminous Brotherhood* examines the practice of Spiritualism among a nonwhite male audience, but unlike *Radical Spirits*, this text places readers in the séance action of the Cercle Harmonique.

27. Andrew Jackson Davis, *Beyond the Valley*, 64.

28. Carroll, *Spiritualism in Antebellum America*, 37.

29. Braude, *Radical Spirits*; Carroll, "'A Higher Power to Feel'"; Moore, "The Spiritualist Medium"; Tromp, "Spirited Sexuality"; Owen, *The Darkened Room*.

30. Additionally, Finley, Guillory, and Page, eds., *Esotericism in African American Religious Experience* explores African American esoteric religion but not nineteenth-century American Spiritualism.

31. In *Ghosts of Futures Past: Spiritualism and the Cultural Politics of Nineteenth-Century America*, Molly McGarry investigates how the "ambivalent affiliations" Anglo-American Spiritualists developed with the Native American spirits they channeled reflected their "romantic attachments to an ideal or imagined Indian," but *Ghosts of Futures Past* stops short of offering nonwhite voices. McGarry, *Ghosts of Futures Past*,

66–93. For another work that considers the relationship between Spiritualism and Native Americans, see Bridget Bennett, "Sacred Theatres."

32. The example of the Cercle Harmonique aligns with the traditional focus on resistance and politics in the historiography of African American religions and yet does not easily subscribe to the subfield's emphasis on mainline Protestantism and Evangelicalism. In recent years scholars have expanded the historiography by taking seriously what Curtis Evans called the "burden of black religion" and identifying the "surprises, paradoxes, and ironies" in this historically contingent category. Evans, *The Burden of Black Religion*, 4–6; x.

33. For a small sampling of examples, see Glaude, *Exodus!*; Montgomery, *Under Their Own Vine and Fig Tree*; Raboteau, *Slave Religion*; Stowell, *Rebuilding Zion*.

34. Caribbean and Francophone studies scholar Richard Burton describes the transition of African to Afro-Creole as involving "at the same time cultural loss, cultural retention and reinterpretation, cultural imitation and borrowing, and cultural creation." Burton, *Afro-Creole*, 5. Also see Robert Farris Thompson, *Flash of the Spirit*; Joyner, *Down by the Riverside*; Young, *Rituals of Resistance*.

35. For example, see Dominguez, *White by Definition*; Dubois and Melançon, "Creole Is, Creole Ain't"; Eble, "Creole in Louisiana"; Dawdy, *Building the Devil's Empire*.

36. Shirley Thompson, *Exiles at Home*, 17.

37. Schmidt, "From Demon Possession to Magic Show," 302. Also see, Schmidt, *Hearing Things*.

38. Schmidt, *Restless Souls*, 15; Noll, *America's God*.

39. Grandjean Collection, Reg. 85-38, 2 January 1872, message signed Ambroise.

40. Israel, *Revolutionary Ideas*, 11.

41. Howe, *What Hath God Wrought*, 52.

42. Spiritualism as a whole has been examined as a transnational tradition, but the United States is typically absent from this historiographical thread. See note 30 in Cox, *Body and Soul*, 242. Bridget Bennett's *Spiritualism and Nineteenth-Century American Literature* is the exception.

43. Earlier histories identified New Orleans, its culture, and its history as exceptional. For example, in the introduction to *Creole New Orleans: Race and Americanization*, editors Arnold R. Hirsch and Joseph Logsdon identified New Orleans as "a very peculiar city" and "a strange province in the American South." Hirsch and Logsdon, "Preface," ix–xi.

44. Thus, *A Luminous Brotherhood* builds on the conclusions of Paul Johnson and Charles Long in *New Territories, New Perspectives*. Long classified New Orleans as a quintessential American city because it provides the best vantage point from which to script a more accurate and full narrative of American religious history. Though it is seldom mentioned in stories of America's founding, a variety of Native American, European, and African peoples forged relationships and exchanged ideas in New Orleans history, as Long emphasized. Charles Long, "New Orleans as an American City"; Paul Johnson. "Vodou Purchase."

45. Tweed, "Introduction," 17. Another historian who pushes against the story of New Orleans exceptionalism is Emily J. Clark. See, Clark, "How American is New Orleans?" and "Moving from Periphery to Centre." Also see Frymer, Strolovitch, and Warren, "New Orleans is Not the Exception."

46. The Cercle Harmonique has not been thoroughly investigated. To date, sections in two published books, one master's degree thesis, and one journal article complete the group's primary historiography. For previous examinations of the Cercle Harmonique see Bell, *Revolution, Romanticism, and the Afro-Creole Protest Tradition in Louisiana*, 215–21; Cox, *Body and Soul*, 171–88; Daggett, "Henry Louis Rey;" Daggett, "Spiritualism Among Creoles of Color in Nineteenth-Century New Orleans."

47. Parts of their archive are nearly unreadable due to faded ink.

48. Grandjean Collection, Reg. 85-44, 25 August 1872.

49. Grandjean Collection, Reg. 85-57, 15 September 1874.

50. Grandjean Collection, Reg. 85-31, 12 March 1869.

51. Grandjean Collection, Reg. 85-38, 8 February 1872.

52. Grandjean Collection, Reg. 85-31, 24 February 1869.

Chapter One

1. The *Daily True Delta* reported that "Miss Emma Hardinge" would begin delivering free lectures on Spiritualism in December. *Daily True Delta*, 27 November 1859.

2. Grandjean Collection, Reg. 85-64, Grandjean notes.

3. Britten, *Modern American Spiritualism*, 428–29.

4. Ibid., 205.

5. *The Daily Picayune*, 31 March 1843, 5 November 1842.

6. *The Daily Picayune*, 4 April 1842, 23 February 1843. In July 1843, the *Daily Picayune* adopted the language of animal magnetism to refer to the city's current state and interest: "The city at the present time is in a perfect state of mesmerism." *The Daily Picayune*, 16 July 1843.

7. Bell, *Revolution, Romanticism, and the Afro-Creole Protest Tradition*, 198.

8. Quoted in Braude, *Radical Spirits*, 29–30.

9. Tomlinson and Perret, "Le Mesmérisme á la Nouvelle-Orléans de 1845 á 1861."

10. "Prospectus," *Le Propagateur Catholique*, 12 November 1842.

11. Bell, *Revolution, Romanticism, and the Afro-Creole Protest Tradition*, 201–9.

12. This comes from the tagline of *Le Spiritualiste de la Nouvelle-Orléans*: "Ils ne sont pas morts. Parlez-leur, ils vous répondront" ("They are not dead. Talk to them, they will answer"). Issues of *Le Spiritualiste de la Nouvelle-Orléans* were later published in yearly volumes for its short publication tenure.

13. Barthet, *Le Spiritualiste*, 3.

14. One long article responding to Perché's remarks includes a mention of how the Spiritualists tried to correct Perché. The article informs readers that a letter was sent

to *Le Propagateur Catholique* for the priest that responded to his claims regarding Spiritualism, and that Perché chose to continue to misspeak about Spiritualism.

15. Barthet, *Le Spiritualiste*, 143–47.

16. For example, *The Daily Picayune*, 24 November 1853.

17. Testut, *Le Vieux Salomon*, 95.

18. The worldview of Testut's characters and of Testut himself also resembled that of Hugues-Félicité Robert de Lamennais, a French revolutionary priest who frequently visited the Cercle Harmonique. Abel, *Charles Testut's Le Vieux Salomon*, 8.

19. Bell, *Revolution, Romanticism, and the Afro-Creole Protest Tradition in Louisiana*, 201–6.

20. Grandjean Collection, Reg. 85-31, 10 December 1865, message from Mesmer.

21. Barthet, quoted in Bell, *Revolution, Romanticism, and the Afro-Creole Protest Tradition*, 206.

22. Desdunes, *Our People and Our History*, 53. Valmour's funeral announcement refers to him as "VALMOUR (medium)." *New Orleans Tribune*, 7 February 1869.

23. Bell, *Revolution, Romanticism, and the Afro-Creole Protest Tradition in Louisiana*, 187.

24. Grandjean Collection, Notebook 85–92. Grandjean notes include other stories of Valmour's successful cures. Grandjean Collection, Reg. 85-36 notes include cures of others, including Lavigne. For the story with the bishop, Grandjean Collection, Reg. 85-47, Grandjean notes.

25. In a short 1907 publication entitled *A Few Words to Dr. Dubois: "With Malice toward None,"* Creole of color and political figure Rodolphe Lucien Desdunes differentiated between the "Anglo-Saxon or American Negro" and the "Latin Negro." What Desdunes noted was a philosophical and political difference between the two kinds of blacks in the South whom the 1896 Supreme Court case *Plessy v. Ferguson* legally categorized together. According to Desdunes: "The Latin Negro differs radically from the Anglo-Saxon in aspiration and in method. One hopes, the other doubts. Thus we often perceive that one makes every effort to acquire merits, the other to gain advantages. One aspires to equality, the other to identity. One forgets he is a Negro in order to think that he is a man; the other will forget that he is a man in order to think that he is a Negro. These radical differences act on the feelings of both in direct harmony with those characteristics. One is a philosophical Negro, the other practical." He associated identity politics with the "American Negro" and equality with the "Latin Negro." Whether or not this was an accurate distinction, some Afro-Creoles continued to maintain an ethnic and cultural boundary between themselves and non-Creole blacks. Rodolphe Lucien Desdunes, *A Few Words to Dr. Dubois: "With Malice toward None,"* March 1907, Tureaud Papers, Box 37, Amistad Research Center, Tulane University.

26. Bell, *Revolution, Romanticism, and the Afro-Creole Protest Tradition*, 215.

27. Desdunes, *Our People and Our History*, 10–60; Cheung, "'Les Cenelles' and Quadroon Balls"; Haddox, "The 'Nous' of Southern Catholic Quadroons"; Jerah Johnson,

"Les Cenelles"; Bell, *Revolution, Romanticism, and the Afro-Creole Protest Tradition,* 105–23.

28. The most active years were 1872 and 1873, with 1871 and 1874 following as the next most active.

29. Grandjean Collection, Reg. 85-38, 31 January 1872, message from "Delauney (father)"; Grandjean Collection, Reg. 85-34, Grandjean notes; Grandjean Collection, Reg. 85-36, Grandjean notes; Grandjean Collection, Reg. 85-57, Grandjean notes; Daggett, "Henry Louis Rey," 48–49; Grandjean Collection, Reg. 85-45, 6 September 1872, message from E. Darcantel; Grandjean Collection, Reg. 85-45, 7 September 1872, message from Ludenberg; Grandjean Collection, Reg. 85-60, 10 November 1875.

30. All the names that Grandjean lists as regular members are men. Grandjean Collection, Reg. 85-36, Grandjean notes. Message after message addressed the group as "mes frères" or "my brothers." An example of a message that refers to "mes frères et sœurs" was from a female spirit, the former medium Louise, at whose home Rey first transcribed a message. Grandjean Collection, Reg. 85-33, 9 June 1871. A few days later when "Boniface" appeared, he also referred to "mes Frères et Sœurs."

31. Grandjean Collection, Reg. 85-33, 9 June 1871; Grandjean Collection, Reg. 85-70, 2 March 1873.

32. Grandjean Collection, Reg. 85-40, 28 April 1872; Grandjean Collection, Reg. 85-34, 8 December 1871; Grandjean Collection, Reg. 85-43, 3 August 1872, message from *"L'Inconnu"* (The Unknown); Grandjean Collection, Reg. 85-44, 8 August 1872.

33. Pension records describe Rey in this manner, quoted in Daggett, "Henry Louis Rey," 33.

34. Grandjean Collection, Reg. 85-30, 26 October, 1859. Barthélemy referenced this experience in some of his later messages. Grandjean Collection, Reg. 85-35, 11 December 1871. "I communicated with my son, May 29, 1852, the day of my departure." Grandjean Collection, Reg. 85-41, 27 May 1872, message from Abner; Grandjean Collection, Reg. 85-51, 28 March 1873, message from "a brother"; Grandjean Collection, Reg. 85-30, 29 November 1858.

35. Bell, *Revolution, Romanticism, and the Afro-Creole Protest Tradition,* 216.

36. Carolyn Morrow Long, "Marie Laveau," 290; Carolyn Morrow Long, *A New Orleans Voudou Priestess,* 66, 167. For Glapion/Crocker genealogy, see Carolyn Morrow Long, *A New Orleans Voudou Priestess,* 183. A message from a spirit identified as "A. Glapion" was recorded on 25 July 1872. Crocker and Glapion had a daughter named Adelai Aldina who died in 1871. Grandjean Collection, Reg. 85-43.

37. Desdunes, *Our People and Our History,* 101–8.

38. *Prospectus de L'Institution Catholique des Orphelins Indigents.*

39. DeVore and Logsdon, *Crescent City Schools,* 42.

40. Grandjean Collection, Reg. 85-30, 26 October, 1859. This particular entry in the register book is a long autobiographical essay detailing the Rey family's interactions with Spiritualism.

41. Bell, *Revolution, Romanticism, and the Afro-Creole Protest Tradition*, 216. In some of his notes, René Grandjean describes Sœur Louise (her last name is not given) as having dark black skin. Grandjean Collection, Notebook 85–92. Louise would later come to the table as a spirit.

42. Some of Rey's registers contain pages of what appears to be pencil scribbling.

43. Grandjean Collection, Reg. 85-45, Grandjean notes.

44. Grandjean Collection, Reg. 85-30, 28 November 1859.

45. In a message received on 29 May, 1871, Barthélemy Rey expressed his joy of seeing both Henri and Octave at the séance table. Grandjean Collection, Reg. 85-33.

46. Grandjean Collection, Reg. 85-53, Grandjean notes. Desdunes reports that Octave Rey was a Metropolitan Police captain and that his superiors spoke highly of him. Desdunes, *Our People and Our History*, 114.

47. In 1874, a Corporal Reading was "sorry" that "Capt. R your brother" (meaning Rey's brother, Octave) was not using his powers "as a medium between us and your world." Grandjean Collection, Reg. 85-56, 24 August 1874. Message recorded in English.

48. Dunn was busy at the time—"immersed in reflections on his past life"—but the spirit of "Lucile la vieille" (Lucile the old) assured Lucia that Dunn would come some other time. Grandjean Collection, Reg. 85-34, 30 November 1871.

49. The involvement of free blacks in the Confederate volunteers has puzzled some historians. Many blacks undoubtedly enlisted with the Confederacy fearing that they otherwise would be suspected as traitors. Others may have volunteered in order to defend their home city, and at least a few did so to maintain the economic and racial status quo in Louisiana. The black soldiers' defensive explanation for joining the Confederate troops was not fully developed and widely deployed until some were forced to give official statements regarding their volunteer enlistment with the Confederacy.

50. Desdunes, *Our People and Our History*, 118–19.

51. Hollandsworth, *The Louisiana Native Guards*, 120.

52. *L'Union*, 27 September 1862.

53. Daggett, "Henry Louis Rey," 46, 52.

54. Vincent, "Aspects of the Family and Public Life of Antoine Dubuclet"; Desdunes, *Our People and Our History*, 74–75; Christian, "Let Freedom Ring," in "The Negro in Louisiana," unpublished manuscript (1942), Christian Collection, Louisiana and Special Collections, Earl K. Long Library, University of New Orleans, available online: http://cdm16313.contentdm.oclc.org/cdm/landingpage/collection/p15140coll42.

55. Though this particular spirit always signed "Lamenais," the spirit was that of French priest Hugues-Félicité Robert de Lamennais. Even though the Cercle Harmonique was educated, they occasionally spelled things incorrectly. All subsequent references to the spirit or the historical priest will spell his name correctly.

56. Grandjean Collection, Reg. 85-31, Grandjean notes; Grandjean Collection, Reg. 85-31, 8 January 1869, message from "Nelson DesBrosses and others"; Grandjean

Collection, Reg. 85-31, 6 February 1869; Grandjean Collection, Reg. 85-41, 7 May 1872; Grandjean Collection, Reg. 85-43, 23 July 1872, message from Bilvana.

57. Grandjean Collection, Reg. 85-42, 22 June 1872; Grandjean Collection, Reg. 85-34, 27 November 1871; Grandjean Collection Reg. 85-31, 7 April 1869. Valmour shouts that he missed Petit in two short back-to-back messages.

58. Grandjean Collection, Reg. 85-35, 19 December 1871, message from Valmour signed "your brother and friend."

59. Grandjean Collection, Reg. 85-64.

60. Grandjean Collection, Reg. 85-56, 16 August 1874; Grandjean Collection, Reg. 85-32, 3 September 1874, message signed X; Grandjean Collection, Reg. 85-44, 25 August 1872; Grandjean Collection, Reg. 85-40, 4 April 1872, message from Lamennais.

61. Grandjean Collection, Reg. 85-40, 2 May 1872, message from Joanni; Grandjean Collection, Reg. 85-53, 1 February 1874, message from a "devoted sister." But on one occasion, Rey disregarded a message he received. Once, Rey reported to Valmour that a spirit asked Rey to transcribe a message that was "against" his beliefs. Valmour advised him to "write, always write" and afterward they would "consider" it. If the message was inconsistent with other messages and their beliefs in general, they would "reject" it. Grandjean Collection, Reg. 85-42, Grandjean notes.

62. Grandjean Collection, Reg. 85-30, 20 February 1859, message marked "Seul" and from Swedenborg; Grandjean Collection, Reg. 85-46, 4 November 1872, message from Joseph Rey; Grandjean Collection, Reg. 85-30, 19 June 1858, message from Sophia Jacisto; Grandjean Collection, Reg. 85-48, 23 December 1872, message from Celena Durel; Grandjean Collection, Reg. 85-56, 20 July 1874, message from Vincent de Paul; Grandjean Collection, Reg. 85-36, 27 May 1872, message from Volney; Grandjean Collection, Reg. 85-37, 22 November 1875. For example, Père Antoine reminded Rey of his earlier messages at the circle of Louise. Grandjean Collection, Reg. 85-63, 13 May 1877. Since Rey was likely practicing alone at this time, the messages he and others had compiled for years were consulted and regarded like a treasured friend.

63. Grandjean Collection, Reg. 85-31, Grandjean notes; Grandjean Collection, Reg. 85-49, Grandjean notes. Grandjean wrote in his notes that Sister Francis Degruy was a local mother of eight whom Valmour introduced to Spiritualism. He did not note the regularity or irregularity of her attendance at the Cercle Harmonique. Grandjean Collection, Reg. 85-51, Grandjean notes.

64. *New Orleans Tribune*, 25 April 1865; *New Orleans Tribune*, 30 July 1867.

65. Grandjean Collection, Reg. 85-33, 17 June 1871, message from "*L'Inconnu*"; Grandjean Collection, Reg. 85-39, Rules to be followed for the Harmonic Séance; Grandjean Collection, Reg. 85-36, 1 April 1872; Grandjean Collection, Reg. 85-43, 14 July 1872; Grandjean Collection, Reg. 85-44, 13 August 1872.

66. Grandjean Collection, Reg. 85-45, 6 September 1872, message from E. Darcantel; Grandjean Collection, Reg. 85-40, 9 April 1872; Grandjean Collection, Reg. 85-57,

Grandjean notes; Grandjean Collection, Reg. 85-43, 3 August 1872, message from "*L'Inconnu*"; Grandjean Collection, Reg. 85-60, 4 October 1875, message from Jeanne Dastugue. In the case of the Webster message, the circle had recently welcomed a "child" to the table and since then had "very little success." Webster's advice was first to "procure, if possible, a well-developed medium; so that we may insinuate our ideas with more facility." Secondly, and perhaps more importantly, the circle should make sure that the child understood the purpose of Spiritualism and possessed a supportive family. If the child's relatives, "especially of the father and mother," held contrary beliefs, this could be the problem. However, the child's presence at the table and hearing "this wholesome lecture" should help rectify the problem. Grandjean Collection, Reg. 85-31, 23 January 1866.

67. Grandjean Collection, Reg. 85-34, 19 November 1871; Grandjean Collection, Reg. 85-42, Grandjean notes; Grandjean Collection, Reg. 85-31, 20 March 1867. Grandjean Collection, Reg. 85-32, 5 April 1870, message from Sister Louise; Grandjean Collection, Reg. 85-33, 17 May 1871; Grandjean Collection, Reg. 85-46, 20 October 1872, message from Mesmer; Grandjean Collection, Reg. 85-59, 8 March 1875, message from a spirit signed as X; Grandjean Collection, Reg. 85-36, 25 July 1872, message from Abner.

68. Grandjean Collection, Reg. 85-32, 8 October 1872; Grandjean Collection, Reg. 85-40, 3 May 1872.

69. Grandjean Collection, Reg. 85-34, 19 November 1871; Grandjean Collection, Reg. 85-44, 23 August 1872, message in English from Thomas Warrick; Grandjean Collection, Reg. 85-38, 6 February 1872, message from Bonnaventure Dénis; Grandjean Collection, Reg. 85-63, 22 July 1877, message from John Hoffman; Grandjean Collection, Reg. 85-36, 14 June 1872, message from Victoire Bonnecaze; Grandjean Collection, Reg. 85-56, 10 June 1874, message from James O'Brook; Grandjean Collection, Reg. 85-56, 19 June 1874, message from Maximilien; Grandjean Collection, Reg. 85-58, 10 December 1874, message from John Augustin; Grandjean Collection, Reg. 85-59, 4 January 1875, message from Paul Dubrue; Grandjean Collection, Reg. 85-51, 26 April 1873, message from Joseph Lucas.

70. While Confucius's presence may be unexpected, Chinese laborers worked in and around New Orleans after the Civil War. The name Confucius also makes occasional appearances in local newspapers during the late nineteenth century.

71. Grandjean Collection, Reg. 85-31, 20 November 1865. The day before, Mesmer also came before the circle to encourage their "spiritual growth." Grandjean Collection, Reg. 85-32, 1 June 1871; Grandjean Collection, Reg. 85-32, 1 June 1871; Grandjean Collection, Reg. 85-32, 6 October 1872; Grandjean Collection, Reg. 85-30, 20 February 1859; Grandjean Collection, Reg. 85-40, 23 April 1872, message from Alpha; Grandjean Collection, Reg. 85-36, 2 September 1872; Grandjean Collection, Reg. 85-35, 13 December 1871.

72. McGarry, *Ghosts of Futures Past*, 21–28; Lutz, "The Dead Still among Us"; Cox, *Body and Soul*, 127–31.

73. Grandjean Collection, Reg. 85-31, 12 December 1865; Grandjean Collection, Reg. 85-48, 9 December 1872; Grandjean Collection, Reg. 85-38, 15 January 1872, message from "your devoted brother, Lunel, who watches"; Grandjean Collection, Reg. 85-32, message from B. Brion (père).

74. Grandjean Collection, Reg. 85-31, 25 December 1865. Henriette Lavinge also delivered more general messages of encouragement and advice, see Grandjean Collection, Reg. 85-48, 7 December 1872 and 12 December 1872. Grandjean Collection, Reg. 85-33, 17 June 1871. For more from Joseph Rey, also see Grandjean Collection, 85-38, 2 February 1872. See Grandjean Collection, Reg. 85-34, 19 November 1871, for a message from Pierre. See Grandjean Collection, Reg. 85-35, 13 December 1871, for a message from Rose Crocker immediately followed by one from Pierre. Grandjean Collection, Reg. 85-48, 17 December 1872, message signed Rose Gignac (Rose Crocker). Grandjean Collection, Reg. 85-36, 12 February 1872, message from Charles identifying "courage and patience" and "magic words." Grandjean Collection, Reg. 85-38, 3 February 1872. Grandjean Collection, Reg. 85-36, 10 May 1872.

75. Grandjean Collection, Reg. 85-31, 3 February 1867; Grandjean Collection, Reg. 85-31, 4 March 1867; Grandjean Collection, Reg. 85-31, 20 May 1866 and Grandjean notes; Grandjean Collection, Reg. 85-31, Grandjean notes; Grandjean Collection, Reg. 85-31, 18 February 1869.

76. Grandjean Collection, Reg. 85-31, 13 February 1869; Grandjean Collection, Reg. 85-38, 25 January 1872; Grandjean Collection, Reg. 85-35, 25 December 1871; Grandjean Collection, Reg. 85-39, 22 February 1872. For Lorenzo Dow's message in English during which he attested that he was in the "light," see Grandjean Collection, Reg. 85-52, 9 November 1873. Grandjean Collection, Reg. 85-35, 18 December 1871, two messages from Montezuma. Grandjean Collection, Reg. 85-35, 27 December 1871, spirits named Pacoha, Poloah, and Piloho followed Pocahontas. Grandjean Collection, Reg. 85-63, 14 September 1877. Grandjean Collection, Reg. 85-58, 13 December 1874.

77. Grandjean Collection, Reg. 85-37, Grandjean notes; Grandjean Collection, Reg. 85-47, 7 November 1872; Grandjean Collection, Reg. 85-35, 11 December 1871; Grandjean Collection, Reg. 85-47, 10 November 1872; Grandjean Collection, Reg. 85-51, 14 June 1873; Grandjean Collection, Reg. 85-54, 7 April 1874. For a message where Joanni [Questy] served as intermediary, see Grandjean Collection, Reg. 85-59, 5 March 1875; Grandjean Collection, Reg. 85-41, 15 May 1872; Grandjean Collection, Reg. 85-43, 15 July 1872; Grandjean Collection, Reg. 85-44, 27 August 1872; Grandjean Collection, Reg. 85-63, 18 October 1877. Grandjean noted that a message from a spirit identified as E. Marc was a member of Barthet's circle. Grandjean Collection, Reg. 85-63, 23 October 1877, Grandjean notes. On another occasion, a spirit simply identified as Barthet accompanied two other spirits in a brief message of encouragement. Grandjean Collection, Reg. 85-31, 8 December 1865; Grandjean Collection, Reg. 85-33, 9 June 1871; Grandjean Collection, Reg. 85-51, 14 June 1873; Grandjean Collection, Reg. 85-36, 1 April 1872.

78. Grandjean Collection, Reg. 85-38, 6 February 1872.

79. Blassingame, *Black New Orleans*, 108, 136; Desdunes, *Our People and Our History*, 68; Bell, *Revolution, Romanticism, and the Afro-Creole Protest Tradition in Louisiana*, 215–20; Shapiro and Weiss, "Duhart, Adolphe." A message signed by Lelia Duhart told the Afro-Creole Spiritualists not to grieve over the dead, for in death the spirit passes into the glorious world of the spirits. Grandjean Collection, Reg. 85-40, 30 March 1872.

80. For example, the spirit of Paul Mateo, a "good boy" from Bayou Lafourche, informed the circle that he was "calm and happy." Grandjean Collection, Reg. 85-54, 8 April 1874. The same day as his death in Baton Rouge, the spirit of Henry Shephard reported his happiness in the spirit world. Grandjean Collection, Reg. 85-58, 23 November 1874.

81. According to Grandjean's notes next to a message from Leaumont received on 12 April 1872, Leaumont must have owned copies of Andrew Jackson Davis's works because he once saw copies with "Charles Leaumont" written on the inside cover. Grandjean Collection, Reg. 85-36.

82. Grandjean Collection, Reg. 85-58, 28 October 1874; Grandjean Collection, Reg. 85-38, 8 February 1872.

83. Grandjean Collection, Reg. 85-31, Grandjean notes; Grandjean Collection, Reg. 85-55; Grandjean Collection, Reg. 85-58, 25 November 1874. Not surprising considering that Dunn was African American in background rather than Afro-Creole, his messages arrived in English.

84. Grandjean Collection, Reg. 85-31, 20 May 1869.

85. Grandjean Collection, Reg. 85-38, 8 February 1872, message from Assitha; Grandjean Collection, Reg. 85-31, 9 January 1870, message from Ambroise; Grandjean Collection, Reg. 85-33, 1 June 1871, message from Lacour; Grandjean Collection, Reg. 85-38, 2 January 1872, message from Ambroise which cites all themes/trends in one sentence as "movements in humanity" that will "produce" a "good result"; Grandjean Collection, Reg. 85-39, 25 February 1872, message from Fénélon Boguille; Grandjean Collection, Reg. 85-34, 10 December 1871.

86. Grandjean Collection, Reg. 85-34, 11 August 1871; Grandjean Collection, Reg. 85-31, 15 October 1869; Grandjean Collection, Reg. 85-31, 25 October 1869; Grandjean Collection, Reg. 85-51, 17 March 1873, message from "a brother"; Grandjean Collection, Reg. 85-51, 24 March 1873, message from "a devoted sister."

87. Grandjean Collection, Reg. 85-31, 18 April 1869; Grandjean Collection, Reg. 85-36, 1 April 1872, message from Claire Pollard; Grandjean Collection, Reg. 85-33, 1 June 1871, message from Lacour; Grandjean Collection, Reg. 85-34, 4 December 1871, message from Vincent de Paul; Grandjean Collection, Reg. 85-31, 18 April 1869, message from Ambroise.

88. Grandjean Collection, Reg. 85-34, 25 July 1871; Grandjean Collection, Reg. 85-31, 19 February 1869; Grandjean Collection, Reg. 85-31, 24 December 1865, message from Henriette Lavinge; Grandjean Collection, Reg. 85-50, 7 March 1873, message from Augustine Daboval; Grandjean Collection, Reg. 85-31, 20 May

204 Notes to Chapter 1

1866, message from Rosalie Dubuclet; Grandjean Collection, Reg. 85-56, 7 June 1874, message from "a luminous brother"; Grandjean Collection, Reg. 85-52, 2 November 1873, message from Paul Hecaud.

89. Grandjean Collection, Reg. 85-36, 23 February 1872; Grandjean Collection, Reg. 85-46, 25 October 1872, message from Swedenborg; Grandjean Collection, Reg. 85-38, 17 January 1872; Grandjean Collection, Reg. 85-41, 19 May 1872, message from Volney; Grandjean Collection, Reg. 85-60, 28 June 1875, message from "a beloved sister."

90. Grandjean Collection, Reg. 85-56, 10 August 1874, message from Vincent de Paul; Grandjean Collection, Reg. 85-54, 3 April 1874, message from "a devoted sister"; Grandjean Collection, Reg. 85-63, 26 August 1877, message from Jesus; Grandjean Collection, Reg. 85-47, 27 November 1872, message from F. Escoffier; Grandjean Collection, Reg. 85-43, 21 July 1872; Grandjean Collection, Reg. 85-43, 25 July 1872, message from Volney; Grandjean Collection, Reg. 85-31, 16 April 1867.

91. Grandjean Collection, Reg. 85-40, 14 April 1872; Grandjean Collection, Reg. 85-41, 9 May 1872; Grandjean Collection, Reg. 85-59, 15 January 1875, message from "a devoted sister"; Grandjean Collection, Reg. 85-39, 1 March 1872, message from Père Ambroise; Grandjean Collection, Reg. 85-50, 9 March 1873, message from "a devoted brother"; Grandjean Collection, Reg. 85-56, 21 June 1874, message from X; Grandjean Collection, Reg. 85-58, 7 November 1874, message from Père Antoine; Grandjean Collection, Reg. 85-60, 20 September 1875, message from "André, a brother."

92. Grandjean Collection, Reg. 85-35, 13 December 1871; Grandjean Collection, Reg. 85-50, 22 February 1873, message from Alfred Delavigne; Grandjean Collection, Reg. 85-50, 2 March 1873, message from J. Lespinasse; Grandjean Collection, Reg. 85-52, 30 October 1873, message from "a brother."

93. Grandjean Collection, Reg. 85-59, 8 March 1875, message from a spirit signed as X; Grandjean Collection, Reg. 85-52, 3 December 1873; Grandjean Collection, Reg. 85-34, 9 November 1871; Grandjean Collection, Reg. 85-34, 27 November 1871.

94. Grandjean Collection, Reg. 85-33, 5 June 1871; Grandjean Collection, Reg. 85-31, 18 March 1870; Grandjean Collection, Reg. 85-31, 12 December 1869; Grandjean Collection, Reg. 85-33, 28 May 1871, message from Jesus; Grandjean Collection, Reg. 85-31, 18 April 1869.

95. Grandjean Collection, Reg. 85-40, 4 May 1872, message from Absalon; Grandjean Collection, Reg. 85-56, 9 June 1874, message from "a luminous brother"; Grandjean Collection, Reg. 85-60, 7 June 1875, message from "a luminous brother"; Grandjean Collection, Reg. 85-51, 18 March 1873, message from John Salvant.

96. Grandjean Collection, Reg. 85-42, 22 June 1872, message from Lamennais; Grandjean Collection, Reg. 85-35, 21 December 1871; Grandjean Collection, Reg. 85-51, 19 March 1873, message from "Lunel, the devoted brother"; Grandjean Collection, Reg. 85-40, 1 April 1872; Grandjean Collection, Reg. 85-41, 13 May 1872; Grandjean Collection, Reg. 85-32.

Chapter Two

1. "The Louisiana Question," *New York Times*, 25 January 1875.

2. Grandjean Collection, Reg. 85-59, 29 January 1875, message recorded in English from William Weeks.

3. Orsi, "Crossing the City Line," 6.

4. Grandjean Collection, Reg. 85-44, 8 August 1872, message signed "Lunel, the devoted brother."

5. Grandjean Collection, Reg. 85-34, 28 July 1871, message from P. L. Lareschi.

6. Hanger, *Bounded Lives, Bounded Places*; Ingersoll, "Free Blacks in a Slave Society," 180.

7. Article XXXIV of the Louisiana *Code Noir*, 1724.

8. Governor Miró first required the headdress in 1785 and the restriction remained in place during U.S. rule. Christian, "The Free Colored Class," in "The Negro in Louisiana." The tignon later would be associated frequently with New Orleans Creole women. For example, images of Marie Laveau almost always feature a tignon.

9. Rothman, *Slave Country*, 73–117.

10. La Société Catholique pour l'Instruction des Orphelins dans l'Indigence was left intact only because it had the support of the Catholic Church.

11. Louisiana Legislature, *Acts Passed at the First Session of the Second Legislature of the State of Louisiana*, 90.

12. Schafer, *Becoming Free, Remaining Free*, 150; Schafer, *Slavery, the Civil Law, and the Supreme Court of Louisiana*, 179.

13. Grandjean Collection, Reg. 85-59, 8 January 1875, message signed X.

14. Hogue, *Uncivil War*, 4.

15. Vincent, *Black Legislators in Louisiana during Reconstruction*, 18–20; Hennessey, "Race and Violence in Reconstruction New Orleans," 79–80.

16. *The New Orleans Weekly Times*, 26 March 1864.

17. Immediate emancipation passed with a final count of sixty-seven to sixteen.

18. Delegate Edmund Abell's proposed amendment, Christian, "Ballots or Bullets," in "The Negro in Louisiana."

19. Connor, "Reconstruction Rebels."

20. Grandjean Collection, Reg. 85-38, 8 February 1872.

21. *New Orleans Tribune*, 19 December 1865.

22. Convention resolution quoted in Christian, "The Mechanics' Hall Riot of 1866," in "The Negro in Louisiana;" Vincent, *Black Legislators in Louisiana during Reconstruction*, 40–41.

23. Tunnell, *Crucible of Reconstruction*, 111.

24. Convention resolution, quoted in Christian, "The Mechanics' Hall Riot of 1866," in "The Negro in Louisiana."

25. Grandjean Collection, Reg. 85-38, 9 February 1872, message signed "Victor Lacroix and others."

26. *New Orleans Daily Crescent*, 27 July 1866.

27. Hollandsworth Jr., *An Absolute Massacre*, 50.

28. Vandal, "The Origins of the New Orleans Riot of 1866."

29. Quoted in Christian, "The Mechanics' Hall Riot of 1866," in "The Negro in Louisiana."

30. Report from F. W. Tilton, quoted in Vandal, "The Origins of the New Orleans Riot of 1866," 150.

31. *The Daily Picayune*, 16 April 1865.

32. Reed, *Life of A. P. Dostie*, 298; Christian, "The Mechanics' Hall Riot of 1866," in "The Negro in Louisiana."

33. Hogue, *Uncivil War*, 39; Christian "The Mechanics' Hall Riot of 1866," in "The Negro in Louisiana;" *Times-Picayune*, 28 July 1866.

34. Hollandsworth, *An Absolute Massacre*, 3; Bell, *Revolution, Romanticism, and the Afro-Creole Protest Tradition*, 262.

35. Reed, *Life of A. P. Dostie*, 313–14.

36. Select Committee on the New Orleans Riots, *Report of the Select Committee on the New Orleans Riots*, 30.

37. Ibid., 10–11.

38. Grandjean Collection, Reg. 85-32, 9 November 1870, message recorded in English from W. R. Meadows; Grandjean Collection, Reg. 85-31, 21 February 1869. There is a reference to Lacroix's participation in Rey's circle in Daggett, "Henry Louis Rey," 14. François was likely in attendance during the meetings featuring his martyred son's spirit.

39. Grandjean Collection, Reg. 85-31, 25 October 1869.

40. Grandjean Collection, Reg. 85-34, 18 November 1871.

41. Theatricality and descriptions of a martyr's gruesome death from witnesses have been significant in the history of Catholic martyrs. See Castelli, *Martyrdom and Memory*, 104–33; Greer, "Colonial Saints."

42. Grandjean Collection, Reg. 85-38, 1 January 1872, message recorded in English and signed Horton.

43. Grandjean Collection, Reg. 85-32, 26 October 1870, message signed V. Lacroix; Grandjean Collection, Reg. 85-34, 9 December 1871, message recorded in English; Grandjean Collection, Reg. 85-36, 30 July 1872; Grandjean Collection, Reg. 85-37, 30 July 1875; Grandjean Collection, Reg. 85-52, 1 December 1873; Grandjean Collection, Reg. 85-63, 30 July 1877, message recorded in English and signed A. Dostie.

44. Grandjean Collection, Reg. 85-32, 28 July 1870, message signed DuBuys; Grandjean Collection, Reg. 85-32, 26 October 1870; Grandjean Collection, Reg. 85-32, 4 April 1870; Grandjean Collection, Reg. 85-32, 4 April 1870, Dostie's message recorded in English.

45. In Louisiana and South Carolina, the majority of delegates were not white. Hume and Gough, *Blacks, Carpetbaggers, and Scalawags*, 158.

46. Quoted in Christian, "Let Freedom Ring," in "The Negro in Louisiana."

47. Grandjean Collection, Reg. 85-33, 28 June 1871, message from P. Galle; Grandjean noted next to this message that Galle was a Creole native to New Orleans. Grandjean Collection, Reg. 85-32, 9 November 1870, message recorded in English from W. R. Meadows.

48. Vincent, *Black Legislators in Louisiana during Reconstruction*, 47–85.

49. Grandjean Collection, Reg. 85-37, 22 November, 1872, message from Dunn and recorded in English.

50. Quotation from House Misc. documents, quoted in in Nystrom, *New Orleans after the Civil War*, 75.

51. Hogue, *Uncivil War*, 61–65.

52. Vincent, *Black Legislators in Louisiana during Reconstruction*, 92.

53. Grandjean Collection, Reg. 85-32, 9 November 1870, message from W. R. Meadows and recorded in English.

54. Nystrom, *New Orleans after the Civil War*, 106–8.

55. Sumner, quoted in English, " 'That Is All We Ask For,' " 63.

56. Dunn was not the only local political figure to appear at the Cercle Harmonique's table. Others who came but did not deliver politically-charged messages are listed here. Plantation owner, governor of Louisiana (1853–56), and brigadier general for the Confederate Louisiana militia Paul Hébert was another local politician and Confederate who visited the Cercle Harmonique, and his message was received before his physical death in 1880. In 1872, when his message was recorded, he was a backer of the Warmoth Republican faction and later hoped Grant would run for a third term. Cowan and McGuire, *Louisiana Governors*, 81–82. It is Grandjean's notes that identified the Paul Hébert behind the spirit as the local Acadian, as opposed to anything in the message itself—which is a message endorsing Spiritualism and its "magnificence"— and so it is possible that the spirit was another Hébert. Grandjean Collection, Reg. 85-39, 20 February 1872. A. Fabre, mayor of the city in 1855, visited the Cercle Harmonique. Grandjean Collection, Reg. 85-42, 31 May 1872. Grandjean Collection, Reg. 85-38, 12 February 1872. Paul Bertus, who briefly served as New Orleans mayor in 1838 and again in February 1843, instructed listeners to "help many beings." Grandjean Collection, Reg. 85-55, 3 June 1874. He promised that kindness and selflessness like this would be rewarded in the spiritual spheres, and he also lamented how "erroneous principles" had "dominated" many "misfortunates" in the country. Upon joining the spiritual world, those formerly oppressed would be "refreshed and happy." Grandjean Collection, Reg. 85-61, 25 January 1875; Grandjean Collection, Reg. 85-57, 4 September 1874. Alfred Wiltz, the father of local politician and democrat Louis Alfred Wiltz, also appeared. Grandjean Collection, Reg. 85-40, 17 April 1872.

57. The message was recorded in English. The flip-flop of "true and tried friends" may indicate that English was the scribe's and/or medium's second language. Grandjean Collection, Reg. 85-34, 22 November 1871.

58. Grandjean Collection, Reg. 85-34, 8 December 1871, message recorded in English; Grandjean Collection, Reg. 85-34, 9 December 1871, message recorded in

English; Grandjean Collection, Reg. 85-35, 26 December 1871, message recorded in English.

59. Hogue, *Uncivil War*, 80–85; Handbill, 19 January 1872, quoted in Christian, "Let Freedom Ring," in "The Negro in Louisiana."

60. Gill, *Lords of Misrule*; Nystrom, *New Orleans after the Civil War*, 117–20.

61. Grandjean Collection, 85-38, 3 February 1872.

62. Hogue, *Uncivil War*, 91–96.

63. Christian, "Let Freedom Ring," in "The Negro in Louisiana."

64. Grandjean Collection, Reg. 85-36, 27 September 1872, message recorded in English.

65. Grandjean Collection, Reg. 85-37, 22 November, 1872.

66. Grandjean Collection, Reg. 85-63, 2 November 1877, message recorded in English.

67. Mistick Krewe of Comus 1873, Missing Links Parade Costume Designs, The Louisiana Digital Library, http://cdm16313.contentdm.oclc.org/cdm/landingpage /collection/p15140coll3.

68. Hogue, *Uncivil War*, 104–6.

69. Eric Foner, *Reconstruction*, 437.

70. *Daily Picayune*, 30 June 1874; *Daily Picayune*, 4 July 1874.

71. *Daily Picayune*, 13 September 1874.

72. Nystrom, *New Orleans after the Civil War*, 171.

73. Christian, "Let Freedom Ring," in "The Negro in Louisiana"; Emberton, "The Limits of Incorporation"; Taylor, "New Orleans and Reconstruction."

74. Quoted in Nystrom, *New Orleans after the Civil War*, 175.

75. Grandjean Collection, Reg. 85-57, 15 September 1874, message from "a devoted sister." Grandjean Collection, Reg. 85-57, 16 September 1874.

76. Quoted in Nystrom, *New Orleans after the Civil War*, 176.

77. For more details on the Battle of Liberty Place, see Nystrom, *New Orleans after the Civil War*, 170–76; Hogue, *Uncivil War*, 131–43.

78. Grandjean Collection, Reg. 85-57, 15 September 1874; Grandjean Collection, Reg. 85-57, 20 September 1874, message signed Paul Lacroix (possibly related to Mechanics' Institute Riot martyr Victor Lacroix).

79. Grandjean Collection, Reg. 85-57, 15 September 1874.

80. Grandjean Collection, Reg. 85-57, 15 September 1874; Grandjean Collection, Reg. 85-57, 15 September 1874, message from André, a brother.

81. Grandjean Collection, Reg. 85-57, 20 September 1874.

82. Ibid.

83. Grandjean Collection, Reg. 85-57, 22 September 1874.

84. Christian, "Let Freedom Ring," in "The Negro in Louisiana."

85. *New Orleans Times*, 10 November 1874.

86. Otten, "The Wheeler Adjustment in Louisiana;" Hogue, *Uncivil War*, 148–57; Vincent, *Black Legislators in Louisiana during Reconstruction*, 206.

87. Grandjean Collection, Reg. 85-61, 26 November 1875, message recorded in English from O. J. Dunn.

88. Hogue, *Uncivil War*, 165–76.

89. Grandjean Collection, Reg. 85-36, 5 February 1872, message from Vincent de Paul.

90. James D. Davidson, "A Journey through the South in 1836," 357.

91. Charles R. Schultz, "New Orleans in December 1860."

92. Grandjean Collection, Reg. 85-51, 3 September 1873, message from "a brother"; Grandjean Collection, Reg. 85-43, 25 July 1872, message from François Estèves; Grandjean Collection, Reg. 85-51, 19 March 1873; Grandjean Collection, Reg. 85-38, 30 December 1871, message from "Lunel, a devoted brother"; Grandjean Collection, Reg. 85-41, 29 May 1872; Grandjean Collection, Reg. 85-51, 12 March 1873, message from "a brother."

93. Grandjean Collection, Reg. 85-48, 25 December 1872, message from Edmond Capdeville, the devoted brother; Grandjean Collection, Reg. 85-40, 29 March 1872, message from Lamennais; Grandjean Collection, Reg. 85-32, 1 October 1871; Grandjean Collection, Reg. 85-32, 26 October 1870; Grandjean Collection, Reg. 85-32, 26 October 1870; Grandjean Collection, Reg. 85-31, 29 March 1869, message from Lacenair.

94. Grandjean Collection, Reg. 85-49, 9 February 1873, message from "a brother friend"; Grandjean Collection, Reg. 85-36, 12 April 1872, message from Alpha; Grandjean Collection, Reg. 85-51, 15 March 1873, message from John Hamilton; Grandjean Collection, Reg. 85-51, 17 March 1873, message from "another devoted brother"; Grandjean Collection, Reg. 85-34, 4 September 1871; Grandjean Collection, Reg. 85-47, 3 December 1872, message from Duquesnay.

95. Grandjean Collection, Reg. 85-30, 30 November 1858, message signed A. Lanna and received "alone"; Grandjean Collection, Reg. 85-34, 29 October 1871, message from "Relf!"; Grandjean Collection, Reg. 85-50, 10 March 1873, message from Henri Lacroix; Grandjean Collection, Reg. 85-38, 8 February 1872, message from Assitha; Grandjean Collection, Reg. 85-35, 12 December 1871, message from "*L'Inconnu.*"

96. Grandjean Collection, Reg. 85-51, 17 March 1873, message from Philip D'Aulnay; Grandjean Collection, Reg. 85-38, 17 January 1872, message from "your brother, Paul Hécaud"; Grandjean Collection, Reg. 85-42, 22 June 1872, message from Lamennais; Grandjean Collection, Reg. 85-31, 28 March 1869, message from Sévigné; Grandjean Collection, Reg. 85-38, 6 February 1872, message from Robert Sévérin; Grandjean Collection, Reg. 85-35, 22 December 1871, message from Clovis Bauver; Grandjean Collection, Reg. 85-51, 20 March 1873, message from C. Boudreau; Grandjean Collection, Reg. 85-31, 4 March 1869, message from "a spirit"; Grandjean Collection, Reg. 85-50, 8 March 1873, message from a brother.

97. Grandjean Collection, Reg. 85-36, 5 February 1872; Grandjean Collection, Reg. 85-32, 15 October 1870, message from Vincent de Paul; Grandjean Collection,

Reg. 85-47, 4 December 1872, message from Emile Rabouin; Grandjean Collection, Reg. 85-45, 15 September 1872, message from L. Bmy Rey; Grandjean Collection, Reg. 85-59, 2 March 1875, message from X; Grandjean Collection, Reg. 85-47, 27 November 1872, message from Amédée Rapp; Grandjean Collection, Reg. 85-47, 27 November 1872, message from F. Escoffier; Grandjean Collection, Reg. 85-52, 17 November 1873, message from Vincent de Paul. Looking back on his life, one spirit asked, "Here! what would I do with these material goods?" He wished he had understood the temporary nature of material things during his time on earth, but the "vile combination" of fear and greed kept him captive to things. Grandjean Collection, Reg. 85-52, 26 November 1873, message from M. Morano.

98. Grandjean Collection, Reg. 85-45, 6 October 1872, signature unclear; Grandjean Collection, Reg. 85-40, 24 April 1872, message from Annette Bouligny; Grandjean Collection, Reg. 85-51, 20 March 1873.

99. Grandjean Collection, Reg. 85-40, 29 April 1872; Grandjean Collection, Reg. 85-34, 9 November 1871; Grandjean Collection, Reg. 85-32, date unclear.

100. Schafer, "New Orleans Slavery in 1850"; Baptist, " 'Cuffy,' 'Fancy Maids,' and 'One-Eyed Men.' "

101. Cheung, " 'Les Cenelles' and Quadroon Balls," 8; Couch, "The Public Masked Balls of Antebellum New Orleans," 412.

102. Christian, "Negro Periodicals, Literature, and Art in Louisiana," in "The Negro in Louisiana."

103. The way the male Afro-Creole authors of *L'Album littéraire* and *Les Cenelles* portrayed *placées* was similar to white authors. The critical content and the quality of writing in *L'Album littéraire* and *Les Cenelles* were similar to white counterparts. See Zanger, "The 'Tragic Octoroon' in Pre–Civil War Fiction"; Raimon, *The "Tragic Mulatta" Revisited*; Reid, *The Quadroon*; Sollors, " 'Never Was Born.' "

104. Grandjean Collection, Reg. 85-34, 22 July 1871, message from "a woman who suffered."

105. Grandjean Collection, Reg. 85-41, 29 May 1872; Grandjean Collection, Reg. 85-30, November 1858, message from Labeyre; Grandjean Collection, Reg. 85-51, 30 August 1873; Grandjean Collection, Reg. 85-35, 23 December 1871, message from Marie Delauney; Grandjean Collection, Reg. 85-33, 13 June 1871. Though many messages affiliate drinking with wife-beating or neglecting one's family, a spirit named Marcelles linked "the use of strong drink" to cowardice in general. Grandjean Collection, Reg. 85-34, 18 November 1871.

106. In this sense, the spirit of Valmour seemed to reiterate what is commonly referred to as the Madonna-whore complex. For a more complex exploration of similar issues, see Fessenden, "The Convent, the Brothel, and the Protestant Woman's Sphere."

107. Grandjean Collection, Reg. 85-39, 15 March 1872; Grandjean Collection, 85-52, 19 October 1873, message from Jeanne Dastugue; Grandjean Collection, Reg. 85-35, 18 December 1871, message from "a wise and devoted mother."

Chapter Three

1. Grandjean Collection, Reg. 85-46, 25 October 1872, message from Lamennais.

2. This particular spirit, Père Ambroise, occasionally signed his messages with the description "ex-Capuchin" following his name. The spirit was possibly that of Ambroise de Reims, a French Capuchin from the early seventeenth century. Luria, *Sacred Boundaries*, 70–71. Or the spirit was maybe Ambroise of Preuilly, a French Capuchin who served as a missionary in India in the mid-seventeenth century. Yasuyuki, "The French Travellers and the Mughal Empire in the 17th Century," 85–86.

3. Grandjean Collection, Reg. 85-49, 25 January 1873.

4. Carroll, *Spiritualism in Antebellum America*, 79–81. In *A Republic of Mind and Spirit*, Albanese references Catholicism only in passing and typically in relation to a metaphysic's Catholic upbringing. The main reference to Catholicism in Ann Braude's *Radical Spirits* is a brief citation of Andrew Jackson Davis's dislike of Catholic infant baptism.

5. This did not necessarily mean Catholic orthodoxy. Clerics did not always find Louisiana to be an easy place to evangelize, administer the sacraments, and oversee parishes. The frontier could be harsh, the laity could be disinterested, and the institutional infrastructure took time to build. Additionally, even though baptism of slaves was legally required, this did not ensure that it would happen. Pasquier, *Fathers on the Frontier*.

6. Article III of the Louisiana *Code Noir*.

7. For example, the Ursulines offered their free black plantation overseer a small farm in return for his service but refused to allow his heirs to inherit the farm after his death. See *Jacobs et al. v. Ursuline Nuns*, 328–31.

8. Ingersoll, "Free Blacks in a Slave Society," 187–99.

9. Not all in New Orleans were Catholic, though it was the primary religious orientation of the Afro-Creole community. As a large port city, New Orleans was racially diverse as well as religiously diverse, particularly with the beginning of U.S. rule. Following the Louisiana Purchase, various forms of Protestantism officially arrived in the city with black American and Anglo-American migrants. While some black Protestants in the South embraced the opportunity for racially separate churches and complete control over the religious sphere, many Methodists in New Orleans, along with Catholics, held onto their racially integrated congregations. Further complicating the city's religio-racial scene, Congregationalist, Presbyterian, and Methodist missionaries from the American Missionary Association flooded into Louisiana following the Civil War, opened schools for African Americans, and hoped to attract converts. Despite Protestants' attempts, many of the city's Creoles of color continued to identify with the Catholicism of their families. See James Bennett, *Religion and the Rise of Jim Crow in New Orleans*; Richardson, *Christian Reconstruction*. Also see the extensive American Missionary Association archives at the Amistad Research Center, Tulane University.

10. Bell, "French Religious Culture in Afro-Creole New Orleans"; Bell, *Revolution, Romanticism, and the Afro-Creole Protest Tradition in Louisiana.*

11. Alberts, "Origins of Black Catholic Parishes in the Archdiocese of New Orleans," 43; Bell, "French Religious Culture," 8–9.

12. However, Sedella's decision to stay was contentious. In the time leading up to his decision, Father Patrick Walsh, the vicar general for Louisiana and the Floridas, declared himself the pastor of the parish. Their dual claim of the pastorate led to the Schism of 1805 with most of the laity and the parish's *marguilliers* (lay trustees) siding with Sedella. Walsh withdrew to the Ursulines' chapel and laid an interdict upon St. Louis Cathedral. Both sides appealed to Rome and to the nearby archdioceses in Havana and Baltimore. Even Walsh's death in 1806 did not end the conflict, but with the support of the primarily Creole laity, Sedella eventually was affirmed as the cathedral's pastor. Sedella's European ties, particularly to the Spanish monarchy that paid his salary for several years even after the Louisiana Purchase, rendered him suspect to some. It was not until he swore an oath of loyalty to the United States in 1806 in front of Governor William C. C. Claiborne that Sedella was allowed to officially continue as pastor. For more, see the Antonio de Sedella Collection; O'Neill, "'A Quarter Marked by Sundry Peculiarities'"; Faye, "The Schism of 1805 in New Orleans."

13. Bell, *Revolution, Romanticism, and the Afro-Creole Protest Tradition in Louisiana,* 70–73. Stephen Ochs also references the revered status of Sedella among the city's black population due to his "pastoral attention to them" and his "zealous ministry among the slaves and free people of color." Ochs, *A Black Patriot and a White Priest,* 24, 50.

14. Though historians should be more critical of the universalism proclaimed by their subjects. There is much secondary literature on the ideal of universalism in New Orleans Catholicism. See Alberts, "Origins of Black Catholic Parishes in the Archdiocese of New Orleans"; Bell, "French Religious Culture"; Clark, *Masterless Mistresses*; Clark and Gould, "The Feminine Face of Afro-Catholicism in New Orleans," 448; Ochs, "A Patriot, a Priest and a Prelate."

15. Grandjean Collection, Reg. 85-30, 25 December 1858; Grandjean Collection, Reg. 85-38, 10 February 1872; Grandjean Collection, Reg. 85-30, 19 November 1858; Grandjean Collection, Reg. 85-30, 25 November 1858.

16. Grandjean Collection, Reg. 85-46, 1 November 1872; Grandjean Collection, Reg. 85-30, 12 December 1858; Grandjean Collection, Reg. 85-38, 9 February 1872.

17. Grandjean Collection, Reg. 85-38, 6 January 1872; Grandjean Collection, Reg. 85-56, 9 June 1874.

18. Grandjean Collection, Reg. 85-31, 12 March 1871; Grandjean Collection, Reg. 85-32, 18 March 1870; Grandjean Collection, Reg. 85-58, 7 November 1874; Grandjean Collection, Reg. 85-31, 6 February 1870.

19. Grandjean Collection, Reg. 85-31, 12 March 1871; Grandjean Collection, Reg. 85-31, 25 October 1869. Moni was not the only spirit to compare priests to cock-

roaches. Grandjean Collection, Reg. 85-35, 18 December 1871, message from Felix Deville; Grandjean Collection, Reg. 85-31, 7 February 1869.

20. Grandjean Collection, Reg. 85-47, 7 November 1872.

21. Grandjean Collection, Reg. 85-30, 29 November 1858; Grandjean Collection, Reg. 85-31, 18 February 1869; Grandjean Collection, Reg. 85-34, 5 December 1871. The content of this last message is reminiscent of nineteenth-century anti-Catholic literature about women religious. Nancy Schultz, *Veil of Fear*.

22. Grandjean Collection, Reg. 85-36, 21 June 1872; Grandjean Collection, Reg. 85-36, 15 April 1872; Grandjean Collection, Reg. 85-38, 1 January 1872; Grandjean Collection, Reg. 85-40, 30 April 1872; Grandjean Collection, Reg. 85-51, 18 July 1873; Grandjean Collection, Reg. 85-41, 13 May 1872, message from "Vve Bernard Couvent" (Widow Bernard Couvent).

23. Grandjean Collection, Reg. 85-45, 8 September 1872, message from Lamennais; Grandjean Collection, Reg. 85-50, 12 February 1873; Grandjean Collection, Reg. 85-34, 4 September 1871.

24. References to a local chapter of the Society of Saint Vincent de Paul begin to appear in the local New Orleans newspapers in 1853. The current society's website lists 1852 as its founding year. "Feast of St. Vincent de Paul," *Times-Picayune*, 18 July 1857; "St. Vincent de Paul," *The Daily Picayune*, 18 July 1860.

25. There were fourteen publication dates, and on each day the segment on de Paul ranged from one newspaper page to a quarter of a page.

26. Bell, "French Religious Culture in Afro-Creole New Orleans," 2.

27. *L'Union*, 9 April 1863; *L'Union*, 15 January 1863.

28. Bell, "French Religious Culture in Afro-Creole New Orleans," 3, 5.

29. Grandjean Collection, Reg. 85-52, 17 November 1873; Grandjean Collection, Reg. 85-32, 15 October 1871.

30. Grandjean Collection, Reg. 85-31, 1 December 1865; Grandjean Collection, Reg. 85-31, 7 December 1865; Grandjean Collection, Reg. 85-31, 7 December 1865; Grandjean Collection, Reg. 85-52, 27 October 1873.

31. Grandjean Collection, Reg. 85-36, early 1872.

32. Barthet, *Le Spiritualiste*, 136 (this was not a spirit message but rather an editorial on Spiritualism); Message from Husson, printed in Barthet, *Le Spiritualiste*, 193. Message from L. Bourdaloue, printed in Barthet, *Le Spiritualiste*, 222–23.

33. Grandjean Collection, Reg. 85-32, 15 October 1871; Grandjean Collection, Reg. 85-32; Grandjean Collection, Reg. 85-53, 8 March 1874; Grandjean Collection, Reg. 85-52, 17 November 1873; Grandjean Collection, Reg. 85-33, 5 June 1871.

34. Grandjean Collection, Reg. 85-32, 5 May 1871; Grandjean Collection, Reg. 85-34, 19 November 1871; Grandjean Collection, Reg. 85-52, 17 October 1873.

35. Grandjean Collection, Reg. 85-31, 5 April 1869.

36. An Edmond Capdeville fought in the eighth regiment of the Louisiana militia during the War of 1812. Pierson, *Louisiana Soldiers in the War of 1812*, 21.

37. Grandjean Collection, Reg. 85-48, 18 December 1872; Grandjean Collection, Reg. 85-52, 26 November 1873, message from "a brother"; Grandjean Collection, Reg. 85-32, 1 October 1870, message from Vincent de Paul; Grandjean Collection, Reg. 85-48, 18 December 1872.

38. The spirit Lunel was likely the spirit of a tobacco agent in early French colonial Louisiana. Of Swiss origin, Lunel was a Protestant and was allowed to practice despite the fact that Protestantism was outlawed in French Louisiana. For this denial of Catholicism's supremacy, the Cercle Harmonique would have admired him. Giraud, *History of French Louisiana*, 135–36.

39. Grandjean Collection, Reg. 85-35, 21 December 1871; Grandjean Collection, Reg. 85-36, 23 February 1872; Grandjean Collection, Reg. 85-40, 30 March 1872; Grandjean Collection, Reg. 85-40, 30 April 1872, message from "a devoted brother, Romain"; Grandjean Collection, Reg. 85-44, 13 August 1872.

40. Carroll, *Spiritualism in Antebellum America*, 22, 78; Albanese, *Republic of Mind and Spirit*, 142, 151, 154.

41. Grandjean Collection, Reg. 85-34, 21 October 1871; Grandjean Collection, Reg. 85-34, 21 October 1871.

42. Grandjean Collection, Reg. 85-52, 1 December 1873, message from "Andre, a brother"; Grandjean Collection, Reg. 85-57, 4 September 1874; Grandjean Collection, Reg. 85-32, 6 October 1872, message from A. Rousseau; Grandjean Collection, Reg. 85-52, 1 December 1873, message from "a brother"; Grandjean Collection, Reg. 85-52, 1 December 1873; Grandjean Collection, Reg. 85-46, 1 November 1872, message from Père Antoine; Grandjean Collection, Reg. 85-49, 5 February 1873, message from Pierre Crocker; Grandjean Collection, Reg. 85-49, 9 February 1873, message from Emile Forstall; Grandjean Collection, Reg. 85-52, 27 November 1873, message from "a brother."

43. Grandjean Collection, Reg. 85-50, 8 March 1873, message from "a brother"; Grandjean Collection, Reg. 85-51, 22 March 1873, message from "Robert, a delegate"; Grandjean Collection, Reg. 85-50, 12 March 1873, message from Emile Bertrand.

44. For example, the historian Jay P. Dolan frequently mentioned discussions of hellfire during the colonial period in *The American Catholic Experience*, but hellfire largely dropped out of the narrative as the nineteenth century progressed. Dolan, *The American Catholic Experience*; Goddard, "Converting the 'Sauvage.'"

45. Considering the Cercle Harmonique's French influence seen in the language of the séance records, the spirits who visited, and their own cultural heritage, the French Catholics' move away from preaching hellfire and damnation seems significant. Gibson, "Hellfire and Damnation in Nineteenth-Century France." French Spiritists also rejected the Catholic notion of hell. Sharp, "Fighting for the Afterlife," 287.

46. This negative regard for hell was not confined to the Cercle Harmonique. The spirit of Pére Ambroise informed Barthet's circle in April 1857 that the church's notion of hell was absurd, for God was merciful and did not want to torture his children. Rather, hell was a construct of the Catholic Church meant to

"inspire terror" and "subject" the laity. Published message in Barthet, *Le Spiritualiste*, 88–91.

47. Grandjean Collection, Reg. 85-34, 2 June 1871.

48. Grandjean Collection, Reg. 85-34, 6 July 1871, message from Lamennais; Grandjean Collection, Reg. 85-35, 16 December 1871, message from Voltaire; Grandjean Collection, Reg. 85-43, 2 August 1872; Grandjean Collection, Reg. 85-34, 21 October 1871; Grandjean Collection, Reg. 85-51, 17 March 1873; Grandjean Collection, Reg. 85-31, 16 February 1869, message from "one."

49. Grandjean Collection, Reg. 85-38, 2 January 1872; Grandjean Collection, Reg. 85-34, 10 October 1871; Grandjean Collection, Reg. 85-33, 11 June 1871.

50. Desdunes, *Our People and Our History*, 109–22.

51. Grandjean Collection, Reg. 85-30, 28 November 1858.

52. Grandjean Collection, Reg. 85-30, 28 July 1858.

53. Carroll, *Spiritualism in Antebellum America*, 40–41, 79–81.

54. For a longer history of the Catholic Church's support of slavery and the racial status quo of the South, see Pasquier, "'Though Their Skin Remains Brown'"; Pasquier, *Fathers on the Frontier*, 167–202. For a more national look at the Catholic Church's support of slavery and Democratic politics, see Klement, "Catholics as Copperheads during the Civil War."

55. A spirit identifying himself as "Odin" visited the group in July 1874 and encouraged the circle to prepare for a world "of love and charity." Grandjean Collection, Reg. 85-56, 7 July 1874, message from "Odin." Though the spirit did not apologize, as other former Catholic clerics often did, there is a good chance that the spirit was that of New Orleans archbishop Jean-Marie Odin. Odin died on May 25, 1870, four years before the receipt of this message.

56. Jean Marie Odin, Pastoral Letter for the Lent of 1862, quoted in Pasquier, "Catholic Southerners, Catholic Soldiers," 26.

57. "Religion Accommodating Politics," *L'Union*, 6 December 1862.

58. Wilson, *Baptized in Blood*.

59. Pasquier, "Catholic Southerners, Catholic Soldiers," 36–46.

60. Napoléon Joseph Perché, Pastoral Letter, quoted in Pasquier, "Catholic Southerners, Catholic Soldiers," 44.

61. Bishop James Oliver Van de Veld to Archbishop Antoine Blanc, quoted in Ochs, *A Black Patriot and a White Priest*, 99.

62. For example, though diocesan regulations ordered the segregation of parish sacrament registers for whites, slaves, and free persons of color, Maistre began to integrate the St. Rose of Lima registers in January 1863. When Archbishop Jean-Marie Odin ordered Maistre to return to "normal" practice, Maistre ignored his request.

63. Baudier, *Centennial*, 21.

64. "Messe A Sainte-Rose de Lima," *L'Union*, 14 April 1863.

65. "Religion Accommodating Politics," *L'Union*, 6 December 1862.

66. During the Holy Name of Jesus's first year (1864), Maistre claimed 150 baptisms—all black—nearly tripling his numbers from his final year at St. Rose. When the archdiocese reopened St. Rose under new pastoral care in early 1864, the parish's more powerful white Creole families had their children baptized there. According to Archbishop Odin, Maistre had offended many of the white Creole families of St. Rose with his support of emancipation, and the families who stopped attending the parish would return only after Maistre left it. Baudier, *Centennial*, 25–26.

67. "John Brown; M. Maistre," *New Orleans Tribune*, 1 December 1867.

68. Grandjean Collection, Reg. 85-33, 11 June 1871.

69. In 1833, British visitor Thomas Hamilton wrote, "Both Catholic and Protestant agree in the tenet that all men are equal in the sight of God, but the former gives practical exemplification of this creed. In a Catholic Church . . . the slave and master, kneel before the same altar in temporary oblivion of all worldly distinctions." Five years later Harriet Martineau identified the Catholic Church as the one place "where all men meet together as brethren." Writing later in life, Dr. Thomas L. Nichols, a social reformer from the North, noted that he had never before seen such a "mixture of conditions and colours" as he did at St. Louis Cathedral in 1845. "White children and black, with every shade between, knelt side by side" without "distinction of rank or colour." He could imagine no better example of "perfect equality." Hamilton, *Men and Manners in America*, 209–10; Martineau, *Society in America*, 153; Nichols, *Forty Years of American Life*, 127–28.

70. *L'Union*, 5 May 1863; Bell, *Revolution, Romanticism, and the Afro-Creole Protest Tradition in Louisiana*, 243.

71. Grandjean Collection, Reg. 85-31, 25 March 1869.

72. Grandjean Collection, Reg. 85-43, 25 July 1872; Grandjean Collection, Reg. 85-31, 9 January 1870; Grandjean Collection, Reg. 85-39, 18 February 1872, for message where he signs off as "Père Ambroise, ex-Capucin"; Grandjean Collection, Reg. 85-34, 10 October 1871; Grandjean Collection, Reg. 85-39, 22 February 1872.

73. Grandjean Collection, Reg. 85-31, 12 March 1869; Grandjean Collection, Reg. 85-35, 17 December 1871; Grandjean Collection, Reg. 85-35, 25 December 1871; Grandjean Collection, Reg. 85-39, 22 February 1872.

74. Grandjean Collection, Reg. 85-49, 6 February 1873, message from Armand Boutin; Grandjean Collection, Reg. 85-35, 16 December 1871, message from Voltaire.

75. "The Archbishop's Return. A Grand Pageant," *The Daily Picayune*, 23 May 1871.

76. Grandjean Collection, Reg. 85-32; Grandjean Collection, Reg. 85-32, 22 May 1871; Grandjean Collection, Reg. 85-32, date unknown.

77. Grandjean Collection, Reg. 85-34, 26 October 1871; Grandjean Collection, Reg. 85-31, 24 February 1869.

78. Grandjean Collection, Reg. 85-32, Grandjean notes on loose-leaf paper and glued into book.

79. Grandjean Collection, Reg. 85-31, 13 February 1869, message from Voltaire; Grandjean Collection, Reg. 85-34, 10 October 1871, message from Ambroise; Grandjean

Collection, Reg. 85-39, 19 March 1872, message from Voltaire; Grandjean Collection, Reg. 85-34, 10 October 1871, message from Ambroise; Grandjean Collection, Reg. 85-41, 7 May 1872, message from Clement XIV; Grandjean Collection, Reg. 85-33, 13 June 1871.

80. Grandjean Collection, Reg. 85-48, 23 December 1872.

81. Grandjean Collection, Reg. 85-34, 10 December 1871; Grandjean Collection, Reg. 85-62, 24 February 1876, message from "a friend"; Grandjean Collection, Reg. 85-48, 20 December 1872; Grandjean Collection, Reg. 85-36, 18 July 1872, message from Valdermar Gauthier; Grandjean Collection, Reg. 85-31, 11 March 1869.

82. Grandjean Collection, Reg. 85-62, 24 February 1876, message signed a "Friend!"; Grandjean Collection, Reg. 85-32, 24 February 1871, message from De Sevigne.

83. Grandjean Collection, Reg. 85-32, 5 April 1869; Grandjean Collection, Reg. 85-49, 25 January 1873.

84. Grandjean Collection, Reg. 85-32, 13 July 1870.

85. Grandjean Collection, Reg. 85-49, 25 January 1873.

86. Grandjean Collection, Reg. 85-39, 6 March 1872; Grandjean Collection, Reg. 85-34, 28 November 1871. (Another spirit, Pierre Dante, also referred to Catholic theology as "nonsense preached for centuries" that unfortunately had been accepted by many. Grandjean Collection, Reg. 85-35, 20 December 1871.) Grandjean Collection, Reg. 85-47, 27 November 1872, message signed A. Villemain.

87. Grandjean Collection, Reg. 85-48, 23 December 1872; Grandjean Collection, Reg. 85-33, 10 June 1871.

88. McGreevy, *Catholicism and American Freedom*, 22–23.

89. Grandjean Collection, Reg. 85-48, 23 December 1872.

90. Grandjean Collection, Reg. 85-51, 20 March 1873; Grandjean Collection, Reg. 85-30, 28 November 1858; Grandjean Collection, Reg. 85-34, 4 March 1871.

91. Grandjean Collection, Reg. 85-31, 13 February 1869; Grandjean Collection, Reg. 85-32, 26 October 1870.

92. D'Agostino, *Rome in America*, 1.

93. Ibid., 20.

94. Grandjean Collection, Reg. 85-33, 11 June 1871; Grandjean Collection, Reg. 85-34, 23 September 1871; Grandjean Collection, Reg. 85-38, 2 January 1872; Grandjean Collection, Reg. 85-35, 17 December 1871; Grandjean Collection, Reg. 85-36, 26 January 1872.

95. Grandjean Collection, Reg. 85-33, 16 June 1871, message recorded in English, which, considering Crowder's background, is not surprising.

96. *The Daily Picayune*, 11 June 1871, 16 June 1871, 17 June 1871, 20 June 1871.

97. He also called priests "hypocrites" and identified "secrets" as Catholicism's reason for success. Grandjean Collection, Reg. 85-33, 18 June 1871; Grandjean Collection, Reg. 85-33, 19 June 1871, message from "*L'Inconnu*."

98. Grandjean Collection, Reg. 85-42, 22 June 1872, message from Valmour; Grandjean Collection, Reg. 85-50, 12 March 1873; Grandjean Collection, Reg. 85-51,

17 March 1873; Grandjean Collection, Reg. 85-52, 27 October 1873, message from Anna Marte, J. W. Hutchinson, and Cornelius Hutchinson.

99. Grandjean Collection, Reg. 85-59, 15 March 1875; Grandjean Collection, Reg. 85-68, 25 July 1872, message from Abner; Grandjean Collection, Reg. 85-59, 8 March 1875; Grandjean Collection, Reg. 85-56, 9 June 1874; Grandjean Collection, Reg. 85-32, 18 February 1869.

Chapter Four

1. *New Orleans Daily Picayune,* 30 July 1863; *New York Times,* 8 August 1863; *Harper's Weekly,* 29 August 1863.

2. Grandjean Collection, Reg. 85-32, date unknown; Grandjean Collection, Reg. 85-30, 8 July 1863; Grandjean Collection, Reg. 85-34, 2 June 1871; Grandjean Collection, Reg. 85-36, 12 February 1872.

3. Maffly-Kipp, *Setting Down the Sacred Past,* 8–11.

4. For more on the theme of exodus in African American religions, see Glaude, *Exodus!;* Raboteau, *A Fire in the Bones,* 17–36.

5. Rable, *But There Was No Peace;* Mathews, "The Rite of Human Sacrifice."

6. Paddison, *American Heathens,* 5.

7. Grandjean Collection, Reg. 85-32, date unknown, message from Andre Cailloux, J. P. Lana, Anguies Pédéslaux.

8. Article X of the Louisiana *Code Noir.*

9. Schafer, "New Orleans Slavery in 1850 as Seen in Advertisements," 34.

10. James D. Davidson, "A Journey through the South in 1836," 358.

11. Walter Johnson, *Soul by Soul,* 2. For example, Frederick Law Olmsted spends more space discussing New Orleans than anywhere else in Olmsted, *A Journey in the Slave States,* ix.

12. Schafer, " 'Open and Notorious Concubinage.' " In regard to the tourism element, Olmstead writes about the racial landscape of New Orleans within the first few pages of the city's chapter. Also see Elliott, *Sinfulness of American Slavery,* 151–52; the travel journal of Emil Deckert compiled and translated by Frederic Trautmann, "New Orleans, the Mississippi, and the Delta through a German's Eyes"; Featherstonhaugh, *Excursion through the Slave States,* 141; and the travel journal of James D. Davidson compiled by Herbert A. Kellar, "A Journey through the South in 1836."

13. Schafer, *Becoming Free, Remaining Free,* 145–62.

14. 1850 Slave Schedule of the 1st Ward, 3rd Municipality in the Parish of Orleans, quoted in Daggett, "Henry Louis Rey," 14.

15. Vincent, "Aspects of the Family and Public Life of Antoine Dubuclet," 27.

16. For the numbers, see Christian, "The Free Colored Class," in "The Negro in Louisiana."

17. Grandjean Collection, 85-31, 25 March 1869, message from Lamennais; Grandjean Collection, Reg. 85-40, 24 April 1872, message from Annette Bouligny.

18. Douglass, *My Bondage and My Freedom*, 416.

19. Grandjean Collection, Reg. 85-31, 13 February 1869.

20. Grandjean Collection, Reg. 85-31, 27 January 1866, message arrived in English; Grandjean Collection, Reg. 85-31, 3 February 1866.

21. Here, the idea of a judgment and punishment from God seems to be endorsed, as opposed to how retribution typically was described in spirit messages.

22. Grandjean Collection, Reg. 85-35, 11 December 1871, both messages recorded in English.

23. In her memoir, New Orleans socialite Eliza Ripley wrote that "no subsequent [Civil War] funeral was more largely attended than Charles Dreux's." Ripley, *Social Life in New Orleans*, 156.

24. Jones, *Lee's Tigers*, 12.

25. Grandjean Collection, Reg. 85-40, 3 May 1872; Grandjean Collection, Reg. 85-34, 28 November 1871, message from Joanni.

26. Grandjean Collection, Reg. 85-31, 25 October 1869; Grandjean Collection, Reg. 85-36, 12 February 1872, message from Ambroise and Vincent de Paul; Grandjean Collection, Reg. 85-35, 27 December 1871.

27. Grandjean Collection, Reg. 85-34, 19 November 1871; Grandjean Collection, Reg. 85-39, 15 March 1872. Grandjean notes that this spirit, B., might be that of Booth. Grandjean Collection, Reg. 85-34, 28 November 1871, message in English from "General Williams (federal)." Grandjean Collection, Reg. 85-36, 26 April 1872, message from "Jacques Stanislas—a devoted brother."

28. Blum, "'The First Secessionist was Satan.'"

29. Bell, *Revolution, Romanticism, and the Afro-Creole Protest Tradition*, 41–64; Rasmussen, *American Uprising*.

30. Waitz, *The Journal of Julia Le Grand*, 40.

31. Desdunes, *Our People and Our History*, 118; Christian, "The Negro as Soldier, 1860–1865," in "The Negro in Louisiana."

32. *Daily Picayune*, 22 February 1863.

33. *Daily Picayune*, 2 August 1863; *L'Union*, 1 August 1863. Also see Everett, "Free Persons of Color in New Orleans."

34. Grandjean Collection, Reg. 85-30, 31 August 1864.

35. Grandjean Collection, Reg. 85-32. Recorded into the register book on 10 January 1872, cited as being received by Rey on 20 October 20, 1862, at the Gentilly Station of Camp Strong.

36. William Wells Brown, *The Negro in the American Rebellion*, 171.

37. "Funeral of a Colored Captain," *The New York Herald*, 8 August 1863.

38. *New Orleans Era*, 20 July 1863.

39. Ochs, "A Patriot, a Priest, and a Prelate"; *Harper's Weekly*, 29 August 1863.

40. Cailloux's spirit stated, "I succumbed, but the flag flatters." Grandjean Collection, 85-32, 4 April 1870, message signed "Capt. A. Caillou."

41. Grandjean Collection, Reg. 85-33, 4 June 1871; Grandjean Collection, Reg. 85-32, 4 April 1870; Grandjean Collection, Reg. 85-34, 20 November 1871; Grandjean Collection, Reg. 85-32, 4 April 1870. Final message signed "And. Jackson." Considering Jackson's role in the Battle of New Orleans and his welcoming of the black militia in the fight, it is likely that this spirit's identity was that of the former general and president.

42. Grandjean Collection, Reg. 85-32, 26 October 1870; Grandjean Collection, Reg. 85-38, 8 February 1872; Grandjean Collection, Reg. 85-40, 4 May 1872 (spirit signed as "Sydney Johnson"); Grandjean Collection, Reg. 85-43, 14 July 1872.

43. Grandjean Collection, Reg. 85-32, 4 April 1870, message in English from "Col. Dreux"; Grandjean Collection, Reg. 85-32, 4 April 1870, message in English from "Capt. Cailloux"; Grandjean Collection, Reg. 85-53, 23 February 1874, message signed R. E. Lee.

44. Grandjean Collection, Reg. 85-32, 19 November 1870; Grandjean Collection, Reg. 85-32, 29 September 1871, message from Lopez; Grandjean Collection, Reg. 85-32, 26 October 1870; Grandjean Collection, Reg. 85-43, 25 July 1872, message from Laplume; Grandjean Collection, Reg. 85-43, 25 July 1872, message from Simon; Grandjean Collection, Reg. 85-31, 13 February 1869, message from Ambroise; Grandjean Collection, Reg. 85-32, 26 October 1870, message from "Crowder, 1st La Native Guards."

45. Grandjean Collection, Reg. 85-36, 19 July 1872, message from Robert Preaux.

46. Nystrom has encouraged other scholars to examine the motivations of Reconstruction political actors without bias, be it of the Dunning school variety or the revisionists. The main question Nystrom asks historians to answer is, "To what degree were Reconstruction politics a struggle between freedom and white supremacy as opposed to being merely a bare-knuckle struggle for power?" Nystrom, *New Orleans after the Civil War*, 83–85.

47. Eric Foner, *Free Soil*; McPherson, *Battle Cry of Freedom*, 178–88; Kaczorowski, "To Begin the Nation Anew"; Blight, *Race and Reunion*.

48. Grandjean Collection, Reg. 85-34, 28 November 1871, message in English from "General Williams (federal)."

49. Grandjean Collection, Reg. 85-33, 30 June 1871, message from Pascal, perhaps French mathematician Blaise Pascal (1623–62) in light of the circle's French influence. Additionally Pascal's *Lettres Provinciales* (Provincial Letters, 1656) was critical of the Jesuits.

50. Financial issues plagued Louisiana following the war because slaves were no longer taxed property. Throughout Reconstruction, various tax ideas were presented in the legislature to ameliorate the state's financial quagmire.

51. Grandjean Collection, Reg. 85-38, 12 February 1872. This was the second message from A. Fabre on that day.

52. Grandjean Collection, Reg. 85-59, 20 March 1875, message from Frank; Grandjean Collection, Reg. 85-56, 9 June 1874.

53. Grandjean Collection, Reg. 85-32, 1 October 1871, message from Brown; Grandjean Collection, Reg. 85-38, 12 February 1872, first message from A. Fabre that day; Grandjean Collection, Reg. 85-34, 29 October 1871, message from "Relf!"

54. Grandjean Collection, Reg. 85-39, 6 March 1872; Grandjean Collection, Reg. 85-39, 18 February 1872, message from "Père Ambroise, ex-Capucin"; Grandjean Collection, Reg. 85-33, 10 June 1871, message from Eugene Sue.

55. Grandjean Collection, Reg. 85-32, 1 December 1871; Grandjean Collection, Reg. 85-52, 27 October 1873, message from Anna Marte, J. W. Hutchinson, Cornelius Hutchinson. Lunel, "the devoted brother," stated that in uniting together, loving one another, and working in peace they would "be elevated splendidly." Grandjean Collection, Reg. 85-51, 19 March 1873; Grandjean Collection, Reg. 85-57, 22 October 1874.

56. Grandjean Collection, Reg. 85-38; 2 January 1872, message from Ambroise; Grandjean Collection, Reg. 85-35; 29 December 1871, message from Confucius; Grandjean Collection, Reg. 85-30; 30 December 1859; Grandjean Collection, Reg. 85-31, 6 February 1870, message signed Booth; Grandjean Collection, Reg. 85-32, 26 October 1870; Grandjean Collection, Reg. 85-41, 9 May 1872, message from Alcée Labranche.

57. Grandjean Collection, Reg. 85-32, 12 July 1870.

58. Grandjean Collection, Reg. 85-34, 2 June 1871; Grandjean Collection, Reg. 85-34, 13 September 1871.

59. Grandjean Collection, Reg. 85-36, 19 July 1872, message from Robert Preaux; Grandjean Collection, Reg. 85-33, 24 June 1871; Grandjean Collection, Reg. 85-53, 23 February 1874, message signed A. Lincoln; Grandjean Collection, Reg. 85-57, 20 September 1874, message from Simon. This message arrived the same day as a message from Alexandre Pétion and Auguste Brouard, who were Haitian spirits, and so it is also possible that Simon was Simón Bolívar, the Venezuelan republican and revolutionary. See the section on "Caribbean Revolutions" in chapter 5 for more on Pétion, Brouard, and Bolívar. Grandjean Collection, Reg. 85-31, Grandjean notes for Dubuclet's life details. Grandjean Collection, Reg. 85-31, 13 February 1869.

60. Grandjean Collection, Reg. 85-48; 11 December 1872; Grandjean Collection, Reg. 85-38, 30 December 1871; Grandjean Collection, Reg. 85-34, 28 November 1871, message signed Joanni; Grandjean Collection, Reg. 85-39, 7 March 1872, message from D'Apremont; Grandjean Collection, Reg. 85-30, 5 February 1860.

61. In *Ghosts of Futures Past*, McGarry explores how Native American spirits' ethnic identity as Native Americans was significant for the white mediums who contacted them. In *Body and Soul*, Cox examines how some American Spiritualists supported slavery as a means for harmony and for promoting the "sympathetic union in the nation," 153. Among some practitioners, the spirit of George Washington "spoke of immediate abolition and leveling equality, but also of social hierarchy

and racial subordination," 137. If the spirits visiting this particular group of Spiritualists supported a racial hierarchy, this suggests that racial differences remained in the
spiritual world.

62. For example, Swedenborgian physician William Henry Holcombe labeled the
indigenous populations of Native Americans and Africans as the most primitive
races. Above them in the racial hierarchy were Asians, with Caucasians of course on
the top. Cox, *Body and Soul*, 153–54; Ferguson, "Eugenics and the Afterlife."

63. Grandjean Collection, Reg. 85-40, 24 April 1872, message from Annette Bouligny; Grandjean Collection, Reg. 85-31, 6 May 1870; Grandjean Collection, Reg. 85-
41, 6 May 1872; Grandjean Collection, Reg. 85-42, 6 June 1872.

64. Grandjean Collection, Reg. 85-31, 21 February 1869; Grandjean Collection,
Reg. 85-36, 19 July 1872.

65. Grandjean Collection, Reg. 85-34, 7 November 1871. See Grandjean Collection,
Reg. 85-39, 12 March 1872 for a short message from Marigny describing the glories of
the spirit world. Full poem from "a black man, once" repeated here:

> Black in the land of America,
> But my hands pure in the spirit-land.
> I look with joy that from Africa
> No Americans, to spirit-land.
> Are sent.
> I went
> Forgiving
> And Helping.
> For I was right
> From darkness, light
> I received.
> Never deceived
> Are men in the spirit-land.
> Oh, Come and join our band
> White men of America
> Join the sons of Africa.
> In love we live
> In love forgive
> White men
> Black men.

Grandjean Collection, Reg. 85-32, 26 October 1870, message recorded in English;
Grandjean Collection, Reg. 85-61, 25 January 1876, message from Joseph Rey.

66. Grandjean Collection, Reg. 85-42, 16 June 1872; Grandjean Collection,
Reg. 85-42, 16 June 1872, message from F. D.

67. Grandjean Collection, Reg. 85-41, 27 May 1872, message from Abner.

68. Joseph G. Tregle Jr. "Creoles and Americans," 173.

69. *Le Moniteur*, 13 July 1873, quoted in Dubois and Melançon, "Creole Is, Creole Ain't," 242.

70. For example, Gayarré's popular and later printed 1885 lecture "The Creoles of History and the Creoles of Romance" defended the Creole's white racial purity and favorable contributions to New Orleans history. Contemporary negative mythologizing about old French creole culture by authors such as George Washington Cable in *The Grandissimes: A Story of Creole Life* had made the boundaries of Creole identity a contentious issue. Cable, a New Orleans native but of Anglo-American background, wrote popular novels and short stories about New Orleans Creoles that often depicted them as backward, ignorant, illiterate, and dishonorable.

71. Deckert and Trautmann, "New Orleans, the Mississippi, and the Delta through a German's Eyes," 87.

72. Grandjean Collection, Reg. 85-42, 18 June 1872, message from Raoul Daunoy; Grandjean Collection, Reg. 85-42, 16 June 1872; Grandjean Collection, Reg. 85-44, 25 August 1872; Grandjean Collection, Reg. 85-56, 8 June 1874, message from "a bright brother"; Grandjean Collection, Reg. 85-59, 2 March 1875, message from X; Grandjean Collection, Reg. 85-46, 30 October 1872, message from Elina Laporte; Grandjean Collection, Reg. 85-57, 20 September 1874; Grandjean Collection, Reg. 85-52, 5 December 1873, message from a brother; Grandjean Collection, Reg. 85-42, 20 June 1872, message signed "L'official." Though racial differences did not exist in the spirit world, some spirits felt it was necessary to "manifest . . . according to their previous earthly state." Spirits would appear different after undergoing spiritual "changes and transformations." One reason some spirits chose to appear similar to their material envelopes was for the sake of human understanding. Out of concern that their former friends might not recognize or understand their spiritual forms, many spirits looked similar to their material appearances when communicating with mediums. Communication between spirits and the living occasionally could be better facilitated if the spirit manifested akin to his or her living self. The spirits could see "beyond what you are allowed to glimpse." This was true in terms of human progress but also physical sight. Spirits could see in ways those on earth, still limited by their physical bodies, could not. Grandjean Collection, Reg. 85-32, 8 October 1872, message from Sophia; Grandjean Collection, Reg. 85-47, 10 November 1872, message from Joanni Questy.

73. For example, see Blum, Fessenden, Kurien, and Weisenfeld, "Forum." Additionally Blum and Paul Harvey track Jesus's visual development in U.S. history from "light" in the colonial era to white in the early republic in Blum and Harvey, *The Color of Christ*.

74. Grandjean Collection, Reg. 85-32, 9 November 1870, message recorded in English. The grammatical error in the message ("no race" instead of "nor race") unveils a bit more about the men seated at the séance table. It would seem that French was the primary language of the Cercle Harmonique member who transcribed this message.

75. Grandjean Collection, Reg. 85-35, 12 December 1871, message signed "The Unknown"; Grandjean Collection, Reg. 85-35, 27 December 1871.

76. Grandjean Collection, Reg. 85-31, 23 December 1869, message from Ambroise; Grandjean Collection, Reg. 85-35, 12 December 1871; Grandjean Collection, Reg. 85-53, 23 February 1874, message signed R. E. Lee.

77. Grandjean Collection, Reg. 85-31, 25 March 1869, message from Lamennais.

78. Other famous people who appeared to the Cercle Harmonique possibly include a British figure. A spirit who signed off as Arnold Benedict equated stories about ghost hauntings to "fairy tales." Grandjean Collection, Reg. 85-40, 27 April 1872; Grandjean Collection, Reg. 85-32, 26 October 1870; Grandjean Collection, Reg. 85-36, 26 January 1872; Grandjean Collection, Reg. 85-31, 9 January 1870, message from Ambroise.

79. Grandjean Collection, Reg. 85-31, 23 December 1869, message from Ambroise.

80. James Madison, *A Discourse on the Death of General Washington*, quoted in Crowe, "Bishop James Madison and the Republic of Virtue" 59–64.

81. Grandjean Collection, Reg. 85-57, 20 September 1874, message from Paul Lacroix; Grandjean Collection, Reg. 85-36, 12 February 1872, message from Ambroise and Vincent de Paul. Ambroise and de Paul referenced "the glorious birth of Lincoln, as you celebrate today." Grandjean Collection, Reg. 85-50, 18 February 1873, message from Lucile Bienvenue.

82. Grandjean Collection, Reg. 85-31, 25 March 1869, message from Lamennais.

83. Grandjean Collection, Reg. 85-57, 4 September 1874; Grandjean Collection, Reg. 85-35, 27 December 1871; Grandjean Collection, Reg. 85-32, date unknown.

84. Grandjean Collection, Reg. 85-31, 7 December 1865; Grandjean Collection, Reg. 85-31, 7 December 1865.

85. The Cercle Harmonique seemed to have forgiven the historical Lincoln for his earlier speeches and comments that did not support universal equality. While debating Stephen Douglas in 1858, Lincoln stated: "I will say then that I am not, nor ever have been in favor of bringing about in any way the social and political equality of the white and black races . . . and I will say in addition to this there is a physical difference between the white and black races which I believe will forever forbid the two races living together on terms of social and political equality." Abraham Lincoln, Lincoln-Douglas Debates, quoted in Schwartz, *Abraham Lincoln and the Forge of National Memory*, 3. Clearly, this was not the Lincoln who advised the Cercle Harmonique.

86. *New York Times*, 22 April 1876.

87. Schwartz, "Collective Memory and History," 476.

88. Grandjean Collection, Reg. 85-39, 19 February 1872, message from John Brown; Grandjean Collection, Reg. 85-39, 19 February 1872, message from Lincoln; Grandjean Collection, Reg. 85-34, 28 November 1871; Grandjean Collection, Reg. 85-42, 18 June 1872, message from Raoul Daunoy; Grandjean Collection, Reg. 85-36, 26 April 1872, message from "Jacques Stanislas—a devoted brother."

89. Cooke and De Witt, *The Life, Trial, and Execution of Captain John Brown*, 47.

90. Grandjean Collection, Reg. 85-59, 11 January 1875.

91. Grandjean Collection, Reg. 85-38, 8 February 1872.

92. Laderman, *The Sacred Remains*, 90.

93. Fine, "John Brown's Body," 229.

94. Ibid., 235.

95. Meyer, "Thoreau's Rescue of John Brown from History."

96. "The Delegation to Washington," *New Orleans Tribune*, 31 May 1865.

97. "Address Delivered to the Citizens of Louisiana," *New Orleans Tribune*, 15 September 1865.

98. Grandjean Collection, Reg. 85-33, 13 June 1871; Grandjean Collection, Reg. 85-34, 6 September 1871, message recorded in English; Grandjean Collection, Reg. 85-32, 29 October 1870; Grandjean Collection, Reg. 85-37, 27 June 1873; Grandjean Collection, Reg. 85-58, 13 December 1874; Grandjean Collection, Reg. 85-32. Additionally, though a Catholic in life, Cailloux was pleased to find his "old companions seated at the Holy Table of Truth." Grandjean Collection, Reg. 85-38, 8 February 1872.

99. Lamennais reported that "Hutchinson" watched over the Cercle Harmonique. Grandjean Collection, Reg. 85-51, 24 March 1873.

100. John W. Hutchinson lived beyond the tenure of the Cercle Harmonique; in January 1859 Jesse committed suicide. Gac, *Singing for Freedom*, 238.

101. Albanese, *Nature Religion in America*, 4. They knew Andrew Jackson Davis, who received a series of visions at the Hutchinson cottage in Massachusetts during the summer of 1852. Cox, *Body and Soul*, 237, note 1.

102. John W. Hutchinson, *Hutchinson's Republican Songster*.

103. The spirit also referenced a local black New Orleans legislator, James H. Ingraham. Ingraham was an organizer and captain of the Louisiana Native Guards, an active member of the "Convention of Colored Men of Louisiana," and a delegate of the Constitutional Convention of 1867–68. J. W. Hutchinson dictated, "So Ingraham / In Light I am / And for ever!" Grandjean Collection, Reg. 85-39, 22 February 1872.

104. Additionally, Hutchinson would not be the only musical spirit guest at the table. A spirit identified as L. Gabici appeared in October 1875 and congratulated "Henri" for being a Spiritualist. L. Gabici was the same name as a music composer associated with the Union side of the Civil War and a local music teacher in New Orleans. Gabici composed the music for the song "Stand By Our Flag," a song that celebrated the country's dedication to freedom and justice. He published sheet music of this song and others he composed from downtown New Orleans. Grandjean Collection, Reg. 85-60, 21 October 1875. L. Gabici, *Stand By Our Flag*, L. Gabici: New Orleans, 1857. http://www.loc.gov/item/ihas.200001118/. 5 May 2015.

105. Douglass, *My Bondage and My Freedom*, 441.

106. Grandjean Collection, Reg. 85-31, 5 April 1869; Grandjean Collection, Reg. 85-30, 8 July 1863. Grandjean Collection, Reg. 85-31, 18 April 1869.

107. Grandjean Collection, Reg. 85-59, 14 January 1875; Grandjean Collection, Reg. 85-59, 14 January 1875, message recorded in English from Sumner. Two earlier spirit messages lauded Sumner as an exemplar. One referred to him as a kind of stand-in for republicanism, and the other styled him as one who continued Lincoln's work. Grandjean Collection, Reg. 85-31, 22 May 1870, message from Pierre Soulé; Grandjean Collection, Reg. 85-36, 12 February 1872, message from Ambroise and Vincent de Paul; Grandjean Collection, Reg. 85-59, 14 January 1875, message recorded in English from O. J. Dunn; Grandjean Collection, Reg. 85-59, 14 January 1875, message recorded in English from L'Official.

108. Grandjean Collection, Reg. 85-32.

109. The freedom of newspapers was one reason for this progress, and P. B. delighted in independent journalism's rise in Louisiana. It helped destroy "the slave aristocracy of late memory" by providing a forum for speech. The whip, the prison, or the gallows could not stop the righteous from exposing the horrors of "fraternal suffering." Grandjean Collection, Reg. 85-33, 7 June 1871.

110. Bloch, *Visionary Republic*, xiii.

111. Hutchins, *Inventing Eden*, 223–30.

112. Grandjean Collection, Reg. 85-33, 4 June 1871, message signed "Your friend, Henry Clay"; Grandjean Collection, Reg. 85-32, 14 July 1870; Grandjean Collection, Reg. 85-38, 9 February 1872, message from Père Antoine.

113. Grandjean Collection, Reg. 85-36, 12 February 1872, message from Ambroise and Vincent de Paul; Grandjean Collection, Reg. 85-34, 2 June 1871; Grandjean Collection, Reg. 85-34; Grandjean Collection, Reg. 85-34, 4 July 1871.

114. Grandjean Collection, Reg. 85-31, 22 February 1869, message from Jefferson.

115. Whitman, *Democratic Vistas*, 2.

Chapter Five

1. Preaux's family emigrated to New Orleans, where he became an active member of the masonic community. Bell, *Revolution, Romanticism, and the Afro-Creole Protest Tradition in Louisiana*, 162–64. His name appears in listings of masons in antebellum New Orleans. Grand Lodge, *Proceedings of the W. M. Grand Lodge Free and Accepted Masons of the State of Louisiana* (New Orleans: A. W. Hyatt Stationary Manufacturing Co. 1912).

2. Grandjean Collection, Reg. 85-41, 8 May 1872, message from Robert Preaux.

3. Historians disagree on how quickly this happened. For example, in *Religion and the Rise of Jim Crow in New Orleans*, James Bennett sets the endpoint of Americanization with the rise of Jim Crow, while the contributors to *Creole New Orleans* place it sooner, and in *The Battle of New Orleans* Robert V. Remini links the Americanization with the 1815 Battle of New Orleans. Hirsch and Logsdon, *Creole New Orleans*; Remini, *The Battle of New Orleans*.

4. Gilroy, *The Black Atlantic*, 19. Also see Chambers, "The Black Atlantic."

5. These are the characteristics of the Atlantic age of revolutions laid out in the editors' introduction in Armitage and Subrahamanyam, *The Age of Revolutions in Global Context*, xii–xxxii.

6. John Thornton's work has done the most to advocate for an Atlantic world understanding that recognizes the agency of Africans and their diasporic descendants. Thornton, *Africa and Africans in the Making of the Atlantic World*.

7. Historian Sophia Rosenfeld discusses the productivity and significance of revolutionary pamphlets in this manner in *Common Sense*:

> It matters little, then, from our perspective, that the representative of the people, speaking to and from *le gros bon sens* or *le bon sens populaire* or *le bon sens villageoise* failed to exist as a sociological reality behind every text that assumed this authorial voice. It is not authenticity that is our chief concern . . . Rather, it is the way that the perceived common sense of peasants or women or any social group deemed closer to nature than the old ruling elite helped to foster a new populist ideal, a stereotype to be favorably contrasted with the aristocrat, the wordsmith, the sophist, and all others whose erudition or self-interest had caused them to lose sight of the simplicities that ostensibly unite most other humans. (Rosenfeld, *Common Sense*, 192)

8. Article 1, Declaration of the Rights of Man and of the Citizen, http://avalon.law .yale.edu/18th_century/rightsof.asp.

9. For U.S. South parallel and context, see Fox-Genovese and Genovese, "The Divine Sanction of Social Order."

10. Grandjean Collection, Reg. 85-34, 18 November 1871, message from Hughes Pedesclaux. Pedesclaux, a white Creole who lived in the Tremé neighborhood, acknowledged his mixed-race children and freed his slaves in 1841. Toledano and Christovich, *Faubourg Tremé and the Bayou Road*, 99.

11. Grandjean Collection, Reg. 85-57, 17 September 1874, message from Perique Angelo.

12. Despite John Locke's influence on liberalism and republicanism, his spirit is absent from the pages of the Cercle Harmonique's séance records.

13. Chartier, *The Cultural Origins of the French Revolution*, 20–37.

14. Neely, *A Concise History of the French Revolution*, 17.

15. Ian Davidson, *Voltaire*; Ian Davidson, *Voltaire in Exile*.

16. Grandjean Collection, 85-33, 18 June 1871.

17. Montesquieu, "Of the Principle of Democracy," in "Of the Principles of the Three Kinds of Government," Book 3 *The Spirit of Laws*.

18. Kessler, "Religion & Liberalism in Montesquieu's Persian Letters," 381.

19. Grandjean Collection, Reg. 85-32, 1 October 1871.

20. Wolfe, "The Confederate Republic in Montesquieu."

21. Boesche, "Fearing Monarchs and Merchants."

22. Voltaire advocated top-down reform because he believed "the thinking part of mankind is confined to a very small number." Montesquieu defended the nobility and advocated imperial governmental structures in some cases (such as Asia). Voltaire, quoted in Neely, *A Concise History of the French Revolution*, 18.

23. Rousseau, *Rousseau*, 41.

24. Neely, *A Concise History of the French Revolution*, 23.

25. Rousseau, *Rousseau*, 48.

26. Grandjean Collection, Reg. 85-34, 7 November 1871, message from J. J. Rousseau.

27. Grandjean Collection, Reg. 85-56, 25 June 1874, message from André, a brother.

28. Preamble, Declaration of the Rights of Man and of the Citizen, http://avalon.law .yale.edu/18th_century/rightsof.asp.

29. Other translations read "social distinctions can be based only on public utility," perhaps allowing for the nobility and remaining monarchy to maintain their status. Neely, *A Concise History of the French Revolution*, 86.

30. Grandjean Collection, Reg. 85-49, 6 February 1873, message from Armand Boutin.

31. Grandjean Collection, Reg. 85-38, 2 January 1872, message from Ambroise; Grandjean Collection, Reg. 85-38, 29 January 1872, message from Montesquieu; Grandjean Collection, Reg. 85-38, 1 February 1872, message from Montesquieu.

32. Grandjean Collection, Reg. 85-44, 31 August 1872, message from Beaumarchais; Grandjean Collection, Reg. 85-60, 25 September 1875, message from "a friend"; Grandjean Collection, Reg. 85-41, 21 May 1872, message from Volney; Grandjean Collection, Reg. 85-39, 18 February 1872, message from "Père Ambroise, ex-Capucin"; Grandjean Collection, Reg. 85-38, 9 February 1872, message from X; Grandjean Collection, Reg. 85-44, 15 August 1872, message from Mesmer.

33. Public speech of Robespierre, quoted in Neely, *A Concise History of the French Revolution*, 207.

34. Andress, "Living the Revolutionary Melodrama."

35. Robespierre speech, quoted in Sagan, *Citizens and Cannibals*, 427.

36. Hunt, "The Rhetoric of the Revolution in France," 88.

37. Grandjean Collection, Reg. 85-33, 28 May 1871.

38. Noir's own funeral has been identified as a "key moment" in the left's development leading up to the Paris Commune. Gluckstein, *Paris Commune*, 73.

39. Grandjean Collection, Reg. 85-31, 9 January 1870, message from Ambroise.

40. Generality, meaning "the rejection of intermediary bodies and the aspirations to achieve a single, unified society," emerged as a significant civil desire in France following the Revolution. Rosanvallon, *The Demands of Liberty*, 4.

41. Grandjean Collection, Reg. 85-45, 17 September 1872, message from Volney.

42. Rosanvallon, *The Demands of Liberty*, 130.

43. Michelet, *History of the French Revolution*, 18. Also see Mitzman, "Michelet and Social Romanticism." Rosanvallon described this religion of Michelet's as "rather vague, little more than a diffuse spiritualism serving as a sort of prop to the democratic ideal." Rosanvallon, *The Demands of Liberty*, 130.

44. Grandjean Collection, Reg. 85-45, 22 September 1872, message from Volney.

45. Mitzman, "Michelet and Social Romanticism," 663.

46. Together the works of these men represented an "alliance of disenfranchised popular elements," "critical intellectuals," and "left-liberal and republican elements." Mitzman, "Michelet and Social Romanticism," 663.

47. Grandjean Collection, Reg. 85-38, 10 February 1872.

48. Mitzman, "Michelet and Social Romanticism," 680–81.

49. King, *New Orleans*, 142–43.

50. For a closer look at the aggression in the lyrics and singing in "Ça ira," see Mason, *Singing the French Revolution*, 42–50.

51. Hanger, "Conflicting Loyalties."

52. Pitot, *Observations on the Colony of Louisiana from 1796 to 1802*, 3.

53. Court testimony of Don Luis Declouet about Pedro Bailly, quoted in Hanger, *Bounded Lives, Bounded Places*, 158.

54. Bell, *Revolution, Romanticism, and the Afro-Creole Protest Tradition*, 25. Also see Paul F. Lachance, "The Politics of Fear"; Liljegren, "Jacobinism in Spanish Louisiana."

55. Meadows, "Engineering Exile."

56. Quotation is from the poem "Le Retour de Napoleon" by Creole of color Victor Séjour and published in *Les Cenelles*. English translation of the poem provided in Desdunes, *Our People and Our History*, 32.

57. Volney, *The Ruins*, 177.

58. The prefaces to English editions of his songs also sing his praises. For example, see Graven Langstroth's translator's note in *Songs from Béranger*. The translator's "Memoir" of Béranger preceding the translations of songs describes the lyrics as not only embodiments of "a nation" but also "the microcosm of a life" and "the macrocosm of a society." Béranger, *Songs from Béranger*, 21.

59. Ibid., 272.

60. Tilby, "Pierre-Jean de Béranger."

61. Phelan, "The British Reception of Pierre-Jean de Béranger," 7.

62. Grandjean Collection, Reg. 85-32, 26 October 1870.

63. Béranger, *Songs from Béranger*, 104–6.

64. Joyaux, "The Reception of Pierre-Jean de Béranger in America," 271.

65. In August 1865 a group known as "les disciples de Béranger" held a ball and concert in honor of his birthday. *The New Orleans Times*, 6 August 1865.

66. *The Daily Picayune*, 7 December 1843.

67. *The Daily Picayune*, 5 January 1851; *The Daily Picayune*, 1 January 1856; *The Daily Picayune*, 7 August 1856; *Times-Picayune*, 12 August 1857; *Times-Picayune*, August 1857; *Times-Picayune*, 16 August 1857; *The Daily Picayune*, 12 December 1858.

68. Grandjean Collection, Reg. 85-32, 9 February 1871.

69. Michelet, *The People*, 172.

70. Ibid., 182.

71. *The Daily Picayune*, 16 September 1845; *The Daily Picayune*, 13 February 1846; *The Daily Picayune*, 11 January 1845; *The Daily Picayune*, 27 June 1857; *The Daily Picayune*, 21 February 1863; *New Orleans Tribune*, 19 December 1867.

72. *The Daily Picayune*, 29 March 1874; *New Orleans Weekly Louisianian*, 28 January 1873; *The Daily Picayune*, 21 February 1875; *The Daily Picayune*, 29 August 1875.

73. *The New Orleans Times*, 6 November 1865; *The Sunday Delta*, 26 September 1858; *The Sunday Delta*, 28 August 1859; *The Daily True Delta*, 28 April 1861.

74. *Black Republican*, 13 May 1865.

75. *The Daily Picayune*, 7 March 1869.

76. Daut, "'Sons of White Fathers'"; James Allen Smith, *Popular French Romanticism*, 178–98; Bell, *Revolution, Romanticism, and the Afro-Creole Protest Tradition*, 89–106.

77. Of Louverture, Lamartine wrote, "This man is a nation." Lamartine, quoted in Bell, *Revolution, Romanticism, and the Afro-Creole Protest Tradition*, 99.

78. Grandjean Collection, Reg. 85-41, 14 May 1872; Grandjean Collection, Reg. 85-33, 9 June 1871.

79. Quoted in Bell, *Revolution, Romanticism, and the Afro-Creole Protest Tradition*, 106–7.

80. Desdunes, *Our People and Our History*, 10–60; Kress, "Pierre-Aristide Desdunes"; Haddox, "The 'Nous' of Southern Catholic Quadroons"; Bell, *Revolution, Romanticism, and the Afro-Creole Protest Tradition*, 115–23.

81. Quotation from Lamennais, *What Catholicism Will Be in the New Society*, quoted in Stearns, *Priest and Revolutionary*, 176.

82. Kselman, "State and Religion," 67–68.

83. Ibid., 84.

84. Grandjean Collection, 85-40, 25 April 1872; Grandjean Collection, Reg. 85-41, 21 May 1872, message arrived in English.

85. Stearns, *Priest and Revolutionary*; Ellis, "The Abbe Lamennais on Freedom"; Oldfield, "The Evolution of Lamennais' Catholic-Liberal Synthesis."

86. The Papal Encyclical *Singulari nos* (7 July 1834), subtitled "On the Errors of Lamennais" condemned *Paroles d'un Croyant* as corrupt, wicked, and dangerous.

87. Excerpt from *Paroles d'un Croyant* in Stearns, *Priest and Revolutionary*, 181–87.

88. La Mennais, *Words of a Believer*, 14.

89. Ibid., 20–23.

90. Grandjean Collection, Reg. 85-43, 25 July 1872.

91. La Mennais, *Words of a Believer*, 74, 34–35, 95, 57.

92. *The Daily Picayune*, 4 June 1848, 24 September 1848.

93. "La Liberté," *L'Union*, 18 October 1862.

94. Lamennais's death was even local news, including mention of his current intellectual work (a translation of Dante's Inferno). *The Daily Picayune*, 21 June 1855.

95. Grandjean Collection, Reg. 85-34, 6 October 1871, message from Lamennais; Grandjean Collection, Reg. 85-34, 6 July 1871, message from Lamennais.

96. Crook, "The French Revolution and Napoleon," 27.

97. Grandjean Collection, Reg. 85-33, 4 June 1871. Grandjean Collection, Reg. 85-32, 26 October 1870.

98. Jefferson, *Notes on the State of Virginia*, 204–6.

99. Letter, Thomas Jefferson to Henri Grégoire, 25 February 1809, http://teach ingamericanhistory.org/library/document/letter-to-henri-gregoire/. (5 May 2015).

100. Grégoire, *An Enquiry Concerning the Intellectual and Moral Faculties, and Literature of Negroes*, 248.

101. Grandjean Collection, 85-32, 5 April 1870.

102. Klooster, *Revolutions in the Atlantic World*, 4.

103. Klooster, "The Rising Expectation of Free and Enslaved Blacks in the Greater Caribbean," 57.

104. Political scientist James C. Scott defined a hidden transcript as "a critique of power spoken behind the back of the dominant." Scott, *Domination and the Arts of Resistance*, xii.

105. Grandjean Collection, Reg. 85-38, 7 January 1872, message from Toussaint Louverture.

106. Clavin, *Toussaint Louverture and the American Civil War*, 122.

107. *The Daily Picayune*, 19 March 1863.

108. *New Orleans Tribune*, 12 July 1865.

109. Bellegarde, "Alexandre Pétion."

110. Grandjean Collection, Reg. 85-38, 11 February 1872, message from Pétion; Grandjean Collection, Reg. 85-43, 25 July 1872, message from Pétion; Grandjean Collection, Reg. 85-46, 25 October 1872, message from Swedenborg.

111. Laurent Dubois, "Dessalines Toro d'Haïti," 543.

112. Sheller, " 'You Signed My Name, but Not My Feet,' " 74.

113. Nicholls, "A Work of Combat."

114. Bellegarde-Smith, "Haitian Social Thought."

115. Sheller, " 'You Signed My Name,' " 80.

116. The spirit "Jeffrard" appeared the same day as other Haitian spirits, such as Pétion, M. De St. Méry, and Auguste Brouard. Grandjean Collection, Reg. 85-43, 25 July 1872.

117. Grandjean Collection, Reg. 85-43, 25 July 1872; Grandjean Collection, Reg. 85-47, 30 November 1872, message signed General Auguste Brouard; Grandjean Collection, Reg. 85-35, 23 December 1871, message signed Auguste Brouard.

118. Bellegarde-Smith, "Haitian Social Thought," 21.

119. Ardouin's *Etudes sur l'histoire d'Haïti*, quoted in Nicholls, "A Work of Combat," 24.

120. Saint-Rémy, *Pétion et Haïti*.

121. Nicholls, "A Work of Combat," 16. Though Madiou was a mulatto himself, his work did the least to propagate the "mulatto legend."

122. Fenton, *Religious Liberties*, 103–20.

123. Additionally, for many African Americans outside New Orleans, Haiti was seen as "a New World exemplar and redeemer for the race." In short, Haiti was a place of divine potential. See Maffly-Kipp, *Setting Down the Sacred Past*, 109–53.

124. Sheller, *Democracy after Slavery*, 5.

125. Sheller does not argue that these ideologies meant total liberty for all in the immediate aftermath of the Haitian Revolution or the emancipation in Jamaica. For example, her focus in Haiti was the Liberal Rebellion, the Piquet Rebellion in 1843–44, and the radicalism of the peasant classes on the island. Following the Haitian Revolution, the island possessed a "*limited* liberal democracy." Sheller, *Democracy After Slavery*, 10.

126. Grandjean Collection, Reg. 85-43, 25 July 1872, message from M. De St. Mery.

127. Garraway, "Race, Reproduction and Family Romance in Moreau de Saint-Méry's Description."

128. Much of López's recruitment took place in the United States, and his rebel efforts were akin to invasions of Cuba from the United States gulf. Caldwell, *The Lopez Expeditions to Cuba*; Chaffin, *Fatal Glory*.

129. In the years leading up to and following López's failed attempts, Cuban exiles living in the Northeast also echoed the ideas of the French Revolution by quoting Montesquieu, Lamennais, and Rousseau and supporting liberty and abolition in their writings, both fictional and not. Luis-Brown, "An 1848 for the Americas."

130. Grandjean Collection, Reg. 85-34, 10 December 1871, message from Lopez; Grandjean Collection, Reg. 85-34, 21 October 1871, message from Lopez.

131. A *New York Herald* correspondent in New Orleans reported in August 1849 that the object of his expedition was to "carry out the formation of the Republic of the Sierra Madre, to separate that territory from the Mexican republic, proclaim its independence, and maintain it by force." *New York Herald,* quoted in Chaffin, *Fatal Glory*, 63.

132. Caldwell, *The Lopez Expeditions to Cuba*, 90.

133. Grandjean Collection, Reg. 85-31, 25 March 1869, message from Lamennais. The spirit Pierre Soulé also spoke favorably of Cuban freedom. Grandjean Collection, Reg. 85-31, 22 May 1870.

134. Chaffin, *Fatal Glory*, xxii.

135. Cisneros and Thrasher, "Addresses Delivered at the Celebration of the Third Anniversary in Honor of the Martyrs for Cuban Freedom at the Mechanic's Institute Hall."

136. Grandjean Collection, Reg. 85-30, 5 February 1860, message from "Virgile."

137. Tocqueville, *The Old Regime and the Revolution*, 11.

138. Grandjean Collection, Reg. 85-32, 15 October 1871, message from Vincent de Paul; Grandjean Collection, Reg. 85-33, 2 June 1871; Grandjean Collection, Reg. 85-46, 1 November 1872, message from Bach.

139. Grandjean Collection, Reg. 85-51, 16 March 1873, message from "Lunel, the devoted brother"; Grandjean Collection, Reg. 85-32, 18 February 1869; Grandjean Collection, Reg. 85-31, 13 October 1869, message from Moni; Grandjean Collection, Reg. 85-31, 14 July 1870, joint message from Robespierre and André Chenier; Grandjean Collection, Reg. 85-34, 26 October 1871, message from Voltaire; Grandjean Collection, Reg. 85-64, message from Lamennais.

140. Grandjean Collection, Reg. 85-35, 17 December 1871, joint message from Montesquieu and Ambroise; Grandjean Collection, Reg. 85-34, 4 March 1871; Grandjean Collection, Reg. 85-40, 29 March 1872, message from Lamennais; Grandjean Collection, Reg. 85-35, 28 December 1871, message from N. Debrosses, on behalf of Geo. B. Dubuclet; Grandjean Collection, Reg. 85-32, 29 September 1871, message from Lopez.

141. Grandjean Collection, Reg. 85-40, 26 March 1872; Grandjean Collection, Reg. 85-38, 27 January 1872.

142. Grandjean Collection, Reg. 85-43, 14 July 1872; Grandjean Collection, Reg. 85-38, 27 January 1872; Grandjean Collection, Reg. 85-45, 20 September 1872.

143. Grandjean Collection, Reg. 85-34, 4 December 1871, message from Lamennais; Grandjean Collection, Reg. 85-44, 27 August 1872, message from Lamennais; Grandjean Collection, Reg. 85-38, 2 January 1872, message from Ambroise; Grandjean Collection, Reg. 85-51, 29 June 1873, message from "a sister." The spirit criticized those who claimed to be descendants of Charlemagne when really their fathers were just "poor devils." Grandjean Collection, Reg. 85-38, 6 February 1872; Grandjean Collection, Reg. 85-38, 4 February 1872, message from Jean Duvernay; Grandjean Collection, Reg. 85-35, 17 December 1871; Grandjean Collection, Reg. 85-35, 14 December 1871, message from Mesmer; Grandjean Collection, Reg. 85-33, 5 June 1871, message from Lamennais; Grandjean Collection, Reg. 85-31, 25 October 1869, message from Béranger.

144. Grandjean Collection, Reg. 85-32, 9 February 1871; Grandjean Collection, Reg. 85-51, 5 July 1873, message recorded in English.

145. Wolff, "Religious Devotion and Maternal Sentiment in Early Modern Lent," 361.

146. Ravenel, "The Great Tradition," 745; Conley, "Marie de Rabutin-Chantal, Marquise de Sévigné."

147. Her letters were selected as the inaugural publication of the renowned *Les Grands Ecrivains de la France* series begun by the Hachette publishing company in Paris in the mid-nineteenth century.

148. *The Daily Picayune*, 29 January 1854 and 17 July 1850.

149. Madame De Sévigné, *The Letters of Madame De Sévigné to Her Daughter and Friends*, iii.

150. Farrell, *Performing Motherhood: The Sévigné Correspondence*, 2.

151. Grandjean Collection, Reg. 85-31, 38 March 1869; Grandjean Collection, Reg. 85-38, 26 January 1872.

152. Grandjean Collection, Reg. 85-32, 11 September 1870, message from Victor Noir.

153. Grandjean Collection, Reg. 85-39, 7 March 1872; Grandjean Collection, Reg. 85-34, 8 November 1871; Grandjean Collection, Reg. 85-42, 19 June 1872; Grandjean Collection, Reg. 85-44, 18 August 1872; Grandjean Collection, Reg. 85-47, 8 November 1872, message from Oscar St. Felix.

154. Grandjean Collection, Reg. 85-32, 11 September 1870; Grandjean Collection, Reg. 85-36, 29 July 1872.

155. In Grandjean's notes, he explained that Soulé left France during the reign of Napoleon III for Saint-Domingue before arriving in New Orleans. Grandjean Collection, Reg. 85-31, 22 May 1870.

156. Grandjean Collection, Reg. 85-31, 24 February 1869.

157. *The Daily Picayune*, 13 June 1845.

158. *The Daily Picayune*, 26 July 1848; *The Daily Picayune*, 5 October 1848; *The Daily Picayune*, 30 October 1848. A correspondent from Europe bitterly reported that "the memory of Our Saviour and of Robespierre were toasted in the same breath" during a toast at the new National Assembly. *The Daily Picayune*, 1 June 1849.

159. *The Daily Picayune*, 12 September 1861. Also during the Civil War, the *New Orleans Daily True Delta* deemed Horace Greeley "a little Robespierre" for his demands for a "traitor" during the Confederacy's rebellion. The periodical's office happily offered him some rope and then sardonically suggested that he "hang himself to the nearest lamp post, and thus at once satisfy his desire to hang a traitor, and greatly gratify the loyal public." *The Daily True Delta*, 13 April 1862.

160. *The New Orleans Times*, 2 August 1868 and 13 August 1868.

161. Grandjean Collection, Reg. 85-31, 24 February 1869.

Conclusion

1. Grandjean Collection, Reg. 85-30, 8 July 1863.

2. Grandjean Collection, Reg. 85-32, message from Mesmer.

3. Grandjean Collection, Reg. 85-34, 28 September 1871, message from Crocker. Those who committed suicide not only set a poor example, but they were "unhappy and miserable" in the spiritual world. Grandjean Collection, Reg. 85-43, 2 August 1872, message from Alfred Morant, accompanied by J. St. Hubert and others.

4. Grandjean Collection, Reg. 85-34, 19 November 1871; Grandjean Collection, Reg. 85-59, 15 January 1875, message from Louis Lacroix; Grandjean Collection, Reg. 85-32, message from Rose Crocker; Grandjean Collection, Reg. 85-39, 18 February 1872, message from "Père Ambroise, ex-Capucin"; Grandjean Collection, Reg. 85-45, 29 September 1872, message from Auguste; Grandjean Collection, Reg. 85-45, 5 September 1872, group message from: Edmond Capdeville, Clément Ramos, Alphonse de Buys, Philippe Avegne Jr., Robert Severin, A. Dubrouille, and Louis Bernard; Grandjean Collection, Reg. 85-36, 7 June 1872, message from Daux Barriere; Grandjean

Collection, Reg. 85-57, 16 September 1874, message from "A Guide"; Grandjean Collection, Reg. 85-36, 4 March 1872, message recorded in English from J.

5. Grandjean Collection, Reg. 85-51, 1 April 1873, message from Moni; Grandjean Collection, Reg. 85-49, 4 February 1873, message from Louisa Leblanc; Grandjean Collection, Reg. 85-31, 6 March 1869, message from "your father and your mother"; Grandjean Collection, Reg. 85-51, 18 July 1873, message from Rosalie Dubuclet; Grandjean Collection, Reg. 85-31, 6 July 1870, message from Luc; Grandjean Collection, Reg. 85-31, 7 March 1869, message from Père Antoine; Grandjean Collection, Reg. 85-60, 4 June 1875, message from "a bright brother"; Grandjean Collection, Reg. 85-31, 12 March 1869, message from Moni; Grandjean Collection, Reg. 85-31, 25 March 1869, message from Lamennais; Grandjean Collection, Reg. 85-43, 14 July 1872, message from Augustin Carrière; Grandjean Collection, Reg. 85-52, 17 November 1873, message from Vincent de Paul.

6. Grandjean Collection, Reg. 85-52, 22 November 1873, message from a devoted brother; Grandjean Collection, Reg. 85-30, 28 November 1858; Grandjean Collection, Reg. 85-41, 6 May 1872, message from Confucius; Grandjean Collection, Reg. 85-57, 4 September 1874, message from Paul Bertus; Grandjean Collection, Reg. 85-52, 28 November 1873, message from Anais Syndreybranchet [spelling unclear]; Grandjean Collection, Reg. 85-53, 24 January 1874, message from Charles Lévègue; Grandjean Collection, Reg. 85-43, 25 July 1872, message from Volney; Grandjean Collection, Reg. 85-56, 8 June 1874, message from "a bright brother"; Grandjean Collection, Reg. 85-51, 20 July 1873.

7. Eric Foner, *Reconstruction*, 604.

8. Grandjean Collection, Reg. 85-31, 2 March 1865, message signed Vincent de Paul.

9. Grandjean Collection, Reg. 85-37, 8 October 1875.

10. Grandjean Collection, Reg. 85-37, Grandjean notes; Grandjean Collection, Reg. 85-61, Grandjean notes.

11. Grandjean Collection, Reg. 85-63, 12 November 1877, message from "Beaucoup" (many); Grandjean Collection, Reg. 85-63, 21 November 1877, message from "Friend!"; Grandjean Collection, Reg. 85-63, 20 November 1877, message from "Rite"; Grandjean Collection, Reg. 85-63, 6 November 1877; Grandjean Collection, Reg. 85-63. Grandjean Collection, Reg. 85-63, Grandjean notes following final message.

12. Grandjean Collection, Reg. 85-63, Grandjean notes.

13. Grandjean Collection, Reg. 85-32, 30 August 1906, 29 October 1906, 11 November 1906, and 2 December 1906, messages all recorded in French.

Bibliography

Manuscript Collections

New Orleans
    Amistad Research Center, Tulane University
        George Longe Papers
        Charles Barthelemy Rousseve Papers
        Alexander Pierre Tureaud Papers
    Historic New Orleans Collection, New Orleans
        Free Persons of Color in Louisiana Collection
        New Orleans Church Ephemera Collection
    Howard-Tilton Memorial Library, Tulane University
        Edna B. Freiberg Papers, 1800–1981
        Zoe Posey Papers, 1822–1934
        Antonio de Sedella Collection, 1778–1816
        Voodoo Notes, Undated
        John Minor Wisdom Collection, 1710–1960
    Louisiana and Special Collections, Earl K. Long Library, University of New Orleans
        Marcus B. Christian Collection
        René Grandjean Collection

Periodicals

L'Album littéraire: Journal des jeunes gens, amateurs de literature
Black Republican
Le Moniteur de la Louisiane
New Orleans Daily Crescent
The New Orleans Daily Delta
New Orleans Daily True Delta
The New Orleans Daily Picayune
New Orleans Era
New Orleans L'Union
New Orleans Times
The New Orleans Times-Picayune
The New Orleans Tribune
New Orleans Weekly Louisianian
The New Orleans Weekly Times

Le Propagateur Catholique
Le Spiritualiste de la Nouvelle-Orléans
The Sunday Delta

Published Sources

Abel, Sheri Lyn. *Charles Testut's Le Vieux Salomon: Race, Religion, Socialism, and Freemasonry*. Lanham, Md.: Lexington Books, 2009.

Agee, Gary B. *A Cry for Justice: Daniel Rudd and His Life in Black Catholicism, Journalism, and Activism, 1854–1933*. Fayetteville: University of Arkansas Press, 2011.

Albanese, Catherine L. *Nature Religion in America: From the Algonkian Indians to the New Age*. Chicago: University of Chicago Press, 1990.

———. "On the Matter of Spirit: Andrew Jackson Davis and the Marriage of God and Nature." *Journal of the American Academy of Religion* 60, no. 1 (1992): 1–17.

———. *A Republic of Mind and Spirit: A Cultural History of American Metaphysical Religion*. New Haven, Ct.: Yale University Press, 2007.

Alberts, John Bernard. "Origins of Black Catholic Parishes in the Archdiocese of New Orleans, 1718–1920." Ph.D. diss., Louisiana State University, 1998.

Anderson, Emma. *The Death and Afterlife of the North American Martyrs*. Cambridge, Mass.: Harvard University Press, 2013.

Andress, David. "Living the Revolutionary Melodrama: Robespierre's Sensibility and the Construction of Political Commitment in the French Revolution." *Representations* 114, no. 1 (Spring 2011): 103–28.

Anthony, Arthé Agnes. "The Negro Creole Community in New Orleans, 1880–1920: An Oral History." Ph.D. diss., University of California, Irvine, 1978.

Apter, Andrew. "Of African Origins: Creolization and Connaissance in Haitian Vodou." *American Ethnologist* 29 (2002): 233–60.

Armitage, David. "Three Concepts of Atlantic History." In *The British Atlantic World, 1500–1800*, edited by David Armitage, and Michael J. Braddick, 13–29. New York: Palgrave Macmillan, 2002.

Armitage, David, and Sanjay Subrahamanyam, eds. *The Age of Revolutions in Global Context, c. 1760–1840*. New York: Palgrave MacMillan, 2010.

Aslakon, Kenneth. "The 'Quadroon-Plaçage' Myth of Antebellum New Orleans: Anglo-American (Mis)interpretations of a French-Caribbean Phenomenon." *Journal of Social History* 45, no. 3 (Spring 2012): 709–34.

Baker, Kelly J. *Gospel According to the Klan: The KKK's Appeal to Protestant America, 1915–1930*. Lawrence: University Press of Kansas, 2011.

Baptist, Edward E. " 'Cuffy,' 'Fancy Maids,' and 'One-Eyed Men': Rape, Commodification, and the Domestic Slave Trade in the United States." *American Historical Review* 106, no. 5 (December 2001): 1619–50.

Barthet, Joseph. *Le Spiritualiste de la Nouvelle-Orléans*. Vol. 1. New Orleans, La: J. L. Sollée, 1857.

Baudier, Roger, Sr. *Centennial: St. Rose of Lima Paris.* New Orleans, La., 1957.

Bell, Caryn Cossé. "French Religious Culture in Afro-Creole New Orleans, 1718–1877." *U.S. Catholic Historian* 17, no. 1 (1999): 1–16.

———. *Revolution, Romanticism, and the Afro-Creole Protest Tradition in Louisiana, 1718–1868.* Baton Rouge: Louisiana State University Press, 1997.

Bellegarde, Dantes. "Alexandre Pétion: The Founder of Rural Democracy in Haiti." *Caribbean Quarterly* 3, no. 3 (1953): 167–73.

Bellegarde-Smith, Patrick. "Haitian Social Thought in the 19th Century." *Caribbean Studies* 20, no. 1 (1980): 5–33.

Bellegarde-Smith, Patrick, and Claudine Michel, eds. *Haitian Vodou: Spirit, Myth, and Reality.* Bloomington: Indiana University Press, 2006.

Bennett, Bridget. "Sacred Theatres: Shakers, Spiritualists, Theatricality, and the Indian in the 1830s and 1840s." *Drama Review* 49, no. 3 (2005): 114–34.

———. *Spiritualism and Nineteenth-Century American Literature.* New York: Palgrave MacMillan, 2007.

Bennett, James B. *Religion and the Rise of Jim Crow in New Orleans.* Princeton, N.J.: Princeton University Press, 2005.

Béranger, Pierre-Jean de. *Songs from Béranger.* Translated by Craven Langstroth Betts. New York: Frederick A. Stokes & Brother, 1888.

Berlin, Ira. "From Creole to African: Atlantic Creoles and the Origins of African-American Society in Mainland North America." *William and Mary Quarterly* 53, no. 2 (1996): 251–88.

Berry, Mary F. "Negro Troops in Blue and Gray: The Louisiana Native Guards, 1861–1863." *Louisiana History: The Journal of the Louisiana Historical Association* 8, no. 2 (Spring 1967): 165–90.

Blassingame, John W. *Black New Orleans, 1860–1880.* Chicago: University of Chicago Press, 1973.

Blight, David W. *Race and Reunion: The Civil War in American Memory.* Cambridge, Mass.: Harvard University Press, 2001.

Bloch, George. *Mesmerisms: A Translation of the Original Scientific and Medical Writings of F. A. Mesmer.* Los Alitos, Calif.: William Kaufmann, 1980.

Bloch, Ruth. *Visionary Republic: Millennial Themes in American Thought, 1756–1800.* Cambridge, U.K.: Cambridge University Press, 1985.

Blum, Edward J. "'The First Secessionist was Satan': Secession and the Religious Politics of Evil in Civil War America." *Civil War History* 60, no. 3 (2014): 234–69.

———. *Reforging the White Republic: Race, Religion, and American Nationalism, 1865–1898.* Baton Rouge: Louisiana State University Press, 2005.

Blum, Edward J., Tracy Fessenden, Prema Kurien, and Judith Weisenfeld. "Forum: American Religion and 'Whiteness.'" *Religion and American Culture* 19, no. 1 (2009): 1–35.

Blum, Edward J., and Paul Harvey. *The Color of Christ: The Son of God and the Saga of Race in America.* Chapel Hill: University of North Carolina Press, 2012.

Boesche, Roger. "Fearing Monarchs and Merchants: Montesquieu's Two Theories of Despotism." *Western Political Quarterly* 43, no. 4 (1990): 741–61.

Botein, Barbara. "The Hennessy Case: An Episode of Anti-Italian Nativism." *Louisiana History: The Journal of the Louisiana Historical Association* 20, no. 3 (1979): 261–79.

Braden, Waldo Warder, ed. *Building the Myth: Selected Speeches Memorializing Abraham Lincoln.* Champaign: University of Illinois Press, 1990.

Braude, Ann. "News from the Spirit World: A Checklist of American Spiritualist Periodicals, 1847–1900." *Proceedings of the American Antiquarian Society* 99 (1989): 399–462.

———. *Radical Spirits: Spiritualism and Women's Rights in Nineteenth-Century America.* Boston: Beacon Press, 1989.

Brett, Edward T. *The New Orleans Sisters of the Holy Family: African American Missionaries to the Garifuna of Belize.* Notre Dame, Ind.: University of Notre Dame Press, 2012.

Britten, Emma Hardinge. *Autobiography of Emma Hardinge Britten.* London: John Heywood, 1900.

———. *Modern American Spiritualism: A Twenty Years' Record of the Communion between Earth and the World of the Spirits.* New York, 1870.

Brown, Ras Michael. *African-Atlantic Cultures and the South Carolina Lowcountry.* Cambridge, U.K.: Cambridge University Press, 2012.

Brown, William Wells. *The Negro in the American Rebellion: His Heroism and His Fidelity.* Boston: Lee and Shepard, 1867.

Burton, Richard D. E. *Afro-Creole: Power, Opposition, and Play in the Caribbean.* Ithaca, N.Y.: Cornell University Press, 1997.

Butler, Jon. *Awash in a Sea of Faith: Christianizing the American People.* Cambridge, Mass.: Harvard University Press, 1990.

Cable, George Washington. "Creole Slave Songs." *Century Magazine,* 31, no. 6 (1886): 807–27.

———. "The Dance at Place Congo." *Century Magazine,* 31, no. 4 (1886): 519–32.

Cadwallader, Jen. "Spirit Photography and the Victorian Culture of Mourning." *Modern Language Studies* 37, no. 2 (2008): 8–31.

Caldwell, Robert Granville. *The Lopez Expeditions to Cuba, 1848–1851.* Princeton, N.J.: Princeton University Press, 1915.

Carroll, Bret E. "'A Higher Power to Feel': Spiritualism, Grief, and Victorian Manhood." *Men and Masculinities* 3, no. 1 (2000): 3–29.

———. *Spiritualism in Antebellum America.* Bloomington: Indiana University Press, 1995.

Castelli, Elizabeth. *Martyrdom and Memory: Early Christian Culture Making.* New York: Columbia University Press, 2004.

Chaffin, Tom. *Fatal Glory: Narciso López and the First Clandestine U.S. War Against Cuba.* Baton Rouge: Louisiana University Press, 2003.

Chambers, Douglas B. "The Black Atlantic: Theory, Method, and Practice." In *The Atlantic World 1450–2000*, edited by Toyin Falola and Kevin D. Roberts, 151–73. Bloomington: Indiana University Press, 2008.

Chartier, Roger. *The Cultural Origins of the French Revolution.* Translated by Lydia G. Cochrane. Durham, N.C.: Duke University Press, 2004.

Cheung, Floyd D. "*Les Cenelles* and Quadroon Balls: 'Hidden Transcripts' of Resistance and Domination in New Orleans, 1803–1845." *Southern Literary Journal* 29, no. 2 (1997): 5–16.

Chireau, Yvonne P. *Black Magic: Religion and the African American Conjuring Tradition.* Berkeley: University of California Press, 2003.

Cisneros, Gaspar Betancourt, and J. S. Thrasher. "Addresses Delivered at the Celebration of the Third Anniversary in Honor of the Martyrs for Cuban Freedom at the Mechanic's Institute Hall, New Orleans, Sept. 1, 1854." New Orleans, La.: Sherman, Wharton, 1854.

Clark, Emily J. "How American is New Orleans?: What the Founding Era Has to Tell Us." In *Place, Identity, and Urban Culture: Odesa and New Orleans*, edited by Samuel C. Ramer and Blair A. Ruble, 27–34. Washington, D.C.: Woodrow Wilson International Center for Scholars, 2008.

———. *Masterless Mistresses: The New Orleans Ursulines and the Development of a New World Society, 1727–1834.* Chapel Hill: University of North Carolina Press, 2007.

———. "Moving from Periphery to Centre: The Non-British in Colonial North America." *Historical Journal* 42, no. 3 (1999): 903–10.

———. *The Strange History of the American Quadroon: Free Women of Color in the Revolutionary Atlantic World.* Chapel Hill: University of North Carolina Press, 2013.

Clark, Emily, and Virginia Meacham Gould. "The Feminine Face of Afro-Catholicism in New Orleans, 1727–1852." *William and Mary Quarterly* 59, no. 2 (2002): 409–48.

Clark, Emily Suzanne. "Catholics, Creoles, and Color Lines." *Journal of Africana Religions* 2, no. 2 (2014): 263–70.

Clavin, Matthew J. *Toussaint Louverture and the American Civil War: The Promise and Peril of a Second Haitian Revolution.* Philadelphia: University of Pennsylvania Press, 2011.

Clifford, James, ed. *Writing Culture: The Poetics and Politics of Ethnography.* Berkeley: University of California Press, 1986.

Conley, John J. "Marie de Rabutin-Chantal, Marquise de Sévigné (1626–96)." In the *Internet Encyclopedia of Philosophy*, edited by James Fieser and Bradley Dowden. http://www.iep.utm.edu/sevigne/#H5. 5 May, 2015.

Connor, William P. "Reconstruction Rebels: The *New Orleans Tribune* in Post-War Louisiana." *Louisiana History: The Journal of the Louisiana Historical Association* 21, no. 2 (1980): 159–81.

Cooke, John Edwin, and Robert M. De Witt, *The Life, Trial, and Execution of Captain John Brown, Known as "Old Brown of Ossawatomie" with a Full Account of the Attempted Insurrection at Harper's Ferry.* New York: R. M. De Witt, 1859.

Couch, R. Randall. "The Public Masked Balls of Antebellum New Orleans: A Custom of Masque Outside the Mardi Gras Tradition." *Louisiana History: The Journal of the Louisiana Historical Society* 35, no. 4 (1994): 403–31.

Cowan, Walter Greaves, and Jack B. McGuire. *Louisiana Governors: Rulers, Rascals, and Reformers.* Oxford: University Press of Mississippi, 2008.

Cox, Robert S. *Body and Soul: A Sympathetic History of American Spiritualism.* Charlottesville: University of Virginia Press, 2003.

Crook, Malcolm. "The French Revolution and Napoleon, 1788–1814." In *Revolutionary France, 1788–1880*, edited by Malcolm Crook, 8–35. Oxford: Oxford University Press, 2002.

Crowder, John H. "The Civil War through the Eyes of a Sixteen-Year-Old Black Officer: The Letters of Lieutenant John H. Crowder of the 1st Louisiana Native Guards." Edited by Joseph T. Glatthaar. *Louisiana History: The Journal of the Louisiana Historical Association* 35, no. 2 (1994): 201–16.

Crowe, Charles. "Bishop James Madison and the Republic of Virtue." *The Journal of Southern History* 30, no. 1 (1964): 58–70.

Cummings, Kathleen Sprows. "American Saints: Gender and the Re-Imaging of U.S. Catholicism in the Early Twentieth Century." *Religion and American Culture* 22, no. 2 (2012): 203–31.

Curran, Andrew S. *The Anatomy of Blackness: Science & Slavery in an Age of Enlightenment.* Baltimore: Johns Hopkins University Press, 2011.

D'Agostino, Peter. *Rome in America: Transnational Catholic Ideology from the Risorgimento to Fascism.* Chapel Hill: University of North Carolina Press, 2004.

Daggett, Melissa L. "Henry Louis Rey, Spiritualism, and Creoles of Color in Nineteenth-Century New Orleans." M.A. thesis, University of New Orleans, 2009.

———. "Spiritualism among Creoles of Color in Nineteenth-Century New Orleans: The Life and Times of Henry Louis Rey." *Louisiana History: The Journal of the Louisiana Historical Association* 55, no. 4 (2014): 409–31.

Daut, Marlene L. " 'Sons of White Fathers': Mulatto Vengeance and the Haitian Revolution in Victor Séjours's 'The Mulatto.' " *Nineteenth-Century Literature* 65, no. 1 (2010): 1–37.

Davidson, Ian. *Voltaire: A Life.* New York: Pegasus Book, 2010.

———. *Voltaire in Exile: The Last Years, 1753–78.* New York: Grove Press, 2004.

Davidson, James D. "A Journey through the South in 1836: Diary of James D. Davidson." Edited by Herbert A. Kellar. *Journal of Southern History* 1, no. 3 (1935): 345–77.

Davis, Andrew Jackson. *Beyond the Valley; A Sequel to "The Magic Staff": An Autobiography of Andrew Jackson Davis.* Boston: Colby & Rich, 1885.

————. *The Great Harmonia; Being a Philosophical Revelation of the Natural,
Spiritual, and Celestial Universe*. Boston: Benjamin B. Mussey, 1851.

————. *The Magic Staff: An Autobiography of Andrew Jackson Davis*. New York: J. S.
Brown, 1857.

————. *The Present Age and Inner Life; Ancient and Modern Spirit Mysteries Classified
and Explained*. Boston: Colby & Rich, Banner Publishing House, 1886.

————. *The Principles of Nature, Her Divine Revelations, and a Voice to Mankind*.
New York: S. S. Lyon, and Wm. Fishbough, 1851.

Davis, Cyprian. "Black Catholics in Nineteenth Century America." *U.S. Catholic
Historian* 5, no. 1 (1986): 1–18.

————. *The History of Black Catholics in the United States*. New York: The Crossroad
Publishing Company, 1995.

Dawdy, Shannon Lee. *Building the Devil's Empire: French Colonial New Orleans*.
Chicago: University of Chicago Press, 2008.

Deckert, Emil. "New Orleans, the Mississippi, and the Delta through a German's Eyes:
The Travels of Emil Deckert, 1885–1886." Edited by Frederic Trautman. *Louisiana
History: The Journal of the Louisiana Historical Society* 25, no. 1 (1984): 79–98.

Declaration of the Rights of Man and of the Citizen, Yale Law School Avalon
Project. http://avalon.law.yale.edu/18th_century/rightsof.asp. 5 May, 2015.

Deggs, Sister Mary Bernard. *No Cross, No Crown: Black Nuns in Nineteenth-Century
New Orleans*. Edited by Virginia Meacham Gould and Charles E. Nolan.
Bloomington: Indiana University Press, 2002.

Delp, Robert W. "Andrew Jackson Davis: Prophet of American Spiritualism." *Journal
of American History* 54, no. 1 (1967): 43–56.

Desdunes, Rodolphe L. *Our People and Our History: Fifty Creole Portraits*. Translated
by Sister Dorothea Olga McCants. Baton Rouge: Louisiana State University
Press, 1973.

De Sévigné, Madame. *The Letters of Madame De Sévigné to Her Daughter and Friends*.
Edited by Mrs. Hale. Boston: Roberts Brothers, 1889.

Dessens, Nathalie. *From Saint-Domingue to New Orleans: Migration and Influences*.
Gainesville: University Press of Florida, 2007.

Deveney, John Patrick. *Paschal Beverly Randolph: A Nineteenth-Century Black
American Spiritualist, Rosicrucian, and Sex Magician*. Albany: State University of
New York Press, 1997.

DeVore Donald E., and Joseph Logsdon. *Crescent City Schools: Public Education in
New Orleans, 1841–1991*. Lafayette: University of Southwestern Louisiana, 1991.

Dolan, Jay P. *The American Catholic Experience: A History from Colonial Times to the
Present*. Notre Dame, Ind.: University of Notre Dame Press, 1992.

————. *In Search of an American Catholicism: A History of Religion and Culture in
Tension*. Oxford: Oxford University Press, 2002.

Dominguez, Virginia. *White By Definition: Social Classification in Creole Louisiana*.
New Brunswick, N.J.: Rutgers University Press, 1986.

Donaldson, Gary A. "A Window on Slave Culture: Dances at Congo Square in New Orleans, 1800–1862." *Journal of Negro History* 69, no. 2 (1984): 63–72.

Doorley, Michael. "Irish Catholics and French Creoles: Ethnic Struggles within the Catholic Church in New Orleans, 1835–1920." *Catholic Historical Review* 87, no. 1 (2001): 34–54.

Douglass, Frederick. *My Bondage and My Freedom.* New York: Miller, Orton & Mulligan, 1855.

Dubois, Laurent. "Dessalines Toro d'Haïti." *William and Mary Quarterly* 69, no. 3 (2012): 541–48.

———. "An Enslaved Enlightenment: Rethinking the Intellectual History of the French Atlantic." *Social History* 31, no. 1 (2006): 1–14.

Dubois, Sylvie, and Megan Melançon. "Creole Is, Creole Ain't: Diachronic and Synchronic Attitudes toward Creole Identity in Southern Louisiana." *Language in Society* 29, no. 2 (2000): 237–58.

DuBois, W. E. B. *Black Reconstruction in America, 1860–1880.* New York: Simon and Schuster, 1999.

Dunn, Marie S. "A Comparative Study: Louisiana's French and Anglo-Saxon Cultures." *Louisiana Studies* 10 (1971): 131–69.

Eble, Connie. "Creole in Louisiana." *South Atlantic Review* 73, no. 2 (2008): 39–53.

Elliott, Charles. *Sinfulness of American Slavery.* Cincinnati, Ohio: L. Swormstedt & J. H. Power, 1850.

Ellis, Frederick E. "The Abbe Lamennais on Freedom." *Harvard Theological Review* 41, no. 4 (1948): 251–71.

Emberton, Carole. "The Limits of Incorporation: Violence, Gun Rights, and Gun Regulation in the Reconstruction South." *Stanford Law & Policy Review* no. 615 (2006): 615–34.

English, Linda. " 'That Is All We Ask For—an Equal Chance': Oscar James Dunn, Louisiana's First Black Lieutenant Governor." In *Black Reconstruction Era Politicians: The Fifteenth Amendment in Flesh and Blood.* Vol. 2 of *Before Obama: A Reappraisal of Black Reconstruction Era Politicians,* edited by Matthew Lynch, 63–85. Santa Barbara, Calif: ABC-CLIO, 2012.

Evans, Curtis J. *The Burden of Black Religion.* Oxford: Oxford University Press, 2008.

Everett, Donald E. "Ben Butler and the Louisiana Native Guards, 1861–1862." *Journal of Southern History* 24, no. 2 (May 1958): 202–17.

———. "Free Persons of Color in New Orleans, 1803–1865." Ph.D. diss., Tulane University, 1952.

Fandrich, Ina J. "The Birth of New Orleans' Voodoo Queen: A Long-Held Mystery Resolved." *Louisiana History: The Journal of the Louisiana Historical Association* 46, no. 3 (2005): 293–309.

———. "Yoruba Influences on Haitian Vodou and New Orleans Voodoo." *Journal of Black Studies* 37 (2007): 775–91.

Farrell, Michèle Longino. *Performing Motherhood: The Sévigné Correspondence.* Hanover, N.H.: University Press of New England, 1991.

Faye, Stanley, ed. "The Schism of 1805 in New Orleans." *Louisiana Historical Quarterly* 22 (January 1939): 98–141.

Featherstonhaugh, George William. *Excursion through the Slave States.* New York: Harper & Brothers, 1844.

Fenton, Elizabeth. *Religious Liberties: Anti-Catholicism and Liberal Democracy in Nineteenth-Century U.S. Literature and Culture.* Oxford: Oxford University Press, 2011.

Ferguson, C. "Eugenics and the Afterlife: Lombroso, Doyle, and the Spiritualist Purification of the Race." *Journal of Victorian Culture* 12, no. 1 (2007): 64–85.

Fessenden, Tracy. "The Convent, the Brothel, and the Protestant Woman's Sphere." *Signs* 25, no. 2 (2000): 451–78.

———. "The Sisters of the Holy Family and the Veil of Race." *Religion and American Culture* 10, no. 2 (2000): 187–224.

Fick, Carolyn E. *The Making of Haiti: The Saint Domingue Revolution from Below.* Knoxville: University of Tennessee Press, 1990.

Fiehrer, Thomas. "Saint-Domingue/Haiti: Louisiana's Caribbean Connection." *Louisiana History: The Journal of the Louisiana Historical Association* 30, no. 4 (1989): 419–37.

Fine, Gary Alan. "John Brown's Body: Elites, Heroic Embodiment, and the Legitimation of Political Violence." *Social Problems* 46, no. 2 (1999): 225–49.

Finley, Stephen C., Margarita Simon Guillory, and Hugh R. Page Jr., eds. *Esotericism in African American Religious Experience: "There is a Mystery" . . .* Leiden, Netherlands: Brill, 2014.

Fischer, Roger A. "Racial Segregation in Antebellum New Orleans." *American Historical Review* 74, no. 3 (1969): 926–37.

Foner, Eric. *Free Soil, Free Labor, Free Men: The Ideology of the Republican Party before the Civil War.* Oxford: Oxford University Press, 1995.

———. *Reconstruction: America's Unfinished Revolution, 1863–1877.* New York: Harper Collins, 2002.

Foner, Laura. "The Free People of Color in Louisiana and St. Domingue: A Comparative Portrait of Two Three-Caste Slave Societies." *Journal of Social History* 3, no. 4 (1970): 406–30.

Fox-Genovese, Elizabeth, and Eugene D. Genovese. "The Divine Sanction of Social Order: Religious Foundations of the Southern Slaveholders' World View." *Journal of the American Academy of Religion* 55, no. 2 (1987): 211–33.

Frey, Sylvia. "Acculturation and Gendered Conversion: Afro-American Catholic Women in New Orleans, 1726–1884." In *Beyond Conversion and Syncretism: Indigenous Encounters with Missionary Christianity, 1800–2000,* edited by David Linderfeld and Miles Richardson, 213–41. New York: Berghahn Books, 2012.

Frink, Sandra Margaret. "Spectacles of the Street: Performance, Power, and Public Space in Antebellum New Orleans." Ph.D. diss., University of Texas at Austin, 2004.

Frymer, Paul, Dara Z. Strolovitch and Dorian T. Warren. "New Orleans is Not the Exception: Re-politicizing the Study of Racial Inequality." *Du Bois Review* 3 (2006): 37–57.

Gabici, L. *Stand By Our Flag*. L. Gabici: New Orleans, La., 1857.

Gac, Scott. *Singing for Freedom: The Hutchinson Family Singers and the Nineteenth-Century Culture of Reform*. New Haven, Ct.: Yale University Press, 2007.

Garraway, Dorris. "Race, Reproduction and Family Romance in Moreau de Saint-Méry's Description . . . de la partie française de l'isle Saint-Domingue." *Eighteenth-Century Studies* 38, no. 2 (2005): 227–46.

Geggus, David Patrick, ed. *The Impact of the Haitian Revolution in the Atlantic World*. Columbia: University of South Carolina Press, 2001.

Gibson, Ralph. "Hellfire and Damnation in Nineteenth-Century France." *Catholic Historical Review* 74, no. 3 (1988): 383–402.

Gill, James. *Lords of Misrule: Mardi Gras and the Politics of Race in New Orleans*. Jackson: University of Mississippi Press, 1997.

Gilroy, Paul. *The Black Atlantic: Modernity and Double Consciousness*. New York: Verso, 1993.

Giraud, Marcel. *History of French Louisiana: The Company of the Indies, 1723–1731*. Baton Rouge: Louisiana State University Press, 1974.

Glaude, Eddie S. *Exodus!: Religion, Race, and Nation in Early Nineteenth-Century Black America*. Chicago: University of Chicago Press, 2000.

Gluckstein, Donny. *Paris Commune: A Revolution in Democracy*. Chicago: Haymarket Books, 2011.

Goddard, Peter A. "Converting the 'Sauvage': Jesuit and Montagnais in Seventeenth-Century New France." *Catholic Historical Review* 84, no. 2 (1998): 219–39.

Gordon, Michelle Y. " 'Midnight Scenes and Orgies': Public Narratives of Voodoo in New Orleans and Nineteenth-Century Discourses of White Supremacy." *American Quarterly* 64, no. 4 (2012): 767–86.

Greer, Allan. "Colonial Saints: Gender, Race, and Hagiography in New France." *William and Mary Quarterly* 57, no. 2 (2000): 323–48.

———, ed. *The Jesuit Relations: Natives and Missionaries in Seventeenth-Century North America*. New York: Bedford/St. Martin, 2000.

Grégoire, Henri. *An Enquiry Concerning the Intellectual and Moral Faculties, and Literature of Negroes*. Translated by D. B. Warden. Brooklyn: Thomas Kirk, 1810.

Guthrie, John J., Jr., Phillip Charles Lucas, and Gary Monroe, eds. *Cassadega: The South's Oldest Spiritualist Community*. Gainesville: University Press of Florida, 2000.

Haddox, Thomas F. "The 'Nous' of Southern Catholic Quadroons: Racial, Ethnic, and Religious Identity in *Les Cenelles*." *American Literature* 73, no. 4 (2001): 757–78.

Hall, David, ed. *Lived Religion in America: Toward a History of Practice*. Princeton, N.J.: Princeton University Press, 1997.

Hall, Gwendolyn Midlo. *Africans in Colonial Louisiana: The Development of Afro-Creole Culture in the Eighteenth Century*. Baton Rouge: Louisiana State University Press, 1992.

Hamilton, Thomas. *Men and Manners in America*. Vol. 2. Edinburgh: W. Blackwood, 1833.

Hanger, Kimberly S. *Bounded Lives, Bounded Places: Free Black Society in Colonial New Orleans, 1769–1803*. Durham, N.C.: Duke University Press, 1997.

———. "Conflicting Loyalties: The French Revolution and Free People of Color in Spanish New Orleans." *Louisiana History: The Journal of the Louisiana Historical Association* 34, no. 1 (Winter 1993): 5–33.

Hare, Robert. *Lecture on Spiritualism: Delivered Before an Audience of Three Thousand, at the Tabernacle, in the City of New York, in November 1855: Comprising an Account of the Manifestations which Induced the Author's Conversion to Spiritualism, and Confirmed His Hope of Immortality*. Philadelphia, Pa.: Samuel Barry, 1855.

Hart, Francis Borgia. *Violets in the King's Garden: A History of the Sisters of the Holy Family of New Orleans*. New Orleans, La., 1976.

Hazen, Craig James. *The Village Enlightenment in America: Popular Religion and Science in the Nineteenth Century*. Urbana: University of Illinois Press, 2000.

Hennessey, Melinda Meek. "Race and Violence in Reconstruction New Orleans: The 1868 Riot." *Louisiana History: The Journal of the Louisiana Historical Association* 20, no. 1 (1979): 77–91.

Hirsch, Arnold R., and Joseph Logsdon, eds. *Creole New Orleans: Race and Americanization*. Baton Rouge: Louisiana State University Press, 1992.

Hogue, James K. *Uncivil War: Five New Orleans Street Battles and the Rise and Fall of Radical Reconstruction*. Baton Rouge: Louisiana University Press, 2006.

Hollandsworth, James G., Jr. *An Absolute Massacre: The New Orleans Race Riot of July 30, 1866*. Baton Rouge: Louisiana State University Press, 2001.

———. *The Louisiana Native Guards: The Black Military Experience during the Civil War*. Baton Rouge: Louisiana State University Press, 1998.

Howe, Daniel Walker. *Making of the American Self: Jonathan Edwards to Abraham Lincoln*. Oxford: Oxford University Press, 2009.

———. *What Hath God Wrought: The Transformation of America, 1815–1848*. Oxford: Oxford University Press, 2007.

Hume, Richard L. and Jerry B. Gough. *Blacks, Carpetbaggers, and Scalawags: The Constitutional Conventions of Radical Reconstruction*. Baton Rouge: Louisiana State University Press, 2008.

Hunt, Lynn. "The Rhetoric of the Revolution in France," *History Workshop*, no. 15 (Spring 1983): 78–94.

Hurston, Zora Neale. "Hoodoo in America." *Journal of American Folklore* 44, no. 174 (1931): 317–417.

———. *Mules and Men*. New York: Harper Perennial, 1990.

Hutchins, Zachary McLeod. *Inventing Eden: Primitivism, Millennialism, and the Making of New England*. Oxford: Oxford University Press, 2014.

Hutchinson, John W., ed. *Hutchinson's Republican Songster, for the Campaign of 1860*. New York: O. Hutchinson, 1860.

Ingersoll, Thomas N. "Free Blacks in a Slave Society: New Orleans, 1718–1812." *William and Mary Quarterly* 48, no. 2 (1991): 173–200.

Israel, Jonathan. *Revolutionary Ideas: An Intellectual History of the French Revolution from* The Rights of Man *to Robespierre*. Princeton, N.J.: Princeton University Press, 2013.

Jacobs, Claude F. "Spirit Guides and Possession in the New Orleans Black Spiritual Churches." *Journal of American Folklore* 102, no. 403 (1989): 45–56, 65–67.

Jacobs, Claude F., and Andrew J. Kaslow. *The Spiritual Churches of New Orleans: Origins, Beliefs, and Rituals of an African-American Religion*. Knoxville: University of Tennessee Press, 1991.

Jacobs et al. v. Ursuline Nuns. In *Martin's Reports of the Cases Argued and Determined in the Superior Court of Territory of Orleans, and in the Supreme Court of the State of Louisiana*. New Orleans: Samuel M. Stewart, 1846.

Jefferson, Thomas. *Notes on the State of Virginia*. Boston: David Carlisle, 1801.

Johnson, Jerah. "*Les Cenelles*: What's in a Name?" *Louisiana History: The Journal of the Louisiana Historical Association* 31, no. 4 (1990): 407–10.

———. "New Orleans's Congo Square: An Urban Setting for Early Afro-American Culture Formation." *Louisiana History: The Journal of the Louisiana Historical Association* 32, no. 2 (1991): 117–57.

Johnson, Paul Christopher. "An Atlantic Genealogy of 'Spirit Possession.'" *Comparative Studies in Society and History* 53, no. 2 (2011): 393–425.

———. *Diasporic Conversions: Black Carib Religion and the Recovery of Africa*. Berkeley: University of California Press, 2007.

———. "Vodou Purchase: The Louisiana Purchase in the Caribbean World." In *New Territories, New Perspectives: The Religious Impact of the Louisiana Purchase*, edited by Richard J. Callahan Jr., 146–65. Columbia: University of Missouri Press, 2008.

Johnson, Sylvester. *The Myth of Ham in Nineteenth-Century American Christianity: Race, Heathens, and the People of God*. New York: Palgrave MacMillian, 2004.

Johnson, Walter, *Soul by Soul: Life Inside the Antebellum Slave Market*. Cambridge, Mass.: Harvard University Press, 2001.

Jones, Terry L. *Lee's Tigers: The Louisiana Infantry in the Army of Northern Virginia*. Baton Rouge: Louisiana State University Press, 2002.

Joyaux, Georges J. "The Reception of Pierre-Jean de Béranger in America: 1818–1848." *French Review* 26, no. 4 (1953): 268–77.

Joyner, Charles. *Down by the Riverside: A South Carolina Slave Community.* Urbana: University of Illinois Press, 1984.

Kaczorowski, Robert J. "To Begin the Nation Anew: Congress, Citizenship, and Civil Rights after the Civil War." *American Historical Review* 92, no. 1 (1987): 45–68.

Kane, Paula M. " 'She Offered Herself up': The Victim Soul and Victim Spirituality in Catholicism." *Church History* 71, no. 1 (2000): 80–119.

Kaplan, Louis. "Where the Paranoid Meets the Paranormal: Speculations on Spirit Photography." *Art Journal* 62, no. 3 (2003): 18–29.

Kein, Sybil, ed. *Creole: The History and Legacy of Louisiana's Free People of Color.* Baton Rouge: Louisiana State University Press, 2000.

Kerber, Linda. "Separate Spheres, Female Worlds, Woman's Place: The Rhetoric of Women's History." *Journal of American History* 75, no. 1 (1988): 9–39.

Kessler, Sanford. "Religion & Liberalism in Montesquieu's Persian Letters." *Polity* 15, no. 3 (1983): 380–96.

King, Grace Elizabeth. *New Orleans: The Place and the People.* New York: MacMillan and Co., 1896.

Klement, Frank L. "Catholics as Copperheads during the Civil War." *Catholic Historical Review* 80, no. 1 (1994): 36–57.

Klooster, Wim. *Revolutions in the Atlantic World: A Comparative History.* New York: New York University Press, 2009.

———. "The Rising Expectation of Free and Enslaved Blacks in the Greater Caribbean." In *Curaçao in the Age of Revolutions: 1795–1800,* edited by Wim Klooster and Gert Oostindie, 57–74. Leiden, Netherlands: KITLV Press, 2011.

Krause, Sharon. "The Spirit of Separate Powers in Montesquieu." *Review of Politics* 62, no. 2 (2000): 231–65.

Kress, Dana. "Pierre-Aristide Desdunes, *Les Cenelles,* and the Challenges of Nineteenth-Century Creole Literature." *Southern Quarterly* 44, no. 3 (2007): 42–67.

Kselman, Thomas. "State and Religion." In *Revolutionary France, 1788–1880,* edited by Malcolm Crook, 63–92. Oxford: Oxford University Press, 2002.

Kucich, John J. *Ghostly Communion: Cross-Cultural Spiritualism in Nineteenth-Century American Literature.* Hanover, N.H.: Dartmouth College Press, 2004.

Lacerte, Robert K. "The First Land Reform in Latin America: The Reforms of Alexander Pétion, 1809–1814." *Inter-American Economic Affairs* 28, no. 4 (1975): 77–85.

Lachance, Paul F. "The Politics of Fear: French Louisianans and the Slave Trade, 1786–1809." *Plantation Society in the Americas* 1, no. 2 (1979): 162–67.

Lachance, Paul L. "The 1809 Immigration of Saint-Domingue Refugees to New Orleans: Reception, Integration and Impact." *Louisiana History: The Journal of the Louisiana Historical Association* 29, no. 8 (1988): 109–41.

Laderman, Gary. *The Sacred Remains: American Attitudes toward Death, 1799–1883.* New Haven, Ct.: Yale University Press, 1999.

La Mennais, F. De. *Words of a Believer.* Translator not listed. New York: Charles De Behr, 1834.

Landau, Emily Epstein. *Spectacular Wickedness: Sex, Race, and Memory in Storyville, New Orleans.* Baton Rouge: Louisiana State University Press, 2013.

Leumas, Emilie Gagnet. "Mais, I Sin in French, I Gotta Go to Confession in French: A Study of the Language Shift from French to English Within the Louisiana Catholic Church." Ph.D. diss., Louisiana State University, 2009.

Liljegren, Ernest R. "Jacobinism in Spanish Louisiana." *Louisiana Historical Quarterly* 22, no. 1 (1939): 47–97.

Lipsitz, George. "Mardi Gras Indians: Carnival and Counter-Narrative in Black New Orleans." *Cultural Critique* 10 (Autumn 1988): 99–121.

Long, Alecia. *The Great Southern Babylon: Race, Sex, and Respectability in New Orleans, 1865–1920.* Baton Rouge: Louisiana State University Press, 2004.

Long, Carolyn Morrow. "Marie Laveau: A Nineteenth-Century Voudou Priestess." *Louisiana History: The Journal of the Louisiana Historical Association* 46, no. 3 (2005): 262–92.

———. *A New Orleans Voudou Priestess: The Legend and Reality of Marie Laveau.* Gainesville: University Press of Florida, 2006.

———. "Perceptions of New Orleans Voodoo: Sin: Fraud, Entertainment, and Religion." *Nova Religio: The Journal of New and Emergent Religions* 6, no. 1 (2002): 86–101.

Long, Charles. "New Orleans as an American City: Origins, Exchanges, Materialities, and Religion." In *New Territories, New Perspectives: The Religious Impact of the Louisiana Purchase,* edited by Richard J. Callahan Jr., 203–22. Columbia: University of Missouri Press, 2008.

Louisiana Legislature. *Acts Passed At the First Session by the Second Legislature of the State of Louisiana.* New Orleans, La.: Office of the "Louisiana Courier," 1848.

———. *Official Journal of the Proceedings of the House of Representatives of the State of Louisiana.* New Orleans, La.: A. L. Lee, State Printer, 1870.

Luis-Brown, David. "An 1848 for the Americas: The Black Atlantic, 'El negro mártir,' and Cuban Exile Anticolonialism in New York City." *American Literary History* 21, no. 3 (2009): 431–63.

Luria, Keith P. *Sacred Boundaries: Religious Coexistence and Conflict in Early-Modern France.* Washington, D.C.: Catholic University Press, 2005.

Lutz, Deborah. "The Dead Still among Us: Victorian Secular Relics, Hair Jewelry, and Death Culture." *Victorian Literature and Culture* 39 (2011): 127–42.

Maffly-Kipp, Laurie. *Setting Down the Sacred Past: African-American Race Histories.* Cambridge, Mass.: The Belknap Press of Harvard University Press, 2010.

Marotti, Frank. *The Cana Sanctuary: History, Diplomacy, and Black Catholic Marriage in Antebellum St. Augustine, Florida.* Tuscaloosa: University of Alabama Press, 2012.

Martineau, Harriet. *Society in America*. Vol. 2. Paris: Baudry's European library, 1837.

Mason, Laura. *Singing the French Revolution: Popular Culture and Politics, 1787–1799*. Ithaca, N.Y.: Cornell University Press, 1996.

Mathews, Donald G. "The Southern Rite of Human Sacrifice," *Journal of Southern Religion* 3 http://jsr.fsu.edu/mathews.htm. 5 May, 2015.

Matory, J. Lorand. *Black Atlantic Religion: Tradition, Transnationalism, and Matriarchy in the Afro-Brazilian Candomblé*. Princeton, N.J.: Princeton University Press, 2005.

McCartin, James P. "The Sacred Heart of Jesus, Thérèse of Lisieux, and the Transformation of U.S. Catholic Piety, 1865–1940." *U.S. Catholic Historian* 25, no. 2 (2007): 53–67.

McGarry, Molly. *Ghosts of Futures Past: Spiritualism and the Cultural Politics of Nineteenth-Century America*. Berkeley: University of California Press, 2008.

McGreevy, John T. *Catholicism and American Freedom: A History*. New York: W. W. Norton, 2003.

McPherson, James. *Battle Cry of Freedom: The Civil War Era*. Oxford: Oxford University Press, 1988.

McPherson, Natasha L. " 'There Was a Tradition among the Women': New Orleans's Colored Creole Women and the Making of a Community in the Tremé and Seventh Ward, 1791–1930." Ph.D. diss., Emory University, 2011.

Meadows, R. Darrell. "Engineering Exile: Social Networks and the French Atlantic Community, 1789–1809." *French Historical Studies* 23, no. 1 (2000): 67–102.

Meyer, Michael. "Thoreau's Rescue of John Brown from History." *Studies in the American Renaissance* (1980): 301–16.

Michelet, Jules. *History of the French Revolution*. Translated by C. Cocks. London: G. Bohn, 1847.

———. *The People*. Translated by G. H. Smith. New York: D. Appleton, 1846.

Mills, Gary B. *The Forgotten People: Cane River's Creoles of Color*. Baton Rouge: Louisiana State University Press, 1977.

Mistick Krewe of Comus, 1873 Missing Links Parade Costume Designs, The Carnival Collection, Tulane University Digital Library, Louisiana Digital Library, http://cdm16313.contentdm.oclc.org/cdm/landingpage/collection/p15140coll3. 5 May, 2015.

Mitzman, Arthur. "Michelet and Social Romanticism: Religion, Revolution, Nature." *Journal of the History of Ideas* 57, no. 4 (1996): 659–82.

Modern, John Lardas. *Secularism in Antebellum America*. Chicago: University of Chicago Press, 2011.

Monroe, John Warne. "Cartes de Visite from the Other World: Spiritism and the Discourse of Laicisme in the Early Third Republic." *French Historical Studies* 26, no. 1 (2003): 119–53.

———. *Laboratories of Faith: Mesmerism, Spiritism, and Occultism in Modern France*. Ithaca, N.Y.: Cornell University Press, 2008.

Montesquieu. *The Spirit of Laws*. University of Virginia Library. http://etext.lib
.virginia.edu/toc/modeng/public/MonLaws.html. 5 May, 2015.

Montgomery, William E. *Under Their Own Vine and Fig Tree: The African-American Church in the South 1865–1900*. Baton Rouge: Louisiana State University Press, 1993.

Moore, R. Laurence. "The Spiritualist Medium: A Study of Female Professionalism in Victorian America." *American Quarterly* 27, no. 2 (1975): 200–21.

Moran, Maureen. "The Art of Looking Dangerously: Victorian Images of Martyrdom," *Victorian Literature and Culture* 32, no. 2 (2004): 475–93.

Morita, Sally. "Unseen (and Unappreciated) Matters: Understanding the Reformative Nature of 19th-Century Spiritualism." *American Studies* 40, no. 3 (1999): 99–125.

Morrow, Dianne Batts. *Persons of Color and Religious at the Same Time: The Oblate Sisters of Providence, 1828–1860*. Chapel Hill: University of North Carolina Press, 2002.

Mossiker, Frances. *Madame de Sévigné: A Life and Letters*. New York: Columbia University Press, 1983.

Murphy, Joseph M. *Working the Spirit: Ceremonies of the African Diaspora*. Boston: Beacon, 1994.

Nartonis, David K. "The Rise of 19th-century American Spiritualism, 1854–1873." *Journal for the Scientific Study of Religion* 49, no. 2 (2010): 361–73.

Neely, Sylvia. *A Concise History of the French Revolution*. New York: Rowman & Littlefield, 2008.

Nicholls, David. *From Dessalines to Duvalier: Race, Colour and National Independence in Haiti*, 3rd ed. New Brunswick, N.J.: Rutgers University Press, 1996.

———. "A Work of Combat: Mulatto Historians and the Haitian Past, 1847–1867." *Journal of Interamerican Studies and World Affairs* 16, no. 1 (1974): 15–38.

Nichols, Thomas Low. *Forty Years of American Life*. 2nd ed. London: Longmans, Green, and Co., 1874.

Noll, Mark. *America's God: From Jonathan Edwards to Abraham Lincoln*. Oxford: Oxford University Press, 2002.

Nystrom, Justin A. *New Orleans after the Civil War: Race, Politics, and a New Birth of Freedom*. Baltimore: Johns Hopkins University Press, 2010.

Ochs, Stephen J. *A Black Patriot and a White Priest: André Cailloux and Claude Paschal Maistre in Civil War New Orleans*. Baton Rouge: Louisiana State University Press, 2000.

———. "A Patriot, a Priest and a Prelate: Black Catholic Activism in Civil War New Orleans." *U.S. Catholic Historian* 12, no. 1 (1994): 49–75.

Oldfield, John J. "The Evolution of Lamennais' Catholic-Liberal Synthesis." *Journal for the Scientific Study of Religion* 8, no. 2 (1969): 269–88.

Olmsted, Frederick Law. *A Journey in the Slave States, with Remarks on Their Economy*. New York: Mason Brothers, 1861.

O'Neill, Charles Edwards. "'A Quarter Marked by Sundry Peculiarities': New Orleans, Lay Trustees, and Père Antoine." *Catholic Historical Review* 76, no. 2 (1990): 235–77.

Orsi, Robert. "2 + 2 = Five, or the Quest for an Abundant Empiricism." *Spiritus: A Journal of Christian Spirituality* 6, no. 1 (2006): 113–21.

———. *Between Heaven and Earth: The Religious Worlds People Make and the Scholars Who Study Them.* Princeton, N.J.: Princeton University Press, 2005.

———. "Introduction: Crossing the City Line." In *Gods of the City*, edited by Robert Orsi, 1–78. Bloomington: Indiana University Press, 1999.

Otten, James T. "The Wheeler Adjustment in Louisiana: National Republicans Begin to Reappraise Their Reconstruction Policy." *Louisiana History: The Journal of the Louisiana Historical Association* 13, no. 4 (1972): 349–67.

Owen, Alex. *The Darkened Room: Women, Power, and Spiritualism in Late Victorian England.* Chicago: University of Chicago Press, 2004.

Ownby, Ted. *Subduing Satan: Religion, Recreation, and Manhood in the Rural South, 1865–1920.* Chapel Hill: University of North Carolina Press, 1993.

Paddison, Joshua. *American Heathens: Religion, Race, and Reconstruction in California.* Berkeley: University of California Press, 2012.

Palmer, R. R. *Twelve Who Ruled: The Year of the Terror in the French Revolution.* Princeton, N.J.: Princeton University Press, 2005.

Pasquier, Michael. "Catholic Southerners, Catholic Soldiers: White Creoles, the Civil War, and the Lost Cause in New Orleans." M.A. thesis, Florida State University, 2003.

———. "Creole Catholicism before Black Catholicism: Religion and Slavery in French Colonial Louisiana." *Journal of Africana Religions* 2, no. 2 (2014): 271–79.

———. *Fathers on the Frontier: French Missionaries and the Roman Catholic Priesthood in the United States, 1789–1870.* Oxford: Oxford University Press, 2010.

———. "'Though Their Skin Remains Brown, I Hope Their Souls Will Soon Be White': Slavery, French Missionaries, and the Roman Catholic Priesthood in the American South, 1789–1865." *Church History* 77, no. 2 (2008): 339–70.

Perron, Paul. "Isaac Jogues: From Martyrdom to Sainthood." In *Colonial Saints: Discovering the Holy in the Americas*, edited by Allan Greer and Jodi Bilinkoff. New York: Routledge, 2003.

Peterson, Anna L., and Brandt G. Peterson. "Martyrdom, Sacrifice, and Political Memory in El Salvador." *Social Research: An International Quarterly* 75, no. 2 (2008): 511–42.

Peterson, Merrill D. *Lincoln in American Memory.* Oxford: Oxford University Press, 1994.

Pettinger, Alasdair. "From Vaudoux to Voodoo." *Forum of Modern Language Studies* 40, no. 4 (2004): 415–25.

Phelan, Joseph. "The British Reception of Pierre-Jean de Béranger." *Revue de littérature comparée* 313 (2005): 5–20.

Pierson, Marion John Bennett. *Louisiana Soldiers in the War of 1812*. Baton Rouge: Louisiana Genealogical and Historical Society, 1963.

Pitman, Bambra. "Culture, Caste, and Conflict in New Orleans Catholicism: Archbishop Francis Janssens and the Color Line." *Louisiana History: The Journal of the Louisiana Historical Association* 49, no. 4 (2008): 423–62.

Pitot, James. *Observations on the Colony of Louisiana from 1796 to 1802*. Translated by Henry C. Pitot. Baton Rouge: Louisiana State University Press, 1979.

Porterfield, Amanda, and John Corrigan, eds. *Religion in American History*. Malden, Mass.: Wiley-Blackwell, 2010.

Prospectus de L'Institution Catholique des Orphelins Indigents. New Orleans, La., 1847.

Prothero, Stephen. "From Spiritualism to Theosophy: 'Uplifting' a Democratic Tradition." *Religion and American Culture* 3, no. 2 (1993): 197–216.

Rable, George C. *But There Was No Peace: The Role of Violence in the Politics of Reconstruction*. Athens: University of Georgia Press, 2007.

Raboteau, Albert J. *A Fire in the Bones: Reflections on African-American Religious History*. Boston: Beacon, 1995.

———. *Slave Religion: The "Invisible Institution" in the Antebellum South*. Oxford: Oxford University Press, 2004.

Raimon, Eve Allegra. *The "Tragic Mulatta" Revisited: Race and Nationalism in Nineteenth Century Antislavery Fiction*. Piscataway, N.J.: Rutgers University Press, 2004.

Rasmussen, Daniel. *American Uprising: The Untold Story of America's Largest Slave Revolt*. New York: Harper Perennial, 2011.

Ravenel, Florence Leftwich. "The Great Tradition: Madame de Sévigné." *North American Review* 200, no. 708 (1914): 743–57.

Reed, Emily Hazen. *Life of A. P. Dostie, or, The Conflict in New Orleans*. New York: Wm. P. Tomlinson, 1868.

Reid, Thomas Mayne. *The Quadroon; or, A Lover's Adventure in Louisiana*. 3 vols. London: George W. Hyde, 1856.

Remini, Robert V. *The Battle of New Orleans: Andrew Jackson's and America's First Military Victory*. New York: Penguin, 2001.

Richardson, Joe M. *Christian Reconstruction: The American Missionary Association and Southern Blacks, 1861–1890*. Tuscaloosa: University of Alabama Press, 1986.

Ripley, Eliza. *Social Life in New Orleans: Being Recollections from my Girlhood*. New York: D. Appleton, 1912.

Rosanvallon, Pierre. *The Demands of Liberty: Civil Society in France since the Revolution*. Translated by Arthur Goldhammer. Cambridge, Mass.: Harvard University Press, 2007.

Rose, Al. *Storyville, New Orleans: Being an Authentic, Illustrated Account of the Notorious Red-Light District*. Tuscaloosa: University of Alabama Press, 1974.

Rosenfeld, Sophia. *Common Sense: A Political History*. Cambridge, Mass.: Harvard University Press, 2011.

Rothman, Adam. *Slave Country: American Expansion and the Origins of the Deep South*. Cambridge, Mass.: Harvard University Press, 2005.

Rousseau, Jean-Jacques. *Rousseau: The Social Contract and other later political writings*. Edited by Victor Gourevitch. Cambridge, U.K.: Cambridge University Press, 2003.

Sagan, Eli. *Citizens and Cannibals: The French Revolution, the Struggle for Modernity, and the Origins of Ideological Terror*. Lanham, Md.: Rowman and Littlefield, 2001.

Saint-Rémy, Joseph. *Pétion et Haïti: Etude monographique et historique*. Edited by François Dalencour. Paris: Librairie Berger-Levrault, 1956.

Schafer, Judith K. *Becoming Free, Remaining Free: Manumission and Enslavement in New Orleans, 1846–1862*. Baton Rouge: Louisiana State University Press, 2003.

———. *Brothels, Depravity, and Abandoned Women: Illegal Sex in Antebellum New Orleans*. Baton Rouge: Louisiana State University Press, 2011.

———. "New Orleans Slavery in 1850 as Seen in Advertisements." *Journal of Southern History* 47, no. 1 (1981): 33–56.

———. " 'Open and Notorious Concubinage': The Emancipation of Slave Mistresses by Will and the Supreme Court in Antebellum Louisiana." *Louisiana History: The Journal of the Louisiana Historical Association* 28, no. 2 (1987): 165–82.

———. *Slavery, the Civil Law, and the Supreme Court of Louisiana*. Baton Rouge: Louisiana State University Press, 1997.

Schmidt, Eric Leigh. "From Demon Possession to Magic Show: Ventriloquism, Religion, and the Enlightenment." *Church History* 67, no. 2 (1998): 274–304.

———. *Hearing Things: Religion, Illusion, and the American Enlightenment*. Cambridge, Mass.: Harvard University Press, 2000.

———. *Restless Souls: The Making of American Spirituality*. New York: HarperCollins, 2005.

Schultz, Charles R. "New Orleans in December 1860." *Louisiana History: The Journal of the Louisiana Historical Association* 9, no. 1 (Winter 1968): 53–61.

Schultz, Nancy Lusignan ed. *Veil of Fear: Nineteenth-Century Convent Tales by Rebecca Reed and Maria Monk*. West Lafayette, Ind.: Purdue University Press, 1999.

Schwartz, Barry. *Abraham Lincoln and the Forge of National Memory*. Chicago: University of Chicago Press, 2000.

———. "Collective Memory and History: How Abraham Lincoln Became a Symbol of Racial Equality." *Sociological Quarterly* 38, no. 3 (1997): 469–96.

Scott, James C. *Domination and the Arts of Resistance: Hidden Transcripts*. New Haven, Ct.: Yale University Press, 1990.

Scott, Rebecca J. "The Atlantic World and the Road to *Plessy v. Ferguson*." *Journal of American History* 94 (December 2007): 726–33.

Sensbach, Jon F. *Rebecca's Revival: Creating Black Christianity in the Atlantic World*. Cambridge, Mass.: Harvard University Press, 2005.

———. "'The Singing of the Mississippi': The River and Religions of the Black Atlantic." In *Gods of the Mississippi*, edited by Michael Pasquier, 17–35. Bloomington: Indiana University Press, 2013.

Shapiro, Norman R., and M. Lynn Weiss, "Duhart, Adolphe." In *Creole Echoes: The Francophone Poetry of Nineteenth-Century Louisiana*, edited by Norman R. Shapiro, with translations by M. Lynn Weiss, 67–74. Champaign: University of Illinois Press, 2004.

Sharp, Lynn L. "Fighting for the Afterlife: Spiritists, Catholics, and Popular Religion in Nineteenth-Century France." *Journal of Religious History* 23, no. 3 (1999): 282–95.

Sheller, Mimi. *Democracy after Slavery: Black Publics and Peasant Radicalism in Haiti and Jamaica*. Gainesville: University Press of Florida, 2003.

———. "'You Signed My Name, but Not My Feet': Paradoxes of Peasant Resistance and State Control in Post-Revolutionary Haiti." *Journal of Haitian Studies* 10, no. 1 (2004): 72–86.

Slauter, Eric. *The State as a Work of Art: The Cultural Origins of the Constitution*. Chicago: University of Chicago Press, 2009.

Smith, James Allen. *Popular French Romanticism: Authors, Readers, and Books in the 19th Century*. Syracuse, N.Y.: Syracuse University Press, 1981.

Smith, Mark M. "Remembering Mary, Shaping Revolt: Reconsidering the Stono Rebellion." *Journal of Southern History* 67, no. 3 (2001): 513–34.

Smith-Rosenberg, Carol. *Disorderly Conduct: Visions of Gender in Victorian America*. Oxford: Oxford University Press, 1985.

Sollors, Werner. "'Never Was Born': The Mulatto, an American Tragedy?" *Massachusetts Review* 27, no. 2 (1986): 293–316.

Spear, Jennifer M. *Race, Sex, and Social Order in Early New Orleans*. Baltimore, Md.: Johns Hopkins University Press, 2009.

Stearns, Peter N. *Priest and Revolutionary: Lamennais and the Dilemma of French Catholicism*. New York: Harper & Row, 1967.

Stolow, Jeremy. "The Spiritual Nervous System: Reflections on a Magnetic Cord Designed for Spirit Communication." In *Deus in Machina: Religion, Technology, and the Things Between*, edited by Jeremy Stolow, 83–113. New York: Fordham University Press, 2012.

Stowell, Daniel W. *Rebuilding Zion: The Religious Reconstruction of the South, 1863–1877*. Oxford: Oxford University Press, 1998.

Sweet, James H. *Domingos Álvares, African Healing, and the Intellectual History of the Atlantic World*. Chapel Hill: University of North Carolina Press, 2011.

Swedenborg, Emanuel. *Heaven and Its Wonders and Hell*. Philadelphia, Penn.: J. P. Lippincott Company, 1890.

Taylor, Joe Gray. "New Orleans and Reconstruction." *Louisiana History: The Journal of the Louisiana Historical Association* 9, no. 3 (1968): 189–208.

Testut, Charles. *Le Vieux Salomon: ou, Une Famille d'esclaves au XIX siècle.* New Orleans, 1872.

Thompson, Robert Farris. *Flash of the Spirit: African & Afro-American Art & Philosophy.* New York: Vintage Books, 1984.

Thompson, Shirley. "'Ah Toucoutou, ye conin vous': History and Memory in Creole New Orleans." *American Quarterly* 53, no. 2 (2001): 232–66.

———. *Exiles at Home: The Struggle to Become American in Creole New Orleans.* Cambridge, Mass.: Harvard University Press, 2009.

Thornton, John. *Africa and Africans in the Making of the Atlantic World, 1400–1800.* Cambridge, U.K.: Cambridge University Press, 2006.

———. "African Dimensions of the Stono Rebellion." *The American Historical Review* 96, no. 4 (1991): 1101–13.

———. *The Kongolese Saint Anthony: Dona Beatriz Kimpa Vita and the Antonian Movement, 1684–1706.* Cambridge, U.K.: Cambridge University Press, 1998.

———. "On the Trail of Voodoo: African Christianity in Africa and the Americas." *Americas* 44, no. 3 (1988): 261–78.

Tilby, Michael. "Pierre-Jean de Béranger." In *Encyclopedia of the Romantic Era, 1760–1850,* edited by Christopher John Murray, 75–78. New York: Taylor & Francis, 2004.

Toledano, Roulhac, and Mary Louise Christovich. *Faubourg Tremé and the Bayou Road.* Vol. 6 of *New Orleans Architecture.* Gretna, La.: Pelican, 2003.

Tomlinson, Wallace K., and J. John Perret. "Le Mesmérisme á la Nouvelle-Orléans de 1845 á 1861." *Histoire des sciences médicales* 8, no. 4 (1974): 842–47.

Toplin, Robert Brent. "Between Black and White: Attitudes toward Southern Mulattoes, 1830–1861." *Journal of Southern History* 45, no. 2 (1979): 185–200.

Tocqueville, Alexis de. *The Old Regime and the Revolution.* Translated by John Bonner. New York: Harper & Brothers, 1856.

Tregle, Joseph G., Jr. "Creoles and Americans." In *Creole New Orleans: Race and Americanization,* edited by Arnold R. Hirsch and Joseph Logsdon, 131–86. Baton Rouge: Louisiana State University Press, 1992.

Tromp, Marlene. "Spirited Sexuality: Sex, Marriage, and Victorian Spiritualism." *Victorian Literature and Culture* 31, no. 1, (2003): 67–81.

Trouillot, Michel-Rolph. *Haiti: State Against Nation: The Origins and Legacy of Duvalierism.* New York: Monthly Review Press, 1990.

Tunnell, Ted. *Crucible of Reconstruction: War Radicalism and Race in Louisiana 1862–1877.* Baton Rouge: Louisiana State Press, 1984.

Turner, Richard Brent. *Jazz Religion, the Second Line, and Black New Orleans.* Bloomington: Indiana University Press, 2009.

Tweed, Thomas. "Introduction: Narrating U.S. Religious History." In *Retelling U.S. Religious History,* edited by Thomas Tweed, 1–23. Chapel Hill: University of North Carolina Press, 1997.

United States Congress. House. Select Committee on the New Orleans Riots. *Report of the Select Committee on the New Orleans Riots.* Washington, D.C.: U.S. Government Printing Office, 1867.

Vandal, Gilles. "The Origins of the New Orleans Riot of 1866, Revisited." *Louisiana History: The Journal of the Louisiana Historical Association* 22, no. 2 (1981): 135–65.

Vincent, Charles. "Aspects of the Family and Public Life of Antoine Dubuclet: Louisiana's Black State Treasurer, 1868–1878." *The Journal of Negro History* 66, no. 1 (1981): 26–36.

———. *Black Legislators in Louisiana during Reconstruction.* Baton Rouge: Louisiana State University Press, 1976.

Volney, Constantin-François. *The Ruins; Or, Meditation on the Revolutions of Empires: And The Law of Nature.* New York: Peter Eckler, 1890.

Waitz, Julia Ellen Le Grand. *The Journal of Julia Le Grand, New Orleans, 1862–1863.* Richmond, Va.; Everett Waddey Co., 1911.

Walker, David. "The Humbug in American Religion: Ritual Theories of Nineteenth-Century Spiritualism." *Religion and American Culture* 23, no. 1 (2013): 30–74.

Warner, Michael. *Publics and Counterpublics.* New York: Zone Books, 2010.

Webb, Clive. "The Lynching of Sicilian Immigrants in the American South, 1886–1910." *American Nineteenth Century History* 3, no. 1 (2002): 45–77.

Wehmeyer, Stephen C. "Indian Altars of the Spiritual Church: Kongo Echoes in New Orleans." *African Arts* 33, no. 4 (2000): 62–69, 95–96.

Wilson, Charles Reagan. *Baptized in Blood: The Religion of the Lost Cause, 1865–1920.* Athens: University of Georgia Press, 2009.

Whitman, Walt. *Democratic Vistas, and Other Papers.* Walter Scott: London, 1888.

Wolfe, Christopher. "The Confederate Republic in Montesquieu." *Polity* 9, no. 4 (1977): 427–45.

Wolff, Larry. "Religious Devotion and Maternal Sentiment in Early Modern Lent: From the Letters of Madame de Sévigné to the Sermons of Père Bourdaloue." *French Historical Studies* 18, no. 2 (1993): 359–95.

Yasuyuki, Ona. "The French Travellers and the Mughal Empire in the 17th Century." In *Cultural and Economic Relations between East and West: Sea Routes,* edited by Prince Takahito Mikasa, 82–88. Wiesbaden, Germany: Otto Harrassowitz Verlag, 1988.

Young, Jason R. *Rituals of Resistance: African Atlantic Religion in Kongo and the Lowcountry South in the Era of Slavery.* Baton Rouge: Louisiana State University Press, 2007.

Zanger, Jules. "The 'Tragic Octoroon' in Pre-Civil War Fiction." *American Quarterly* 18, no. 1 (1966): 63–70.

Index of Spirits

This index provides an abridged overview of the spirits who appear in the Cercle Harmonique's séance records. The name of the spirit is followed by a short description if necessary and the page numbers where readers can find messages from that particular spirit.

General Index

MIX
Paper from
responsible sources
FSC® C013483

www.fsc.org